Institute of Commonwealth

Social Science Library
Oxford University Library Services
Manor Road
Oxford OX1 3UQ

WITHDRAWN

C
59
.7
MCC

9 FEB 1987

3008983390

PATHS TO PROGRESS

Other Books by the Author

PATHS TO PROGRESS

---

*Bread and Freedom
in Developing Societies*

WILLIAM McCORD

with

ARLINE McCORD

W · W · NORTON & COMPANY
New York   *London*

Copyright © 1986 by William McCord and Arline McCord

All rights reserved

Published simultaneously in Canada by Penguin Books Canada Ltd,
2801 John Street, Markham, Ontario L3R 1B4
Printed in the United States of America

The text of this book is composed in Times Roman, with display type set in Janson.
Composition and manufacturing by the Maple-Vail Book Manufacturing Group.
Book design by Jacques Chazaud.

First Edition

Library of Congress Cataloging-in-Publication

McCord, William Maxwell, 1930–
    Paths to progress.

Bibliography: p.
    Includes index.
        1. Developing countries—Economic conditions.
2. Developing countries—Economic policy.
3. Developing countries—Politics and government.
I. McCord, Arline, 1934–   II. Title.
HC59.7.M358   1986   330.9172′4   85–29809

ISBN 0-393-02307-9

W. W. Norton & Company, Inc., 500 Fifth Avenue, New York, N.Y. 10110
W. W. Norton & Company Ltd., 37 Great Russell Street, London WC1B 3NU

1 2 3 4 5 6 7 8 9 0

FOR OUR CHILDREN

Contents

PATH TO PROGRESS

Initial Reflections

I should have loved freedom, I believe, at all times, but the time
in which we live I am ready to worship it.

—ALEXIS DE TOCQUEVILLE, 1857

The Stoics, perhaps the most rational and balanced of men, witnessed the downfall of Roman civilization to German barbarians. They knew that history offers only one permanent lesson: all atoms, all men, all worlds change. At no time has the extent of change become more apparent than in the twentieth century.

In 1900, the average person could not possibly imagine our present world: a globe encircled by superhighways and Concorde jets, yet threatened by total destruction from hydrogen bombs and the overheating of our ecosphere. He could not have known that we would create unparalleled prosperity and yet cannot find the means to feed a quadrupled population. He would not have envisioned a new technology that encourages an increasing gap between rich and poor nations and simultaneously cloisters scientists who think of shooting space colonies up into the sky as the best means of saving the earth's peoples.

In 1900, only the most impractical of visionaries would have predicted the fall of London and the rise of Peking as world powers. The man of that period, except for a Jules Verne, did not foresee the suffering inflicted by poison gas at Amiens, by Stuka bombers leveling Guernica, or of napalm bombs dropped on Vietnam. He could not have anticipated the megalomania of Hitler, the erosion of liberalism, the growth in fanatical collectivisms, or the fact that every time our pulse beats today a baby sees light—and usually survives. Radio, television, space flights, the triumph and betrayal of Marxism, the four-minute passage of a missile from Washington to Moscow, kidney dialysis, heart transplants, deadly laser beams—all of these were unknown to the man of 1900. And surely he could not have foreseen the decline in Western power and the rise of new imperialisms. After all, in 1907, the empire required only twenty-one British civil servants and twelve British police officers to rule the 17.5 million people of Dacca and Chittagong.

Born in 1930, I grew up in an environment that seems unreal today: a time when horse-drawn vehicles crowded the streets and bread lines of the unemployed stretched through America's cities. Fifty percent of the nation's productive capacities remained idle. It was a period when typhus, influenza, and sleeping sickness took a deadly toll; and refrigerators, indoor plumbing, automobiles, and air travel remained the prerogatives of the rich. A child of that time could hardly anticipate the spread of totalitarianism, a word coined by Mussolini only in 1929.

In manhood, fortune took me throughout the developing world. To West Africa, when Nkrumah proclaimed his vision of Pan-Africanism. To Egypt, while Nasser tried vainly to stem the population flood with the Aswan dam. To India, that vast subcontinent where untouchables swept up the dung from an "Old Cows' Home" while women and children died in the streets. To Indonesia, a land of beauty and unparalleled cruelty. To China, after Deng attempted to free his people from the bitter heritage left by Mao. To Nigeria, a cauldron of tribal loyalties which condemned one million children to the idiot-producing effects of kwashioekor. To Southeast Asia, where garden islands bloomed with prosperity. And to those "developing" sections of the West—Belfast's alleys, Mississippi's jails, and decaying American cities where despairing blacks rioted.

Voyages over the last twenty-five years, however disillusioning or frightening, convinced me of one fact: the twentieth century is, above all, a paramount epoch in the advance of freedom.

In 1965, I wrote *The Springtime of Freedom* in an attempt to defend this position. The forthright intent of the book was to counteract the prevailing notions of that time:

That dictatorship is inevitable in developing nations;

That economic development cannot be achieved without recourse to dictatorship and a centralized economy;

That new nations are incapable of sustaining a democratic system.

These theses proved highly controversial. Expectedly, both Marxists and Fascists rejected the argument. A segment of American intellectuals (then mistakenly devoted to "dependency" and "world systems" theory) attacked the book.

Some of the diatribes were laughable. At Trinity College, Dublin, a comfortable enclave of intellectual freedom where I was privileged to teach, the "Revolutionary Struggle" group issued pamphlets saying that "alias Big Mac . . . is an intellectual apologist of repression and bourgeois violence." (Supposedly my best friend was the chief of the general staff of the British Army in Ulster, a man whom I had never met). Those were sad days.

Happily, however, more balanced and significant people agreed with a defense of democratic values and realized that the future was in their own hands, rather than being determined by implacable historical or economic forces. Some of these people, whom we am now proud to call friends, took the lead in overthrowing Nkrumah's dictatorship, preserving a rule of law in Southeast Asia, countering Mao's "Cultural Revolution," and contributing a degree of sanity to the Middle Eastern situation. It is precisely these intellectuals, civil servants, and political leaders in developing countries who will really influence the destiny of their societies.

We know well the obstacles they face. Petty dictatorships, à la Amin and Qaddafi, as well as grand totalitarian regimes, still flourish. Poverty continues to affect 70 percent of the world's people. Africa has actually retrogressed economically since 1960. Islamic lands unblessed with oil and huge enclaves of Latin America are starving. Fanatical obscurantist movements—calling for blood in the name of Allah, or the Holy Temple, or "the Revolution"—are on the rise in some parts of the globe. Yet a balanced and reasonable assessment of our century must tally three achievements that have never been matched in prior history:

• *Politically,* since 1960, the peoples of the world have enjoyed the greatest opportunity for independence, a chance to share power, the widest spread of the rule of law, and the greatest number of possibilities for freedom of expression in world history. Whether they took advantage of this new freedom from foreign rule and domestic absolutism is, of course, a matter of record. The collapse of military regimes in Latin America, the democratization of Southeast Asia, the loosening restrictions in China, the sheer survival of bloodied, embattled India—all of these trends undermine the Western school that deplores "the cultural imperialism" of upholding political freedom in the misnamed "Third World."

• *Economically,* some regions of the globe—Southeast Asia, China, sections of India, and parts of Latin America—have benefited from unprecedented economic growth. Omitting the oil-gushing nations, all of the twenty fastest-growing nations on the earth in the 1970s and 1980s resided in the Third World. Singapore, Taiwan, Hong Kong, Mexico, Brazil, South Korea, Malaysia, even the Dominican Republic and Trinidad averaged over a 9 percent increase in their gross national product each year during this period.*

By 1982, the "underdeveloped" countries exported more manufactured goods than supplies of basic commodities. By 2000, these nations will acount for more than 30 percent of the world's industrial production in crucial sectors such as steel, railroad equipment, machinery, textiles, oil refineries, automobiles, electronics, and computer technology: The "tilt" toward the Pacific Basin in manufacturing has allowed some nations, such as Singapore, to jump a further stage ahead into the "age of information." This expansion in wealth allows a vast widening in freedom to choose one's destiny.

Economic growth means that people read more, travel more, purchase better housing, and learn more—or waste their increased monies on *ghee* and liquor, cigarettes, or other baubles. Nonetheless, at base, the increment in economic resources results in an (often bewildering) array of choices among new alternatives.

Critics will object that such nations often started from a base of absolute poverty in 1960. That is true but only serves to underline the achievements. Critics will also point out that growth has taken place in some areas under the aegis of dictatorial regimes that did not hesitate to squeeze capital from their peoples and keep their wages low. This is also true, but as we will contend, such regimes are not a necessary propellent of economic advance. Critics may also argue that such phenomenal growth results in intolerable "dependency," elimination of indigenous industries, higher unemployment, and increased inequality among classes. This position is generally untrue.

• *Socially,* people in the developing world live longer, are freer from disease, have lower infant mortality, and learn more than ever before.

---

*Critics will object that such nations often started from a base of absolute poverty in 1960. That is true but only serves to underline the achievements. Critics will also point out that growth has taken place in some areas under the aegis of dictatorial regimes that did not hesitate to squeeze capital from their peoples and keep their wages low. This is also true, but as I will contend, such regimes are not a necessary propellent of economic advance. Critics may also argue that such phenomenal growth results in intolerable "dependency", elimination of indigenous industries, higher unemployment, and increased inequality among classes. This position is generally untrue, as I will demonstrate.

Women, especially, have a wider range of choices; peasants are often no longer irretrievably locked to their land; children can usually expect to attend a school, however rudimentary; and everyone has become acutely aware of a world that extends far beyond their villages.

Twentieth-century technology, among its other miracles, now allows the production of some 100,000 book titles a year, the diffusion of newspapers to millions of readers a day, and the broadcast of a television spectacle to 100 million people at one time. This massive explosion of the media both reflects and shapes opinion.

We must remember that all of these changes—political, economic, and social—have taken place in the last three decades. The pace and scope of change is unmatched in any other previous era—even in Europe, Japan, and America during their most buoyant times.

We must try to understand the scope and direction of these changes, particularly as they have transformed the so-called Third World. The task is grim and urgent. The time is short, for this much is clear: if man cannot understand and control the forces he has unleashed, he is doomed. The invention of the hydrogen bomb alone ensures that.

THE IRONIES OF THE
TWENTIETH CENTURY

Our century will be chiefly remembered by future generations as an age in which human society dared to think of the welfare of the whole human race.

—ARNOLD TOYNBEE

The people of this century have welcomed the advance of science, the decline of blatant imperialism, and the growth in medical care. This unmatched progress has, however, brought in its wake new disorders: the menace of nuclear destruction, the multiplication of fledgling states that might resort to "nuclear blackmail" if industrialized nations do not help to meet their aspirations, and the time bomb of population expansion. The double-edged nature of twentieth-century development has led some perceptive commentators into a profound pessimism about the future. As Robert Heilbroner wrote in 1974:

There is a question in the air, more sensed than seen, like the invisible approach of a distant storm, a question that I would hesitate to ask aloud did I not believe it existed unvoiced in the minds of many: "Is there hope for man?"

> The answer to whether we can conceive of the future other than as a continuation of the darkness, cruelty, and disorder of the past seems to me to be no; and to the question of whether worse impends, yes.[1]

Such despair would hardly have been evident in 1900 when people greeted the new century with a confident expectation that harmony among nations, the humanization of peoples, and the advance of science would proceed in a stately, inevitable march. By the middle of the century, however, a few brilliant men perceived the illusory nature of these hopes. Hans Kohn observed in 1950 that the men of his generation could remember an extremely varied set of experiences; the seemingly serene first decade; the thunderstorm of the first war; the interval in which wishful thinking and anxiety were so strangely mixed; and finally, the catastrophe and the bitterness of the 1940s.

We do not share the gloom that pervades the Western World today for we believe that mankind possesses wells of ingenuity, rationality, and yes, even compassion, which have yet to be fully tapped. We think such twentieth-century prophets of doom as Spengler, Sorokin, and Toynbee, were wrong.

The purpose of this book is to put forward the bases for optimism about the future of mankind in developing nations.

To accomplish this goal, we will sketch some of the facts about people and forces that have molded the twentieth century. The goal of the book is to provide the rudimentary knowledge that will allow people of the year 2000 to judge rationally the alternatives facing them and to choose between different models of development.

We do not aim at the prediction of global events, an impossible task in any case, but rather at the provision of a basic set of facts which will better allow the man of the future to fashion his own fate. As Antoine Saint-Exupéry, the great philosopher and pioneer of aviation, said before his mysterious death on a transcontinental flight: "As for the future, your task is not to foresee, but to enable it."

AN AFFIRMATION OF "THE WEST": AN EMERGING WORLD CULTURE

> The central problem for modern civilization is to preserve humanistic values and the possibility of freedom in a world now driven by the sovereign powers of science and technology.
>
> —CHARLES FRANKEL

The fratricidal wars of the twentieth century, the emergence of Slavic and Asian nations as world powers, the eclipse of arrogant colonialism, and the unanticipated effects of scientific advance—particularly the invention of machine guns and poison gas, of death chambers and the hydrogen bomb—have eroded the faith of many in Western civilization. In fact, the fashionable intellectual (at least since 1918) has repeatedly portrayed the decadence and imminent downfall of "the West."

However liberating they may have been, Darwin showed modern man that he was hardly a unique creation, the logical positivists jettisoned MORAL certainty, and both Freud and Marx questioned man's rationality. Inadvertently, at times, physicists and anthropologists contributed to a pervasive atmosphere of relativism. The intellectual "enemies from within," motivated precisely by the hope of advancing the ideals of the Enlightenment, succeeded too often in undermining the central assumptions of Western civilization.

Above all, the cataclysm of World War I destroyed man's belief in automatic progress. Oswald Spengler, an obscure German school-teacher, first proclaimed the fall of our civilization in his still popular *Decline of the West;* Jacques Maritain, the Catholic philosopher, berated the modern age for its lack of faith in absolutes; and Pitirim Sorokin—a Russian who escaped from six condemnations to death by the tsar, and six more from the Bolsheviks—declared that the West had entered a "sensate" period which marked the terminal illness of a civilization.

Another generation, witnessing the rise of Nazism and Stalinism, succumbed even more to despair. Arnold Toynbee warned of the probable end of Western civilization; George Orwell, his throat pierced by Fascist shrapnel during the Spanish civil war, foresaw the bleak prospects of a totalitarian 1984; Jean-Paul Sartre, who maintained his comfortable life even during the Nazi occupation of Paris, embraced a philosophy of "absurdity"; and theologian Rheinhold Niebuhr condemned Westerners for forgetting that "original sin" tainted all of man's efforts at progress. We cannot ignore, too, the Marxists of different breeds who predicted the inevitable collapse of "bourgeois" civilization while ex-Marxists bemoaned "The God That Failed."

During the 1960s and the 1970s, the popular culture mirrored a portrait of the West as feeble and stricken by a mortal disease. Teenagers danced to "punk rock," crime rates soared, pornography flourished, churches opened their doors to yawning indifference, fathers and mothers increasingly deserted their families, petty dictators murdered schoolchildren for not wearing the proper uniforms, pollution desecrated the land, the threat of nuclear obliteration hung over the globe, energy resources seemed strained to the limit, and bureaucrats in every country treated people as numbers.

American presidents led the nation into the quagmire of Indochina, Richard Nixon violated elementary standards of decency. Jimmy Carter bemoaned America's lack of self-confidence. And Ronald Reagan blusteringly confronted the ''evil empire''—but only in its tiniest enclaves of Grenada and Nicaragua.

Ostensibly, in the 1980s, many leaders of ''Third World'' nations turned their backs on the West. The Ayatollah Khomeini proclaimed a *jihad* on Western mores; Zaire's Mobutu sought a return to African ''authenticity''; Sudanese leaders re-established the *Sharia* as the basic law of the land and proceeded to amputate the limbs of criminals.

The list of the West's frailties—perceived by Indian, African, Islamic, Latin, and Marxist leaders, and not least by European and American intellectuals—filled many books.

Every period of history, of course, harbored its prophets of doom, but the twentieth century seems to have produced more than its share of Cassandras.

Admittedly, the critics can present much evidence for their stance. Subverting the great hope of nineteenth-century liberals, the Nazis put science to use in building gas ovens for killing Jews. The Soviet's practice of psychiatry to stifle dissent and the American pilots who burned people to a crisp with napalm put an end to the genial assumption that increased knowledge or advanced technology go hand in hand with improvements in morality.

The crass manipulations of bureaucracies, corporations, and states have undermined the Victorian hope that an age of individual autonomy would soon blossom. ''An urban and technological civilization has progressively isolated individuals,'' Charles Frankel wrote, ''making their relations more formal and impersonal, their experience more private and lonely.'' And Frankel, who stood as one of the few intellectuals who has defended modern civilization recognized that ''The faith in science, the belief in progress, the ideals of liberty, equality and fraternity, have all been paraded before us in a murderer's masquerade.''[2]

Ironically, burglars slaughtered Frankel and his wife in 1979.

Frankel's death at the hands of mindless killers would appear to symbolize the failure of modern man to achieve the values espoused in the West. All too often, events in the twentieth century confirmed the fears

of the few men who, at the beginning of this period, had already succumbed to a *fin-de-siècle* mood. "I have the imagination of disaster,"
Henry James wrote as early as 1896, "and see life as ferocious and
sinister."[3] At times, a premonition of tragedy overwhelmed visions of
progress.

As the year 2000 crept even closer, realists could not ignore four
possibilities:

First, some maniac in any nation—or simply a computor malfunc-
tion—might unleash nuclear warfare and destroy all of the advances
made by both Western and modernizing nations. The reluctance of Israel
and Egypt, India and China, as well as the continuing failure of super-
powers to disarm, made this nightmare all too possible.

Second, racists might unite the "yellow" and "black" groups of the
world against the "whites." Japan, for example, could lend her technology to China, India, and Africa in return for mass labor and gigantic
markets. Misguided leaders might then involve themselves in a policy
of "nuclear blackmail" aimed at extorting more technology and food
from Europe, the United States, Latin America, and even Russia.

Such a policy would hardly be novel. Since 1945, after all, the United
States put its nuclear forces on "red alert" seventeen times in such
diverse areas as Korea, Indochina, and the Middle East.

Racism dies hard and modern technology has made it ever more lethal.

Third, nationalism or religious fanaticism might well lead some
developing regions to reject Western values, science, technology, and
medicine. The dawn of a new "dark ages," a real possibility in the
Islamic and African worlds, cannot be dismissed lightly. Peoples caught
in the agonizing process of modernization yearn for a home that offers
them unquestioned meaning.

Fourth, some scientists argued that the advance of technology itself,
as epitomized in industrialization, might overheat the earth, melt the ice
caps, dramatically change our climate, and result in human extermination—if an overpopulated world had not already eaten up all of the
available food.

In spite of the prevailing gloom and the risk of being labeled ethno-
centric, we remain pragmatic optimists about the future's possibilities
and defenders of the principles of Western civilization.

On certain simple standards, Western civilization has achieved
unprecedented progress over the last one hundred years. Basic conditions of human life—food, shelter, literacy, health, work conditions,
life expectancy—have changed for the better over this period, and almost

beyond recognition. Moreover, it was the values and technology first invented in the West which made this progress possible.

Western civilization's central features—a demand for evidence to support one's beliefs, a break from the dead hand of fatalism, a conviction that government should rest on consent, an adherence to the rule of law, a broad concept of human rights, the tolerance characteristic of an open society, a cautious optimism that human institutions can reconcile societies beset by conflicting interests, a belief that all men, however flawed, are brothers, and the ideal of individual autonomy combined with social equity—these ideas have now been adopted by many of the world's peoples.

After all, as Peter Berger has cogently argued, "there are fundamental human rights that all or nearly all human societies recognize: the right of an individual not to be subjected to arbitrary and cruel punishment by his own rulers in the absence of any crime; the right of parents to keep their children; the right of people to go on living in the place of their birth." Western civilization has created the most extensive set of institutions for protecting these and other rights. As Berger noted, "A reasoned stand for the human achievements of Western civilization, including the monumental achievements of political democracy, is long overdue."[4]

At first, the precious Western ideals remained in the hands of a few Greek, Judaic, Hellenic, Christian, and Roman prophets; a handful of Renaissance men, the founders of the Enlightenment, and isolated aristocrats from Montaigne to Jefferson. Today, even supposedly alien cultures such as that of Japan, have fashioned a similar ethos, blending with their own tradition.

Most of the leaders of the world (and their prime audiences, those who have received a secondary or university education) publicly espouse the same values, even if they do not always follow them and even when they loudly condemn the "cultural imperialism" of the West. Posters in Peking, the Helsinki agreements on human rights, American presidents, United Nations declarations—all proclaim the same values, however shallow in practice. It would be cultural condescension for any leader to say that his people actually prefer dictatorship to genuine self-determination.

And, although not systematically representative, we have heard the "common people" throughout the world—Polish intellectuals, Indonesian peasants, Indian village chiefs, Egyptian women—whisper or loudly proclaim very similar thoughts. Literacy, newspapers, the radio, movies, and television have created a common ground of discourse. Even enemies—Israel and the PLO, the Pope and the Communists, the Americans and the Sandanistas—announced their dedication to similar aims, while quietly or violently disagreeing on the means of fulfilling their ideals.

To be sure, bureaucrats in Washington and dictators in Africa, the Ku Klux Klan in Texas and secret policemen in Moscow, apartheid supporters in South Africa and generals in Latin America have grievously violated these ideals. Yet they have absorbed them and, more often than not, they excused their most execrable actions on grounds that they must use distasteful means in order to achieve (some indefinite day) the end of a civilized, humane order.

In fact, Western civilization in our time has not declined but is the world's most vigorous, progressive, and revolutionary culture. We are, as Wendell Wilkie predicted in the 1940s, about to become "one world."

Further, we see little reason to believe that this new world culture will shortly come to the end of its tether. With courage, a measure of optimism, and reasoned actions, our children should live to see the ideals of this new world culture fulfilled in the twenty-first century.

Such a statement will undoubtedly elicit criticism from three groups:

First, those who follow Max Weber in attempting to create a "value free" social science will condemn this view. As Weber's pronouncements before World War I indicated—when he described the coming catastrophe as a "splendid event"—such an ambition is unattainable for mortals and, even if it were, it would amount to an abdication of responsibility.

Second, people who believe that their particular cultures should triumph (whether they be Stalinists in Albania, advocates of a *Jihad* in Iran, or Sikhs in India) will obviously reject the assumption that a new, universalistic world culture is emerging. Only time will provide the answer to our disagreement.

Third, those gentle folk who think that all values are relative and all cultures are equal will undoubtedly recoil. For these latter, having lived in Africa, Asia, and the Middle East, we would be foolish to deny the magnificence of Benin bronzes, the calming influences of Hinduism, or the mathematical achievements of Arabic culture. We suggest only that these contributions have been adapted by the "West"—or rather, a common world culture—which has superseded all others.

The advance of Western values has entailed radical changes in indigenous cultures: the abolition of slavery in Africa, the end of *suttee* in India, a ban on the blinding of criminals in Saudi Arabia. In Japan, fathers cannot sell their female children into prostitution. In China, millions no longer die in floods, famines, and epidemics. In Thailand, the king now lacks the power to dispense death at his whim. Dyaks in Borneo are forbidden to hunt human heads for trophies. The cruel indifference of the world has been transformed into an era where an individual existence makes a difference.

We do not regret these changes, any more than we deplore the demise of child labor, the Inquisition, the burning of "witches," or the destruction of Nazism and Stalinism in the West. Admittedly, such social changes have involved many deaths and the erosion of ancient cultures and hoary traditions. These social changes were often carried out by blood-stained warriors, imperialists, haughty capitalists, or the common "Tommy Atkins" of the world who may not have realized what they were doing.

Dreadful as the costs may have been, the expansion of a new, more humane, and universal ethic during the last century is apparent in its materialistic benefits. Contemplate, for example, the extension of Western science and technology into virtually every hamlet of the globe.

To a greater or lesser degree, each nation in the world now possesses technology originally invented in the West, and people have developed an insatiable appetite for its produce. As Raymond Aron once argued, "In terms of productivity, technical innovation, living standards, scientific progress and human freedom, it is the West—the United States and Europe together—which took the lead during the course of the last thirty years."[5]

Western "materialism" has infuriated some, including many young people in America and France, Scandinavia and Japan. They admired the passive ethos of the East (idolized by Herman Hesse, who never actually visited India). They called for a return to the land. And they renounced the pagan idolatry of technology.

Such antimaterialists ignored the fact that scientific advance is not inimical to humane values or to the survival of the human race. By its nature, the scientific process—now engaging and enlightening the minds of people throughout the world—is at its base both self-critical and self-correcting. Science's demand for evidence, its preference for qualified judgments and pragmatic results, and its awareness that our actions must test and revise the most sweeping of generalizations reinforces some of the values of the new world culture.

We must admit, too, that the use of new technology in agriculture, industry, and medicine raised the standard of living of the average man throughout the world to the highest level ever attained. Famines, of course, still plagued Bangladesh, the waterless deserts of sub-Saharan Africa, and the poverty-ridden peasants of northeastern Brazil. This suffering cried out for our continued attention. Disparities in wealth, particularly between the "north" and the "south", grew at an unprecedented rate.

The fact remains, however, that the adoption of Western technology throughout the world has measurably improved the daily life of most people. "I am no believer in automatic progress. I have experienced too much to wear blinders readily." Max Lerner said, "But I can point to the real revolutions in process—in research, in access to life chances, in sexual attitudes, in awareness of the phases of the life cycle, in values and life-styles."[6]

Thus, the specter that haunts the world is not Communism (as Marx said) or "The Yellow Peril" (as Hearst wrote). It is the steady advance of Western technology and Western values into the most obscure sections of the globe. And for this we should be grateful to all of those individuals, great and unknown, who have sought to reduce the toll of callousness, misery and cruelty in the world.

This book is a defense of the revolution of modernity and of the emergence of a new world culture. Through an examination of model regions that have achieved great progress, it is our attempt to show that the counsels of despair so prominent in our time are unwarrented.

The book is, above all, an expression of a belief that Prometheus' gift of understanding, compassion, and a portion of reason to mankind has not doomed us but has offered man a vision by which we can guide our course.

William McCord

PART I

THE CRUEL

DILEMMAS

I

The Human Challenges

When we enumerate all the difficulties in which the human species can become embroiled, it would appear a priori that the probability of successful transition along any path would be extremely small.

—HARRISON BROWN, 1956

Ahmed Said, a suffragi in Cairo, tried to raise his ten children in a two-room slum apartment in Shubra. He earned E£40 a month, a munificent sum for a man who came from peasant roots, but it was not enough to sustain six of his children who died before the age of five. "It was the will of Allah," he said, glancing around furtively for blue-eyed people, "Or perhaps someone cast the evil eye on them." His remaining children had little food and no milk. They had their grandest dinners on lamb bones thrown away by opulent restaurants.

Ahmed had fled his village near Aswan when the great dam arose. Aswan offered the possibility of electrifying Egypt's four thousand villages and freshly irrigating their fields. For Ahmed, however, the dam was a disaster. It created Lake Nasser, a huge basin of 165 billion cubic meters of water straddling earthquake faults. As the lake threatened to innundate Ahmed's village, he was forced to flee. "The soldiers came one day and loaded us on boats. I cried. The spirits of my ancestors lived in our village and now they are drowned."

The army moved him first to a "model village" below the dam but he could not survive as a farmer. Unexpected silt from the dam ruined the village lands and a corrupt bureaucrat in Cairo stole the monies which could have provided the machines for purification.

Like millions of others, Ahmed sought his fortune in Cairo. Fortunately, he secured a job in the French embassy and, being a highly intelligent if totally uneducated man, he learned French. The city exposed him to a wider world: he cheered lustily for Nasser when the great man passed by in an open car (''But what can he do when he hasn't known hunger?''); he spit on a poster of Sadat (''He betrayed us to the Jews''); and he developed a taste for his master's gin (''The Koran forbids it but what can we do when life is so sad?'')

Ravaged by tuberculosis, Schistosomiasis, and cirrhosis of the liver, Ahmed died at forty-two. He left behind an illiterate wife and four sons. Only one son could find work in Cairo.

Ahmed's sad life—an uprooted, starved existence devoid of meaning and satisfaction—too often typified the Egyptian and other developing peoples during the latter half of the twentieth century.

Egypt's food shortage, its overpopulation, its suppurating urban blight, its bumbling bureaucracy and stifling superstitions caught Ahmed in circumstances beyond his comprehension or control.

To understand the cruel dilemmas of development, we must begin by portraying in the bleakest of terms the challenges that almost every developing region faced. Although some countries overcame these challenges, they remained formidable barriers to the progress of some 70 percent of the world's people.

INVIGORATING THE ECONOMY

How can one look through the picture window with enough vision to see the starving men, bundled in rags, lying on Calcutta's pavements? Just so did the nobles of France ignore the peasants starving at their castle gates.

—BARBARA WARD

Once, while living in Uttar Pradash, I visited a village which was heavily subsidized by the Ford Foundation. The village had new wells, a paved road, a school, and a clinic. A young doctor, who had sacrificed a lucrative practice in Bombay, showed me around.

I noticed an untouchable sweeping up cow dung and, after collecting it, picking out pieces of grain which the cows had not digested.

''He and his family eat it,'' the doctor said sadly. ''It's their only real food. The *harijans* here are not allowed in the fields. They can't drink at the well. The women walk ten miles a day to get buckets of water.'' The doctor guided me on to his clinic and proudly displayed sterilizing equipment, a pharmacy, and a modern surgical theater furnished by American aid.

Such contrasts symbolized the contradictions throughout developing nations: a modern, Westernized but thin elite has been struggling to overcome centuries of poverty, disease, and ignorance. The scope of this economic challenge is almost beyond imagination:

• The money spent on women's cosmetics in America alone during the last twenty years equaled the income of all Black African nations during the same period.

• The money used for a single American aircraft carrier, that obsolete symbol of military strength, could have built and sustained 40,000 village pharmacies in Latin America.

• The money spent by the United Kingdom in the Falklands war was 60 percent greater than India's entire national income during that period, although India's people outnumbered Englishmen by fifteen to one.

• In 1984, the people of Mozambique barely subsisted on an annual average income of $270. Research-rich Zaire doled out $220 a year, Ethiopia $140, Bangladesh $120, and mountainous Bhutan $80. The total average income of people in these nations equaled the yearly expenditure of French families for table wine.

How could the peoples of developing lands fulfill their newly aroused, if modest, dreams with such an economic base? Their aspirations were limited: a piece of land to call their own, hope that their children would not die in infancy, a desire to escape from money lenders, a cautious optimism that their sons might attend school. But how to attain these goals?

The ramifications of the economic challenge were endless and overlapping:

The Need for Food

In most developing lands, 70 percent of the people toiled in the fields trying, sometimes hopelessly, to escape the specter of starvation. They faced major obstacles:

In China, arable land had been cultivated for centuries and yet the population of hungry people continued to grow under Mao.

In Chad (per capita income in 1984 of $120), Bedouin herders tried to nourish their flocks while the Saharan desert inexorably encroached on their grasslands.

In Latin America during the 1970s, 1,000 children died each day simply because of a lack of potable water.

In India, rodents and insects ate up as much as 50 percent of imported grain before it left shoddy depots for isolated villages.

Rampant urbanization made it increasingly difficult to put more grain in the empty bowls of Asian and African villagers. Imported food and foreign gifts of grain too often went to city dwellers rather than peasants. In the 1970s, Dacca, the capital of Bangladesh, swelled by 400,000 people. The government established 4,300 soup kitchens but nevertheless city street sweepers collected the bodies of dead peasants each morning.

In India, the sheer lack of transport from the cities forced famished peasants in the north to strip the trees of edible bark. The cities had ample stores of grain.

In central Africa, during a typhoid epidemic, parents refused shipments of drugs. They believed it would be better for their children to die quickly than to suffer from hunger or the stunted minds created by malnutrition. Again, some cities had food but road systems often extended only fifty miles into the hinterlands.

While there was a wealth of potential solutions to the continuing food crisis, world trends—beyond the horizon of the peasantry—hindered their implementation. Shortages of oil and phosphate sometimes crippled the production of fertilizers. (A pound of fertilizer applied to India's nutrient-starved land yielded three times as much food as when used on America's saturated soil.) Massive grain purchases by the Soviet Union inflated world prices while, in America, the affluents' hunger for beef ate up grain reserves. (The world's cattle consumed as much grain annually as would have fed 8.7 billion people.)

Within developing nations, frightened dictators—unresponsive to peasant demands—often subsidized food for volatile city dwellers while depressing the price in the countryside for produce. Thus, the peasants often lacked an incentive to learn about new technology or to join the "green revolution" in hybrid wheat and rice.

Social conditions within the villages of Latin America, Asia, and Africa also played a part. Regardless of geography, the rural areas over the last quarter of a century have displayed a drab similarity. The villagers were self-contained, sick, ignorant, and—due to variations in growing seasons and a lack of industry—often idle.

In Latin America, 50 percent of the population ate less than 1,500 calories a day while North Americans consumed 3,200. Seventy percent of peasants in Latin America could not read.

In Africa, during the 1980s, almost every villager was habitually unwell from smallpox or malaria, sleeping sickness, or malnutrition. This was perhaps the worst fate, for constant illness prevented the average peasant from participating in intellectual commerce with other men or altering his condition of stint and poverty.

In India, 30 percent of village men worked only eight days a month. This enforced idleness was an enormous waste of human talent. The caste system condemned another 10 percent of untouchable Indians to perform such useless tasks as meticulously cleaning temple steps with toothbrushes.

The average village was socially isolated, cut off from the modern world, convoluted upon itself. Sir Charles Metcalf's observations on India in 1832 applied with little modification to the twentieth century: "Dynasty after dynasty tumbles down; revolution succeeds revolution . . . but the village community remains the same."[1]

Hierarchical, traditional relationships have often dominated village life, condemning a lowly innovator to scorn or even exile and the landless peasant to perpetual servitude. The prevalence of authoritarianism in the village—the conviction that the patron or Brahmin or chief was always correct—often prevented the peasant from learning about the government located in some far off capital, of its hopes, and its "five year plans." Indeed, the peasant often had only a vague awareness that a larger state existed beyond his village border. Kussum Nair, the brilliant social critic, once questioned Indian villagers about the dominant Congress party. One peasant enthusiastically replied:[2]

"Yes, we have heard of the Congress. We have heard of the Congress, yes. Everyone talks of it."

"But," he paused, gravely puckering his bushy eyebrows, "but now that you mention it, we do not know whether Congress is a man or a woman."

Fatalism and conservatism also pervaded village life. The very fact that life was so precarious, as Tawney noted in the China of the 1930s, made any potential change from ancient ways a grave risk. Some religious systems—particularly Islam, Hinduism, Buddhism, and some life-denying versions of Latin Christianity—also encouraged peasants to consign themselves to their implacable fate.

While acknowledging these aspects of peasant life, we should add that they were not inevitable or unchanging features of the world's peasantry: the original societies of the Egbas and Yorubans in Nigeria were vigorous "village republics," subverted by colonization; the peasants of the Ivory Coast, Taiwan, and Korea have adopted immensely productive agricultural techniques as they responded to land reform and market incentives; the Sikhs in the Punjab and their Hindu cousins in Haryana and Uttar Pradash carried out a revolution in agriculture within six years.

Progress has occurred and, at times, it has come dramatically and quickly—but only when prompted by new knowledge, scientific techniques, a turn toward the market economy, and an infusion of money.

Finding the Money

The need for capital presented most developing nations with another basic economic dilemma. Put in its simplest yet compelling terms, Colin Clark has demonstrated that investment in productive activities had to exceed increases in population by a ratio of four to one, if a people's true standard of living was to improve. (This ratio changed, of course, if a country's leaders invested in Volta dams or automated steel industries, mechanized agriculture or high-cost computers.)

Where could abysmally poor nations find the money to initiate development? Here, the options were grim and limited for, as Marx once observed. "If money . . . comes into the world with a congenital bloodstain in one cheek, capital comes dripping from head to foot, from every pore, with blood and dirt."[3]

There were only eight ways in which the nations of the globe accumulated the capital to launch economic growth—and each of these had its detractors and critics:

1. *Keeping wages low:* English entrepreneurs in the eighteenth and nineteenth centuries—after borrowing capital from commercial coffers and other trading states—created an industrial base by crowding peasants into the cities, squeezing profits from pitifully low industrial wages, and investing them in new enterprises at home and throughout the Empire. In an age which had yet to develop a concept of rights for women, children, or laborers, such a brazen policy "worked"—in the sense that English industry and commerce grew remarkably.

2. *Expropriation and taxation:* The Bolsheviks in Russia after 1917

followed their own path to modernization by confiscating from the rich, and by taking over a well-developed infrastructure of railroads, steel factories, and armaments plants largely constructed with French capital. Entranced by a vision of heavy industry, the Leninists and Stalinists strangled the peasants with heavy "turnover taxes" and rural collectivization. With its huge costs—millions of executions (Stalin estimated 10 million deaths), the building of prison camps, the creation of man-induced famine, and a virtually permanent stifling of Soviet agriculture—this approach also "succeeded". Russia built a massive steel and armaments industry from the proceeds of exploitation. Since 1917, diverse leaders from the Shah of Iran to Mao attempted to follow the Stalinist path. With their demise, however, few governments in developing nations seriously entertained the idea of copying Russia's approach.

3. *Attracting foreign capital:* Some countries have lured large amounts of foreign capital from richer countries as a stimulus to their own economies. British capital played an important role in the original development of America, India, and Argentina; the Belgians, with great human cruelty, opened up Zaire's resources; Europeans, Americans, and Japanese have poured monies and technology into Southeast Asia.

"Dependency theorists" argued that such investments served only to exploit cheap labor, destroy indigenous industries, corrupt the political system, distort the native economy, rape nations of their natural resources, and benefit the foreign guzzlers of profit.

In fact, in times of economic crisis such as the 1980s—an era characterized by high interest rates, low commodity prices, and trade restrictions dictated by the lending countries—such developing areas as Mexico, Brazil, Argentina, and South Korea amassed unprecedented, unpayable debts.

By the 1980s, most experts recognized that the debts encumbered during an earlier period of booming oil revenues and consequent optimism could not be repaid. In 1984, for example, Mexico borrowed $4 billion to meet critical needs but it had to pay interest of $12 billion. By 1985, debt service jumped to an impossible $22 billion.

Since nations like Mexico could respond only by cutting imports from industrialized regions, the rich nations suffered too. Between 1981 and 1983, for example, US exports to debt-ridden Latin America dropped by 40 percent.

Politically under intense pressure from the International Monetary Fund, leaders such as Raul Alfonsin of Argentina tried to dismantle military rule, restore human rights, and reduce an annual inflation rate of 500 percent. Yet, in 1985, the IMF demanded more: a reduction in real income for Argentinians, an increase in taxes, a cut in government spending for health, and less investment. How could any democratic country have responded to such foreign demands? As Henry Kissinger admitted, the debtor countries could not sustain economic growth while simultaneously maintaining social and political order—and paying their international debts.

In the 1980s, it had become increasingly apparent that American, European, and Arab banks had to write off or depreciate many of their loans, allowing nations to repay them at lower interest rates over an extended period of grace. The central banks of the West had to bear the increased burdens, obscuring the fact that the debt crisis was in fact a way of redistributing wealth from the rich to the poor regions.

4. *Commodity trade:* Many developing nations sought foreign monies (or bartered goods and technology) through the export of raw commodities which were then processed in the West, Japan, or Russia. Too often, this policy (whether pursued under socialist or capitalist aegis) involved dependence on a single export, such as sugar in Cuba, cocoa in Ghana, copper in Chile, coffee in Kenya, or jute in Bangladesh.

If world prices for particular commodities declined—as did the terms of trade for Central America's agricultural products by 40 percent between 1977 and 1982—such economies lost all hope for diversification and creation of "import substitution" industries. Although hotly debated, some experts claimed that commodity prices had steadily declined since 1900, condemning certain developing nations to a worsening trade position.

5. *Establishment of cartels:* Oil-producing countries, the OPEC group, hoarded capital by trying to establish a cartel over the supply of oil and demanding higher prices. On paper, this created unmatched prosperity: in 1983, per capita income in Saudi Arabia reached $11,000 a year, $23,000 in Kuwait, $26,000 in Qatar, and over $30,000 annually in the United Arab Emirates. This gush of wealth resulted in new schools, hospitals, airports, palaces, and roads. In the 1970s, it represented the greatest movement of wealth in history from developed to underdeveloped regions. Some of the riches even spread out to other states who possessed no oil; in the 1980s, Saudi Arabia distributed 10 percent of its income to other Arab countries.

Nonetheless, problems plagued the member nations of the cartel. Much of the money found its way into lush haciendas, Swiss banks, and Florida real estate rather than into productive domestic activities. Lacking an infrastructure, an honest bureaucracy, a free press, and an educated populace, many of the oil states could not (or would not) use the money at home. Other nations such as Mexico and Nigeria lavished their windfall revenue on "prestige" projects such as superhighways and skyscrapers that had to be abandoned when oil prices turned down in 1982–83. Fratricidal conflicts between Iraq and Iran further diminished the cartel's effectiveness.* And, in any case, nature required an end to the temporary bonanza. Iran, for example, would run out of oil reserves in 2050 if it continued its pace of extraction.

6. *Substitution of labor:* In a desperate search for self-sufficiency, some countries—Mao's China is an exemplar—used unpaid human labor as the direct source of capital. During the Cultural Revolution, Mao directed intellectuals, doctors, students, and other urbanites to return to the countryside and join the peasants (80 percent of the population) in creating a more vibrant economy. Some of the results—more small factories, dams, canals, roads, and orchards—were admirable. Yet Mao's successors after 1976 admitted that the Cultural Revolution was, as a whole, a great leap backward. Without trained laborers, industry suffered; without the technology to improve food production, whole areas of the countryside starved; without untrammeled scientists, research in advanced techniques came to a halt. Inspired by an ideology of egalitarianism, midwives became doctors, surgeons did the duties of orderlies. All sectors of the economy suffered from this enforced equality.

7. *Compulsory savings:* A few countries adopted compulsory savings plans as a source of capital. Singapore, for example, required employees to donate 25 percent of their income (doubled by their employers) to a Central Provident Fund. This served as a bank for home loans and an eventual source of social security. The Fund paid the donor interest at an inflation-adjusted rate of 6.5 percent. Until the donors collected their monies at age fifty-five, the government (often in alliance with multinational companies) used the capital to create productive enterprises. Although critics admitted that this policy resulted in unprecedented savings and held down the inflation rate, they argued that the

*Even if the oil cartel held together, there were severe doubts that similar monopolies on other commodities could be established by developing regions. Too many diverse interests inhibited such a development as well as the fact that industrialized nations could easily find substitutes for specific commodities. Even in the case of a rare mineral such as chromium, the United Nations could not maintain an effective embargo on Rhodesia since the Soviet Union and South Africa quickly filled world demand for that product with their own reserves.

system suffered from all of the problems of a state-dominated enterprise: the use of monies for unproductive activities such as advanced jet fighters, early warning defense systems, and a showy, but unnecessary subway network.

8. *Foreign gifts:* Direct foreign aid, a new creation derived from the Marshall Plan era, represented one other source of capital. At times, the transfer of goods, services, technology, and expertise from generous nations such as Sweden and the Netherlands wrought miracles in developing nations. In the Middle East, one million fruit trees blossomed in formerly barren deserts. In Peru, a comprehensive sewage system was built in the 1960s. In Venezuela, as a result of the Alliance for Progress, a majority of people began to enjoy literacy. The discoveries of the Rockefeller Foundation, disseminated from Mexico to the Philippines, increased the world's food supply to unparalleled levels. UN family planning programs, reinforced by growing prosperity in some regions, resulted in the first decline in the world's population growth rate in 1984.

Nonetheless, one must admit that foreign aid was not a panacea to the problem of capital formation. The original Marshall Plan was a great success but it was, after all, devoted to the reconstruction of a modern Europe and Japan which already had the skills, the technological knowledge, the mineral resources, the managerial experience, and even the work ethic necessary for re-industrialization. With such advantages, Japan and Germany could readily absorb the most advanced technology of the 1950s and, in fact, emerge as "miracles" of economic growth.

In contrast, inefficient, dictatorial, or corrupt governments in the "third world" have often wasted foreign aid. At times, "gifts" have been totally inappropriate to a nation's needs; Russia once gave tropical Guinea two snowplows. At other times, foreign aid—such as donations of food to Africa—have been used by despotic governments to distort a natural market economy and depress returns to the nation's farmers. At other times, foreign aid has been wasted totally by tyrants in developing regions; in the 1960s, for example, France paid $11 million merely for the coronation of Emperor Bokassa of the Central African Empire who soon lost his throne. Too often, foreign aid has served as a well of corruption and a reinforcement to dictatorial regimes. Witness the cases of Tanzania and Bangladesh:

By 1980, Tanzania had received more aid per capita than any other nation in Africa. Foreign gifts constituted 18 percent of recorded gross national product, 107 percent of tax receipts, and 153 percent of gross earnings. Yet, in 1981, Julius Nyerere (an unquestioned dictator and elder statesman of "African Socialism") publicly admitted that his country had grown progressively poorer than ten years earlier. Nyerere had forced millions of peasants to leave their homes, collectivized agriculture with disastrous effects, expropriated private productive groups, invaded Uganda, and kept more political prisoners in jail than did South Africa. He was primarily responsible for the spoilation of his potentially rich land. Nonetheless, Nyerere blamed the West for his nation's devastation and called for even more foreign aid as recompense for the West's supposed guilt.

Similarly, in Bangladesh during the 1980s, huge amounts of food poured in to help the destitute peasantry. The food seldom reached the people for whom it was intended since it had to be filtered through the central government. The leaders of the government were intensely fearful of discontent among the army, police, and the other urban classes; the peasantry, on the other hand, did not mobilize and passively accepted its fate. Consequently, the government doled out foreign grain at extremely low prices only to those groups such as the army which had the potential for revolution. The countryside was untouched and, according to some observers, foreign aid served only to entrench the power of urban despots and feudal landlords.

Thus, any policy of capital formation—squeezing the industrial workers or peasants, total confiscation of the rich, dependence on foreign trade or multinational companies, and even outright gifts from more prosperous nations—proved to have serious drawbacks and even bloody results.

Sweeping reform policies such as the "new economic order" advocated by the Group of 77, the UN, and the Brandt Commission in the 1980s met with little practical response. Each specific suggestion encountered adamant opposition. Developing nations themselves could not agree on the establishment of a "commodity bank" (a reserve which could be used to stabilize world prices) since their leaders feared that they would not reap the benefits of a rise in price for their products. Groups within the rich nations, including workers and trade unions, opposed a "world tax" (which might be used to bolster foreign aid) and turned to protectionism as a way to ensure their own welfare. Some economists regarded even a "world food bank" (such as gigantic warehouses of grain to be used in times of famine) as a hindrance to capital formation and rural development.

Yet, from whatever source—domestic restrictions on consumption, foreign exchange, foreign investment, or direct aid—the fact remained that every country had to save and reinvest at least 20 percent of its national income if progress was to be made.

We must realize, too, that this prosaic matter of capital accumulation—supposedly, a strictly economic concern—was, at base, a volatile social and political issue.

Who should get the biggest slice of the economic pie?

Setting Priorities

The third economic imperative was the need to allocate capital, whether through government decisions or the vagaries of a free market, in such a way that it would be used to increase economic productivity and minimize human suffering. Even if a nation had the grand luck to stumble upon a treasure of capital, how would it be invested?

Nigeria presented one example of this problem. Nigeria was the largest nation in Black Africa, blessed with a great pool of oil, potentially abundant food, and impressive mineral resources. The inrush of oil revenue from the 1960s through the 1970s, however, went hand in hand with successive military revolutions which overthrew the nation's parliamentary system. Corruption and assassinations, urban blight and religious massacres, tribal hatreds and a civil war which consumed at least one million people accompanied the inflow of new capital. At its birth as a nation, Nigeria easily fed her people; by 1980, Nigeria had to expend declining foreign reserves in importing food. By 1984, when oil revenues fell, thousands of students studying abroad who might have formed a new generation of technocrats, suddenly found that their stipends from home had disappeared. What went wrong?

Essentially, both the government and the private sector lacked the ability or will to allocate monies in ways which the people regarded as just, honest, and beneficial.

Ibos in the East, where oil fields lay, balked at having crude oil refined in Yoruban territory and they disliked paying oil taxes to a government dominated by Hausas and Fulanis.

The northern region, largely illiterate in the 1960s, demanded the creation of costly technical institutes and universities to match educational expenditures in the south.

Lagos, the capital, multiplied its population tenfold in twenty years but no one provided adequate housing, medical care, or even a sewage system for the newcomers. Consumer spending on Mercedes, Dior dresses, and stereos went unchecked while inflation soared. In the 1980s,

Lagos had the world's highest cost of living.

"Dash" (bribery) encouraged but not originated by the oil revenues, corrupted officers and bureaucrats, businessmen and politicians. As a result, entire skyscrapers built of shoddy materials suddenly collapsed on their inhabitants, new highways developed gaping potholes, and hospitals never received the medicines which had been ordered.

Peasants deserted their fields to seek riches in Nigeria's cities while jungle devoured their once verdant crop lands.

In short, the oil revenues—which would never again reach the splendid heights of the early 1970s—were stolen, misallocated, or frittered away. Where should this cash have gone? To building refineries? Or, first, to training the workers and engineers that would be required? Or, perhaps, to modernizing the transport system? Maybe food production should have preceeded all else since oil workers, teachers, and engineers had to be fed. A choice had to be made, since there was not money available for every option: each *naira* spent on a school meant that much less for agriculture or industry—or for the corrupt bureaucrat.

No group had made these hard choices in an honest and fair manner. Free marketeers catered to consumer demands and the requirements of foreign trade, ignoring the nation's more basic needs such as mass education, sanitation, and medicine. Civilian bureaucrats lacked the knowledge, even the most rudimentary statistics, to create a stable government plan. After declaring that bribe takers should be hung, the military proved no more capable of running the economy or avoiding temptations than did civilians. In consequence, Nigeria ricocheted back and forth between anarchy and military suppression, democracy, and civic discord.

To its peril, Nigeria ignored advice such as that given by John Kenneth Galbraith:

> The importance of political stability in the sequence of development cannot be too strongly emphasized. There is today no country with a stable, participatory and honest government that does not have—or has not had—a reasonably satisfactory state of economic progress.[4]

PROVIDING POLITICAL FREEDOM
AND A RULE OF LAW

> My legacy to India? Hopefully, it is 400,000,000 people capable of governing themselves.
>
> —NEHRU

On June 5, 1984, Indian troops swept into the holiest of Sikh shrines, the Golden Temple of Amritsar. At least a thousand people died, caught in machine gun, mortar, and tank fire. Among the bodies lay Sant (Saint) Bhindranwale, a leader of Sikh terrorists, who may have committed suicide, and Shabeg Singh, a cashiered former general who had taught and armed guerilla forces.

The Sikhs had relatively minor political demands: the recognition of Sikhism as a unique religion and of Amritsar as its holy city; establishment of Chandrigarh as a purely Punjabi capital; a greater share in Punjabi river waters; and a slice of the neighboring state of Haryana.

Indira Gandhi had agreed verbally to most of these requests, yet it did not satisfy Sikh extremists. For the preceeding two years, they had assassinated opponents, murdered innocent Hindus, blown up railways, and threatened to cut off wheat, water, and electricity from other parts of India. Sadly, Mrs Gandhi had to act: murderous violence which threatened the survival of India's constitution, its freedoms, and the lives of all was met with bullets.

Although Sikh army units (16 percent of India's armed forces) staged abortive revolts and remnants of Sikh rebels blew up dams, terrorism was temporarily subdued. Whether Amritsar would turn into an influential symbol of martyrdom—as it did in 1919 when a General Dyer fired on unarmed protestors and sparked Mahatma Gandhi's drive for Indian independence—only historians of the next century will know. In October, 1984, Mrs. Gandhi paid with her life for the invasion.

Violence in the Punjab represented in brutal terms the crucial dilemma of many leaders: how to preserve political liberties and civic order in the face of intense political, religious, and economic hatreds? At what point should dictatorial means—the imposition of censorship, a curfew, a ban on travel and, finally, a resort to force—be used to defend democracy and uphold the rule of law?

The Punjab illustrated an ironic lesson for our century: vast economic and social advances can inflame violence and political discontent.

By 1984, the Punjab had emerged as the richest state in India; its golden fields of wheat produced most of India's food reserve; its people enjoyed literacy, television, and a record life expectancy; its cities boasted advanced ''miracle chip'' computer industries; its untouchables had escaped from the worst of caste humiliations.

Yet, this prosperity brought with it a feeling that Sikhs had not received their ''just'' rewards, that New Delhi unfairly favored the poorer regions of India, and that Hindus were deadly oppressors.

Economic progress alone had not ensured a spread in political freedoms, a stable rule of law, or an end to civic anarchy—this was, perhaps, the lesson from the Punjab.

In spite of this fact, authoritarians of the left or right—even when unthreatened by domestic violence—have argued that the search for economic progress *required* a "temporary" abolition of a free press, the shackling of courts, the stifling of political opposition, and the destruction of autonomous groups from trade unions to entrepreneurs. If every peasant or tribal leader or capitalist had a political voice, so the argument went, how could a government impose austerity measures, redistribute land, or reduce useless consumer imports? How could an illiterate population often inflamed by religious, tribal, caste, or linguistic hatreds cooperate freely in the pursuit of a common good?

Supporters of Argentine and Chilean generals, revolutionaries such as Nkrumah and Touré, and charismatic leaders from Mao to Sukarno clung to a tattered hope that a dictatorship which sponsored economic reform and social justice would evolve into a "new" and "higher" form of freedom.

Now, at the end of the century, we know that they were wrong: economic advance, even when it occurred, has not automatically blossomed into political liberty—no matter how many millions were sacrificed to this illusion. Indeed, in many nations, dictatorship served only to shatter once promising, even abundant economies and eroded what little political participation the people once exercized.

The clear task of liberal and social democrats in developing nations was to seek economic advance while stalwartly defending the rudimentary principles of a liberal polity: a rule of law independent of the whims of an elite; a tolerance for nonviolent political opposition; a willingness to consult the people's judgment; a recognition that mediating institutions—the family, the church, unions, even the tribes or castes—have a right to function outside the state's embracing arms; a guarantee of open criticism from the press, pulpit, or assembly; and a marked hesitancy on the part of government to invade a man's privacy and to treat his work, village, family, and self as mere extensions of state policy.

To fulfill these ideals in any developing nation was, to be sure, a complex and often grim task. Among the paramount obstacles, one must consider the following:

Calming Traditional Hostilities

Ethnic divisions—exacerbated by caste, class, religious, and linguistic differences—made the business of government a tenuous enterprise.

Few people in developing nations thought of themselves in terms of their national identity. Thus, calls for sacrifices for the country's welfare—as opposed to the immediate interests of one's tribe, caste, village, or region—often fell on deaf ears.

Too often the original unity of developing nations, as well as the concept of nationalism itself, was an artificial by-product of colonialism. In fact, during the time of their rule some colonial powers encouraged ethnic divisiveness as a method of controlling their populations.

As a result, India underwent the bloody partition of 1947 and subsequent ethnic and religious revolts in Asaam, the Punjab, Kerala, and Bombay.

Indonesia suffered armed revolts in Sumatra, the Celebes, the Moluccas, New Guinea, and Timor.

Malaysia, a nation governed by Muslims but financially managed by Straits Chinese, strained to improve relations between the impoverished Malays and the relatively prosperous Chinese. (Ironically, the rich Chinese who fought beside British guerrillas during World War II led the Communist insurgency of the 1950s.)

Unfortunately, advocates of dictatorship often ignored their own ethnic traditions of self-government. In Ghana, for example, Nkrumah and later military regimes justified despotism as the only means of creating a new social democracy. In fact, as one Ghanaian noted during the last years of Nkrumah's tyranny:

> Abettors of Nkrumah's regime implicitly tell us that we are incapable of appreciating . . . values based on the sanctity of human life and personal freedom. They do not realize what an insult this is to some of us . . . who have had personal experience of the values which informed our most primitive governmental arrangements before the White man set foot in ghana . . . values derived from the belief that above everything else, men matter.

Reducing Ignorance

Eradicating traditional hatreds and sustaining vestiges of self-government were even more difficult in nations where people did not share the same language, were illiterate, and were unable to understand objective reports about each other or their nation's condition.

In village India, despite mass education, only 40 percent of men and 25 percent of women were able to read; in absolute numbers by 1985, there were 130 million *more* illiterates than at the time of independence. Only three percent of India's people understood the lingua franca—English.

In Africa, literacy rates often retrogressed as the century moved on. Sekou Touré declared in 1980 that "we in Guinea have concentrated on developing the mentality of our people."

Nonetheless, at the time of his death, only 21 percent of adult Guineans could claim to read, less than that at independence.

Even in China, where Mao succeeded in creating a new generation of literates, the people were allowed to read only slogans and political pap until 1976.

Under such circumstances, the enforcement of a reasonable, fair, and understandable system of laws—assuming that the governing elite truly desired equity—became a monumental task.

Enforcing Law

During Mao's reign, the Chinese cadres simply abandoned law and handed out swift, drum-head "justice" to any who had been condemned.

Under Suharto in Indonesia and military regimes throughout Latin America, death squads executed supposed criminals, dissidents, or just personal enemies without benefit of trial.

In Central Africa, Bokassa proclaimed his own set of arbitrary laws including one which condemned children to death for not wearing school uniforms made in a factory which he owned.

Even in India, a nation dedicated to constitutional rule, Mrs. Gandhi suspended the law by declaring "emergency rule" in 1975 and again in 1984 when she invoked "preventive detention" without trial for thousands of (presumed) Sikh terrorists.

During the most pacific of times, the rule of law in India developed a blemished record. In 1952, police arrested a man for riding a train without a ticket, imprisoned him, and forgot his case. He spent thirty years in a Bihar prison awaiting trial. In 1980, police in Bhagalpur blinded thirty-one prisoners with needles. In the city of Varanasi, policemen stomped on the knees of alleged criminals, shattering their bones. Many had their legs amputated.

Such atrocities at the hands of a hated police force would not have come to light without a vigorous, investigative Indian press.

Freeing the Press

Unfortunately, as UNESCO's recommendations for a "new information order" in the 1980s indicated, the elites in many developing areas had contempt for a free press. The mass media in developing nations, so the rulers said, should educate and not stir political controversy or spread news of "troubles." In consequence, most developing countries established a state-owned mass media or a heavily censored press.

Admittedly, lax libel laws and a thirst for sensation did, at times, lead to irresponsibility on the part of a private press. Nonetheless, the surest guarantee against tyranny, corruption, and cruelty remained a free and responsible press. Without the assistance of a privately controlled mass media, even benevolent despots could not learn the truth about simmering ethnic hostilities or grievous economic problems plaguing their nations. Exactly at a point when more people can read than ever before and had the ability to assess their own condition, the need for active and critical movies, newspapers, radio, and television was never more apparent.

More often than not, however, the military and political popinjays of developing nations have gagged their mass media, jailed the Jacob Timermans of the world, expelled foreign correspondents, and turned mass communication into an endless paean to those in power.

Too late, the rulers of the status quo have often discovered that they mistook silence for acquiescence and sycophancy as a cover for incipient revolution. Nkrumah, Sukarno, and Amin learned this lesson tardily, just as their peoples or armies toppled their statues.

Conquering Corruption

Among other problems, the absence of free and responsible criticism encouraged corruption, favoritism, and nepotism—universal failings of "third world" governments. Corruption, the need for "tea money," "backshish," "dash," or "mahmool" undermined both the polities and the economies of nearly every developing nation.

Even during its supposedly most idealistic period, China's economy functioned by *zou-hou-men,* "taking the back door": pretending to be a party cadre to obtain privileges, accepting bribes in Swiss banks for purchasing oil equipment, or trading medical care to ensure that one's son entered a university.

In Egypt, special functionaries (who specialized in the arcane trade of estimating the exact scale of bribes for each bureaucracy) served in every enterprise. They had no other purpose than to pay off the proper ministers for large or small favors.

In many African nations, sheer survival depended on giving "dash" to local officials in charge of food or medicines.

In Nigeria, $10,000 served to get a chief customs inspector to look the other way when a container ship full of contraband entered a port. Contractors destroyed office buildings to hide their use of inadequate materials. In 1981, someone burned down the foreign ministry itself to conceal evidence of shoddy construction. In 1983, arsonists set fire to the main telecommunications office in Lagos for the same reason. Neighboring, impoverished Benin emerged as one of the world's largest importers of French champagne. Porous borders, lubricated by bribes, allowed gallons of the liquor to be smuggled into Nigeria where its import was forbidden. Roadside border markets openly sold champagne for $50 a bottle in the 1980s.

In Colombia, brave men tried to destroy the traffic in illicit drugs. In 1984, the young minister of justice pursued the corruption into the highest ranks of Parliament. Someone had him assassinated.

Pervasive corruption was neither an inevitable facet of development (Singapore effectively abolished it after 1964); nor was it a unique characteristic of the "third world" (as Tammany Hall and "Abscam" aptly demonstrated in the United States). Nevertheless, the practice commonly received traditional support and even approval from some elements in non-Western cultures. Among certain African tribes, for example, it was an honorable and open custom to profer gifts to one's chief; the practice only became counterproductive when practiced in an industrializing society. In India, where the "fixing" of licenses, contracts, and permissions was an outcome of family and caste pressures, corruption was considered as a privilege of public office, even a part of one's duty in life. The corruption of public officials came naturally in Hindu culture where the gods themselves expect bribes. As Trevor Fishlock has observed:

> . . . Hindus have a good idea of their obligations, and they also have a fairly easygoing and businesslike arrangement with their gods: they offer sacrifices and gifts to ask for favours, give substantial homage in gratitude if prayers are answered, and hurl abuse at the deities if things go wrong.[5]

Transforming Feudal Manors

Unchecked by criticism or political opposition, despots and petty bureaucrats, landowners and money lenders were often able to ignore the most desperate pleas for rural reform.

In São Tomé, a typical village in northeastern Brazil, most people worked as marginal farmers or landless laborers. The patrons despised them and paid them a minimal wage in script which could only be used at the plantation store. Occasionally, people struck for better wages but the feudal rulers used hired thugs to keep the helots under control. The peasants in São Tomé were aware of the electoral process but the local gangsters barred them from the polls. The farmers knew their rights and that the central Brazilian government had initiated a crash program to launch a new era in the northeast, but they could not sweep aside the power of the landholders. Under such a system where the profits from agricultural produce went largely to the local lord, the peasants had absolutely no reason to increase their production. Many of the young men chose to flee to the cities burgeoning *favelados* (urban slum dwellers).

Curbing Urbanization

Rampant urbanization created another set of political problems. During the last twenty years, it became clear that cities can teach tolerance but, in too many case, they were merely refugee stations on the outer edge of civilization. Newly arrived from the countryside, the anomic urbanites sought solace in crime or a cult, alcohol or drugs. They often succumbed to authoritarian political appeals for once they had witnessed the collapse of a traditional order, the "true believers" sought frantically for a new idol. Revolutions, after all, originate in the urban areas of Shanghai, Paris, or St. Petersburg—not in the countryside.

Handling the desperate turmoil of urbanization often seemed beyond the capacity of governments.

In Calcutta, for example, "the city of dreadful night" as Rudyard Kipling once described it, millions of peasants flooded the city as a result of India's partition in 1947, the creation of Bangladesh in the early 1970s, and Bengal's continuing rural poverty. They descended on a putrifying city of 10 million that was hardly prepared to welcome them. Until the 1970s, no new water lines had been built for a hundred years, the last major road in 1930, and the last sewage drain in 1896. The open sewers carried typhoid and cholera. Some hundred thousand beggars, often purposively multilated, lined its streets. Women and children sifted through garbage for food. A continuing expansion in population at the rate of 25 percent a decade threatened to worsen the plight of a city that Clive once described as "the most wicked place in the universe."

Mexico City was another example of the catastrophes produced by "third world" development models based on rapid industrialization, a neglect of agriculture, and uncontrolled urbanization.

World War II and a subsequent oil boom encouraged Mexico to follow a policy of instant industrialization which naturally concentrated in Mexico City, the traditional seat of government and commerce. The ruling PRI (Institutional Revolutionary Party) ignored the rural areas while waves of migrants swept into the capitol.

In the last decades of the century, the city's population crept toward 31 million people. By the 1980s, the city's population had increased sixteen-fold in the prior five decades but the government, almost bankrupt in the 1980s, could not provide new housing, transportation, electricity or sanitation.

Children played in open sewers; 30 percent of the city's 10,000 tons of garbage went uncollected each day; slum dwellers tried to burn the rubbish (a vain effort to control the multiplying population of rats) but this only contributed to the poisonous yellow pall which constantly hung over Mexico City.

In 1983, officials estimated that eight hundred thousand people had no homes and that 51 percent of families (averaging six people) slept in a single room. Settlements of squatters had no water, drainage, or electricity. The ex-peasants had no motive for improving their jerry-built shacks since the government could evict them at a moment's notice.

As the unemployed multiplied, President de la Madrid recognized in 1983 that chaos pervaded Mexico City and that "some days are truly catastrophic"—yet the government had few choices and no strategies.

Lagos, the capital of Nigeria, was another unplanned sprawl of huts and skyscrapers built on a malodorous swamp. Once a port where African chiefs deposited their slaves for sale to the Portuguese, Lagos grew from about 400,000 people in 1963 to 5 million in 1983. Spurred by a temporary oil boom, people flooded the city. Municipal services could not cope with the sudden growth: latrines flushed out on the streets, shantytowns sprung up over night, cars were licensed to drive only every other day to avoid crushing traffic jams, and mobs took justice into their own hands by dousing thieves with gasoline and setting them afire.

Oil money in the 1970s poured into the city at the rate of $55,555 a minute but it was drained away from services into incomplete superhighways and the building of Abuja, a shiny new national capital. (In 1983, arsonists burned down the buildings that housed the Abuja Capital Authority to cover up for slipshod construction.)

The oil money went above all into the ubiquitous "commissions" characteristic of West Africa. The government did not even channel the oil riches into Lagos's broken-down general hospital where patients had to pay bribes to attendants in order to receive prescribed drugs. In the 1980s, when a world oil glut dried up Lagos's revenues, whatever dreams the ex-peasants had of an urban future evaporated.

The problems of a Lagos swamped with refugee Ghanaians, of a Mexico City awash with unemployed, unhoused peasants, and of a Calcutta full of starving Bengalis were aggravated by waves of immigrants from other countries.

Coping with Refugees

A central problem for the next century will be dealing with an increasing wave of "illegal" immigrants who disregard boundaries and border niceties in escaping from poverty and repression.

In 1982, India futilely tried to build a fence across Assam to keep out hundreds of thousands of destitute people fleeing from Bangladesh. The people came, even when the Assamese took out hatchets and knives to massacre 5,000 helpless migrants.

In 1983, faced with rising unemployment, Nigeria abruptly expelled two million West Africans who had been working illegally. They fled by truck, ship, or foot. Dozens died on the 300-mile trek through Benin and Togo to Ghana. When one million Ghanaians arrived home, the dictator, Lieutenant Jerry Rawlings, could not offer food, only vague hope.

In 1984, the United States government officially announced that "its borders were out of control." From two to ten million aliens—Mexicans, Haitians, Asians, Cubans, and West Indians—resided in America and their numbers increased by half a million people a year. As a temporary expedient, Congress passed a bill which cracked down on illegal employment but gave amnesty to aliens who had already arrived in America. No one truly believed that this solution would cure the problem.

In 1986, most underpopulated countries such as Australia (fearful of the "yellow peril") and small nations such as Singapore (which reclaimed land to expand its borders into the sea) closed their doors to all except a handful of Vietnamese "boat people" or those with needed skills or huge amounts of capital to invest.

Propelled by the population explosion, political terrorism at home, and joblessness, great waves of migrants tried to seep into the richer or politically freer regions of the globe. Indigenous peoples—racially prejudiced, anxious about job competition, worried about land shortages, or just fearful that the drowning people would swamp their own little "life boat"—bitterly resisted the incursion. Since the world will inevitably contain six billion people by the year 2000, the potential for political turmoil or a militant search for *Lebensraum* has grown implacably.

One other sinister aspect of this problem must be acknowledged. Because of medical advances, the peoples of the more advanced regions are getting steadily older. They could, in theory, use the "new hands" traditionally provided by migrants. And yet, the robotic revolution has given promise of eliminating the need for unskilled (and many skilled) jobs in the industrialized regions.

Meanwhile as the Americans, Japanese, Europeans and Southeast Asians age, a huge mob of young people in other areas restlessly wait in the wings for their opportunity. In some developing countries as many as 50 percent of the population, saved from premature death, were below the age of fifteen. As they reach their twenties, will this energetic group of young people sit passively by while governments debate their fate and talk of the sanctity of their borders?

Tragically, by the 1980s, neither developing nor developed nations had proposed a clear and realistic strategy to meet the imminent challenge of refugees.

There was one fact which our generation tended to ignore: the most vigorous economies and the freest of political orders in history are those which had formerly welcomed strangers.

America, France, Australia, and Canada at various points in their evolution are classic examples. I think, too, of those regions—the Punjab, Singapore, Malaysia, Hong Kong, the Ivory Coast, Costa Rico, Venezuela—that are the models of development in the twentieth century. Until the 1980s, whether by choice or by chance, they all freely welcomed and absorbed migrants, benefiting from an infusion of the newcomers' talents and energy. Countering the advice of both "exclusionists" and some "dependency theorists," P. T. Bauer has argued in the African context:

The control of immigration retards the growth of the volume of trade and activity in West Africa and therefore it works against the economic interests of African consumers, producers and workers. . . . And it stares one in the face that the poorest regions of the less developed world are those that have few or no external contacts.[6]

The evidence suggests that immigrants—who are usually drawn from the ranks of the more adventuresome, risk-taking people in their original societies—bring with them a vital sense of energy and dedication to their new worlds.

Taming the Army

Except for Costa Rica, every nation in the world has maintained an expensive army and a sophisticated air force. Indeed, encouraged by the United States, Russia, France, and Israel, expenditures for these forces have steadily risen during the twentieth century, even in the poorest nations. By 1986, developing nations spent more on importing arms than food.

At times, military groups united ethnically separate peoples, instilled modernizing skills and a sense of nationhood, quelled internal violence, served a genuine defense function, and abstained as professionals from politics.

For many years, as one illustration, the Indian army was a model of this type of military unit. Citing dangers from Pakistan and China, India constructed a trained, disciplined, multi-ethnic, and well-paid army. Its serried ranks of Lancers and Grenadiers, tank drivers and missile launchers contained Madrasis, Rajputs, Assamese, Doghas, proud Sikhs and other Punjabis, as well as the legendary Gurkahs. The Indian army proved its mettle defending the United Kingdom in battles stretching from the Transvaal to Ypres and Burma; it detached Kashmir from Pakistan, created Bangladesh, and staunched rioting in Bombay and Assam. Since the Great Mutiny of 1857, the army sustained a British legacy. As one acute observer of India noted in 1984:

> The cantonments are the smartest settlements in the land, with white painted kerbs, neat roads, buildings and brass. Trouser creases are blades, haircuts a delight to any sergeant major. . . . Officers' messes are as they always were, down to the exquisite manners, old-boy accents, slapped thighs, jaunty pipes and concern for form. There is a strong idea of regiment, of loyalty, tradition, and smartness.[7]

Although three of the four officers who led the invasion of Amritsar's Golden Temple were themselves Sikhs, the Indian army evinced its first signs of deep discontent in 1984. Some Sikh troops revolted and attempted to advance on the Punjab; one group murdered its brigadier. Mrs. Gandhi's estranged daughter expressed fears of an army takeover but the Indian army as a whole maintained its professional aloofness and discipline during that particular crisis.

Obviously, armies have assumed vastly different roles in developing areas. Even in those regions with a British military legacy—Pakistan, Bangladesh, Burma, Uganda, Ghana, Nigeria—the army has stepped in to rule, usually after a period of brutal civilian dictatorship. In the Islamic world, military despotism has been the standard, not the exception. In Latin America, until the 1980s, militarists employed torture and assassination as a way of controlling their peoples. Even in supposedly nonviolent Buddhist lands such as Burma and Thailand, armies have dominated events since, above all, they had control over a basic source of power—lethal weapons.

Some sociologists, such as Irving Louis Horowitz, have brilliantly argued that "a syndrome evolves where military rule guarantees high levels of economic development that yield a democracy rather than a dictatorship."[8] If one considered the military dictatorships in Latin America that crumbled as economic progress occurred during the 1970s, one would have to accept this point of view.

History informs us, however, that military rulers such as Chiang and Tojo have exhibited remarkable resilience and staying power whether in times of temporary prosperity or humiliating defeat. Such military dictatorships have fallen at the hands of overwhelming force, not because of their inner "dialectics." The record of barbarism, ineptitude, and sheer waste displayed by the General Alis and Amins and Nimeiris of the world—and their hungry subordinates from the Lieutenant Rawlings to the Sergeant Does—offered little hope that rule by Praetorian guards automatically ushers in an era of wealth or lays the foundation for a more open, pluralistic society.

Liberals and social democrats have been forced to guard against the political potential of their armies. Sometimes, as in India, independent police and paramilitary forces were deliberately developed as a counterbalance to military prowess. At other times, powerful urban groups, particularly armed labor unions in Latin America, have curbed military excesses. Occasionally, guerrilla forces—such as those of José Figueros in the Costa Rica of 1947—smashed a dictatorial army and then voluntarily relinquished their arms.

Such developments have, however, been rare and almost miraculous. Once they have entered the palace, armies have hesitated to return to their barracks. The lesson of the twentieth century is clear: civilian leaders who are dedicated to a liberal democracy must keep their garrisons on a very short leash, if they waste the money to create them at all. The truth is that the qualities inculcated by armies—authoritarianism, blind obedience, unquestioned loyalty, and an eagerness to kill—are not the virtues of modern men who seek a creative, open, and tolerant society.

TRANSFORMING MEN

Development requires a transformation in the very nature of man, a transformation that is both a means to yet greater growth and at the same time one of the great ends of the development process.

—ALEX INKELES, 1974

In coping with the cruel dilemmas of development—the need to extract capital from a destitute peasantry, the necessity of rewarding one ethnic group while perhaps depriving another, the demand to curb governmental corruption, militarism, and despotism—it is apparent that human cultures, social structures, and even "human nature" itself must undergo change. Without a radical, often wrenching alteration in human attitudes and behavior, there is no hope of creating a more abundant and freer world.

Even a cursory review of the evidence ineluctably leads to the conclusion that man must change his beliefs, habits, and customs before a more humane social order can be created.

In India during the 1950s, for example, a Sikh philanthropist decided to build a technological school. He gave the land and the monies for the school. He recruited a band of teachers. By chance, his land lay right on the border between what became the Punjab (numerically dominated by Sikhs) and the state of Haryana (where Hindus were in the majority by 1966). His generous enterprise involved the creation of a school open to all castes and to both boys and girls.

The best site for the school lay near a Hindu-dominated village. The Sikh philanthropist first offered to build the school in or near the Hindu village. Appalled by the idea of mixing genders and castes, the Hindu village leaders rejected the offer. A Sikh village nearby was more open to such innovations and accepted. There, the benefactor created a fine school which, among other topics, taught about the technology of raising hybrid wheat, the necessity for family planning, and the right of all people to equal opportunity.

By 1986, in spite of similar land and resources, the Sikh villagers had tripled their income, quadrupled their literacy and added six years to their life expectancy at birth.

The adjoining Hindu peasants across the state border remained stagnant and jealously resentful. They had, however, maintained their culture, their caste purities, and their sexual distinctions. At great human cost, an ancient tradition had overcome the influence of a modern innovation.

Egypt offered another illustration of the incompatibility of certain traditional concepts and the demands of modernization. Under Nasser, the government spent scarce foreign revenue in luring the Fiat company to built a plant for "Egyptian" automobiles. The Italians came and created a steel factory, a machine tool complex, and an assembly line for automobiles.

They trained workers, too, but they neglected to instill that sense of precise, quantified timing which is necessary for industrial production. The habit of measuring time in seconds and minutes, ingrained in many Westerners, was almost absent in Islamic culture—a strange lapse since the Arabs virtually invented mathematics. This reluctance to conform to an exact pattern of time had dire consequences in the Fiat plant.

One day an Egyptian worker in charge of a coke oven asked his Italian foreman if he could bank the fires of the oven while he went to the bathroom. I overheard the foreman say yes, asking how long the man would take. "I'll be back immediately," the ex-peasant said insouciantly. Not knowing that that the word "immediately" had very broad, elastic meanings in Arabic, the supervisor agreed and left for another section of the factory.

One hour later, the Italian returned in panic. His worker was still in the latrine. The coke oven had burnt up at a cost of E£3 million. Production of the "Misr" automobile was crippled for a month.

One more example of the tension between some traditional cultures and the drive to modernize: In Ghana, a nation dependent on cocoa exports, the "swollen-shoot" disease infected the cocoa trees. If the sick trees were not cut down, the contagion would have spread throughout the country's forests. And, if Ghana could not export cocoa, its military rulers had no hope of building a self-sufficient economy.

Consequently, the military in Accra ordered that particular villagers should chop down their diseased trees and move across a river to a healthy spot where cocoa trees flourished. An officer sent from the capital informed the villagers of their plight and threatened them with execution if they did not obey. Assuming that the peasants would see the rationality of moving, the officer who issued the commands departed in an air-conditioned Mercedes and left the village without checking on the results of his order.

The peasants, however, did not wish to leave their precious land and, with some justice, they reasoned that their fathers had prospered there and they did not want to incur the costs and risks of moving to a new area.

They stayed in their village. The cocoa crop failed. Ghana starved while the villagers fled as a group to Nigeria hoping for a new start. The officer who had ordered them to cultivate a new area was shot on a moonlit beach after a subsequent coup.

His successor, an Air Force sergeant, now drives the Mercedes.

"Becoming Modern"

As Haryana, Egypt, and Ghana indicated, no set of leaders could successfully avoid the complex but essential process of transforming their people. If people truly wished for material progress, attitudes toward caste distinctions, the status of women, the elasticity of time, and agricultural practices had to change.

Alex Inkeles has eloquently outlined the critical nature of these changes. In a crossnational study of Argentina, Chile, Bangladesh, India, Israel, and Nigeria, Inkeles and his colleagues found a consistent set of traits which characterized people engaged in modern economic activities, who were better educated, more exposed to the mass media, and lived in urban areas. Inkeles conceived of "modern men" as exhibiting nine qualities:

1. They were open to innovation, to change, to risk taking, and to new ideas.

2. They were empathetic and able to form opinions about issues which go beyond the concerns of their immediate environment.

3. The modern man was more "democratic," in the sense that he more often acknowledged and tolerated differences of opinion.

4. Such individuals developed a sense of time oriented to the present and future, rather than the past.

5. The modern man learned how to plan, visualize, and organize his own future.

6. He tended to abandon fatalism and assumed that events in this world are predictable and open to reasonable human control.

7. He more often recognized the dignity of others, despite their traditional status, and consequently changed his view about the role of women and children.

8. The modern person evinced greater faith in science and technology as a means of controlling nature.

9. He held to the view that men should be rewarded for their contribution to society, rather than their particular, often inherited status.

Inkeles argued that such qualities were prerequisite for the operation of an industrialized economy based on scientific technology and a high degree of specialization. In addition, he maintained that these traits were also necessary for people to become active participants in a political order based on a secular, national authority.

In the developing nations which Inkeles studied, exposure to the mass media and working in a factory environment (or in a technologically advanced rural cooperative) were particularly correlated with the development of a "modern" character. Surprisingly, the more modern people in this international sample did not suffer from increased psychosomatic ailments or from symptoms of anomie. Inkeles contended that:

> Neither foreign aid nor domestic revolution can hope successfully to bring an underdeveloped nation into the ranks of those capable of self-sustained growth. . . . The qualities of individual modernity are not a luxury, they are a necessity.[9]

Urbanization, too, seems to have affected the development of a modern mentality. "The city is the teacher of man," Plutarch once commented. And indeed no one who passed through the developing cities of the twentieth century could deny this observation or the contrasts produced by a mingling of modern and traditional cultures. In Cairo, flowing galbiyas mingled with Western clothes, camels competed with buses. In New Delhi, jets flew overhead while snake charmers practiced their art in front of air-conditioned hotels, bars flourished while men fasted to protest the slaughter of sacred cows. In Jakarta, gourmets dined on the cuisine of the Hotel Indonesia, cars blocked the streets, and trucks full of military men darted back and forth—while a few miles away religious instructors taught children how to recite the Koran by rote in classical Arabic.

The cities and all their accompanying appurtenances and contradictions do in fact teach significant lessons. In one piece of research, for example, 3,000 men in the Middle East were interviewed.[10] The men were systematically drawn from desert settlements, peasant villages, and cities. They ranged from sophisticated professionals to illiterate wanderers. Some came from Lebanon, once the most commercialized, richest, and urbanized nation in the Middle East. Others came from Jordan, which had yet to undergo extensive industrialization. Some of the men were drawn from isolated rural areas, others worked in urban occupations but lived in a village, some had been exposed to an urban environment but had not yet been integrated into a factory, and still others lived in an urban environment and were fully engaged in an industrial occupation.

Although the entire sample of Arabs, all of Islamic background, had certain traits in common—a pervasive distrust of others, a surprising aversion to fatalism, and an universal aspiration for better material conditions—those who lived in cities and worked in an industrial occupation had a quite different view of the world than that of rural, traditional people:

• Urbanities were more secularized and less superstitious.

• They more often put their faith in the ultimate efficacy of science and technology.

• Urbanites believed that they could influence the course of events and that man could change his destiny.

• Urbanites were more future-oriented, more convinced that planning rather than luck would determine their future.

• Urbanites seemed more individualistic.

• Urbanites put more emphasis on punctuality in their concept of time.

Beyond the sheer impact of urbanization, as Clark Kerr has argued, industrialized peoples have become more similar, and their ideological differences have lost their virulence as societies coverged in their use of technology, their ways of mobilizing resources, and their patterns of work.

Although recognizing that "every land moves toward its future in terms of its own past, its own institutions and traditions,"[11] Kerr has maintained that industrial, urban societies have grown increasingly alike in their utilization of science, their economic rewards, and their lifestyles. In addition, Kerr has presented evidence to support Weber's belief that bureaucracy would come to dominate industrial societies, Burnham's contention that managers controlled the real levers of power, and Galbraith's argument that public or private groups in all advanced societies engage in a high degree of planning.

This drive towards convergence, Kerr has argued, was no accident: the pursuit of modernization required common social structures, skills, attitudes, and behavior.

In the "third world," Kerr has pointed out, the exact nature and pace of this tendency toward convergence depended on unique historical factors, political ideologies, and particularly the nature of the governing elite. Socialist nations have, in general, stressed economic equality and job security. Capitalist regimes have emphasized productivity, individual freedom, and a high level of consumption:

> What the West seems to have, efficiency and freedom, dissidents in the East want. What the East seems to have, equality and stability, dissidents in the West demand.[12]

Nonetheless, socialist societies have moved toward greater dependence on free market mechanisms, have allocated an increasingly important role to managers, and, to some degree, have provided greater democracy in the work place.

Conversely, capitalist nations have restricted laissez-faire competition, engaged in large-scale planning, and expanded the role of public ownership of property.

For good or evil, this century has been marked by a trend toward uniformity throughout the world as industrialism (or postindustrialism), urbanization, education, and the mass media expanded and transformed previously isolated cultures.

This global change, however necessary for the implementation of new technology, was hardly devoid of tension and conflict. Colin Turnbull has particularly emphasized the costs of modernization in developing societies. Turnbull has described "the lonely African," the person who was in transition between a traditional peasant culture and the new ethic of modernity. In Zaire, an ex-peasant told Turnbull:

> I died the day I left this village. . . . I believed in your world at one time, even if I did not understand it, and I tried to follow your ways. But in doing this I lost my spirit . . . and I am empty.[13]

Another ex-villager said, "For my children it is different, they do not know good and bad as I know it . . . after I am gone there will be no one left."[14]

Similarly, Peter Berger has eloquently argued that the first stages of modernization in the twentieth century have produced a degree of disorganization, anomie, and "homelessness" which have too often resulted in spiritual paralysis:

> Modernity has accomplished many far-reaching transformations, but it has not fundamentally changed the finitude, fragility and mortality of the human condition: What it has accomplished is to seriously weaken those definitions of reality that previously made that human condition easier to bear.[15]

For some, Berger has shown, the ideology of socialism has offered a return to a sense of community and meaning, as well as a "science" for explaining the present, and a prophecy of future happiness.

However much one may lament the passing of old religions and traditions, one must recognize that the comming of new technologies and modern science to the "third world" has increased the length of man's life, preserved man from malignant disease and deformity, opened up new perspectives, freed many from the restrictions of clan, tribe, and caste, and provided new options for both social and geographical mobility.

The coming of factories and mills, clinics and schools, cities and airports has indeed eroded the old cultures and social structures. Social relationships derived from new economic statuses, new occupations, and new political influence have increasingly replaced the old categories based on traditional loyalties. Modernization has also required profound changes in man's perception of causality, his concept of planning, his view of his relation to nature, his sense of time, his worship of inscrutable gods, and his estimate of his own efficacy in changing the world.

In bringing about this transformation of man, all governments have had to face—or have ignored with extreme daring—three critical and interrelated issues:

How should mankind be educated to assume a responsible, creative role in a modernizing society?

How can the "population time bomb" be defused?

How can new scientific approaches be brought to the village level?

The Need for Education

"Education is not something that economic development affords," John Kenneth Galbraith has written. "It is the experience of the older industrial lands that economic development is what education allows."[16]

The hard facts of the last three decades of social change have established a compelling case for education as an instrument for breaking the "vicious cycle" of poverty and its accompanying culture of despair and magic:

First, those regions which have invested most heavily in human beings during this century have later reaped the greatest economic rewards.

The Punjab put much of its capital in all levels of education and turned a largely illiterate state into the most prosperous section of India.

In fits and starts, China educated its peasants in everything from birth control to new agricultural techniques; after 1976, when the government allowed peasants to follow a new "responsibility" system, the birth rate dropped dramatically and the countryside bloomed.

At huge expense, the Ivory Coast created a new generation of francophones and lifted its per capita income fifteen-fold over a thirty-year period.

With no natural resources, Singapore educated hundreds of thousands in the complexities of high technology and achieved an economic level in Asia which almost matched Japan's—a nation which has also put extreme emphasis on education as the propellent of economic growth since 1868.

Since 1960, Taiwan offered universal education to a peasantry which eventually applied their knowledge in creating perhaps the most productive agricultural economy in the world while simultaneously building major export industries.

In contrast, some nations with great economic potential—copper-rich Zaire, Guinea, and Ghana (laden with bauxite and uranium), Indonesia with its vast resources of oil, an Iran bent on extirpating devilish Western influences—neglected education or used their schools as mere agents of political or religious propaganda. They paid an awesome price in economic stagnation and civil strife. In Africa, such nations succumbed to repeated famines and a steady deterioration in economic productivity.

The paramount value of education has been further demonstrated in a series of empirical studies linking educational advances with several unanticipated benefits: the ability of people to deal with economic disequilibria; increased wheat productivity; a more precise calculation of economic risks; an enhanced interest in savings; a willingness to control population growth; and an advance in women's freedom.[17] These side-effects, not consciously planned as results of educational programs, have brought with them great economic advantages.

In addition, an emphasis on education has correlated with a receptivity to the scientific method, an orientation to the future and the fruits of human effort, greater self-awareness, and a more tolerant attitude towards others—all traits which should cause the political or religious despots of the world to tremble.[18]

Leaders in every developing nation, except those that fear "corrupting" influences from the West, have recognized the need for more education. Yet, the statesmen of this century still grappled with cruel dilemmas:

Should the monies allocated for education go first to universal, mass education (as Galbraith argued) or the production of technicians and skilled labor (as Rosenstein–Rodan advocated)?

Should nations launch rapid campaigns of mass literacy as in Cuba, Ghana, and Guinea? Or should governments provide education by more rigorous, but less universal methods as in most of the ex-French colonies of Africa?

Should multinational companies be used as a vehicle for training managers, mechanics, and industrial laborers—following the ways of early Soviet Russia, Brazil, and the Ivory Coast? Or should independent countries shun such foreign training as a form of economic and cultural exploitation, as did China during its Cultural Revolution?

Should governments closely coordinate their educational quotas in accord with national needs, as China sometimes did? Or should educational institutions be allowed to proliferate regardless of economic demands, as in India?

There are no easy answers to such questions. Only the historical experience of differing "model" nations over the last thirty years can offer some reasonable responses.

At this point in our inquiry, however, it is clear that investment in human beings was a distinctive feature of those few areas which have, in fact, grown economically abundant and politically free. Without investment in "human capital," as Theodore Schultz has commented, world history would be nothing more than "the man without skills leaning terrifically against nothing."[19]

Tragically, his description of the human condition still held true for much of Asia, Africa, the Middle East, and Latin America at the twilight of the twentieth century. Indeed, since more people tried to feed themselves on less land, conditions in such areas as Ethiopia, Sahelian Africa, Bangladesh, Tanzania, and Cambodia had actually worsened since the middle of the century.

The Population Problem

In the 1980s, several Asian nations—India, China, Bangladesh, Sri Lanka, Cambodia, and Vietnam—hovered on the edge of starvation despite the fact that cereals production in these areas had increased 3.4 percent in the 1970s.

In Africa, the worst food crisis of the century afflicted twenty-two countries. During the 1980s in Ethiopia alone, two hundred thousand people died from starvation. In many other parts of sub-Saharan Africa, millions of African children suffered permanent brain damage for lack of protein. Since 1960, food production declined while the African population, some half billion in the 1980s, grew at 2.7 percent a year.

In some parts of the world drought devastated crops. In others, flooding caused starvation. In all of Western Latin America and Central America, the basic caloric intake of people was regarded as totally inadequate by the United Nations. In Brazil, two thousand children died daily from a combination of malnutrition and dysentery.

In Egypt, massive investments in the Aswan Dam barely allowed food production to keep pace with population growth.

Those nations which suffered most from starvation had two other central characteristics in common: first, they were governed by corrupt, inefficient and, generally, dictatorial governments which neglected domestic food production. Second, their rates of population growth vastly exceeded their (sometimes impressive) increases in food production.

By 2050, the World Bank reliably estimated, the earth will have to feed ten to eleven billion people. As Robert McNamara, ex-president of the bank recognized, population growth of this magnitude would impose heavy if not impossible economic and social penalties. Nations would be tempted to use coercive measures to control births and individual families would resort to higher rates of abortion and infanticide, particularly of females. (In the 1980s, there were some fifty-five million abortions annually in the "third world.") McNamara foresaw India's population reaching 1.2 billion in 2000, China would also try to feed 1.2 billion, while Indonesia would rise to 216 million people and Bangladesh would have 156 million people.

The facts were simple: the breeding of babies and the aging of the world's population outpaced food production. As Thailand and Singapore, China and Malaysia demonstrated in the 1970s, however, well-financed family planning programs directly affected the birthrate, far beyond the usual reductions which economic progress itself entails. Further, the World Bank estimated in 1984 that an additional US$1 billion a year used for birth control programs—a paltry sum when compared to world "defense" budgets—could go a long way toward finally stabilizing world population growth.

The need to reduce population growth was never so patently obvious. Yet, two ideologically opposed groups expressed grave, potentially crippling opposition to conscious attempts to control the world's population.

"Conservatives," particularly in America, argued that population growth was a natural phenomenon that would actually stimulate economic growth. Aside from their religious objections to abortion (most pronounced in Islamic and Catholic nations), such conservatives said that governmental controls and mismanagement, not simple over-population caused famine. Thus, in 1984, a conservative American government refused to contribute directly or indirectly to any international family planning program which allowed abortion.

The conservatives, allied with Vatican representatives, cited real instances of governmental mismanagement as contributing to famine. In the 1980s, a major part of Ethiopia's famine could be attributed to civil discord and the failures of a Marxist government; in India, the government's policy of subsidizing urban consumers rather than the rural producers of food exacerbated the food problem; and in Africa, corruption and a lack of transport in some countries prevented relief supplies from reaching devastated areas.

Ironically, the conservatives presented almost a mirror image of classical Marxist thought: if only the "right" economic and political system prevailed, the problem of population growth would disappear.

With varying amounts of dogmatism, classical Marxists have opposed birth control programs because they believed that overpopulation was a mere "relative surplus" of labor caused by capitalism's supposed need to maintain high levels of unemployment. In a socialist society, Marxists said, there would be full employment and no superfluous population.

Some Marxists have, at times, argued that family planning programs were merely neocolonialist, racist attempts to reduce the size of ex-colonial peoples. Thus, in United Nations votes, a strange coalition of nations—conservative, Catholic, Marxist, and Africans fearful of "genocide"—united to block international action on family planning.

In reality, the more rational Marxist leaders abandoned their traditional position, but only after a series of ideological reversals. In China, Mao first advocated birth control; in 1958, he demanded more babies from the Chinese and apparently entertained the hope that the sheer size of the Chinese population would allow the nation to survive a nuclear attack. In 1963, he changed again, ordering widespread contraception, sterilization, and abortion. Finally, after the convulsions of the Cultural Revolution, a new Chinese leadership adopted a strict policy of birth control aimed at limiting families to one child. After 1976, laws and economic incentives reinforced persuasive campaigns to reduce the birth rate. At times, the post-Mao rulers may have sanctioned forced abortion in their zeal to curb population growth. In any case, Marxist doctrine was thrown to the winds and China radically decreased its growth rate.

Equally, whatever their rhetoric, most non-Marxist regimes abandoned hope that the invisible hand of economic advance would automatically solve population problems. In spite of great economic progress and a capitalist ideology, for example, Singapore decided to institute family planning in the 1960s and buttressed it with economic rewards and punishments dependent on family size. By the 1980s, the policies had succeeded and Singapore was the first "developing" nation in the world to achieve a zero growth rate. Catholic Mexico, Buddhist Thailand, and Muslim Indonesia all brought about major decreases in birthrates.

Thus, by the 1980s, statesmen in most areas had realized that neither the "green revolution" and economic progress nor the coming of a Marxist "utopia" would allow mankind to keep up with the population expansion. Even the most visionary plans—irrigating the Sahara or packing off "excess" people to space satellites—had given way to the demands of meeting a world food crisis on this small planet.

Here, the battle had to be fought primarily in the world's villages where 70 percent of the earth's population still expended its blood, sweat, and tears.

Transforming Villagers

From the late 1950s through the 1980s, an organization called the Kerala Sastra Sahitya Parished (KSSP) dedicated itself to infusing Indian village life with scientific attitudes and knowledge. They sent cultural groups throughout Kerala's villages, attempting to import new scientific techniques to the Indian peasants and to convince the poor that change was possible and desirable.

The KSSP troupe used an old technique, folk theater, to develop scientific interests and a critical attitude among Kerala's peasants. Perhaps the KSSP's most popular skit, *The Product,* was seen by millions of peasants.

The Product, a short dance-drama, depicted eager smiling children being devoured by the "education machine." In the drama, a half dozen dancers beat the inquiring children with sticks, chanting rote-learned phrases. At the end, the children emerged crippled and stupid—*The Product.*

This critique of formal education took place in Kerala, the most literate state in India (69 percent could read and write in 1986). Kerala's high literacy rates had roots in its unique history: its original Maharajas spent large sums on primary education, its large Christian population valued literacy, and its position on India's coast required the production of large numbers of clerks for keeping export records.

Some experts even talked of the "Kerala model" of development where literacy produced more political organization, greater public demands for health measures, a consequent fall in the birthrate and an improvement in living conditions—without a major increase in industrialization.

The KSSP, however, argued that Kerala's system encouraged only useless knowledge, neglected science, and geared children for farcical exams. Teachers were ill paid and uninspired; supposedly, many bought their positions with bribes. In consequence, only 40 percent of students passed the Indian school-leaving certificate in the 1980s and only a small minority of Kerala university graduates passed all-India competitive exams. Did the results of the "Kerala model" justify the state's major expenditures on formal education? The KSSP thought not.

The KSSP went directly to the peasants, teaching them the newest scientific techniques in agriculture in an exciting, hope-inspiring manner. It criticized not only traditional landowners but the powerful Communist party of Kerala, accusing both of ignoring basic technology.

By 1986, the KSSP boasted of hundreds of village learning centers, a breakthrough of caste and religious barriers, and its ability to fill halls throughout Kerala with eager, critical villagers. More than 300,000 people annually took part in its science competition. Agricultural production bloomed in the state.

By bringing literacy and technology to the village level, the KSSP became India's most popular, innovative movement, adding substance to its motto, "Science for social revolution."

Kerala did not stand alone. Throughout the developing world, new scientific methods—accompanied by intense educational campaigns, changes in economic structures, and additional incentives—transformed both the social structures and the productivity of peasants. The last thirty years of experience have established beyond doubt that the fatalism and resignation characteristic of many peasants was not an unconquerable aspect of their mentalities:

In the southern delta region of Egypt, El Westiani once passively accepted the absolute power of a pasha who owned 3,000 hectares of land. Until 1952, the ten thousand people of El Westiani had to pay the pasha 75 percent of their produce and 50 percent interest rates for loans taken out during periods of drought. When the pasha haughtily drove through the village with bodyguards on the sideboards of his grand touring car, the peasants scattered in terror.

In 1952 and again in 1961, substantial land reforms initiated in Cairo gave El Westiani's people a stake in their production. The Nasser government also encouraged cooperative farming and provided seeds, stock, credit, and advice on crop rotation and marketing.

Later, under Sadat, an agricultural extension center introduced Japanese methods of cultivation, new batches of calves sired by a prize Dutch bull, and television sets to convey educational programs.

Mubarak's government brought in chemical fertilizers and a new road from the markets to El Westiani, as well as irrigation pumps to take advantage of waters released by the Aswan dam. In an area previously dependent on cotton, the peasants diversified into raising cattle, chickens, and even rabbits.

Within one man's lifetime, El Westiani's income doubled, the literacy rate tripled, and people expected realistically to live five years longer. In 1986, even the poorest peasant owned several types of livestock, grew three crops a year on five hectares of his cooperatively owned land and, for the first time in history, voted in a free (if bloody) national election.

Another village, Alipur—a settlement of two thousand people situated on the great plain near New Delhi—showed similar progress over the three decades but for quite different reasons. Alipur, too, adopted hybrid seeds and chemical fertilizers, spurred by the higher prices permitted by the Indian government in the late 1960s.

The villagers built their own school, welcomed a new teacher, and almost abolished illiteracy. The villagers also responded well to government campaigns aimed at the elimination of malaria, yellow fever, and cholera. The *Panchayat Raj* plan, an attempt to create self-government on the village level, resulted in the election of village officials who, for the first time in history, included untouchables.

Alipur's real economic revolution, however, occurred in the 1970s when the Phillips company established a subsidiary in the village. Phillips, a Dutch multinational electronics company, decided to decentralize its operations in India in the hope of encouraging indigenous capitalism. In return for technology, technical advice, and help in marketing, Phillips encouraged small entrepreneurs to invest their capital and to establish new manufacturing plants in Indian villages. Several Alipur Brahmins responded to the opportunity and created a mini-Phillips plant in the village. The factory prospered and eventually hired two hundred landless laborers as factory hands. With guidance from Phillips, the Alipur experiment created a new class of villagers, spawned a group of small merchants who catered to rising consumer demands, and indirectly undermined the caste system by requiring that untouchables should be hired without discrimination.

A fourth illustration of the ways in which villages have been transformed came from Nigeria. Ben Nzeribe, the head of his village in Awgu, led his eastern tribesmen in a determined effort to transform his area. In the 1960s, Awgu grew yams, cassavas, and palm products. In the 1970s Nzeribe, a Ph.D. from Cornell, led the villagers in planting new strains of rice and cashew trees in areas which had previously lain barren. Chemical fertilizers transformed the crops into marketable commodities.

As their incomes increased, the people also donated their labor in constructing a new hospital, school, and a center for the treatment of leprosy. The traditional elder tribesmen grumbled but, as economic advance occurred, they relinquished their elected positions to younger people who had accepted the innovations. Attitudes toward women changed as their new role in a market economy, as tradesmen who took cashew nuts to the markets, demanded more skills and education from them. Taboos on lepers lessened as people realized that leprosy was a disease and not a punishment for past sins; lepers increasingly came forward to seek treatment in the earlier stages of their disease.

Dr. Nzeribe persuaded his people of the rewards for progress, brought experts to the village to reach agricultural and medical techniques, and subtly undermined social and political obstacles to development.

What common lessons could be drawn from Kerala, El Westiani, Alipur, and Awgu?

1. Contrary to pessimists, they showed that village life can be transformed in ways that will end poverty and perpetual disease, ignorance, and superstitious fatalism.

2. Their transformation usually began because of the invasion of "outsiders"—agitators for scientific progress, a multinational company, or agents espousing new government services—all offering new opportunities and fresh ways of viewing the world.*

3. An influx of new scientific knowledge, entrance into a market economy or leadership provided by new religious, political, or educational figures called forth latent entrepreneurial talents. Rapid changes in the villages have indicated that Sir Arthur Lewis was right in arguing that "the underdeveloped countries have no shortage of the commercial instincts. . . . Their peoples demonstrate as great a fondness for trading and taking risks as one can find anywhere."[20]

4. Sustained economic growth on the village level has, however, taken place only when buttressed by outside economic factors: expert advice, credit opportunities, marketing outlets, adequate transport, irrigation canals, and advanced agricultural and scientific knowledge. If these elements were not present (or were provided only briefly during some "big push"), village economies returned to stagnation.

5. Where continued economic progress occurred after the original transformation, it was a voluntary effort—a sustained attempt motivated by religious emotion, political enthusiasm, or more likely, capitalistic greed—informed by scientific knowledge and driven by individual incentives. Massive efforts to compel village change—as in Russia, Mao's China, or Nyerere's Tanzania—have markedly failed to substitute for market forces and adequate knowledge.

One may hope with Richard Critchfield, an astute observer of village life throughout the world, that "a quiet agricultural revolution has begun in the Third World that is likely to have more dramatic effects on more human beings than any revolution that has gone before."[21]

---

*The critical nature of these intrusions partially supported the views of Dutch economist J. H. Boeke and American economist Everett Hagan. In the 1950s, Boeke argued that economic advance in South and Southeast Asia would occur only due to "outside agitation" since, he believed the people of a nation such as Indonesia valued commodities only for their social value, not their economic importance.

Similarly, after experience in Burma, Everett Hagan argued that economic change in nations as diverse as Japan and Colombia took place only when a static elite was forced to relinquish power. A period of "retreatism" ensued until a new class of innovators appeared.

In spite of the advance of science into the remotest village, many leaders in the West and undeveloped countries have given up hope of either economic or political progress.

Manmade famines in Asia and Africa, the worldwide debt crisis, political tyranny and corruption, the pall of illiteracy, the dragging fatalism of traditional cultures, the blind economic policies of the West, the obfuscations of Marxism—all of these stark aspects of the dilemmas of development have contributed to an atmosphere of despair in the last decades of the twentieth century. Whether fallible humans in the "North" and "South" can overcome these challenges remains, at best, questionable.

Beyond the human challenge, however, some prominent scholars have argued that the earth has reached the physical "limits to growth." The more extreme of these prophets of doom, such as Garett Hardin, have argued that the advanced nations must adopt a policy of "triage" and "life-boat ethics" in order to survive an age characterized by the population explosion, famine, energy shortages, a gobbling of finite mineral resources, and the threat posed by an overheated ecosphere.

Are these Cassandras of the earth correct in predicting an apocalypse?

2

The Physical Challenge

There is no doubt in my mind that the human race is hurtling toward disaster.

—AURELIO PECCEI,
founder, Club of Rome

In 1984, the head of World Relief for the Lutheran Church visited the Ethiopian town of Korem. He found dying women, motionless children covered with sores, rows of tents filled with hungry people wrapped in blankets, untended stretchers holding the wounded—but this was not a scene drawn from the wars and revolutions which ravaged that nation.

Korem was merely one example of the toll which population pressure, overgrazing, deforestation, decades of neglect, and the follies of both an uncaring emperor and Marxist militarists had taken in that sad section of Africa. "The problem is larger than Korem," the relief worker wrote. "It also demands rekindled commitment by the international community to fashion a global food system that protects the well-being of all the world's people."[1]

Yet, some responsible scholars argued that no effort—however well financed, concerned, and humane—could save much of the earth's people from disaster. Fashionable commentators said that there was simply not enough food or energy or minerals left to serve the world's burgeoning population. The earth, they believed, had reached the physical "limits of growth."

The panic first publicly surfaced in the West as a reaction to the energy crisis of the 1970s, with "the discovery that the life of nations, nay, the very foundation of industrial civilization cannot rest on abundant cheap oil."[2] By 1977, experts such as D. S. Halacy flatly predicted that "natural gas will be burned up in a matter of years, a decade or two at best. Oil not much longer."[3]

As mineral supplies were exhausted, arable lands depleted, and premature hopes faded that nuclear fussion or fission would offer new sources of energy, some scientists in both the West and the East gave up hope that developing countries could even feed their populations, let alone achieve their ambitious goals of industrialization.

Scientific studies of population growth, pollution, and the decline in energy and mineral resources added to the gloom. The Club of Rome, an organization which combined Western capitalists with some Marxist politicians, used its supposedly infallible computers to gauge the world's food supplies and concluded "the specter of famine is rising again on the planet—but for the first time so huge as to be called megafamine."[4]

An official report to the American president in 1982 asserted that "the world would be more crowded, less stable, more polluted, and have less food by the year 2000." The panel concluded that "the world's people will be poorer in many ways than they are today."[5]

The "greenhouse effect"—an increase in the earth's surface temperature, due to an accumulation of carbon dioxide in the atmosphere from the burning of fossil fuels—added an imminent, unavoidable aspect to prophecies of the earth's collapse. According to some, the warming of the earth's climate in future years could destabilize agriculture, melt ice caps, and flood coastal cities.[6] Supposedly, the current level of the globe's industralization had to come to an abrupt halt. More importantly, all hopes for greater industrialization in the "third world" would inevitably have to be abandoned.

All of these warnings concerning the physical limits of growth contributed to an atmosphere of deep pessimisim. As Fouad Ajami wrote in 1982:

> The sense of political and cultural despair over the Third World—the belief that it can't be taught public order—has its economic counterpart. Now the poverty of the Third World, too, is beyond hope.[7]

The population explosion and the unavailability of sufficient food indicated to certain writers, such as biologist Garrett Hardin, that "the sharing ethic of the spaceship is impossible. For the forseeable future, our survival demands that we govern our actions by the ethics of the life-boat, harsh though they may be."[8]

In effect, Hardin argued against the rich helping the poor nations. In the long run, he believed, such efforts would be worse than useless and the industrialized nations would only deprive their posterity of its privileges.

THE CASE FOR DESPAIR

Everything is irrevocably moving in the direction of random chaos and waste.

—JEREMY RIFKIN, 1980

Hard physical realities contributed to the loss of political nerve and the cultural despair which prevailed during the 1970s and 1980s.

• In 1973, the world awoke to the fact that proven oil reserves would be exhausted in the forseeable future, crippling the thrust toward industrialization. America was the most voracious consumer of oil in the 1970s: the average American used oil at a rate equivalent to 23,000 pounds of coal annually while a Haitian used 68 pounds. If the entire world had drained oil at the American level of 1981, the world's proven reserves would have lasted only until 1986.

In fact, the great oil users, particularly Japan, cut down on their consumption and searched for alternative sources of energy. Their options were severely limited. Exploration of coal reserves, especially abundant in China, required vast amounts of capital, a new infrastructure, and huge amounts of water. Plans for nuclear energy floundered on such problems as the inability of scientists to discover an earthly material capable of withstanding resulting radiation and a temperature of 3 billion degrees centigrade. Solar energy proved difficult to harness: the construction of giant solar satellite generators had to be abandoned when economists estimated that the cost of launching them would consume as much energy as the satellites would deliver for many years in the future.

• Scientists warned that the earth was fast running out of the minerals necessary to highly industrialized regions. In the 1980s, the United States alone used up the world's diminishing supply of minerals at the annual rate of 40,000 pounds per person.

• According to certain scientists, the increased pressure of the world's growing population had strained the basic resources for food production—topsoil, fishing areas, cropland, and grasslands—to the point of near exhaustion. The world's forests declined in productivity since 1967 (and yet people had tripled their use of wood products). The stock of fisheries went down since the 1970s. Crop and grasslands had similarly eroded since 1975.

As early as 1960, such prophets as Karl Sax issued a series of dire warnings concerning the race between population and food supplies. He predicted that "the people of Japan can expect only subsistence living standards," that China would be devastated by famine and, most dramatically: "There is no possibility whatever that Indian industry and agriculture can meet the needs of such a rapidly growing population."[9]

Such forecasts were far off the mark, but only because of the invention of hybrid seeds, new agricultural methods, aquaculture, the success of birth control policies, and changes in economic incentives—all of which created the "green revolution" of the 1970s.

Nonetheless, by the 1980s, such agricultural experts as Lester Brown feared that the "green revolution" might well be using "deficit financing" in its intensive cultivation of land, erosion of soil, and dependence on precious resources.

One source of the "green revolution," for example, had been the extensive use of new fertilizers manufactured from oil. The insatiable requirements for petroleum as a fertilizer base suggested to scholars that the world's food supply—hampered by the inevitable shortage of oil—could not possibly increase sufficiently to support the world's growing population.

• Even if the "third world" peoples miraculously achieved a zero growth rate by the year 2000, demographers estimated that its population will still increase by two and a half times by the year 2050. Such an event would, in turn, quadruple the "third world's" demands for food and energy.

• At the present rate of heat emission from mankind's industries, some experts predicted that the earth's temperature will reach 50 degrees centigrade within 250 years—an impossible condition for human survival. If developing countries succeeded in encouraging industrialization and merely caught up to the West's level in the 1970s, energy use would have to increase twenty- to thirty-fold—again a goal which cannot be reached.

For these reasons, then, observers believed that nature dictated that the battle to feed humanity and improve basic standards of living had already been lost.

"We are living beyond our means, largely by borrowing against our future," so concluded the first of a series of studies in 1984 of the world's ecological and economic conditions. The warning came from the Worldwatch Institute, a monitor of the global resource base. Lester R. Brown, its president, argued that "the world is engaging in wholesale biological and agronomic deficit financing."[10]

In their understandable haste to alert mankind to its frightening prospects, however, the prophets had overlooked salient features of the human condition.

THE CASE FOR HOPE

There is no physical or economic reason why human resourcefulness and enterprise cannot forever continue to respond to impending shortages and existing problems with new expedients.

—JULIAN SIMON, 1981

Aided by science, a balanced vision of human needs, and technological enterprise, the human imagination has repeatedly demonstrated its ability to surmount awesome obstacles:

In 1980, using new methods of exploration and forecasting, Mexico's proven oil reserves increased twenty-fold.

In 1981, the United Nations reported that the overall amount of food available per person had steadily grown since 1900.

In 1982, Japan announced the creation of new sea farms that annually produced 8,000 tons of carp per acre of water.

In 1983, Nigeria's University of Sokoto harnessed solar energy by means of a gigantic field of mirrors, allowing the spread of electric-powered irrigation pumps and the creation of small industries.

In 1984, private American companies experimented with giant "vacuum cleaners" which extracted manganese, phosphates, and nickel nodules from the floor of the Pacific.

Between 1975 and 1985, calling upon a campaign which emphasized humor, Thailand cut its population growth rate in half from 3.3 percent a year to 1.7 percent without the use of coercion.

In 1985, Japan created artificial islands off its coasts and successfully used waves and thermal conversion as a source of energy. The Japanese on these islands developed methods to extract uranium from sea water and to use thermal wastes for nourishing shellfish "farms."

In 1986, the villagers of Al Uyaynah in Saudi Arabia turned on lights for the first time, proudly displayed televisions and toasters, and fully participated in an electronic society based on the sun. They were the first citizens of the world to generate their energy solely from an array of solar mirrors and photovoltaic cells.

These and many other developments offered reasonable hope, although no certain guarantee, that man's ingenuity and innovation—the "ultimate resource," as Julian Simon has called it—could overcome the globe's physical deficiencies.[11] A cautious assessment of the "limits to growth" arguments and their deficiencies indicates that mankind, informed by science and sound economic policies, may well find the resources—on earth, in the ocean, out in space and most importantly within himself—to overcome the most severe of physical limitations.

Even in the 1980s, in spite of the harsh predictions, the earth's energy resources were far from exhausted. Part of the confusion over this matter derived from semantics. Experts based their predictions about an ultimate energy shortage on the concept of "proven reserves" of oil—that is, fields of oil which companies and countries could profitably exploit. These were entirely different from "ultimately recoverable reserves" of oil which were well known, but drillable only at a higher price and with more advanced technology. Such pools contained some 2.2 trillion barrels of oil in the 1980s.

The surplus was particularly great in Asia, Africa, and Latin America. Even in the Middle East, 90 percent of "ultimately recoverable" resources remained untapped and the exploration of the more difficult fields had barely begun.

Oil companies naturally preferred to obtain their product from the least expensive source. In the 1980s, for example, the accessible state of Arkansas in America had three times as many oil rigs as all of Africa. The tiny Sultanate of Brunei produced more oil than all of China. Russia had little desire to expend money on exploration but every reason to encourage the dependence of East Europe on its oil and of West Europe on its natural gas. OPEC countries, whether a socialist revolutionary state such as Libya or a feudal kingdom like Saudi Arabia, had no rational motive for ending their joint monopoly over "proven reserves." Thus, as petroleum expert Peter Odell wrote, "The so-called generally accepted oil shortage is the outcome of commercially oriented interests rather than a statement of the essential realities of the oil resources of the world."[12]

In addition to oil, there were great natural reserves of coal, oil shale, tar sands, and biogas throughout the world. Some of these energy sources, such as oil shale, were relatively expensive to process or had other disadvantages such as a greater tendency to pollute the air than did oil. Other sources, such as biogas, were very inexpensive but offered little profit either to nations or corporations. Although France and Japan built nuclear plants at a fast rate, proponents of nuclear energy faced both financial problems and political opposition because of potential break-downs at their plants and the problem of safely disposing of nuclear waste. In other words, the energy soruces were there but considerations of profit or politics prevented their exploitation. Thus, as Richard Barnet rightly observed in 1980, "the state of world reserves is far more a matter of economics and politics than geology."[13]

Beyond the earth's energy resources lies the sun, the ultimate source of all energy. Man has just begun to tap solar energy directly, but the prospects are limited only by the sun's life expectancy of 4 billion years.

In 1872, an inventor developed the first solar machine for converting salt water into fresh. In 1913, Egyptians used solar irrigations pumps on the Nile. By 1981, Japan had installed 2.5 million solar heating units, while in Africa, Niger used solar energy for all of its hospitals and government offices. By 1984, Indians developed very cheap solar-generated stoves. Throughout the world, single plate conductors and photovoltaic cells demonstrated their ability to convert sun light into electricity.

Technological and economic considerations as well as geography hindered some countries from exploiting solar energy but, as Julian Simon correctly observed, "there is no meaningful limit" to the potential sources "except the sun's energy."[14]

Although there were forecasts during the 1970s that the world would soon use up high-grade, cheap reserves of lead, zinc, iron ore, and aluminium, the fact was that the earth's mineral resources were almost as abundant as the sun's energy. Again, the semantics of profit clouded the issue. Possibly, "proven reserves" of certain rare minerals might be exhausted in the twenty-first century. (Even this is doubtful; diamonds, for example, have been discovered in the ocean bed off Southwest Africa.) Yet, "ultimately recoverable" reserves of such basic resources as bauxite and iron ore were, in fact, unknown. The U.S. Geological Survey dismissed attempts to measure the ultimate reserves as meaningless since bauxite was the most abundant resource on the earth's crust and untapped ore resources were incalculably enormous. Recovery of these resources may become more difficult, man may have to dig deeper into the earth, and costs may rise—but this did not mean that the minerals (or future substitutes) were unavailable.

Beyond these earthly resources, the ocean floor had yet to be combed and the reaches of space remained unexplored. Their possibilities beckoned to the next generation—and also frightened some "third world" governments. Capitalist or socialist, Zambia, Morocco, Chile, and Cuba opposed unrestricted mining of seabeds and wanted them treated as "the common heritage" of mankind. In 1983, such nations called for the establishment of a UN international authority to control the oceans; this authority, in turn, would be dominated by "third world" countries. Whatever humanitarian motives led to this demand, the fact remained that exploitation of seabeds could well depress the prices that these countries (and South Africa) commanded on the world market for their own land-based minerals.

The ocean floor contains manganese deposits, phosphates, and great underwater beds of nickel, copper, and cobalt nodules. By the 1970s, scientists had invented the technology for sweeping and extracting these minerals from the ocean depths. By the 1980s, the threat that exploitation of the ocean minerals might ruin the economies of certain nations emerged in the political realm. Abundance, not scarcity, national self-interest, and not an absence of technology were the underlying issues.

In an ultimate sense, unexplored space represents another "infinite commons" of energy, minerals, and even food. By the 1980s, we knew that asteroids and even other planets could be mined and cultivated. Asteroids offered a particularly attractive source of bauxite, titanium, and magnesium. Space colonies could be built by the end of the twentieth century which would orbit the earth, derive their construction materials from the moon, manufacture certain goods under ideal vacuum conditions, use solar energy and grow their own food—if mankind had the vision.

The unlimited possibilities of space exploration refuted the conclusions of more dismal analysts of the human condition who "tacitly assume that the earth is flat, that there are no other worlds in the universe, that we are stuck on the ground forever."[15] The unresolved issue was whether the industrialized nations would devote sufficient monies to the exploration of space in order to develop its potentialities.

A similar lack of human vision atrophied attempts to end food shortages. It was not the deficiencies of nature but the failures of man which created famine in the late twentieth century. As A. K. Sen has demonstrated, the great famines of 1943 in Bengal, 1974 in Bangladesh, and the African famines of the late 1970s sometimes took place in areas where a food surplus existed.[16] In fact, because of greed, mismanagement, or colonial exploitation, famine-stricken areas often exported food precisely at the moment when the poorest people—those not "entitled" to food—starved.

These tragic ironies persisted even after the "green revolution." That sweeping change in mankind's condition—the introduction of science to villagers, the invention of hyperproductive strains of grain, the creation of new incentives for peasants, the building of irrigation, transport, and storage systems—increased the world's food production per person to unparalleled levels.

By the 1980s, people had begun to utilize great sources of additional food by applying aquaculture in the world's oceans, converting cassava into a high protein food, intensively cultivating algae, and using grains and soybeans for humans rather than cattle.

And yet famine still prevailed in certain beleaguered regions, and some 450 million people suffered from severe malnutrition in 1985.

Why?

Technical failures—a lack of fertilizer, improper irrigation, the wrong seeds, overtilling, deforestation—superficially accounted for some of the devastation. These deficiencies, however, were due to human error and could have been corrected by already known methods.

The truth was that economic miscalculations, often politically motivated, produced famine conditions. Some governments such as Nigeria failed to provide loans or easy credit to peasants. Others such as Mao's China and Tanzania embarked on disastrous experiments in collectivization which destroyed peasant incentives. Still other nations followed policies that encouraged the miniaturization of land holdings, or created an artificial abundance of food in urban areas or simply failed to provide transportation of food supplies from their central cities to more remote areas. During the great Sahelian famine of the 1970s, for example, thousands of tons of millet, dried fish, and cooking oil never reached the starving people, merely because the governments had not built roads to deliver the supplies.

Governments which suffered from revolution or grew dependent on the West's donations of food, countries which failed to provide financial support or incentives to peasants, nations which refused to undergo land reform and devoted only a minuscule portion of their budgets to rural development or agronomic research—these were exactly the lands where people starved to death.

China under Mao provided a salient example of how ideology can degrade the land, pollute the air, and create artificial famines. Under Mao, the drive for industrialization and for local grain self-sufficiency totally ignored the Chinese environment. The extent of China's environmental woes was outlined by Vaclav Smil, who has pointed out that industrial emissions of air pollutants were twice as high in China than in Japan and that only 4 percent of waste water in China's major rivers was processed to remove pollutants.[17] Mao's policies also led to a vicious cycle where peasants cut down forests and planted grain to meet state quotas. The eroded, deforested land yielded sharply lower harvests. The reversal of Mao's stand came in 1980 when a new government encouraged policies of environmental protection and allowed people to grow grain and to plant trees on land which they owned privately or semiprivately.

Floods, droughts, desertification, deforestation, locust plagues, or other obvious causes of food shortages did not "cause" hunger in the twentieth century. Since science had produced the methods to protect the environment and to create the greatest cornucopia of food in history, it was clearly man and his mistaken economic and political policies which ravaged the land, condeming millions to malnutrition and even starvation.

The dreaded "greenhouse effect" was also a matter of man's invention and thus remained potentially under man's control. The thrust for industrialization and the resulting consumption of fossil fuels raised the possibility that the globe's temperature would increase by several degrees centigrade in the next century. As the globe heats up, scientists predicted, there could be a growth in insect populations that would threaten both crops and human health. Conceivably, the warning pattern could melt the Antartic ice sheet, cause unpredictable rains, and turn arable regions such as the American midwest into deserts.

These calamities, dooming all efforts at further industrialization of the globe, might occur in two hundred and fifty years.

Forecasters of meterological disaster, however, tended to ignore the more predictable and more benign influences of the "greenhouse effect." The deserts of the Sahara, the Middle East, central China, and Australia would receive more rain and could blossom as food producing areas. Wetter conditions in India, China, and Southeast Asia would allow multiple cropping and major increases in food production. Whether these crucial areas will benefit from the changes in climate depends on man's ability to cultivate the newly arable regions. The future of industrialization some three centuries from now rests on human decisions about technology, space, and the utilization of solar energy.

"The tragedy will be if the perceived 'threat' leads the rich nations into an ill-conceived and expensive search for solutions," John Gribbin has commented about the future climate. "We should not," he argued, "gobble up resources that could be better used to improve world agriculture."[18]

Thus, a reasonable view of the physical world in the 1980s suggested that people could affect prospective climate changes, steadily increase the globe's food supply, and exploit new and practically unlimited sources of energy and minerals—*if* they acted in a rational political and economic manner to reap and distribute the bounties which the earth, the oceans, and space have bestowed.

The central question remained: could people limit their own population growth? Significant trends which began in the 1970s tentatively indicated that the answer will be yes.

Admittedly, in 1986, the world had not yet defused the population bomb and some regions, even blessed with a high rate of economic growth, seemed on the brink of disaster. Kenya, a land where billboards blatantly advertised drugs which would supposedly enhance male potency, had a birthrate of 4 percent annually in 1986, the highest in the world. Kenya's fertile land could not feed a population that grows at such a rate. Africa in general, a starving continent, will have to feed some 850 million people by the year 2000. Even countries with relatively successful birth control programs, like Thailand, will not reach "replacement fertility" levels (two children per family) until the end of the century. That means that eight million more Thais will have to be fed by the year 2000. Inevitably, Thailand will have to end its rice exports with disastrous implications for its own economy and those of surrounding nations in Southeast Asia.

A few politicians throughout the world held to their obdurate opposition to birth control. In 1985, political groups in Spain, a nominally Catholic country, tried to ban the advertising of male contraceptives; conservatives in the American government and the Vatican succeeded in condemning abortion as a birth control method advocated by UN agencies; and nations such as Malaysia actively promoted more births among segments of their population since the Malay-dominated government wished to increase the power of Malays versus minority groups such as Chinese and Indians.

Yet, developments throughout much of the world—particularly in some Chinese, Catholic, and Islamic cultures which have traditionally encouraged large families—offered hope in the 1970s and 1980s that people would succeed in capping the population volcano.

China's inauguration of a rigorous—and some said, coercive—birth control policy drastically cut the birthrate between 1975 and 1985. By increasing the age of marriage, distributing free contraceptives, encouraging (and sometimes forcing) abortion, by manipulating monetary and food incentives, and by providing better housing for one-child families, a pragmatic post-Mao government gradually brought the world's largest population under control.

Without violence, Islamic Indonesia, Egypt, Tunisia, and Turkey all registered sharp downturns in fertility between 1970 and 1980. Catholic nations such as the Philippines, Mexico, and Colombia managed to introduce effective birth control campaigns. "Confucian" cultures such as South Korea and Taiwan drastically reduced their rate of population growth. Significantly, these changes took place at a speed which exceeded the historical pace experienced in economically growing countries. And, it should be noted, the decrease occurred in diverse cultures where tradition has often dictated that having many children was a symbol of male virility, proof of a mother's fecundity, a religious duty, and an insurance policy for old age. Apparently, cultural and social obstacles to birth control—often described as insuperable—crumbled in the face of well-executed family planning programs and in situations of economic growth.

This was nowhere more evident than in Southeast Asia. By passing out key rings with condoms, sponsoring birth control carnivals, sending out mobile clinics, and putting family planning advisers in 16,000 rural villages, the Thai government convinced 60 percent of its people to practice birth control and cut the rate of fertility in half between 1974 and 1984.

Singapore emerged as the greatest success. Aided by a strong governmental emphasis on family planning, economic incentives, penalties for excessive births (such as an increasing cost of medical care for additional children), and a generally exuberant economy, Singapore was the first developing nation to achieve the goal of a stable replacement rate in 1975. This was essential to the health of this robust island republic since a sheer lack of land already forced 70 percent of the people to live in high-rise apartment buildings.

Thus, in spite of formidable cultural, political, and economic obstacles, there were increasing, if still inconclusive signs that people in many societies were changing their ways in a manner which encouraged a decrease in population pressures and helped to ensure a more bountiful future.

The encouraging facts about the physical challenge—man's increasing ability to control the population explosion, the potential abundance of food, resources, and energy, the unexplored possibilities of the seas and space—should not tempt the human race into complacency. The challenge of the next decades is grim and multifaceted.

In sub-Saharan Africa, for example, the World Food Program estimated in 1984 a shortfall of 1.3 million metric tons of food. The resulting famine, dysentery, measles, meningitis and malaria affected 150 million people. As Robert McCloskey, an official of Catholic Relief Services, remarked about Africa:

> The assessment that there is enough food to feed all the hungry implies the best of possible worlds. The real world, with its projections for huge population increases continuing into the next century, is what must be faced.[19]

Nonetheless, the truth is that nature has not imposed limits to growth. Man's ignorance, venality, and tyranny have created the obstacles. In the short run, technical and material assistance from the West is critical, particularly in Africa. Yet, as McCloskey noted, aid from the West must be matched "by firm commitments on the part of African governments to more enlightened political and economic policies. To pass through the barriers to more productive futures, donor and recipient will have to go arm in arm."[20]

With sufficient knowledge and flexibility, with political will and economic pragmatism, human beings can cope with virtually any physical challenge. Barbara Ward stated the critical issue in 1979: "No problem is insoluble in the creation of a balanced and conserving planet save humanity itself. Can it reach in time the vision of joint survival?"[21]

3

Visions of Development

Most of the great positive evils of the world are in themselves removable, and will, if human affairs continue to improve, be in the end reduced within narrow limits.

—JOHN STUART MILL

As Barbara Ward observed, neither the human nor the physical challenges to world survival are insurmountable. The crucial problem is whether humanity can reach a vision of joint survival. And here we encounter a critical juncture, for mankind has yet to agree either on the means, or more importantly, the goals of "development."

Since 1950, visions of the future have involved a melange of ideologies:

Antimaterialists argued that higher consumption in itself was not a proper goal for any society. In the West, groups such as Germany's Green Party campaigned for "zero growth" in industry, "the greening" of the planet, conservation and, at their extreme, a return to rural existence. In the "third world," believers in various idealistic doctrines emphasized the value of their traditional cultures, the supposed spiritual emptiness of Western life, and the necessity of preserving an "authentic" economic system which they regarded as the "original affluent society."[1]

E. F. Schumacher, an economist who once advised Burma, epitomized this argument in *Small Is Beautiful,* an eloquent plea that the real goal of development should be produce more jobs, not cheaper goods, and that modernization must directly benefit the rural majority in developing nations. He advocated the establishment of decentralized, labor-intensive industries as a way to this end.

Only isolated experimenters and communities responded to this plea. The various national elites largely ignored it, not least because the spread of such small industries might have undermined their own power. Burma may be regarded as the one area which undertook an experiment in "Buddhist economics." Under the strict, isolationalist rule of General Ne Win, Burma's militarists and priests sought to cut the country off from all outside influences and to preserve its Buddhist heritage. Simultaneously, with the most modern weapons. Ne Win fruitlessly tried to subdue various Communist, Christian, and ethnic revolts. The Burmese barely sustained themselves on small industries, traditionally abundant rice and fish, and a flourishing black market trade with Thailand. By the 1980s, no nation in Southeast Asia consciously sought to emulate Burmese stagnation.

At the opposite extreme, neo-Stalinists stressed the necessity for an iron government to increase production, create an egalitarian social order, and eliminate feudal elements. Horrified by the "nasty and brutish" life of their peoples, the neo-Stalinists promised that both a cornucopia of goods and social justice would flow from their policies. The leadership of Mao's China, the Khmer Rouge, and North Korea ruthlessly extirpated traditionalists from their lands; they placed full faith in state planning and measures designed to help the working classes; they did not hesitate to use the repressive methods of police states.

As one illustration, the Albania of Enver Hoxha remained in 1985 as one of a few tiny enclaves of neo-Stalinism. Albania had turned its back on the rest of the world for forty years. The little nation had no unemployment, no inflation, free health care, free education, and enforced self-sufficiency. The leaders refused to compromise their pure principles by encounters with either the capitalist West or the nominally Communist East. In 1985, Albania did not maintain embassies in either the United States or Great Britain, the Soviet Union or China. Religion was eliminated in 1967, and political opposition had disappeared. In a mineral-rich country, however, animals still provided transport and farmers used hoes in the fields. By 1986, Albania desperately sought trade outlets for its abundant, but unused mineral resources.[2]

Few countries, even within the Communist orbit of power, sought to copy the Albanian "model." Instead—as the Prague Spring of 1968, the Hungarian experiments with capitalism, the opening of China in 1976, and the rise of Polish Solidarity in 1980 indicated—there were notable attempts to renew Marxist societies along more democratic and productive lines.

Still another approach—the Fascist model of development—did not die with Hitler and Mussolini, Tojo and Péron. Petty fascists from Somoza to Duvalier tried to maintain their regimes by incorporating various elements from the older fascist examples: "corporatism," inflamed nationalism, centralization of power in one individual or the military, and perhaps, a glorification of a particular race or religion.

In Africa, various military governments dominated the scene, simultaneously proclaiming their opposition to the equally fascist, racist policies of South Africa. During the 1960s and 1970s, many of the nations of Latin America fell prey to their own versions of military fascism. Armies seized power with the claim that only the officer class could subdue Communist terrorism, end corruption, ensure stability, and defend Latin Christianity.

Even in countries which boasted a long tradition of liberal democracy, such as Chile, fascism cast a long shadow. On September 11, 1974, General Augusto Pinochet took power from the only democratically elected Marxist regime in world history. He promptly banned opposition, tortured and killed dissidents, and imposed his own brand of monetarist economics. Pinochet publicly described himself as the reincarnation of a Roman emperor, a defender of Christianity, and as an indispensable leader of his nation. As world copper prices fell, eroding the base of the Chilean economy. Pinochet's rule trembled. By 1986, Pinochet had lifted some censorship on opposition publications and promised parliamentary elections for 1990. Meanwhile, his people rioted in the streets.

In fact, the 1980s marked the demise of fascist regimes and a return, however temporary, of the military to their barracks. Most notably, the military in Argentina and Brazil (perhaps temporarily) handed back the reins of power to civilian leaders. The armies had proved incompetent in ending corruption, meeting the demands of new groups produced by economic growth, correcting the grievances of either labor unionists or businessmen and, in the case of Argentina, they had even failed to conduct a war successfully. The decline of fascism was hastened, too, by the fact that increasing numbers of Latin priests, particularly in Central America, embraced "liberation theology" and undermined the fascist claims to theocracy. Although the international debt crisis imperiled all regimes in Latin America, it appeared that the people (at least, the middle, educated classes) no longer considered fascism as an appropriate or legitimate alternative.

As the old faiths withered, three other grand visions of development—the "Islamic," the "socialist," and the "capitalist"—competed for man's allegiance in different parts of the globe.

THE ISLAMIC RENAISSANCE

An Islamic current from Iran is surging through the world's one billion Muslims.

—HAROON SIDDIQUI, 1984

In 1978, an unlikely candidate for world leadership—an aged, obscure cleric, the Ayatollah Khomeini—emerged from comfortable exile in France to take over Iran. He overthrew the shah, fought with Iraq, tried to break contact with the West (while collecting essential oil revenues), and held off the threat of Russian domination.

Internally, the Ayatollah established an absolute theocracy which theoretically fulfilled the goals not only of Shi'ites but of many other Muslim groups as well. He installed the *Sharia* as the law of the land, attacked minority religions, banned alcohol and frivolous singing, turned mosques into centers for dispensing justice, subordinated women to the Koran's injunctions, and abolished political opposition. This radical priest followed Islamic ideals by ordering women to wear the *hijah,* by dispensing millions of dollars in charity, and by obeying the Koran's command to make mosques the center of life. He fulfilled the longings of many Muslims for the coming of an Islamic renaissance led by a "caliph-like figure, a pious jurist with enormous powers"[3]—a man who combined in one person the Islamic ideals of an indispensable head of the family, a stern leader of the *mullahs,* and a political arbiter.

Externally, the Ayatollah epitomized a crude anti-Western sentiment. "All of the problems of the world," he declared, "stem from foreigners, from the West and from America."[4] He encouraged hatred of Israel and he created a band of Islamic revivalists, including his child soldiers, who were ready to die for their religious ideals.

The Ayatollah, however, merely symbolized a resurgence of Islamic fervor in many countries, a conviction that an Islamic rebirth presented a new force balancing the atheistic challenges of both communism and capitalism:

• In Malaysia, the PAS, a political organization of fundamentalist Muslims, threatened to upset the stability of this multiracial nation. The ruling secular party reacted by breaking up even private meetings of PAS as a threat to public order.

• In Egypt, members of the illegal Muslim Brotherhood slaughtered Anwar Al-Sadat. His successor, Hosni Mubarak, aligned himself increasingly with the Muslim world but allowed free elections. Fourteen members of the Muslim Brotherhood, adherents of an Islamic dictatorship, were elected to parliament in 1984.

• On Egypt's borders, Colonel Muamer Qaddafi installed his own version of an Islamic state. He built a useless river for $11 billion, financed terrorist groups throughout the world, and publicized the hanging of dissenters on television.

• The dictator of Pakistan, Zia ul-Haq, introduced new principles of retribution (*qisas,* an "eye for an eye" form a criminal justice) and stripped women of their theoretical equality with men. (A woman's testimony in court became worth half that of a man's and a murdered woman's family received half of the "blood money" due to a murdered man's.) Following the Koran, sterile universities taught astronomy as a branch of astrology.

• Some Muslim secularist leaders, such as dictator Gaafar Nimeiri of the Sudan, underwent apparent conversions. After suppressing Islam for many years, he suddenly installed the *Sharia* as the basic law of the land in 1983, just before losing power. Other Muslim secularists, like General Suharto of Indonesia, tried to combat fundamentalists among his 147 million Muslims, who rioted, threw bombs, and stoned churchs in the 1980s. In Nigeria, General Mohammed Buhari allowed riot police to shoot down 500 extremist Muslims in the town of Yola. Although ruled by Muslims, Nigeria faced uniquely perplexing problems because of a new prophet who disdained the past and proclaimed himself as the "true" Mohammed.

• Even in Eastern Europe, the messianic vision of a new Islam increased political tensions. Yugoslavia jailed followers of the Ayatollah, and Bulgaria, a nation where mosques were once razed to the ground, increased its persecution of newly inspired Muslims.

• Saudi Arabia and the oil-rich gulf states feared the potential threat of the Ayatollah and of Qaddafi to their own Islamic feudal regimes. In 1980, supporters of the Ayatollah laid siege to the holy mosque of Mecca and in 1984, Libyan pilgrims to mecca tried unsuccessfully to import arms. In response to their concern over these threats, Saudi Arabia and the other gulf kingdoms spent $40 billion in 1984 on defense—half of the war expenditures of the entire "third world." Meanwhile, the Sunni princes of Saudi Arabia claimed the role of sparking an Islamic revival as their own destiny. They expended millions on new mosques and subsidized a set of imans who boycotted pro-Khomeini activists. The Saudi courts continued to enforce harsh laws forbidding adult women from marriage without state permission and punishing adulteresses with a prolonged stoning to death.

For Muslim fundamentalists, there was supposedly one basic model for development: the Islamic state set up by the Prophet in Medina and by the first wave of his successors fourteen centuries ago. In fact, although it has taken many different forms because of the extreme diversities between the Muslim countries, there can be no question that a general Islamic revival surged through the world. Its followers called for the suppression if not death of infidels, a return to an assumed past or a continuation of feudalism, the establishment of theocracies, and the supremacy of Islamic ideals as the basic goals of development. Sometimes, as in Libya and Iran, the leaders linked an Islamic revival with the creation of an egalitarian social order under the guidance of an omnipotent caliph. At other times, as in Malaysia, the fundamentalist leaders refused to announce any specific goals at all except for "Islamization."

Why did the spirit of revival sweep over the Middle East, Africa, and parts of Asia in the 1970s? These stagnant Islamic states had been colonies or feudal fiefdoms for centuries but they stridently burst into life. Part of the answer surely lay in the exploitation of oil. "Until the discovery of oil there," one liberal Muslim observed, "no one spoke of Saudi Arabia as a model for anything."[5] In spite of the Shah's "white revolution," Nasser's "Arab Socialism," or Sukarno's "guided democracy," the same statement held true for Iran, Egypt, and Indonesia as well as Syria, Iraq, Nigeria, and the Gulf Emirates.

The cartelization of oil brought immense new riches to the Islamic regions and with them, new ambitions, weapons, and a sense of power. The oil wealth did not, however, create social equality or inevitably result in an improvement in life for many minor military men, the lower middle classes, students or peasant religious leaders—exactly those disgruntled people who became inflamed with a new vision of establishing a more just Islamic order. In the wings stood men like the Ayatollah and Qaddafi who were eager to exploit the grievances of Muslims: hatred of Israel, an inferiority complex toward the West, an historical distrust of Russia, and a belief that old regimes had betrayed Islamic ideals of charity and social justice. The new leaders, often incorruptible and genuinely identified with the peasants, promised to restore Islam and to create a more abundant, equalizing economy for all.

Will this suffice? As Fouad Ajami has commented:

> It is tempting to cover up decay with claims to authenticity; or to dress up tyranny in the garb of Islam . . . But history has a terrifying velocity today. Reality intrudes; men cannot indefinitely live on frenzy or indefinitely be kept in a trance.[6]

Our skepticism about the Islamic revival, as we have seen it in the Middle East and Asia, comes from four sources:

First, Muslims still could not agree on a coherent vision of an "Islamic society." Some wanted the West's technology but not its ideas. Sufi mystics wished to adopt the hairshirt of absolute poverty. Shi'ite fanatics and Sunni traditionalists offered quite different interpretations of the faith. A minority of Westernized Moslems rejected the claims of all fundamentalists. Hussain Haqqaui dismissed Pakistan's Islamic "reforms" as attempts to reduce women to the status of chattels,[7] while another Islamic liberal described Saudi Arabia as "a dark uncivilized blot on the Islamic map."[8] Such liberals pointed out, for example, that Islam was the first civilization in the world to grant property rights to women. They ridiculed more recent attempts to subjugate women as a betrayal of Islamic traditions.

Amidst such a Babel of interpretations, how could a devout believer discover the "proper" interpretation?

Second, Islamic fundamentalists of any persuasion offered no solution to the problems of pluralistic societies where different faiths competed for adherents. In the largest Islamic country, Indonesia, with its powerful minority of Chinese; in Malaysia where nearly half the people rejected Islam, in the Sudan where the non-Muslim South revolted; in Nigeria where Christian Yorubans and Ibos disliked their Muslim overlords—"Islamization" threatened a return to barbarism. When Muslim leaders in such important regions attempted to impose their particular religious imagery, they created the conditions for civil war and economic disintegration.

Third, the more fervent Islamic leaders had no solutions to the population wave which threatened to engulf them. Fundamentalists of different persuasions generally agreed that the Koran enjoined rich men to support four wives, described children as a gift from heaven, and discouraged birth control and abortion. As a result, Islamic areas had one of the highest birthrates in the world, equivalent to the rapid rate of population expansion in Roman Catholic countries. Islam provided no way to feed these hungry millions and offered only the consolation that whatever happened was the "will of Allah."

Fourth, Muslim villagers throughout the world had tasted the fruits which fundamentalists would forbid: the benefits of Western technology. Would Islam be able to handle the new attitudes and appetites created by this incursion?

By actually or symbolically cutting their ties to the West, some Islamic leaders deprived their peoples of the technology, medicines, scientific knowledge—and ideas—which they urgently required to foster a genuine renaissance.

THE SOCIALIST DREAM

The country that is more developed industrially only shows, to the less developed, the image of its own future.

—KARL MARX

The socialism embraced by some Arabs and, more importantly, by Lenin, Stalin, Mao, and Zhou was perhaps the single most important ideology of development during this century. Allied with nationalist movements, the other prime mover of our times, socialists promised to end exploitation and injustice by abolishing the class system. They deeply believed in "progress," the originally Western concept that man could alter his fate and better his condition by using his reason and by radically changing his economic and social relationships. The great goal of all socialists was the creation of a system of equality where no man would suffer from injustice and where each autonomous individual would creatively blossom. For most socialists, the eradication of poverty and inequality was the central goal of development. Thus, Dudley Sears argued:

> The questions to ask about a country's development are: what has been happening to poverty? What has been happening to unemployment? What has been happening to inequality? If all these have declined from high levels, then beyond doubt, this has been a period of development.[9]

Unlike other believers in the possibility of progress, socialists had the advantage of a single-minded conviction that history was on their side. They claimed that Marx had discovered a science which predicted the inevitable downfall of feudalism and capitalism. Marx, of course, had argued that human labor was the only source of all value in the market-place and that the extraction of "surplus value" (profit) was always exploitation of labor. The dialectical laws of capitalism doomed it to extinction. In their scramble for riches, Marx wrote, capitalists went through an increasingly vicious cycle of crises: they competed for pre-cious workers during periods of prosperity, paid them well (thus reduc-ing their own margin of profit), and belatedly attempted to replace labor with machines (again cutting into their profits). As a capitalist society entered a period of depression, the richer capitalists would gobble up the weaker until a period of monopoly capitalism appeared and most people became members of an impoverished proletariat. Then, an inev-itable revolution would break out, ushering in an era of socialism.

When history failed to fulfill Marxist predictions, such leaders as Lenin, Mao, and Zhou added three important codiciles to the Marxist doctrine. First, revolution would come, they said, only when an intel-lectual vanguard awakened the masses from their lethargy and their "false consciousness." Second, they admitted that capitalist nations had secured a temporary reprieve from their doom by imperialistically (and later, "neo-imperialistically") exploiting Africa, Asia, the Middle East, and Latin America. Only when the "third world" cut all of its dependent relations with capitalistic exploiters, so the argument went, would the less developed nations liberate themselves. Third, Mao and Zhou cre-ated another heresy of classical Marxism: the belief that the peasantry rather than the industrial proletariat in underdeveloped nations such as China could serve as the vanguard of a revolution.

Socialists translated these opinions into a specific strategy for the "third world." Paul Baran, the late economist, was perhaps their most influential spokesman. As did Lenin, Baran predicated all economic progress on revolution against world capitalism: "Economic develop-ment has historically always meant a far-reaching transformation of society's economic, social and political structure."[10] In the present era, said Baran, such revolutions must contain two elements.

First, developing nations had to sever all ties with capitalism since "economic development in underdeveloped countries is profoundly inimical to the dominant interests in the advanced capitalist coun-tries."[11] The advanced capitalist countries, Baran argued, required cheap resources and commodities from poorer lands, inexpensive labor to process certain goods, and helpless markets from which they could extort exhorbitant profits. Thus, Baran contended, "The ruling class in the United States (and elsewhere) is bitterly opposed to the industrialization of the so-called 'source countries.' "[12] The only way for developing countries to escape their disadvantaged position in world trade was to separate themselves from capitalist nations and pursue a goal of self-sufficiency. Eventually, the world would unite in socialist cooperation.

Second, having secured independence from capitalism, leaders in developing nations would create a socialist order where their sole criterion of judgment would be "objective reason."[13] For Baran, "objective reason" required the elimination of all unproductive workers engaged in manufacturing armaments and luxuries, advertising and tax evasion, the law, and religious vocations. The upper social classes, concerned only with conspicuous display and luxury consumption, would disappear. A "rationally ordered" society would devote newfound supplies of wealth and new sources of labor to the welfare of all. A planned economy would be introduced to ensure increasing productivity.

First expressed in 1955, Baran's concern with the dependent position of underdeveloped countries and his faith in planning and "objective reason" affected later generations of social scientists. In the 1960s and 1970s, a collection of "humanistic Marxists," "dependency theorists," and "world systems theorists" voiced their own views on the evils of dependency on a "capitalist core." In economics, a large group of "structuralists," both Marxist and non-Marxist, argued that only state planning and administrative action could overcome the obstacles and constraints which hindered economic change. For those trained before 1960, enthusiasm for these approaches stemmed partially from the apparent success of the Soviet Union in transforming a backward agricultural society into a major industrial and military power. Democratic socialists from the West—Sidney and Beatrice Webb, H. G. Wells, and Harold Laski—all admired the Soviet regime "for getting the job done." Nehru, for one, had an immense respect for the Revolution of 1917 and originally launched India on a path of socialism, state planning, and heavy industrialization modeled on the Soviet example.

Until 1956, Russia did indeed provide one model of development which some poorer nations, particularly Mao's China, temporarily copied. The later history of the twentieth century, however, demonstrated the inapplicability of Soviet methods to the problems of the "third world." Few nations enjoyed the privileges of Russia at the beginning of its development: sparse population, great resources, an already established manufacturing base, and abundant food. After Khrushchev's revelations in 1956, fewer still wished to adopt Stalin's disastrous policies of collectivizing agriculture, exploiting slave labor, and establishing a "command economy" with all of its economic and human costs.

Even China, after its catastrophic convulsions during the Great Leap Forward and the Cultural Revolution abandoned the Stalinist program which Mao had viciously imposed until 1976. For some Chinese leaders such as Deng Xiaoing, a modified form of "neo-capitalism," although still garbed in socialist rhetoric, seemed a preferable option.

THE "INVISIBLE" HAND OF CAPITALISM

Practice is the sole criterion of truth.

—DENG XIAOING

As the twentieth century progressed, such "neoclassical" economists as Milton Friedman, Ian M. D. Little, and P. T. Bauer created a "capitalist" school of thought which diverged from the dominant socialist vision of development.

They contended that the basic goal of development should be to expand free choice rather than to create a classless, egalitarian utopia. Nobel Laureate Arthur Lewis, an advocate of a mixture between socialism and capitalism, stated the basic goal succinctly: "The case for economic growth is that it gives man more control over his environment, and thereby increases his freedom."[14] For capitalist theorists, an expansion in the opportunities available to mankind and a decrease in material and political limits on man's individual judgment were the ends of development.

Capitalists had faith in the capacity of free markets, untrammelled by government restrictions, to increase the prosperity of all. They believed, as Adam Smith first argued in *Wealth of Nations,* that a series of choices made by producers, competing in an international market, and consumers, choosing between the goods and services offered to them, would redound to the greatest prosperity and welfare of all. The "invisible hand" of the free market would weed out the inefficient and ultimately reward those whose acquisitive instincts led to socially beneficial ends. Like Keynes, they may have regretted that individual greed was the motive of economic advance, but they argued that the ultimate result was the common benefit.

Beginning with Ricardo, advocates of capitalism rested their claim for the efficacy of free markets on the doctrine of "comparative advantage." Through accidents of nature and history, some areas of the world can produce goods at a profitable level and exchange them for other products from a different region whose people also gain in the process. Portugal can exchange port wine for English machines; Japan can export cars to Colombia in return for coffee; the Punjab sells its wheat to Bombay for calculators; New York purchases beef from Iowa while midwesterners buy newsmagazines. All the regions profit by maximizing their particular advantage.

Under a system of free trade, so the argument goes, each nation learns its own comparative advantage and the market channels the search for individual profit into a general increase in prosperity.

Capitalists generally deplored the interference of government planning as an inducement to development. Instead, they preferred firm but limited governments which would promote the greatest possible scope for individual initiative and entreprenuerial talent. P. T. Bauer, for example, cited his experience in Malaya and West Africa as indicating that supposedly torpid, illiterate peasants can respond to market incentives very quickly by planting and reaping millions of acres of cash crops. The resulting increase in prosperity was made possible by "voluntary changes in the conduct, attitudes, and motivations of numerous individuals—not by state planning or investment."[15] For the capitalist, the essential tasks of government consist in defense, preserving public security, and the promotion of basic health, educational, and communication services.

Those of capitalist persuasion welcomed the introduction of less developed countries into the world economy and the intrusion of foreign influences, including multinational companies, into the "third world."

Writers such as Ian M. D. Little noted that several Asian economies—particularly Singapore, Hong Kong, Taiwan, and South Korea—made exceptional economic progress because they had "tapped into the world economy," welcomed foreign capital, and eagerly adopted foreign management and technology."[16] Conversely, Lord Peter Bauer argued that the most backward areas of the world—Ethiopia, Liberia, Tibet, Bhutan, Yemen—were seldom touched by colonialism, multinational companies, or invasions by either Western commerce or ideas. This fact led Bauer to assert that "contact with the West has been the prime agent of material progress in the Third World.''[17]

Thus, such thinkers opposed any attempt by developed or nonindustrialized economies to seal off their borders with tariffs or any sort of other restriction on trade. They encouraged an export orientation for developing countries rather than attempts at import substitution or self-sufficiency. Only very large nations—China, India, and Brazil—might profit from creating their own heavy industrial schemes to satisfy internal demands.

People in this ideological camp particularly insisted upon the value of the free market in the agricultural sector. Bauer, for example, argued that famine in some developing countries had nothing to do with a lack of usable land but was the result of low-level subsistence farming and damaging policies pursued by misguided governments.

How well has the capitalist approach worked in the "third world"? Adherents of this position pointed to phenomenal patterns of growth in those parts of Asia, Latin America, India, and even Africa which more or less followed the capitalist doctrine. Yet critics argued that such growth was often introduced by authoritarian political methods, that theories of comparative advantage did not apply to the desperate people at the bottom of the world pyramid of wealth, and that the poor had become poorer in capitalist regions.

Opponents of capitalism cited Brazil—once regarded as a great success story—as a prime example of the doctrine's political implications and its human costs. Until 1930, Brazil was a stagnant, highly unequal economy, dependent on exports from agriculture and mining. Originally, it should be recalled, Brazil like the rest of Latin America, was about on the same economic level as North America in 1850. The Portuguese legacy (which, among other policies, denied Brazilians a higher education), a feudal land-owning pattern, and a church which urged peasants to seek salvation in heaven had hindered Brazil from realizing its potential.

Spurred by the necessities of the great depression, Brazilians broke the mold and adopted a policy of import substitution. Between 1930 and 1964, under a corporatist and populist policy, Brazil created its own industries catering to the tastes of the upper and middle classes. Although the nation grew economically at a fast pace during this era and enjoyed a period of liberal democracy, the poor remained poor and periods of inflation devastated the economy.

In 1964, applauded by the richer classes and perhaps aided by multinational companies, the military took over, abolished democracy, and promised to restore economic stability. The generals introduced a variety of new economic policies, seeking to turn Brazil into a "grand" nation just as the Meiji reformers had once done in Japan. The military expanded Brazilian industry, welcomed foreign investment, and fought inflation with draconian measures. Both state-owned industries and multinational corporations flourished, although smaller private enterprises had difficulty in competing.

The Brazilian rulers followed a monetarist policy, held down expenditures on public welfare, and consciously allowed a growth in economic inequality. They wished to create uniquely Brazilian industries (sometimes in collaboration with multinationals) and invested heavily in manpower training programs and mass literacy. Although Brazil's new capital-intensive industries markedly increased the production of automobiles, television sets, and refrigerators, they could not absorb the unemployed. While industrial production advanced by 90 percent between 1964 and 1970, most of the new wealth went to the rich and to a growing middle class. Between 1970 and 1981, the economy bounded ahead at a dramatic rate of 8 percent annually.

The "stabilization package" offered by the military included a deliberate policy of holding down wages, allowing inefficient firms to go under, balancing the federal budget, and stringently collecting taxes. Brazilian expert Sylvia Ann Hewlett has cogently argued that only a "corporatist state" could impose such austerity since "many of these measures were extremely unpopular and could be carried through only by an authoritarian and repressive government."[18] The militarists of Brazil tortured, imprisoned, or murdered any dissidents who were brave enough to raise critical voices. They ignored starving peasants in the northeast.

By the middle of the 1980s, however, even the military could not shoulder certain new burdens: an increase in petroleum costs, a temporary world recession, and the service of a huge foreign debt which they had incurred.

Too late, they learned that their policy of cultivating indigenous Brazilian "grandeur" had its own economic risks for "import substitution merely shifted demand from imported final consumer goods to a variety of imported industrial inputs."[19] By 1985, the military masters hesitantly and partially returned power to elected civilians but no one guaranteed that the officers would not once again resort to brutality.

In fact, some scholars have argued that the "capitalist model"—at least when carried out in the feudal, militaristic, and unequal society of a Brazil—*required* political repression and poverty for the masses. The existing elite, they contended, would not improve the lot of the poorest.

"No Brazilian government enjoying the support of the contemporary power elite can make a significant dent on social welfare problems," Hewlett argued in 1980, "for a radical improvement in the condition of the poor would seriously threaten the very existence of this elite."[20]

Eliminating obstacles to development and equity, Richard Fagen has argued, "implies 'revolutionary' changes in existing national and international structures." [21] In summarizing the case of Brazil and, by implication, any late-developing nation, Hewlett condemned capitalism because "there is a remorseless logic at work which makes poverty and inequality a *necessary* consequence of economic growth."[22]

Was there any hope for a "fourth path"—one which would avoid the brutal repression of Brazil, the convulsions of a China, and the stifling orthodoxy of an Islamic theocracy?

Was it hopeless to look for pragmatic alternatives which would lead to eventual economic abundance, a degree of social equity, and political freedom? Few statesmen in the "third world" or intellectuals in the West, however humane their intentions, believed that such an ideal could be attained. They had tragically short memories. The early modern histories of certain nations—Denmark, Japan, and Switzerland—indicated that the supposedly "remorseless logic" of economic development does not dictate that the masses must inevitably endure increased suffering, political dictatorship, or the theological conformity before the dawning of a new age.

The histories of these countries suggested two other often neglected facts about development. First, as in Denmark and Switzerland, economic progress proceeded hand in hand with the evolution of liberal institutions—indeed, liberalism preceded and, some would say, "caused" economic growth. A period of intense suffering was not a necessary precursor to political freedom in those nations. Liberal democracy was not a more "mature" stage that evolved only after affluence was achieved. Second, while it did not develop liberal political institutions until after a catastrophic war, Japan showed that great economic development can proceed without uprooting—indeed while reinforcing—traditional culture.

FOURTH WAYS

> We are still haunted by the shadowing thought that by immense
> efforts of will and intelligence . . . mankind may rise above neces-
> sity into the kingdom of freedom, subduing material things to
> humane and rational purposes.
>
> —CHARLES BEARD

In distinct contrast to other historical examples of human development, certain countries in both Europe and Asia followed humane ways
to progress which did not involve the carnage of the French guillotine,
the brutalities of factory life in capitalist England, the devastation of the
Russian revolution, or the wholesale extermination of native ethnic groups
which the Americans practiced.

In Denmark, as one cogent but often neglected example, the monarchy and elements of the aristocracy itself (for their own selfish reasons) took the lead in producing a major land reform in 1794 which, in
turn, invigorated the economy and liberalized the polity.

When a small elite of educated, flexible men dedicated to a rational,
nonviolent transformation of Denmark first exerted their influence, the
country seemed to have little chance for a major economic advance. In
1794 as now, Denmark had few "natural" advantages: no mineral
resources, an impoverished sandy soil, and relatively little industry. At
that time, it had an uneducated population, a feudal tradition, and a low
standard of living for its peasants. By 1986, however, Denmark enjoyed
one of the highest standards of living in the world, universal education,
crèches for infants, retirement cottages for the elderly, free medical
care, a healthy export trade, unrestricted political liberties, and a world
reputation for social welfare.

How did this land, the world's most ancient monarchy, make the
transition? In contrast to the English experience where industrialization
killed off the yeomen, Denmark's peaceful evolution drew its mass support from free peasants who owned their land and allied themselves with
an urban merchant class inspired by the ideas of the Enlightenment.
Their joint economic power undermined the feudal structure and gradually led to an opening of political liberties and economic opportunities.
Unlike their fellows in nineteenth century Germany, Italy, and Russia,
the Liberal party carried out a program which diffused economic opportunity ever more widely through the population while guaranteeing

political rights for all. Later, without destroying the old monarchy or the merchant classes, the Social Democratic Party generated new measures of social welfare. It never sought the collectivization of land advocated by some socialists and only sparingly nationalized major industries. Thus, Denmark followed a careful "fourth way," neither pristinely capitalist nor socialist in content.

Similarly in the 1790s, Switzerland—a land bitterly divided by religious, class, and linguistic hostilities—offered little hope of economic progress. The autocrats who ruled the various cantons subjugated their diverse peoples in a harsh manner. The region was mountainous and had little cultivable land. It had not entered even the first phases of the industrial revolution and, except for minor caches of coal, the country had no mineral resources. The people were illiterate and unskilled. The various cantons had a deserved reputation for belligerence and their major exports were mercenaries who sent back remittances from the various royal courts of the day. Switzerland was like so many countries in the twentieth century: an artificial collection of "tribes"—Germans, French, Italians, Romanesques—who could not speak the same language and detested each other.

All of this changed with the French Revolution and the incursion of Napoleon on the Swiss cantons. Napoleon's armies introduced ideas of progress, the rights of man, and individual liberty which swept over the Swiss middle classes in the French-speaking areas.

Inspired by Voltaire and Rousseau, urban merchants backed by landed peasants adopted a fragile constitution which proclaimed full freedom of religion, liberty of conscience, and universal (male) suffrage. By 1830, a liberal coalition expanded the idea of nationhood, tolerance, and linguistic pluralism by establishing a full-scale Swiss confederation. Even the Italian cantons, lying on the plains below the Alps of central Switzerland, ratified the union and affirmed their allegiance to a newly created nation.

As liberal revolutions shock all of Europe, the year 1848 marked a great ratification of the national compromise. The confederation was solidified by a reform commission which created two legislative houses. The Council of States allowed for the traditional independence of each canton while a freely elected National Council provided unity. Every Swiss citizen was granted guarantees of legal freedoms. Minorities escaped from religious persecution.

Economically, after 1848, Switzerland like Denmark adopted its own mixture of public and private enterprise. The Swiss allowed capitalists, usually Protestants, to take the lead in industrialization but complemented their efforts with public aid. In 1852, for example, private companies built railways, an essential link in Swiss economic development because of the country's strategic position in Europe. The state aided in securing necessary land and, in 1878, a state agency assumed the costs of building rail connections over the Alps, a risky and perhaps unprofitable undertaking. The railways, however, eventually opened up trade possibilities for Switzerland in spite of her rugged mountains.

As prosperity increased, floods of political refugees, including Lenin and Trotsky, migrated to the freedom of Switzerland. Between 1850 and 1930, the population doubled from two million to four million, while the standard of living quadrupled during this period.

By 1986, Switzerland had emerged as the richest country in the world with one of the highest levels of health, longevity, and social welfare. While it had to import food, mineral resources, and oil, the nation became known as a progenitor of social reforms, a land of immense wealth, and a bastion of individual liberties as well as world peace.

In an entirely different context but with equally flexible policies, Japanese samurai sought to transform their nation during the "Meiji restoration." Japan, the first Asian society to end poverty, stirred from its traditional isolation and stagnation in 1868. The West had intruded only intermittently on Japan's deliberate seclusion. In 1863 and 1864, however, European ships demonstrated their devastating fire power by bombarding Sotsuma and Chosu. The "Meiji" samurai—outer clans of minor nobles already alienated from the ruling Tokugawa—felt intensely humiliated by this demonstration of the superiority of Western technology.

In a relatively bloodless transition, this secondary elite replaced the Tokugawa, vowing to restore the glory and power of the emperor. The new rulers made symbolic concessions to the Tokugawa, such as allowing the old nobles to retain their swords, but they vowed to modernize Japan at all costs. Using the Emperor, then a little boy, as their symbolic agent, they set out to transform Japan into a first-class military power.

When Japan began its march forward, she suffered from burdens which afflict only the poorest of nations in the twentieth century. She had almost no mineral or energy resources, little arable land, no export markets, no colonies to exploit, and an ill-fed population. She lacked, too, a technical elite which Europe, America, and Russia already possessed.

Yet, in four decades, this impoverished peasant society emerged as a modernized economy and a military power capable of thrashing tsarist Russia. From 1869 to 1896, the Japanese built, 4,600 industrial concerns while her total national product increased by about 40 percent a decade. Between 1900 and 1930, her national production grew by 50 percent each decade. Because the Meiji particularly stressed education, mass literacy was achieved within the first two decades of the regime, schools and universities sprouted throughout the nation, and the brightest youths went abroad to gain the most advanced knowledge of the time. A fragile system of parliamentary democracy functioned by 1900. Under the Meiji, agricultural production—stimulated by a shift to the growing of rice, silk worms, and the introduction of new forms of irrigation and fertilizer—grew immensely and easily fed the expanding population.

The export of silk emerged as a major industry and, until the turn of the century, Japan actually exported food. Small, often family-based industries formed the foundation for Japan's economy in many sectors up until 1930. Meanwhile, revisions in the law solidified the individual's obligation to support his parents and his ties to his village of origin.

In later years, of course, Japan flexibly shifted its policies toward building heavy industry and, eventually, to the creation of a postindustrial society.

The nature and pace of social change in Japan differed from those nations which had developed earlier. The Meiji, for their own military reasons, wished to Westernize their nation at a fast clip.

Yet, even in their rush to modernity, the Meiji sought to retain some of the useful features and many of the symbols of stable traditional life. They used the emperor as a unifying figurehead, instituted an informal system of social security, encouraged family reverence in the schools, and tried to cement the ties that linked the individual to his community.

As one result, urbanization proceeded slowly. As another effect, factory workers, originally recruited in social and familial units, became tenured members of their companies, privileged employees within a larger, new, paternalistic "family." Trade unions did not emerge until the 1920s and had little power.

Japan adopted, too, the political institutions of the West by creating free courts, a free press, and an elected parliament. Each of these institutions took on a unique Japanese tint. A court, for example, considered a divorce case only after a full family council consented. Newspapers could not question the cult of the emperor, although they were free to discuss any other aspect of the society.

In the 1930s, the avarice of the militarists for colonies and their policy of assassinating dissident politicians stifled this slow but steady advance of political freedoms. They emerged again only after Japan's catastrophe in World War II, the subsequent American military dictatorship, and Japan's eventual rush toward affluence.

In the later decades of the century, Japan, Switzerland, and Denmark had reached a crest in human economic, social, and political welfare. They did it each in their own way, without marked domestic violence or a deepening of poverty for their masses. They responded to economic and military challenges within the context of their idiosyncratic cultures and histories. They achieved unprecedented and sustained success without natural resources, vast lands, energy supplies, abundant food, or a windfall of capital from colonies or war. They did not fashion their destinies according to the dictates of an abstract theological, capitalist, or socialist doctrine.

In spite of their evident differences, the pragmatic fourth way epitomized by these originally poor countries included a number of common elements:

Each began to change because of a "foreign" catalyst. The West's military intrusions or the ideas of the French Revolution shook their stolid status quo and mobilized a significant element in their populations.

All three nations first paid attention to their agriculture, freeing people for the industrialization process and releasing them from starvation.

They adopted mixed economies and gave great latitude to private interests (merchants and freed peasants in Denmark, Calvinist entrepreneurs in Switzerland, and Zaibatsu in Japan) to pursue their opportunities. Nonetheless, the state often played a critical role by offering credit to peasants, gathering productive capital, investing it in new industries, and by providing the necessary infrastructure for economic advance.

The three countries welcomed foreign ideas, techniques, capital, and even refugees.

These successful examples of development stressed education and produced vigorous new "human resources" from clerks to scientists, knowledgeable workers to engineers.

Each region emulated the most modern models of their time but, in general, retained their traditional symbols, social distinctions, and values. Outwardly, their class structures remained in place but in fact, secondary elites—those samurai nobles, or new entrepreneurs, or urban merchants just below the top of their traditional societies—took over real power.

The three countries advanced economically, while simultaneously (if sporadically, in Japan) widening the realm of political freedoms, allowing their middle classes greater political power, and alleviating dire poverty. They chose the path of evolution, not revolution, of moderation rather than violence.

Do these examples from the past offer hope to developing areas in the twentieth century? Clearly, each region suffered from unique historical "accidents" which eventually aided their development: Denmark's king needed money to repair his military fortunes and thus allowed land reform; Switzerland could have remained disunited except that Napoleon invaded on his way to Italy; Japan might have slumbered on if Perry had not sought coal stations for his fleet.

Some social scientists, however, go further in denying the relevance of experience. Economist Hewlett argued that, "there is nothing in the contemporary structure of Third World nations to justify a belief that the 'grand dynamic' of the original industrial revolution will repeat itself."[23] Hewlett argued that five critical elements distinguished the contemporary underdeveloped world from previous times: the population explosion makes it impossible for capital-intensive industries to absorb masses of new labor; no inherent tendencies exist to provide wage increases; feudal structures prohibit the emergence of groups that might demand "social justice"; a labor "aristocracy" has nothing to gain by sharing its wealth with the poor; and nonproductive elites will, in any case, gobble up any economic surplus.

Such a view simply ignored the histories of those regions of the globe that have, in fact, made the "great ascent" without recourse to the violent revolutions advocated by socialists or the "trickle down" theory espoused by some capitalists. Meiji Japan, for example, also faced a severe population crisis and, for that very reason, emphasized labor-intensive industry; wage increases were awarded as a way to spur production for military requirements; the Meiji nobility itself provided greater social equity without dismantling the feudal tradition; the industrial laborers came to identify their individual welfare with that of the emperor, their company, and Japan as a whole, lessening their will to oppose measures which spread the general welfare; and the Meiji elite took the lead in savings and investment.

Why, then, disparage the ability of leaders in contemporary developing nations to make similar decisions?

Naturally, one could reasonably argue that contemporary countries face a new set of severe challenges—the prevalence of new ideologies (socialist, nationalist, or democratic) which might inhibit wise decisions; the growing interdependence of the world economy which makes any particular economy more fragile than in the past; and the exigencies of the "cold war" which render specific nations helpless in determining their fate. These obstacles are genuine but, as we will try to demonstrate, no more formidable than similar barriers in the past.

One new element has, undoubtedly, infiltrated the modern world: the mass media have encouraged a diffusion of knowledge, of new images, and of an ability to compare ourselves to others which was unknown in the world of Danish peasants, Swiss mountaineers, or Japanese silk weavers. Some view this as dangerous since it contributes to the "distribution effect," greed, envy, and an awareness of inequality. At least until the new generation of broadcasting satellites revolutionizes the mass media, their growth has also offered malignant possibilities for mass propaganda.

Nonetheless, the spread of the mass media has increased the awareness, the empathic abilities, the opportunities, and the knowledge of mankind. This broadening of vision has, for good or evil, added a degree of urgency to the tasks of development.

History cannot tell us which vision of development will prevail. It can only inform us that the familiar picture of industrial development and political liberation need not be painted solely in the black or red of inevitable dictatorship. History tells us, too, that even the most impoverished and disadvantaged regions have reason to hope for progress. There is an increasing awareness, as Hans Kohn once put it, that modern man must reject "the utopias of enthusiasm and the utopias of despair," the extremes of socialist centralization, of capitalist efficiency, and of Islamic millenialism.

It is in that uncertain, indefinite middle range of discovering new "fourth ways" that reasonable men find their proper domain in responding to the cruel dilemmas of development.

PART II

———

FOURTH
WAYS

Introduction

It would be easy for us to surrender to pessimism. . . . We must not. . . . We must keep alive the thought that salvation is possible.

—JOHN KENNETH GALBRAITH

The failures and frustrations of the last thirty years have driven idealists to despair and allowed cynics to scoff. Yet, often ignored in the malaise of our "fin de siècle," the truth was that many people in different parts of the globe fashioned their own development without strict adherence to any single theological, philosophical, political or economic vision. These areas, which we call "fourth way" regions or nations, progressed economically at a pace unwitnessed in prior centuries; yet, they satisfied the goals of those who revere freedom:

First, rapid economic advances (at least 6 percent of annual GNP) over the past twenty-five years broadened the life courses of all segments of their population without violent destruction of their social order. Scapegoats—historically a feudal aristocracy, or more often helpless peasants and workers—were not sacrificed in the name of progress or efficiency. Instead, economic affluence went hand in hand with the development of a solid middle class—perhaps entrepreneurs, industrial or urban service workers, technicians, or relatively rich peasants—who enjoyed the material amenities of life as they passed beyond the basic subsistence level and exercised a degree of autonomy over their lives which they had not known before.

Second, the liberating social effects of affluence within these regions were spread to most of their people. The governments of the "fourth way" areas have usually not proclaimed the unrealized goal of equalizing all people. They have, however, brought about measurable improvements in the basic quality of life of their people. Specifically, substantial advances in educational opportunity and literacy were made; the means to save newborn infants from premature death were provided; and the conditions which promoted a greater life expectancy were created. We consider advances in these aspects of life as significant as sometimes misleading statistics of per capita income.

Drawing on the work of M. D. Morris, Clark Kerr has prepared an index using data to produce a combined measure of infant mortality rates, life expectancy, and literacy of a nation's population.[1] On this scale, which we have adopted to measure the basic social welfare of various nations, a high score indicated that a region enjoyed a decent level of nutrition, widespread health care, and good schools while a low score suggested that many of its people were in ill health and often illiterate. Using this combined measure, for example, Sweden ranked highest in the physical quality of life (with a score of 97) while Afghanistan was lowest (18).

Third, while navigating the difficult passage out of their status as "underdeveloped nations," these "fourth way regions" generally, although not always, steered a course between the Scylla of dictatorship and the Charybdis of anarchy.

Some of these nations (Costa Rica, Malaysia, Venezuela, India) were "democracies" in the classical sense of the word (i.e., several political parties competed openly in free elections, except in times of violent insurgency). Other regions (the Ivory Coast and Dengist China) were one-party states, Hong Kong was a colony, and several regions such as Singapore and Colombia had all the trappings of a formal "democracy" but their critics argued that disproportionate power remained in the hands of the elite.

Yet, whether formally described by the often misleading label, "democracy," all of these governments had created or sustained liberal political institutions (regional, religious, ethnic, familial, clan, tribal or economic in origin) which had their autonomy outside of government control.

They also maintained, in their own ways, a basic rule of law. Costa Rica, Venezuela, and India adhered to their own constitutions, however violently they were threatened. Others referred appeals to their own laws to outside monitors. Singapore, Hong Kong, and Malaysia (until

1984) voluntarily submitted the decisions of their supreme courts to the scrutiny of the English Privy Council. Dengist China adopted foreign codes in wholesale fashion to fit the requirements of a country which wished to modernize economically, but had never fashioned its own legal tradition. The Ivory Coast followed the Napoleonic Code. Whatever their differences, the "fourth way" nations adopted formal legal systems which protected the individual from the arbitrary exercise of political or economic power.

In addition, these regions were responsive to the pluralistic nature of their societies and resorted to brute force only when dissident elements in their midsts actually attempted to overturn the entire system with violence.

The "fourth way" governments, then, recognized the independence of courts, created or supported institutions that mediated between the individual and the state, submitted to criticism from outside sources, and tried to conciliate, rather than eliminate religious and ethnic differences. They did not institute reigns of terror at the whim of an elite or a messiah. Their rulers may not have been angels—in fact, they were usually intelligent, urbane, superb, if sometimes arrogant politicians, backed by tough political machines—but they refrained from the practices of the Hitlers and Idi Amins of world history.

Except for Dengist China which tentatively began its internal reforms in 1976, these "fourth way" governments maintained their economic, social, and political progress for at least twenty-five years in a stable, evolutionary fashion.

In judging the political systems of these areas, the reports of Amnesty International provided accounts of the "prisoners of conscience" held in the prisons of the world, their torture, "disappearance," or execution. According to the Amnesty International publications concerning human rights violations, the nations we chose as case histories—with the exception of Dengist China—had among the best, albeit not perfect, records in respecting human dignity.[2]

Each of the advances we have mentioned—an improvement in basic economic standards, substantial changes in the physical quality of life, and the creation of a liberal, stable, more open polity—represented gains in freedom.

Admittedly, as judged by these standards, relatively few areas of the world have progressed on all fronts during the last thirty years. In the twilight of the twentieth century, those areas which most clearly fitted these criteria included: in Southeast Asia, Malaysia and Singapore; in

East Asia, Hong Kong and (debatedly) Dengist China; on the South Asian subcontinent, the Punjab, Haryana, and Uttar Pradash; in Africa, the Ivory Coast; and in South America, Costa Rica, Colombia, and Venezuela. Each of these nations or regions is described in the following chapters. Are there lessons to be discerned from their development?

We do not feel that the rarity of the examples of development invalidates their experience. They are extremely diverse: agricultural and postindustrial, "capitalist" and "socialist," originally resource rich or bleakly poor, blessed with oil or completely dependent on outside sources of energy (even water), "Confucian" and Islamic, Christian and pagan. The differences in their experience should be, in fact, encouraging. As Galbraith observed, "Development is an historical process; all prescriptions must be in keeping with the stage a country or people has reached in that process.[3]

Clearly one could reasonably argue for the inclusion of other countries at different levels of development. We have deliberately omitted those examples which made progress in one sector, but not in another.

Within the "socialist" bloc, for example, Hungary and Romania achieved high levels of social welfare and a modicum of economic progress, but had yet to liberalize their political orders.

On the capitalist "fringe," in contrast, Taiwan and South Korea lunged ahead economically, initiated successful land reforms, and achieved similar levels of social welfare as Singapore and Hong Kong. Yet, while wavering, their dictatorships still held a firm rein.

Maintaining its independence, Yugoslavia tried interesting experiments in worker participation and, in fits and spurts, tended to move toward a politically more open society. Yet, it faltered in maintaining a high rate of economic growth and fell behind such resource poor, blatantly capitalistic regions as Hong Kong in providing social welfare.

In Europe, after the demise of fascist dictatorships, Portugal and Spain peacefully evolved into liberal democracies, but large segments of their populations remained in a poverty much more grim than the peoples of Asia's "miracle economies."

In Latin America, Mexico temporarily enjoyed its oil riches, but unlike Venezuela, failed to share them with the peasant masses or to loosen the grip of its PRI.

In spite of foreign aid, Cuba presented an anomaly: from 1960 onwards, Cuban per capita GNP declined at an average rate of 2 percent a decade (perhaps because of the American embargo and a drop in world sugar prices); the health of Cubans failed to improve (possibly due to an exodus of doctors); and an authoritarian regime retained unquestioned power.

Israel also presented a complex portrait. In spite of a high rate of inflation, the nation made great economic progress. It was difficult, however, to estimate how much of this was due to the approximately $2 billion a year which Israel received in aid from the United States. Further, Israel was, in many ways, a liberal democracy. Yet Amnesty International reported in 1983 that the government held 9,000 Palestinians and Lebanese prisoners at Al Ansar and other prisons and that guards indiscriminately beat them. In addition, Israel jailed "prisoners of conscience" without trial for distributing "subversive" literature, singing forbidden songs, or uttering offensive slogans. During the same year, the Israeli government issued 77 restriction orders which confined people to their villages during the day and to their homes at night. Like South Africa—a country which could also boast of a high standard of living, even for its despised black population—Israel justified political and social oppression as due to a continued state of "emergency."

Thus, whatever their other successes, it was difficult to consider such nations as Israel, South Africa, South Korea, Cuba, Mexico, Hungary, or even Portugal as having fulfilled the three standards which have been outlined.

No doubt changes will occur in the future, but as we hope to make clear, there are no implacable forces which ensure a particular destiny. It is the choices which leaders make in the present that do.

We recognize that each of the "fourth way" regimes advanced according to the drumbeat of its unique history, the dictates of its own culture, resources, and opportunities—and most importantly, to the decisions made by its leaders. Clearly the relatively poor nations of the world were constrained within the straitjacket of the world's economy and the vagaries of superpower politics. It was, however, the decisions and actions of humane, thinking political leaders which created policies that brought their people to their present level of success.

As Engels recognized, but did not emphasize sufficiently, "men make their own history." The cases of the "fourth way" people illustrate the truth of this statement, since their histories have not proven that political liberty must await economic abundance, that economic progress automatically creates political stability, that ethnic divisions doom human development, that "dependency" on outside sources is always harmful (or helpful), or that a particular people or culture has a monopoly on creativity or freedom.

We should be grateful for this very diversity. It suggests that wise leaders and receptive peoples, even in the poorest, most threatened parts of the globe, are able to ascend from the poverty and inequality which had long dominated their lives. In regions as different as Venezuela and the Punjab, Singapore and the Ivory Coast, reasonable people have transformed their nations and the fate of their posterity.

With the death of a particular leader, a convulsion in the world economy, or a military attack, any of these successful regions could revert to the poverty, obscurantism, and despotism which once characterized them. There are no guarantees about their fate at the turn of the century. Nonetheless, they have already demonstrated a staying power which eluded charismatic figures such as Nkrumah, military dictators such as Nimeiri, communist emperors like Mao, or ephemeral democratic regimes such as the Weimar Republic.

Let us first examine Africa, that grand continent which is the largest in the world. It was here, after all, that the exuberant celebrations of the 1960s ended in the prevailing despair of the 1980s.

4

A Wager in West Africa

Something new is always coming from Africa.

—PLINY THE ELDER

In 1984, when a child died every twenty minutes in the Alamata district of Ethiopia, even Mother Teresa of Calcutta recoiled from the remorseless toll of famine. Her nuns had distributed small heaps of grain donated by Europeans. Yet, swirling black columns of dust, sometimes 15 meters high, lept up unexpectedly and covered the previous piles of grain with dirt. A nurse who gave injections to spindly babies summarized the calamity. "We cannot live in this place any more," she said, "We must leave it. But where is there to go?"[1]

Peter Onu, head of the Organization of African Unity, admitted in 1984 that Africa faced an "unparalleled socioeconomic decline . . . a very grim situation that requires some form of radical solutions by our member states."[2]

Over the previous thirty years, with many an oratorical flourish, African states had tried a variety of "radical solutions" in an effort to develop a self-sustaining growth process. With few exceptions, such as the racially tortured regime of South Africa, they had failed. Why?

Africa is a continent that possesses the world's greatest reserves of untapped resources and is four times larger than the United States. Africa's fertile soil could have fed all Africans and Western Europeans; if properly cultivated, it could have produced 130 times what it yielded in the 1980s. Politically, Africa controlled one third of the votes in the United Nations.

What, then, held this continent, the original home of man's progenitors, in a state of starvation and disease, violence and repression? Some observers cited the wretched history of colonial exploitation by Europeans and Arab slave traders. Yet, the tragic experience of colonialism could not explain the desperate situation of Ethiopia, which experienced only six years of Italian rule, or of Liberia, a free state created by American blacks.

Other people preferred a racist explanation. "My dear sir, how can you possibly expect these people to govern themselves?" an irate Boer anthropologist once said to me in Zambia. "Why, they had not even discovered the wheel before we came." Such observations overlooked the fact that Africa had once been home to such great civilizations as Benin and Mali while Caucasians still lived in caves.

On a more practical level, other reasonable observers noted the lack of responsible political leadership, Africa's patchwork of two thousand tribes, its history of illiteracy (imposed alike by colonialists and the emperors of Ethiopia), and its division into unworkable political units as prime sources of economic retrogression and political instability.

Africa had, of course, produced many admirable statesmen during its modern era: Jomo Kenyatta who built a prosperous Kenya and magnanimously welcomed as citizens the whites who had once imprisoned him; Leopold Sedar Senghor of Senegal, the first African leader to resign his presidency voluntarily; and Desmond Tutu, the Anglican bishop who bravely sought racial harmony in South Africa. Yet, the lack of balanced, seasoned leadership in many parts of the continent disturbed those Africans who did not wish to remain hostages to their past and who had lost the romantic zeal of their original quest for independence.

One sympathic foreign observer, David Lamb, exclaimed acerbicly in 1982:

> How do you explain a continent whose heads of state applauded Idi Amin when he walked into a summit wearing his Stetson and six-shooters, having just presided over the massacre of several thousand Ugandans, including the Anglican archbishop? What do you say about the president of Tanzania, who translated Shakespeare into Swahili in his spare time and held more political prisoners than South Africa?[3]

Africa particularly frustrated those who once believed that strong-arm authoritarian governments, imposed by the army or a charismatic leader, would somehow solve the problems of newly independent colonies. The African case indicated just the opposite: the great continent in all of its diversity needed liberal politics that could adjust to the many demands of a society riven by tribal, linguistic, and religious differences—a series of open communities which could cooperate peacefully across the absurdly drawn colonial frontiers. Instead, many Africans had to suffer under the corrupt, callous, or economically unwise leaders who squandered millions of dollars in the purchase of arms, the creation of monuments to their own egos, or the enlargement of their bank accounts from Switzerland to Luxembourg.

The human costs of authoritarian rule were most obvious in the potentially rich areas of Ethiopia and Angola.

In Ethiopia, where millions starved between 1974 and 1986, neither the feudal regime of Haile Selassie nor the Marxist-military rule of Colonel Mengistu Haile Mariam could cope with the country's problems. Local droughts and fragile soil turned the Ethiopian empire into a disaster area. In Alamata refugee camp alone, relief workers tried to feed 100,000 people a day in 1985 on rations adequate for 3,000. Doctors paced up and down the ranks of the starving, placing a cross on the forehead of a person who looked sufficiently healthy to be treated. The others wasted away.

Western nations tried to help, but the air-lifted food was inadequate. In 1983, the United States had embargoed all food aid to Ethiopia. When America reversed its policy in 1984, the food was too late for many. Meanwhile, Russia supplied at least $3 billion in arms to Ethiopia but only 10,000 tons of rice.

Ethiopia's Marxist dictatorship gravely aggravated the crisis, for "it takes acts of men to turn acts of God into calamity."[4] In the midst of famine, the government sponsored a huge party for its tenth anniversary in September 1984. This celebration of dictatorship in Addis Ababa cost $250 million. In response to rebellions in the north, inspired by economic repression, the militarists cut off all food supplies.

Ethiopia's rulers had installed a Stalinist model of agriculture. The Ethiopian junta forbade farmers from saving food or profits from good harvests to carry them over the inevitable bad times. All food had to be channeled through the incompetent central regime; the government condemned investment in agriculture and businesses devoted to the transport of food. Thus, in 1984, *The Economist* reported: "Saving from good years is called hoarding. Saving money earned from past harvests is called capitalist accumulation. Earning a living transporting food is called exploitation. All are punished by official extortion, or worse."[5]

Thus, it was the authoritarian rule of Colonel Mengistu and his mistaken policies which forced Ethiopia into the tragic dilemmas of triage.

Angola, once the jewel of Portugal's cruel empire, suffered a similar fate. In 1975, a revolutionary government in Lisbon cut loose its ties with Angola. A Marxist regime, abetted by Russian aid and Cuban troops, took power and tried to impose minority tribal rule. In a continuing civil war, the dominant Ovimbundu tribe headed by Jonas Savimbi received aid from such diverse allies as South Africa, China, and the United States. Angola collapsed into chaos.

In 1975, the 500,000 Portuguese colonials deserted Luanda, Angola's once beautiful capital, the Rio de Janeiro of Africa. Angola had great promise: it was a temperate country fourteen times the size of Portugal, it had off shore oil rigs (still operating in 1986), a lush coffee crop, diamonds, and iron ore mines. It exported sisal and cotton, as well as food.

By 1986, however, Angola produced little more than oil. It imported half of its food. Coffee as well as mineral exports had dropped by 80 percent. Luanda was littered with mounds of garbage, wrecked cars, and abandoned shops. The city lived under a curfew, 50 percent of its workers were absentee, and the poorest sorted through garbage heaps for food. Officially, the Angola GNP per capita had declined at the rate of 1 percent annually.

The Portuguese had to assume a large measure of responsibility for this disaster. Immediately after independence, all but 25,000 Portuguese left the country, carrying with them cars, telephones, boats, and typewriters. Plantation owners abandoned their fields to rot, bankers left their enterprises to illiterate janitors, medical personnel fled the hospitals. Physically, the Portuguese left the nation in shambles.

More importantly, the shameful colonial policy had left Angola with few human resources. After five centuries of Portuguese rule, 98 percent of the Angolans were still illiterate in 1975. The country had only 250 African schoolteachers, two pilots, and a handful of doctors. The few educated Africans split into three main groups. The MPLA, a Marxist vanguard led by Agostino Neto and other *mestico* urban intellectuals, tried to form a central government and vainly sought help from the United States. Holden Roberto, a descendant of the Kongo monarchy and a mission product, formed his own guerrilla army, while Savimbi, a Swiss-educated tribal leader, called on South Africa for military help.

By 1985, Savimbi's guerrillas aided by the South African army had devastated Angola's southern and eastern provinces. Savimbi's men had sabotaged hydroelectric lines, driven 130,000 refugees from the south, and destroyed all three of the country's rail lines. Negotiations between the tribes, however repugnant to each side, had to commence.

The Marxist government contributed to the disorder. The state marketing board set up to control prices destroyed farmers' initiative and profits; coffee exports fell by 90 percent. A farmer who desired a spare part for his machinery had to process an application through the Ministry of Agriculture and then the Ministry of Planning in Luanda. Agricultural production stalled, and Angola, a land with potentially abundant fields, had to go abroad for food. Meanwhile, the government financed a 65,000-man army by oil exports (largely controlled by Gulf) and maintained 25,000 Cuban troops. By 1984, Angola was "gripped by continuing agony . . . a nation ravaged by chaos and international intervention."[6]

Nowhere were the bitter results of authoritarian rule made more apparent than on the West coast of Africa where several African nations first attained independence. And nowhere else on the continent could one find a better example of a pluralistic, relatively free, benevolent and economically buoyant society than among the swamps and neat fields, the crocodile farms and skyscrapers of modern West Africa.

In 1957, ebullient with independence, Kwame Nkrumah of Ghana challenged Félix Houphouët-Boigny of the Ivory Coast to a "great wager." Predicting eventual disaster for the "neocolonialist," capitalist, and gradualist path already chosen by the Ivory Coast, which would gain its freedom in 1960, Nkrumah confidently asserted that his socialist policies would transform Ghana into an abundant, free society within two decades. In 1958 Guinea, another state on the border of the Ivory Coast, joined in the gamble. Its leader, Sekou Touré, disregarding Charles de Gaulle's pleas that Guinea join the French Community, set out on a course of total self-reliance and "Marxism in African clothes."

At the time, many Westerners were convinced that Nkrumah and Touré would be the winners. The Ivory Coast was, after all, the poorest, least educated of the three nations; it had the weakest agricultural advantages and, relatively speaking, meager mineral resources.

Nonetheless, in their initial days of liberation, the three equatorial countries had several salient features in common: they shared a similar geography and climate; they were heavily dependent upon the export of single crops (cocoa in Ghana, bananas in Guinea, and coffee in the Ivory Coast); and their jungles held unused riches in timber, crops, minerals, and hydroelectric power.

In human terms, too, the regions were somewhat similar. Large proportions of their populations were illiterate and plagued with disease. Their diverse tribes (whose territories overlapped the three national boundaries) were united only by the leadership of a single charismatic figure. They emerged from colonialism in the same era.

It is the political choices they made over a quarter of a century ago, though, not their similarities, that have had the greatest impact on the shape of these societies. Thus the experiences of the contrasting models of development have dramatic importance today not only for Africa but for all of those "Fourth World" areas remaining in the grip of poverty.

As the first African nation to achieve independence, Ghana, well-endowed by nature and boasting the most educated populace, seemed the one likely to come out on top. It had immense foreign exchange resources, large bauxite deposits, cocoa exports of $1 billion a year, and hydroelectric potential. The British had governed "indirectly" during the colonial period. They forbade white settlers, left tribal political structures relatively intact and built an extensive educational system that produced the best civil service on the Dark Continent.

Nkrumah, calling himself "The Redeemer," used his great popularity to have himself elected president for life in 1962. He instituted a police state, crushed dissenters, and set himself up as the leader of Pan-Africanism. Houphouët-Boigny scoffed at the conceit. "What are we supposed to share?" he asked. "Each other's poverty?"

Many Westerners—including Immanual Wallerstein, Patrick O'Donovan, and Sidney Lens—justified Nkrumah's ambitions and his repression by arguing that a social revolution required discipline and that a "fully developed democracy" was impossible in Africa. They viewed anarchy or military dictatorship as the only alternatives to authoritarian rule.

In fact, Nkrumah's megalomania not only destroyed liberal democracy in Ghana but his dictatorship resulted in desperate poverty.

Since Nkrumah's government did not tolerate criticism, corruption in high circles ran rampant. A golden bed imported by one of Nkrumah's cronies, "Crowbar" Edusi, only epitomized the graft which enriched the politicians and stained the civil service.

The lack of responsible criticism and accountability permitted unbridled nationalistic, prestige spending. Nkrumah purchased a $600,000 yacht, remodeled Christianborg Palace (a former slave depot) as his personal home at a cost of $6 million, spent $8 million for a state house, $9 million for a superhighway which went nowhere, $16 million on a hall of African unity, and $20 million for a fleet of Russian jets which carried an average of two persons a flight in grand isolation.

Believing Ghana should become an industrial power, Nkrumah squandered huge sums on fruitless projects: $17 million for a drydock in Tema which was never used, and hundreds of millions on the giant Volta Dam which was designed to power factories which were never built. Between 1958 and 1965, Nkrumah had frittered away $481 million and transformed his surplus in foreign exchange into a $1 billion national debt.

In 1966, while Nkrumah visited China to announce his solutions to the Vietnam crisis, the army overthrew him, the civil service notified INTERPOL that he was wanted for graft, and the people tore down his statue in Accra. His policies—economic waste combined with an intrusion of dogmatism and terror into universities, courts, unions, and the civil service—had decimated Ghana's elite. Five thousand of the best educated Ghanaians fled abroad while another two thousand people spent time in concentration camps. After the coup, those who were left proved incapable of reviving a free government or curing the economy.

As of 1986, Ghana had yet to recover. A civilian government headed by K. A. Busia tried to rebuild the economy between 1969 and 1972 but, confronted with a world drop in cocoa prices, they failed. Disgruntled with the resulting austerity, General Ignatius Aehampong, a drunkard who stole $100 million, and his chief of staff, F. W. K. Akuffo, alternated in office until 1978. That year, a young Air Force Lieutenant, Jerry Rawlings, executed his superiors and installed his own puppet, the former head of Nkrumah's secret police. In 1982, displeased with this man's ineptness, Rawlings seized personal power once again.

In 1984, under military rule, Ghana's national debt had reached $3 billion, inflation topped 100 percent a year, the peasants starved, and 20 percent of the population had fled to neighboring Nigeria (which tried to ship them back in 1983 and again in 1985) and to the Ivory Coast (which still harbored 500,000 Ghanaians). Since 1960, the economy of Ghana actually shrank at an annual rate of 1 percent a year. The once abundant food supply dwindled by more than 1 percent a year, and the price of food increased twenty-five-fold. Ghana's people earned a per capita annual income of $290—less than a dollar a day—which bought much less than thirty years ago. For peasants, a special meal in the Ghana of 1984 was a broiled jungle rat. Favored officers, in contrast, imported (by airplane) Mercedes-Benzes at a cost of $110,000 each for their personal use.

The government devalued the Ghanian *cedi* by 990 percent in 1984 while trade unions demanded a 1,200 percent increase in wages. In one year, prices of staples such as maize and rice rose between 253 and 533 percent. In a nation where cocoa exports had dwindled by 60 percent in twelve years because of artificially low prices for farmers, state controlled agencies went on spending. In 1981, the Ghana National Trading Company, for example, imported $1 million worth of watch straps in a nation which did not produce or import matching stocks. In 1984, the government belatedly ordered the GNTC to dispose of its useless watch bands.

Quite appropriately, considering that he donated $28 million every year to support the government, Nkrumah went into exile in Guinea, where Sekou Touré declared him "co-President." He died there in 1972, after issuing final cabalistic statements about pan-Africanism. Touré, who imposed his own iron rule, survived until 1984.

At the beginning of the "great wager," Guinea too had glittering promise: it was once the richest nation in its corner of the world, its well-tended farmlands fed most of French Africa, its earth contained one third of the world's bauxite reserves, and its hills had major deposits of iron ore, uranium, diamonds, and gold. Conakry, the capital, offered an excellent port, a good transportation system to the inland, and great possibilities for developing industry and hydroelectric power.

But in 1958 Sékou Touré made the first of many disastrous decisions: he severed all relations with France in pursuit of total self-reliance. When de Gaulle flew to Conakry to dissuade Touré, the Guinean leader proclaimed that it was better for his African country to live in poverty than to accept "riches in slavery" as a member of the French Community. To this de Gaulle said, "Then all you have to do is vote 'No.' I pledge myself that nobody will stand in the way of your independence."

Touré advised his people to reject membership in the French Community, and in the only free plebiscite held in the nation, 98 percent of the people voted to follow his lead. Touré became an African and Islamic hero, and the unquestioned radical leader of the only French African territory to opt for autarchy.

De Gaulle responded with vengeful pique, ordering French technicians, doctors, and teachers to leave Guinea within one month of the referendum. All but twenty Frenchmen left. They took with them machines, medical supplies, and even pencils and ceremonial plates.

Western powers refused to help ravaged Guinea. The lure of substantial profits notwithstanding, they distrusted Touré, a Lenin Peace Prize winner and a man with close links to the French Communist Party. By 1978 the tragic rupture—a product of nationalistic pride and ideological blindness on both sides—was partially mended when Touré welcomed French President Valèry Giscard d'Estaing back to Conakry. In July 1982, Touré asked in Washington for American private enterprise to help exploit Guinea's "fabulous economic potential."

During the preceding two decades, Touré had devoted his attention to avoiding assassination attempts, building an army equipped with Czech weapons and instituting a reign of terror and constant indoctrination. As the bodies of opponents swung in the wind over Conakry's bridges, the life expectancy of Guinea's inhabitants declined to forty-one years, its people starved, and only 10 percent of the population learned how to read and write.

According to Amnesty International, Touré's subordinates practiced torture, executed eighteen of his cabinet ministers (including Diallo Telli, once secretary general of the Organization of African Unity), sentenced other ministers to life imprisonment, and periodically displayed the corpses of dissidents as a warning to the masses.

The full scope of Touré's terror only became apparent after his death. A new military dictatorship revealed that thousands of inmates at Conarky's Camp Boiro had undergone electric shock torture and hundreds had died in the "head of death" chamber where they had no food and were hung by their heels over pits of excrement.

During his ascendency, Touré turned to Moscow for aid but received in return only the most blatant form of "neo-colonial exploitation." Russia sent a corps of teachers who spoke only Russian, 10,000 toilet seats, and six combine harvestors to a land which suffered from a surplus of peasants. In return, Russia extracted fishing rights. By 1984, most of the fish consumed in Ghana were sold by Russia but came from Guinean waters. Russia also contracted to mine 90 percent of Guinea's bauxite. Such an arrangement might have resulted in the establishment of indigenous aluminum factories, but instead the ore returned to Russia for processing. Russia paid in rubles used to reduce Guinea's enormous debt for Russian "assistance." Potentially, Guinea's minerals had great value on the world market. A small bauxite mine operated by Western interests, for example, provided 70 percent of Guinea's hard foreign currency in the 1980s.

At the end of Touré's regency, Guinea imported most of its food. Only 12 percent of its once verdant farmland was cultivated. Per capita income had retrogressed at the rate of 0.3 percent annually since 1960.

Its potentially healthy economy produced only $140 a year per person. Some two million Guineans (about 40 percent of the population), emigrated to seek their fortune elsewhere in Africa, particularly in Sierra Leone and the Ivory Coast.

Although still dictatorial and repressive, Touré seemed eager to rejoin the Western economic network after the collapse of his economy became apparent in 1978. Touré sought agricultural expertise from the American midwest and welcomed French capital and advice. After a visit to Guinea, David Rockefeller formed close links with Touré and sponsored business conferences which advertised Guinea's undeveloped resources. Touring the Ivory Coast, Touré openly expressed amazement at the economic marvels which he once denounced as "neo-colonial shams." In 1983, the Ivory Coast's president returned the compliment by speaking of Mr Touré as "my close friend" and citing the Guinean's conversion as proof of the validity of the gradualist approach toward African economic and political development.

By then, the superiority of the Ivory Coast to Guinea was unquestioned. Back in 1957, when the "great wager" began, however, the Ivory Coast seemed an unlikely model of African development. An extraordinarily hot and moist area of West Africa, once checkered with impenetrable jungles, an unnavigable coast, and barren deserts, the Ivory Coast appeared destined, in Henry Kissinger's phrase, to join the ranks of international "basket cases."

The nation lacked the mineral resources, ports, and advanced agriculture which favored Guinea and Ghana. Its people subsisted on about one third the income of those nations. The Ivory Coast's forests and deserts discouraged exploration while its treacherous harbors appeared to prohibit an export trade. The country's meager agriculture depended on the volatile fortunes of one crop, coffee. The capitol, Abidjan, housed twenty thousand people in squalor.

The Ivory Coast also did not have the "human capital" for development, since it did not possess Ghana's well-trained civil service, a unified culture, a stable polity, or broadly educated masses. Its primitive peoples—the Baoulé (refugees from Ghana during the slave-trading epoch), the Senufo, Bete, Wobe, and Guere—each spoke their own languages and had developed their unique cultures, but most had not passed beyond the hunting and gathering state of existence.

Yet, France had governed the Ivory Coast with the announced goal of creating Frenchmen, fully assimilated into French culture. It was direct, central rule, a perhaps arrogant assertion of "cultural imperialism'' far different from rapacious Portuguese and Belgian policies, as well as the British approach of building an African infrastructure of bureaucrats and roads. Houphouët-Boigny, Senghor of Senegal (a fine grammatician in French) and, in his own rebellious way, Touré each joined the world community of Frenchmen. They were educated in France and had the full rights of all Frenchmen, including citizenship, service in government ministries, or membership in the communist party.

As a consequence of this assimilationist policy, the Ivory Coast did have a small African elite epitomized in Félix Houphouët-Boigny, its president, a physician of elegant taste who was the first African to serve metropolitan France at the ministerial level. Although he bitterly opposed the wartime French system of draft labor in Africa, Houphouët-Boigny accepted leadership of his new nation with a degree of reluctance. Like most of the Francophile African aristocrats, he originally believed that his peoples were not yet ready for independence when it was thrust upon them in 1960.

The Ivory Coast also contained approximately 100,000 Lebanese migrants. Houphouët-Boigny carefully nurtured the skills of these people rather than following the lead of other African nations and molesting or expelling them as hated aliens. The Lebanese have since played an important role as small merchants, financiers, and industrialists.

This collection of peoples abetted by ex-patriate Frenchmen and some Israelies transformed the Ivory Coast. The once miserable little country emerged as the ''African miracle,'' a magnet attracting millions of refugees from Guinea and Ghana as well as the starving Sahelian areas.

The economy had surged forward steadily, stimulated particularly by export agriculture. Between 1960 and 1970, the economy grew at a rate of 8 percent annually; between 1970 and 1980, it increased at a pace of 6.7 percent a year. Although plagued by world recession and by a shortage of electrical power in the 1980s, the Ivory Coast managed to expand its GNP by about 6 percent annually. This new wealth reached down to the peasantry: per capita income leapt from $70 annually in 1960 to $1,150 in 1980. The nation claimed the highest per capita income on the continent except for South Africa.

Much of the new prosperity was evident in Abidjan, a city of 900,000 people in 1985, dotted with skyscrapers, highways, and busy docks. Yet, the countryside was not neglected: electricity, roads, and running water appeared in the most remote northern villages.

Agricultural production became highly diversified as the production of all goods tripled between 1965 and 1980. In spite of fluctuations in world trade, coffee production increased three-fold but other products assumed even greater importance as exports. Paloil production increased seven times, making the Ivory Coast one of the largest producers in the world; sugar, cocoa, bananas and pineapples all became leading exports, while the previously arid north yielded sugar cane and cotton. Domestic food production increased simultaneously as export trade, protected by membership in the French community, moved ahead. Unlike Ghana and Guinea, the Ivory Coast not only fed itself but also nourished the migrants from other starving lands.

After an initial concentration on agriculture, the Ivory Coast expanded its industrial production by 10.5 percent a year between 1970 and 1980. In the years since independence, critical measures of the general quality of life also showed important changes: the death rate fell by 33 percent, infant mortality dropped by 40 per cent, and the crude birthrate was reduced by 7 percent. Adult literacy doubled since 1960.

The country devoted an extremely high proportion of its national budget (42 percent) to education. Schooling was free, conducted in French, and virtually devoid of ethnic, tribal, or religious bias. School attendance went up from 22 percent of the school age population at independence to 55 percent in 1980. Because of a strong orientation to French culture, the educational system of the Ivory Coast was criticized as elitist and neocolonial. Yet, adult literacy reached 41 percent in 1977, four times the rate of Guinea, even though Sékou Touré claimed that "for the first twenty years, we in Guinea have concentrated on developing the mentality of our people."[7]

Four factors stood out in explaining this African success:

First, advances in export-oriented agriculture were the lifeblood of economic progress. The government encouraged investment by large landowners (30 percent French) and peasants, diversified into new crops, and opened up fallow lands. The government avoided expenditures on heavy industry, defense, and large-scale monuments to nationalistic prestige. It concentrated its energies on building an infrastructure of roads, electricity, communications, and dredged harbors which would contribute directly to the expansion of the agricultural sector.

Unlike most African nations, the Ivory Coast did not favor city dwellers over the rural population. The government sponsored price supports rather than price ceilings for food, resulting in a steady increase in farm production. Wise land use, investments in new crops, and reasonable marketing policies also supported production. Tribal systems of land tenure were legally modified to provide clear titles needed for bank credits and foreign investments.

Second, Houphouët-Boigny consciously adopted a "gradualist" and state capitalist policy, telling his people, "we must go slowly, my children, for we are in a hurry." His approach opened doors to foreign capital, emphasized export growth, allowed the free movement of profit, slowly built an elite of technicians, and welcomed the expansion of an indigenous and propertied middle class. In pursuing one variant of capitalism, the government's approach involved severe risks: the dangers involved in depending on foreign favor, the risks of shifting world market conditions, and all of the problems inherent in close dealings between a small, poor country and powerful foreign interests. Even in the treacherous trade currents of the 1980s, however, the gamble paid off.

Third, the nationalist movement in the Ivory Coast drew its inspiration from *planteurs,* village people, rather than urban intellectuals, politicians, and administrators as in Ghana. In consequence, the governors at the center of power paid close attention to the needs of peasants, built roads into the interior, and provided incentives and security for peasant farming.

Fourth, Houphouët-Boigny expanded economic dependence on the French: French capital, skills, techniques, markets, managers, and even military power were far more prominent in 1985 than in colonial times. Between 1970 and 1980, the gross inflow of capital, largely French, increased markedly from $77 million annually to $1,426 millions. Between independence and 1985, the number of French nationals in the Ivory Coast grew from 10,000 to 60,000 people, many of them serving in the civil service and education. Frenchmen owned 30 percent of all manufacturing firms and served every function from deputy cabinet minister to maitre d'hotel in Abdijan's elegant restaurants. Exports to France soared, increasing by 6 percent annually between 1960 and 1980. The presence of a contingent of French troops, invited by Houphouët-Boigny, allowed his government to expand large amounts on education and virtually nothing on external security (even during the time when Nkrumah threatened invasion). French concerns tried to exploit offshore oil reserves first discovered in 1977.

The French (and Israeli, Lebanese, and American) presence, so strikingly different from the situation in Guinea, invited bitter charges that the Ivory Coast had surrendered to neocolonialism. "Are the French not the very life and wire of most of its industries?" one Nigerian critic asked of the Ivory Coast. "Liberal capitalism is not African. . . . The Ivorian 'miracle' is a sham."[8] Samir Amin, a neo-Marxist critic, denounced the country's dependence on France, its emphasis on export trade, the supposed unevenness of development, and the profits taken from the country. In 1967, he predicted that Ivorian development "would reach a ceiling which is now near"[9]—a prophecy invalidated by the tripling of average income for villagers since then.

Nonetheless, the issue of neocolonialism rankled many Ivorians, particularly well-educated youth who lost out to Frenchmen in the competition for jobs. Houphouët-Boigny promised eventual "Ivorization" of the economy, but except for the very highest levels in government (and the lower ranks of the peasantry), the French were still dominant in the 1980s. In the uncertain period which follows Houphouët-Boigny's death, demagogues were sure to appeal to racial pride even if it involved crippling the economy.

The dependence on France was great, and Houphouët-Boigny made no secret of it. He admitted that France had gained by the "exploitation" but argued that there would have been nothing at all to "exploit" without French investment. He contended that his economy was vastly sounder and more diversified and his people much better off than in countries such as Guinea or Ghana which had, through choice or mismanagement, remained isolated from the world economy.

His policies were based on the assumption that countries which are short on skills, managers, capital, technology, agricultural scientists, and access to markets must call upon foreign factors of production to invigorate their economies with speed, knowledge, and efficiency. If they do not, he argued, they suffered from the economic stagnation which imprisoned Ghana and Guinea despite the fact that they once enjoyed greater comparative advantages than the Ivory Coast. "If I could have twice as many Frenchmen as we have to help us build the Ivory Coast," he once said, "I would take them."[10]

Despite the unpredictability of the world market and the dangers inherent in dependence on a former imperialist master, the fact that France had major economic and human stakes in the country made French capitalists and the French government tread lightly in the Ivory Coast. The economic links were strong and, for that very reason, the Ivorians were able to exact a price: quota preferences in Europe, generous flows of aid, major continuing investments of private capital, and favored access to export markets. The Franco-Ivorian relationship, symbolized by a statue to an ex-colonial governor in the main square of Abidjan, demonstrated that "dependency" was a two-way street. The Ivory Coast maintained its affluent independence with more dignity and efficacy than a Guinea—and vastly more than a true dependency such as Chad— precisely because it was no longer a mere beggar.

Politically, like many newly formed nations, the Ivory Coast (with some sixty tribes) suffered from ethnic tensions, generational conflict, religious and economic dissensions, and battles between immigrants and native workers. Political issues were fought out in a magical, superstitious atmosphere. During an incipient coup in the 1960s, for example, some rebels planned to kill Houphouët-Boigny by putting needles into minature effigies of him which they carried in suitcases. And Houphouët-Boigny himself was not above shrouding his authority in an aura of mystery.

As V. S. Naipaul observed in his brilliant chornicle of the Ivory Coast, the president had generously donated lands he owned as a chief and transformed his own tribal village of Yamoussukro into a monument to modernity. Yet, he also created an artificial lake in the new complex and stocked it with man-eating crocodiles. Ritually, a government functionary fed them live chickens each day. The significance of the crocodiles remained a mystery; "These are totemic, emblematic creatures and they belong to the president." As Naipaul, a man awed by the Ivory Coast's advances, remarked about the hideous crocodiles in their modern setting: "No one knows precisely what they mean. But to all Africans they speak at once of danger and of the president's, of the chief's, magically granted knowledge, of his power as something more than human, something emananting from the earth itself."[11]

Nonetheless, in this atmosphere of hidden psychic power, in handling plots based on witchcraft, in defusing riots of university students, or in abating the disaffection of army officers over the last thirty years, Houphouët-Boigny consistently relied more on reason, discussion and compromise than force or symbolism as a means of achieving consensus. Instead of executing opponents who planned a coup d'état in the 1960s, for example, Houphouët-Boigny met with them in jail and talked for hours about the future of the Ivory Coast. All were released and the chief conspirator, Jean-Baptiste Mockey, became a friend of the president and served as minister of health, minister of agriculture, and ambassador to Israel. In 1983, Amnesty International reported no incidents of imprisonment, torture, or political executions in the Ivory Coast.

The Parti Démocratique de Côte d'Ivoire had an effective monopoly on political offices at all levels. The party did not, however, brutally repress dissent, try to gain total control over the people, ban elections, dismantle the courts, or kill its opponents. The PDCI government endeavored to change some traditional practices (for example, by amending the law permitting polygamy) but it moved pragmatically and humanely. Most importantly, Houphouët-Boigny preserved all of those mediating instituions—courts, churches, tribal councils, unions of immigrant workers, etc.—which protected individuals from the untrammeled exercise of state power.

At times, such as 1981, Houphouët-Boigny tried to "democratize" his own party. Instead of allowing just a yes or no vote for old party members, the government opened the door to 600 candidates to run for 140 seats in the assembly. Newcomers beat 80 percent of the old deputies who, as former "elders," returned to their villages, stripped of authority and personally degraded. After the election, national television pleaded for "reconciliation" and, in certain villages, there were ceremonies to mark renewed cooperation between the old and the new. For Naipaul, as the observer, "Democracy, people's rule, was the imported idea; reconciliation was the African idea."[12]

The political climate of the Ivory Coast was marked by a relaxed, noncoercive, if highly corrupt, atmosphere. The bribery and favoritism stretched to the highest level and affected all activities. Foreign capitalists bribed the proper ministry to construct a sugar refinery; civil servants bought their jobs from superiors; even taxi drivers paid a price for their permit. Part of this corruption derived from the West African tradition of "dash": the custom of paying for the chief's services with gifts. Endemic in many developing countries—and not unknown in New York's school system, Jersey City courts, or the halls of Congress—corruption in the Ivory Coast had not demonstrably impeded economic growth; it may, in fact, have served useful functions for an entrepreneur eager to cut through red tape or a newcomer to the city seeking favors from the tribal cousins.

Nonetheless, independent Ivorian courts tried to limit corruption by jailing people for such offences as embezzlement and charging the government rents for nonexistent dwellings. In 1984, the courts sentenced seven high government people for ten to twenty years in prison on corruption and ordered them to repay the state millions of dollars.

Where the threat of prosecution or the promise of money and other favors did not succeed in getting lenient, pleasant but rather cynical bureaucrats to do their jobs, dialogue apparently did.

Houphouët-Boigny created a national council which discussed all major issues in face-to-face encounters. Called irregularly, this ingenious invention exercized more real power than the civil administration or the PDCI. It included representatives from the elected national assembly, labor leaders, spokesman for tribes, feminist leaders, heads of religious communities, and even representatives of migrants from Guinea and Ghana. The council was a cross section of the society. Its discussions resulted in the installation of a village well in some distant area, the resolution of a strike in Abidjan, or the dismissal of a cabinet minister who had dipped into the public purse too blatantly.

The council was but one mechanism for the expression of dissent. Courts functioned independently. Scholars and journalists had freedom of movement and of investigation; there were no political prisoners or political executions and no one was forced into exile for political or religious reasons. Students openly criticized the government. Crises—such as a university strike in 1977 when Houphouët-Boigny spent three days listening to student grievances—ended in dialogue and compromise, rather than bloodshed.

Ivorians debated the future of their country after the death of their "old man," Houphouët-Boigny. Although he had not demanded the trappings and obeisance of the charismatic leaders, Houphouët-Boigny had provided decisive leadership and his death left a vacuum. Most observers believed that the fact that Houphouët-Boigny would dare to leave his nation in 1983 for a six-month vacation throughout the world indicated that a stable educated civic class had emerged, capable of pursuing the gradualist, productive policies which their leader initiated. Unlike the rest of Black Africa, the Ivory Coast did not suffer from lethal tribal conflicts, the rise of new fanatical religions (particularly within Islam), or threats from the military class. The greatest danger to the Ivory Coast's future stability and civility arose from urban demagogues who, more often than not, were jealous on-lookers rather than participants in the race for greater wealth.

The Ivory Coast was hardly an unblemished illustration of a liberal or social democracy: the rich francophones in Abidjan participated much more fully in the political process than Muslim tribesmen in the north; civil servants amiably relieved capitalist visitors of "free will" donations; health services and mass literacy needed improvement; a party-owned newspaper, *Fraternité Matin,* spread its coated version of the truth, highlighting "the thoughts of the president" each day; and, as in the time of America's political machines, wise Ivorians consulted their local ward heelers for favors.

Socialists complained that Houphouët-Boigny—a complacent "bourgeois" who did not hide his preference for silk suits and Swiss chalets—was not sufficiently dynamic, charismatic, or "authentically" African. In the conventional sense of the word, as David Lamb has eloquently noted, he was not a revolutionary but he wrought fundamental changes in his country's socioeconomic structure and led a revolution in a climate of open dialogue rather than suppression and bloodshed.

By manipulating a "neocolonial" relationship to his own advantage, by invigorating his peasantry with capitalist incentives, and by making full use of his nation's advantages in the world market, Houphouët-Boigny economically transformed his country. Of equal importance, he did not find it necessary to follow Lenin's dictum that "Liberty is precious—so precious that it must be rationed."

Clearly, whatever the Ivory Coast's shortcomings, it had won "the great wager" with Ghana and Guinea. As Pliny knew long before, Naipaul found Africa in the flux of perpetual change: "It is always on the point of being made something else. So it arouses hope, ambition, frustration, and irritation. And even the success of the Ivory Coast induces a kind of anxiety. Will it last?"[13]

5

An Infidel in Islam: Malaysia

I boasted when in office that I was the happiest Prime Minister in the world and I thank Allah that I am still a happy man.

TUNKU ABDUL RAHMAN, aged 81, 1984

In a land covered by rain forest where king cobras allegedly chased people who angered them, gibbons stole food from human settlements, and most of the 53,000 aborigines were afraid to emerge from the deep jungle, one hardly expected to discover a "model" of economic, social, and political development.

Yet, in 1985, Malaysia with its many tensions and flaws, was such a country.

Indeed, within the Islamic world, it represented the only reasonably successful case of a nation which had followed a "fourth way." Other Muslim areas (Qatar, Kuwait, Saudi Arabia) had vastly higher per capita incomes but had failed to distribute wealth in an equitable fashion or to create political avenues to an open society. Some parts of Islam such as Indonesia had equivalent natural resources but remained under military dictatorship. Iran reverted to Shi'ite orthodoxy, the Lebanon erupted into anarchy, while places like Yemen stood fast as desolate outposts of the faith.

In contrast, Malaysia—a major exporter of tin, timber, rubber, palm oil, natural gas, and cheap petroleum—grew economically at a rate of over 8 percent annually in the 1960s and 1970s. Even during the world recession of the 1980s, the GNP increased at better than 6 percent yearly.

This economic growth proceeded under a singular system of constitutional monarchy where the nine sultans of Malaysia elected a rotating king from among their ranks. Malaysians also voted freely for members of parliament whom they chose from among 12 competing political parties.

Socially, the government attempted to insure that welfare would be spread broadly and that the link between race and economic status would be broken. Among Islamic countries, Malaysia achieved the highest rates of literacy and life expectancy.

Malaysia enjoyed its economic advance and its political freedoms in an atmosphere of ethnic diversity. In 1984, the region's 15 million people contained approximately 50 percent Malays (Moslems of the Sunni faith who spoke Malay), 35 percent Chinese (divided into various religious and political groups), 10 percent Indians, and 5 percent Euroasians, Dyaks, Kadazans, and Nigritos. Uniting this anthropological melange under one flag was not easy.

Between 1948 and 1960, Malaysia experienced its great "Emergency." During World War II, groups of British officers, a few Malays, and thousands of Chinese formed guerrilla units which actively resisted the Japanese occupation. Since Indians and, to some degree, Malays received special privileges from the Japanese who hoped to integrate them within a great "co-prosperity sphere," the Chinese emerged as a majority of the resistance forces. The Japanese persecuted them not only for their guerrilla activities but also because the Japanese identified them with the struggle against mainland China.

After the defeat of the Japanese in 1945, the Chinese Communists created a revolutionary movement and renamed themselves the Malayan Peoples Anti-Japanese Army. They proceeded to organize strikes, to murder European planters and miners, and to disorganize the existing economy in an attempt to topple the government. By 1948, the underground army attacked villages, ambushed travelers, and forced reluctant Malays to furnish supplies and information. Other Malaysians began to identify Chinese by race as both members of a Communist conspiracy and as capitalist exploiters (since the Chinese held a dominant position in the normal economy). This was, of course, a tragic echo of Nazi slogans against Jews.

After the migration of 400,000 refugees, intense jungle operations, and the uncovering of the Secretary General of the Communist party as an agent who absconded with the party's funds, the British and Malaysian armies recovered control of the peninsula. Simultaneously,

Malays formed UMNO in 1951, an organization seeking freedom from British colonial rule. Noncommunist Chinese founded the Malayan Chinese Association and, in 1954, the Indian subgroup created the Malayan Indian Congress. These three parties, devoted to an ideal of a multi-racial and politically free Malaysia, joined together in striving for independence from Great Britain.

This alliance won 80 percent of a free vote in 1955 under the leadership of Tunku Abdul Rahman. "The Tunku," as he became universally known in Malaysia, was a son of the Sultan of Kedah, a graduate of Cambridge, and a popular civil servant. (Technically, any member of a royal family in Malaysia was a "Tunku," or prince, but the leader of UMNO was recognised as the foremost holder of the title.) A Muslim, a tolerant, gentle man, and a gambler who was fond of women, "The Tunku" won the hearts of both Malays and Chinese.

In 1955, the Tunku offered amnesty to all guerrillas and the Communist movement began to disintegrate. In 1956, he led a delegation to London requesting independence from Britain and, in 1957, Malaysia achieved its "Merdeka" (freedom).

His problems had not ended. In 1961, the Tunku proposed a union between various parts of Southeast Asia. Brunei refused. Singapore accepted but, because of the Chinese majority in its area, it was ejected from the federation in 1965. Both the Philippines and Indonesia objected to the absorption of North Borneo by Malaysia. The Indonesians proclaimed a policy of "confrontation" and attacked the territories of Sarawak and Sabah. The violence ended in 1966 when military rulers seized power in Indonesia and acknowledged the existence of a "greater Malaysia," incorporating Malaya, Sarawak, and Sabah.

The Tunku faced perhaps his greatest crisis in 1969. He had consistently preached racial and religious tolerance and had ruled over a country noted for its ethnic harmony. Yet, his dominance rested on an "unwritten understanding": that Malays of the Sunni faith would hold power as politicians and civil servants while the Chinese would be citizens and were allowed to dominate commercial life.[1] The Indians, mainly rubber plantation workers and a few professionals, were left out of this bargain but acted as mediating agents between the two more powerful entities.

In 1969, Malay politicians proposed that Islam become the official religion of the land and that Malay should become the nation's language. The Tunku intervened and tried to calm the predominately Muslim enthusiasm for these measures in parliament. In fact by 1985,

Islam was the official religion of Malaysia and Malay its language. Yet, the government did not apply the strictures of Islam on believers in other religions, and English prevailed as the common medium of communication in the political administration, large-scale commerce, and some of the mass media.

The Tunku became unpopular with many Muslims because of his moderate stand. His tenuous "Alliance" lost power in the elections of 1969. Islamic fundamentalists cast their votes for PAS, an obdurate Islamic party, while some Chinese turned to opposition parties. While the Tunku retained power at the center, some states, such as Selangor, came out of the elections with a tie between the Tunku's alliance and various opposition parties.

Each side celebrated its "victories" with parties which soon broke out into violence. Malays, Chinese, and Indians clashed in unprecedented attacks on others, hundreds died and, reportedly, the Tunku wept. The communal violence, officially referred to as the "May 13th Incident," resulted in a suspension of parliamentary democracy for twenty-one months, a stronger alliance of the more tolerant Malay and Chinese parties, the passage of severe internal security laws, and the fall from grace of the Tunku. Nonetheless, in 1983, all of the nation celebrated the eightieth birthday of the Tunku, "the father of independence."

Although he retired from the prime ministership, the Tunku never relented in his press statements on those who wielded power or in his advocacy of tolerance and compromise.

His successor, Datuk Seri Mahathir Mohamad, took office in 1981. Dr. Mahathir differed from the Tunku on many matters but no one questioned his economic pragmatism or his devotion to liberal principles.

Dr. Mahathir advocated a "clean, efficient, and trustworthy government" and required civil servants (one out of fourteen adults in 1985) to "clock in" their arrivals in government offices. While the Tunku had great admiration for the British ex-colonialists and was a personal friend of Queen Elizabeth, Prince Philip, and the duke of Gloucester, Dr. Mahathir advised his nation to "Look East." He wished Malaysia to emulate the work ethic of Japan and South Korea. In contrast to the Tunku, he counseled his people to adopt the most modern technological and management techniques available in his time—that is, a Japanese approach to work. Perhaps unknowingly, he followed an analogous path of the Meiji rulers of Japan in 1868 who told their people: "Quit Asia. Look West!"

While seeking economic efficiency, Mahathir wished to galvanize his people, encourage a fairer distribution of wealth, and elicit more Malay participation in various areas of the economy. He faced major challenges since Malaysia, with all of its potential wealth, presented great physical obstacles.

Malaya itself is a peninsula covered by dense rain jungle, driven down the middle by a mountainous spine. A few areas on the East coast are mud-flats and mangrove forests inhabited by once fierce pirates. Borneo, a primitive area dominated by Dyaks who were originally famous for head hunting, is covered with jungle which has existed for an estimated one hundred million years. Monitor lizards, elephants, tapirs, and leopards still prowl through the dense undergrowth. Yet, the triple-canopy forest is also a storehouse of immense riches: spices, tin, rubber, palm oil groves, coconuts, and papaya.

The outside world could not ignore Malaysia's riches. The earliest migrants, the *Orang Asli* ("Original Man"), probably were migrants from Southern China who invaded the region seven thousand years ago. By the 1980s, they had fallen into an economically depressed status because other foreigners successively seized the riches of Malaysia from them.

The great kingdom of Srivijaya (A.D. 618–906), located in southeast Sumatra, controlled Malaysia for a century. The kingdom of Malacca, founded by Chinese and Malay merchants who wished to take advantage of the trade route between China and India, gained hegemony around 1400. By the end of the fifteenth century, influenced by Muslim traders from India, Malacca embraced Islam. Malacca's rulers were Malays who wished to benefit from an Arab edict that only Muslim ports could berth Muslim ships. (The first evidence of Muslim activity in Malaysia came from Marco Polo in 1292, but at that time the faith had not spread through the archipelago.)

By the sixteenth century, the Portuguese expanded into Malaya. They sought a mythical priest-king Prester John whom they believed had established a Christian kingdom in the East. Not incidentally, they also wished to control the lucrative trade in Asian spices. Proclaiming a crusade against Islamic influences, Alfonso de Albuquerque conquered Malacca in 1511. His rule was short-lived. Lured by a desire to dominate the Malacca straits, the Dutch stormed into Malacca and destroyed Portuguese influence in 1641.

Meanwhile, the British East India Company enviously surveyed the riches of the sparsely populated, jungle-clad land. In 1786, it seized control of Penang and gradually extended its power throughout Malaya. The bearded "white rajas" continuously expanded their indirect rule over the area, often acting as "advisers" to Malay Sultans.

The British were richly rewarded. By 1861, the British had exploited the huge tin reserves around Kuala Lumpur; by 1888, "Mad Ridley," a botanist who imported rubber seeds from Brazil, made an unexpected fortune in the new rubber industry; by 1920, far-sighted farmers had created large palm oil estates; and by the 1930's British explorers found oil off the shores of Malaysia. Chinese seeking to escape the poverty of their homeland and indentured Indians flooded into Malaysia.

Thus, more than most regions of Southeast Asia, Malaya had established firm contacts with other cultures and a strong base for an export-oriented economy. Foreign influences also brought an end to slavery, a spread in secular education, and a cessation in civil wars between the various principalities.

The advantages of Malaya were not lost on the Japanese. In the 1930s, they infilitrated hundreds of secret agents who, plying a trade as barber, merchant, or photographer, carefully mapped the military and economic topography of Malaysia. On December 8, 1941, the Japanese invaded Malaya. Frustrated by their slow advance in China and a Western embargo on strategic commodities, the Japanese coveted the tin, rubber, oil, and ports of Malaysia. The "little men," as Sir Shenton Thomas, then governor of Singapore, contempuously called them, overan Malaysa in seventy days. Although outnumbered two to one, the Japanese gained supremacy of the air in one day, sank two British warships off Kuantan within two days, and forced the British to surrender Singapore—the "Gibralter of the East"—on February 15, 1942.

Although atom bombs eventually devastated the Japanese war effort in 1945, the occupation made a permanent mark on Malaysia. Persecution of the Chinese, ironically accompanied by economic encouragement for the Malays and the establishment of a puppet Indian National Army, created a new sense of ethnic identity and nationalism in Malaysia.

Inadvertently, the Japanese inspired three groups which soon played an important role in the creation of an independent Malaysia. First, when the tide of war turned against them, the Japanese encouraged a group of Islamic reformers from the Wahabi movement as nascent nationalists. The reformers were educated in Cairo and had absorbed anti-British enthusiasms. The Japanese organized mass demonstrations and pan-Malayan conferences to encourage the nationalist hopes of this group. Second, a new elite of English-educated administrators from the traditional royal families of Malaya, such as the Tunku, viewed themselves as the rightful inheritors of power and as opponents of the Islamic revolutionaries. A third elite consisted of Malay-educated teachers and journalists, including Dr. Mahathir. This intelligentsia emerged primarily from the peasant classes and opposed both British rule and the sultans. As secularists, they also conflicted with the Islamic reformers and became the backbone for the more radical political movements in Malaysia.

In spite of their differences, these three elites united to found an independent Malaysia. Under the leadership of the Tunku, the UMNO-dominated ''Alliance'' succeeded in overcoming the ever present threats of ethnic conflict and, through compromise and tolerance, forged a new, economically healthy nation.

Malaysia's continuing economic success undoubtedly helped in creating a degree of unity in a multiracial society. Both the Japanese and British colonialists, in spite of their exploitation and prejudices, left behind a heritage which offered Malaysia certain distinct advantages. The colonialists had built an infrastructure of ports, roads, and communications; they had created vast plantations based on Western-type land tenure throughout the virgin forests; they dug tin mines, created a rubber industry out of nothing, established research institutes, and provided the rudimentary structure of an educational system.

When freedom came in 1957, the Malays, Indians, and especially the Chinese were ready to build on solid economic foundations. The success of their export-oriented economy since the 1960s became a legend in Southeast Asia. The real economic growth of Malaysia was better than 9 percent annually during the 1960s and 1970s; by the early 1980's, Malaysia enjoyed a healthy growth rate of 5 percent a year; in 1985, Malaysia grew at almost 6 percent a year. Per capita income rose from $500 a year in 1957 to an (inflation-adjusted) rate of $2,100 in 1985. The nation encouraged foreign investment and depended upon the private sector for its growth. Tin, timber, rubber, palm oil, and petroleum were foremost in Malaysia's expansion. Oil production jumped to 440,000 barrels a day in 1984 while the export of natural gas offered a new source of income.

Malaysia's handling of its oil resources illustrated an important application of the principle of comparative advantage. Malaysia's oil happened to be relatively ''clean'' and free of sulphur. Because some nations wanted this particular oil as a way of controlling pollution, Malaysia exported its high-grade petroleum to more industrialized nations. For its own needs, Malaysia imported "dirty" but cheap crude oil and reaped a profit.

An old enemy, Japan, played a major role in Malaysia's development. On the one hand, about 30 percent of OECD investment in Malaysia came from Japan, Malaysia's largest investor, in 1984. On the other hand, Japan received 90 percent of its natural rubber, 90 percent of its tin, 50 percent of its tropical timber, 40 percent of its vegetable oil, and some 10 percent of its crude oil from Malaysia. Japan became Malaysia's largest trading partner and established joint manufacturing ventures in such sectors as ship-building, road construction, and automobile manufacturing.

Malaysia's growth rate might have been even better were it not for certain problems beyond the nation's control or inherent in its social structure. The world recession of the 1980s naturally hurt this export-oriented economy. Nonetheless, because of diversification in its products and trade partners, Malaysia still prospered even when world commodity prices dropped.

Historically the country had been dependent on commodity exports but the post-independence leadership sought ways out of the boom-or-bust vulnerability of natural products.

Manufacturing began in light industry—electronics and textiles—that tended to be capitalized abroad and was located in sheltered free-trade zones. Officials later stressed heavy industry—steel, cement, pulp and paper, and cars—which in 1986 emerged as the single largest sector of the economy.

Paced by the Heavy Industries Corporation of Malaysia (HICOM), development funds poured into high technology, enormous research and development institutes, and an indigenous automaking capacity. The attempt to lead Malaysia into the big leagues of newly industrializing nations was guided as much by highly controversial social goals as by strictly economic ones. Regardless of cost, for instance, HICOM spread heavy industry throughout the land—steel in Trengganu, engine manufacturing in Penang, cars in Selangor.

In addition, the government, inspired by the example of Japan and South Korea, tried to instill new modes of labor management. This did not win the applause of workers attached to English-style craft unions, Chinese entrepreneurs, or the average Malay who treasured a traditional, relaxed way of life.

The modernization drive created many problems. Heavy industries starting up at the end of the twentieth century confronted a worldwide surplus in all their product lines. They therefore required steep protection against imported goods, an expedient that frustrated schemes for cooperation among the countries of Asia.

Further, the lack of export opportunities and the failure of HICOM to tap new natural resources meant that its activities generated little foreign income. Critics worried that HICOM might evolve into a vast, impoverished public corporation "managing" the interests of Malays.

Ethnic tensions, too, undoubtedly hindered economic growth. The government, for example, introduced the "New Economic Policy" in 1971 with the specific goal of increasing the share of Malays in the national wealth. This economic initiative was launched because Malays made up about 75 percent of all people living below the official poverty line while the Chinese ethnic group dominated the upper reaches of the economic hierarchy. In the hope of reducing this disparity, the government founded a number of groups which assisted Malays in entering foreign and Chinese-controlled businesses. The government also created statutory bodies which purchased shares in corporations on behalf of Malays or *bumiputra* (sons of the soil). Supposedly, by 1990, these shares will be distributed among Malays and they will own 30 percent of the corporate sector.

This policy created numerous problems. Some argued, for example, that "there could be in Malaysia a vast public corporation managing the interests of the *bumiputra,* while the private sector remains in the hands of foreigners and the other ethnic communities."[2] The dangers in this approach were illustrated when the great Bank Bumiputra made a number of bad investments and virtually collapsed in 1984. Wealthy businessmen of Chinese background hesitated to risk their capital in the country because of the government's long-range plans to keep giving Malays a bigger role in the economy.

Mahathir's "Look East" policy, initiated in 1981, also drew sharp criticism. Japan's increased presence in Malaysia resulted not only in an upsurge in trade and manufacturing, but attempts to restructure the work force and the economy. Malaysia established large *sogo shoshas* (Japanese style trading houses), sent thousands of workers for training in Japan, and adopted Japanese-style quality control councils.

Malaysian businessmen complained that firms such as Shimizu of Japan and Hyundai of South Korea had attained a virtual monopoly in certain industries. Labor unions, some founded in the 1920s, objected to attempts to transform them into in-house unions, replacing British-style, craft-based unions. Ethnic leaders questioned whether Islamic values could be reconciled with the " Japanese work ethic."

Japanese manufacturers, for their part, continued to have a low opinion of Malaysian work styles. In a 1983 study which surveyed Japanese managers' views of Malaysian workers, only 19 percent rated the workers as "punctual," 5 percent as taking good care in their work, and none considered them highly adaptable to changing conditions.

Nonetheless, the Malaysian economy continued to surge ahead and there were many signs that the Malays, who traditionally controlled the political realm, were also benefiting from a variety of social measures.

In the Clark Kerr measurement of crucial indices of the quality of life (rates of infant mortality, life expectancy, and literacy), Malaysia scored higher than any other Islamic nation with a rating of 66. In contrast, the People's Republic of Yemen stood at 33, Pakistan scored 38, and Indonesia, a country with even greater natural resources, reached 48. Jordan at 47, Syria at 54, and Turkey at 55 had similar incomes, but less equity in their distribution. The rich oil-exporting Islamic countries ranked so low in the physical quality of life (when compared to their income) that they were omitted from Kerr's calculations.[3]

Within the world of Islam, then, it would appear that Malaysia spread educational opportunity, created health facilities, and provided adequate nutrition far more successfully then its Muslim counterparts whether they were of a capitalist or socialist persuasion.

The success of Malaysia can best be illustrated by comparison to Indonesia, its ethnic, religious, linguistic, and geographical neighbor. Larger in population (151 million), enjoying a much greater share of the region's resources of oil, timber, rubber, and rice, and dominated by Islamic Malays, Indonesia failed to match Malaysia's progress since independence.

Economically, by 1986, Indonesia had achieved only about one fifth of Malaysia's income. After a series of booms and depressions, it suffered from heated inflation; in 1966, inflation rose to 839 percent a year; by 1984 it had fallen to a "mere" 22 percent. Villagers, some 80 percent of Indonesia's population did not benefit from the oil boom of the 1970s. By 1978, 75 percent of the village population of Java suffered from severe malnutrition. In 1984, the official life expectancy had reached only fifty years. In the cities, Javanese military men and Chinese merchants enjoyed enormous prosperity, often derived from bribes. Each army unit ran its own business and reaped the profits. The state-owned oil company, for example, charged an under-the-table $5 million "signature fee" when its officials signed contracts with foreign petroleum companies. The overseas Chinese community, a center of entrepreneurial talent as in Malaysia, suffered from riots and persecution while the peasants, swamped in population growth, stagnated.

Indonesia's tattered political course affected the economic situation in this potentially wealthy archipelago.

In 1945, Indonesian nationalists, nurtured by the Japanese occupation, declared their independence from the Netherlands. A bloody civil war ensued, involving the Dutch, dissident ethnic groups, and Indonesian nationalists trained by the Japanese. After crushing a revolution in Sumatra, the charismatic nationalist leader, Sukarno, triumphed. His grandiose visions, economic mismanagement, and "Guided Democracy" ruined the Indonesian economy. By 1965, twenty years after independence, an average laborer's real income had dropped by 40 percent.

In 1965, the Communists, some 3 million strong, may have staged an abortive coup. Rebellious army units did in fact kill six generals and received tentative support from PKI, the Communist party. Assassins did not, however, harm General Suharto, a senior army official or his cronies. Doubts remained about Suharto's role in the coup. Whatever the truth may be, Suharto used the uprising as an excuse for overthrowing Sukarno. Between 1965 and 1966, according to official estimates, the army under General Suharto massacred some 500,000 suspected Communists.

Economically, the nation under Suharto regained momentum and particularly benefited from an upsurge in world oil prices. In the seventies, under the guidance of "the Berkeley Mafia," a group of economists, GNP may have grown at 10 percent per year, inflation was curbed, and the West invested large sums in the economy. Senior officers, controlling various major parts of the economy, benefited enormously; their wives, including Suharto's, served as fronts for businesses which channeled illegal monies into the army's coffers.

Politically, "the years under the Suharto government held a special dimension of hardship and fear."[4] Suharto arrested 750,000 Indonesians and detained most of them without trial. By 1983, according to Amnesty International, some 43,000 people had not regained their civil rights and hundreds of alleged conspirators in the 1965 coup remained in jail after eighteen years. In 1984, as oil revenue fell, the growth rate decreased to 4 percent, and the population of Java ballooned, Suharto faced new political challenges as Muslim activists detonated explosions throughout Indonesia. They sought an end to military rule and corruption, curbs on minority Chinese, and the establishment of an Islamic state. The general responded by jailing 450 Muslims who were allegedly involved in attacking the military regime.

While Indonesia, with all of its great resources, reeled under the corruption and brutality of military rule, the social welfare of Malaysia's people steadily and visibly improved. In the villages where 60 percent of the people still lived, new rice hybrids allowed peasants to reap a second crop during off-season periods, television aerials appeared in the most remote *kampung,* paved roads linked the villages with towns, and universal portable radios allowed people to tune in the news from London or Peking. As they had for centuries, small wooden homes propped up on stilts (a protection from both floods and snakes) dotted the countryside but a higher proportion of peasants owned their own homes in 1985 then ever before. Once completely isolated, peasants in the 1980s routinely took off-station taxis to the nearest town where they could purchase radios and tires, boots and books, all made in Malaysia, as well as traditional batik sarongs. In 1985, surveys of the peasantry indicated that 95 percent believed that life had improved for them over the last twenty years and 90 percent expected a continuing progress in the next ten years.

For most people, migration to cities represented the surest route to progress and the automobile, its vehicle. Between 1980 and 1984, Malaysians added a million new registered motor vehicles to their overburdened roads, mainly in the Kuala Lumpur area. This city, lying at the confluence of the Klang and Gombak rivers, was founded in 1864 by two Chinese merchants who wanted to serve tin miners in the adjoining area. Aptly named the "Muddy Estuary," Kuala Lumpur flourished as a mining center, an export point, and eventually as a capital. Between 1964 and 1984, the city exploded, growing at an annual rate of 6 percent. By 1985, skyscrapers shot up throughout the city, factories flourished in the suburbs, and the gold-plated domes of new mosques sparkled in the sun.

Kuala Lumpur did not fall prey to the ills of many other Asian cities. In 1985, the city was still green, peaceful, and seemingly uncluttered. Half of the homes in the area possessed video cassette recorders; the city's poorest segment (the 13 percent who earned less than M$210 a month) often owned their own tin-roofed houses; and planners debated a mass aerobus system of transport. In the eighties, the government continued to encourage migration to Kuala Lumpur in the belief that the future lay in urban industrialization. Malay ideologues, ignoring the risks, wanted a population of 70 million by the year 2000.

As Malay migrants crowded into Kuala Lumpur (and the government enforced its policy of racial quotas), fears arose that small Chinese merchants might be forced to make way for *bumiputra* residents or that ethnic ghettos might arise in this once peaceful city.

The dangers of ethnic tensions in Kuala Lumpur were but one illustration of the social pressures which faced Malaysia during its period of great economic growth. Indians, in particular, lost economic ground both absolutely and relatively to Chinese and Malays during the 1970s. Indians made up a majority of the demoralized squatters in Malaysia's cities. Some formerly wealthy groups, such as Tamils from Sri Lanka who once enjoyed a privileged position under the British, "felt their world slipping from them."[5]

During the 1980s, for example, Tamil-speaking schools seemed doomed to an irreversible decline. Under the prevailing Malaysian system, Indian and Chinese children were taught in their own languages at primary school. By the secondary level, all schools taught in Bahasa Malaysia, the national language. As a result, children brought up in the Tamil schools were at a great disadvantage; in 1981, 85 percent failed Bahasa Malaysia, 68 percent failed the general science tests, and about 90 percent of Tamil children dropped out of school by age twelve. In 1982, a study of schools on the great rubber and palm oil plantations where a majority of workers were Indian, revealed that only 1.5 percent of students passed the Malaysian Certificate of Education at age seventeen and less than 0.3 percent of Tamil-educated children ever started university-level studies. Most Indian children seemed caught in a system which condemned them to continue as estate workers in a society which increasingly valued technical, professional, and managerial skills.

The Malayan Indian Congress attempted to correct such disparities by a variety of measures. In 1984, for example, it created Maika Holdings, an investment company that pooled Indians' savings to buy into businesses and distribute profits back to its subscribers. This communal investment strategy, it was argued, would increase Indian prosperity and spread social welfare and education within the Indian community. (Both the Chinese and Malay groups had already developed such a policy with a high degree of success.)

Some opposition groups within Malaysia, such as the Democratic Action Party, argued that the remaining poverty in the country was not due to racial or communal problems but to class differences. Four north-eastern states, for example, historically lagged behind Kuala Lumpur's progress even though they were dominated by Malays. Certain important industries, such as fishing, also did not benefit from the general economic progress. Although Malaysia ranked among the top ten nations in the world in fishing reserves, its traditional, inefficient fishing methods left many communities in poverty. For three decades, the fishing villages received grants, loans, and various social benefits but still remained below the poverty line. In 1984, the Mahathir government changed its course and advocated large scale commercial exploitation of the seas. Because of the capital intensive nature of this approach, employment declined in the fishing communities and people were forced to seek other work in urban areas.

Thus, in spite of general economic progress and a wide social distribution of its benefits, Malaysia in the 1980s faced a series of hard choices. Debate over the country's future was often rancorous and prejudiced but it occurred within a relatively open political framework.

Since independence, twelve political parties vied for power in free elections. The dominant group, UMNO, held a central position but only because of a continuing process of negotiation, compromise, and alliance with several Chinese parties and the Malayan Indian Congress. These communal parties often challenged UMNO, modified its stands, gained ministerial posts, and obtained significant influence on the state and local levels. The Democratic Action Party, the parliamentary opposition, played a critical and untrammeled role as an advocate of a multiracial society. In Sabah and Sarawak, indigenous parties, usually espousing the same aims as the opposition, controlled their constituencies.

Change within the ruling elite occurred without bloodshed. After a series of constitutional challenges, the traditional sultans retained their titles, the revolving kingship, and a theoretical veto power on religious issues, but gradually lost influence to a new breed of Malay middle-class technocrats and Chinese entrepreneurs. Dr Mahathir, leader of UMNO in the 1980s, represented the young technocrats. He was the first prime minister of Malaysia who did not come from the aristocracy and had not received a British education. A man of lower middle-class background, he attended the University of Malaya and rose through the ranks of the new Malay meritocracy.

With occasional lapses, other mediating institutions in Malaysia remained free to serve as protectors of the individual from the state and the economic elite. Sometimes heatedly and chaotically, the newspapers, often owned by the competing parties, put forth the views of the various communal and political interests within the country. Churches and temples were not destroyed by Islam, the official religion, because UMNO leaders, while affirming the public purity of their Islamic devotion, privately wished to maintain a secular state. Trade unions stood apart from the state while employers, particularly those of foreign origin or Chinese background, defended their own privileges. Inheritors of Anglo-Indian law, the courts functioned independently and impartially. In a country where corruption often stained commercial activities, the courts remained unblemished. Civilian investigative commissions, such as one charged with unraveling the scandals surrounding Bank Bumiputra, pursued corruption and incompetence with a rigor that sometimes embarrassed the government.

Even when plagued by internal tensions, Malaysia managed to maintain its unique polity while advancing rapidly on both the economic and social levels. Observers attributed the country's success within the Islamic world to several factors:

• Malaysia enjoyed an abundance of resources and access to sea routes. This alone, however, hardly explained its progress since its ASEAN colleague, Indonesia, had even greater natural advantages but faltered in exploiting them.

• The "overseas Chinese," who constituted a higher proportion of the population than in Indonesia, contributed an energetic commercial spirit and perhaps a "Confucian ethic" to Malaysian economic progress. Without them, P. T. Bauer has argued, Malaysia would still be unexplored jungle.

• The remarkably able Malay leaders from the Tunku to Dr. Mahathir sought the maintenance of a plural, secular, open society, precariously balancing the interests of deprived groups, such as estate Malays and Indians, against the priorities of economic growth. It was a difficult path to their goal of creating "a new Malaysian" devoted to national goals, for they had to reassure Malaysia's minorities that Islamic demands would not destroy them while, at the same time, espousing their stance as devout believers. The role of individuals should not be discounted in Malaysia. Clearly, other men in a similar position, such as Sukarno and Suharto, succumbed to impotence or the lure of brute force.

• As a mixed people—influenced by the Arab traders, the Portuguese, Dutch, British, and Japanese as well as by an influx of people from China, Sumatra, Sri Lanka, and India—the modern Malaysians were wordly men, possessed of many skills, and driven by diverse needs. This heady brew of cultures, while potentially lethal, seemed in Malaysia's case to be the best tonic for sustained growth and political tolerance. The durability of an imported system of British law and political life added stability while a continuing Japanese influence and the "Look East" policy helped to ensure economic dynamism. Those areas, such as the northeastern states which were relatively free of contact with cultures other than Islam, remained economically stagnant. Malaysia represented one more case where foreign influences did not contaminate the society: they were the essential ingredients for invigoration.

• Specific economic policies—welcoming foreign investments, trimming government expenditures to meet income, a conscious diversification in trading partners and products, low taxation of the private sector, and encouragement of entrepreneurial, largely Chinese, talent—may well have provided useful ingredients for economic growth, even during periods when the world demand for basic commodities fell temporarily.

Nonetheless, in a country which suffered a civil war, communal riots, and intense racial discrimination, Malaysians had difficulty in maintaining a delicate balance between the demands of the various ethnic groups which participated in their relatively open polity. Without marked success, the Chinese sought recruitment in the armed forces (a traditional Malay preserve) and a larger number of university places. Through MIC, the Indians often acted as mediators between the two major ethnic groups while they sought unsuccessfully to relieve the burdens of Indian unemployment. Muslim fundamentalists tried vainly to impose Islamic laws and ways on all.

Although Malaysia represented a triumph of a multiethnic democracy over the conflicting interests of different communal groups for three decades, various obstacles stood in the way of creating a truly liberal society.

Ethnic and religious tensions within the country too often interacted in creating the more infamous aspects of Malaysian political life. Fears that Islamic fanatics wished to submerge the other minorities led the government of the 1980s to react by restricting foreign (which really meant Iranian) tape recordings and publications. Elements in the government threatened summary incarceration for purveyors of such material. These severe measures served only to increase the fervor of the Islamic faithful who held mass rallies in the northern part of the country, inciting "true" Muslims to violence against the infidels.

Once again in the history of the world, rapid economic growth, although clearly linked with increasing social equity for most, inflamed religious and political passions among those who had been left behind. To illustrate this generalization, one needed only to examine an ominous sequence of political events in the 1980s.

In 1984, the government had yet to dismantle the Internal Security Act (ISA) of 1960, a notorious inheritance from the British during "the Emergency." Originally aimed at those who would violently overthrow the government, this anachronistic law provided for detention without trial of persons whom the state deemed dangerous. Mahathir's government pledged to review the law and, in 1981–83, released 268 "prisoners of conscience." One of these, S. Nada Rajah, convened an open press conference and said that he had been held in solitary confinement for four years. Although the government announced in 1982 that all detainees would be released if they left the country, some 300 reportedly stayed in jail.[6]

Supposedly aimed at Islamic fundamentalists, the Printing Presses and Publications Act reinforced the ISA. The Publications law empowered the government to ban imported printed or audio material which it declared "undesirable." This attack on freedom of speech raised a cry among religious leaders and journalists in Malaysia for they realized that "the elite want acquiescence, not participation" and that the ISA "hangs over newspaper editors." As Tan Boon Kean, a distinguished Chinese reporter, wrote in 1984, "For concerned Malaysian journalists, the time is perhaps coming when they may have to abandon ornate reporting and do what Orwell did: become "pamphleteers."[7]

This limitation on imported literature and cassettes was part of UMNO's intensive attack against the small but influential *Parti Islam* (PAS) which brought in thousands of tape recordings of the Ayatollah Khomeini's preachings and distributed them among devout Moslems.

PAS itself represented an attempt to subvert the political openness of Malaysian society, for the party encouraged violence as a way to an Islamic state, accused Malays who did not subscribe to their position of being *kafir* (infidels), and threatened the Chinese and Indian minorities with the creation of another Iran.

PAS had little electoral support except in the heavily Islamic eastern states and, even there, managed to elect only one member of parliament in the early 1980s (at the same time, the more secular UMNO had seventy MPs out of a total of 212). Nonetheless, fundamentalistic sentiment swept the country. In the northeast, PAS supporters successfully demanded that each mosque should have separate imams and argued that true Muslims should not marry supporters of UMNO or allow their dead to be buried in the same cemetery with "kafir."

A white paper accused Islamic extremists of encouraging their members to throw away TV sets and behead even their parents if they objected. Those of the Buddhist, Hindu, or Christian faiths recoiled at the religious totalitarianism of PAS and treated the movement as a divisive attack on national unity.

Mahathir and other UMNO leaders recognized the serious dangers inherent in the fundamentalist demands, for they too suffered from insults and threats of violence. Once, while driving through Kedah, Mahathir waved to a crowd from his car. Instead of cheering him, the villagers shouted "Kafir!" In the same village, a crowd assaulted Mahathir's wife, turned their backs on her, spat, and called her "kafir."

The secular leaders of Malaysia were indeed infidels to many Muslims. The policies of the nation as a whole—struggling for political tolerance, economic modernization, and a reasonably fair distribution of social benefits—represented a heretical deviation within the Islamic world.

Whether the "kafir" or the "true believers" would eventually prevail in this potentially bounteous land remained in doubt.

6

The Caudillos and the Reformists

"LA CRISIS" IN LATIN AMERICA

Schools will kill militarism or militarism will kill the Republic.

—RICARDO JIMÉNEZ
President of Costa Rica, 1922

In 1821, as Spanish colonials exploded in wars of liberation, North American leaders treated the revolutionaries with disdain. "I wished well to their cause," Secretary of State John Quincy Adams said, "but I had seen and yet see no prospect that they would establish free or liberal institutions of government." Although men like Bolívar looked to the United States as one of their models, Adams argued that "arbitrary power, military and ecclesiastical, was stamped upon their education, upon their habits, and upon all their institution."[1] Other founding fathers of North America including Jefferson and Hamilton found no reason to expect that the social, religious, or political backgrounds of the ex-Spanish colonies had prepared them for genuine independence. At best, in their opinion, Latin America might achieve progress as it gradually fell under the aegis of the United States.

Pessimists in 1985 agreed. Admittedly, huge sections of the continent, most notably Argentina and Brazil, had unexpectedly retired their strong-arm caudillos from power. Yet, observers such as Glen Dealy argued that this was but a temporary reprise from Latin America's tradition of autocratic governments. "In Latin American minds," Dealy wrote, "the vision of freely competing factions all too often seems a choice between chaos and privilege . . . Their political beliefs are based

on the corporatist medieval and Renaissance political theory that pre-
dates the contractarian thought of Locke.''[2] Scholars of this persuasion
contended that a tradition of putting corporate unity ahead of individualism—exacerbated by huge debts, intense class divisions, corruption, and a heritage of violence—would foil those who tried to impose
''alien'' Western concepts on an unwilling and unprepared Latin people.

How valid is this belief? We contend that generalizations about ''the
Latin Mind'' should not blind us to enormously disparate and, at times,
unprecedented trends in Latin America. Differences in historical experience, variations in economic structures, the growth of middle classes
since the 1960s, and even the presumed ''accidents'' of providential
leadership make it impossible to describe a monolithic ''Latin ethic''
or a unilinear pattern of Latin development. Competing visions within
Latin American countries have resulted in many different paths to progress, none of them inevitably doomed to failure. Since 1821, the
triumphs and vicissitues of Costa Rica, Colombia, and Venezuela
illustrated this diversity and offered hope that liberal regimes dedicated
to social and economic advance were not just ephemeral interludes in
a long story of military coups.

COSTA RICA

Oh America! . . . Costa Rica wishes to offer you, with all her
heart, now and always, her love for civility, democracy, and institutional life.

—JOSÉ FIGUERES
President of Costa Rica, 1949

''The whole body of the Central American Republic appears desperate, divided, consumed, covered with blood,'' Juan Mora Fernandez, a
rural teacher who became president of Costa Rica observed in 1829.
''Costa Rica, although small and humble, remains unscathed, enlightened
by the luminous vision of peace.''[3] More than one hundred fifty years
later, his words still held true.

By 1986, amid the political turbulence and brutality of Central America, Costa Rica stood out as a stable polity which had achieved unprecedented levels of liberty, education, and health in Central America.

Economically, Costa Rica lacked precious mineral or energy resources.

With a per capita income of $2,500, Costa Rica possessed a large middle class, a peasantry which usually owned its own land, and an expanding industrial sector. Its industrial workers were, however, poorly paid and it was still an economy dependent on the export of coffee, bananas, and sugar in a wildly fluctuating world market.

In spite of these economic hindrances, Costa Rica broadly spread its limited wealth among 2.4 million "Ticos." Already in 1922, Ricardo Jiménez had proclaimed a virtual national doctrine that education should take first priority in national development. The schools triumphed over military spending and by 1984, Costa Rica had achieved the highest level of literacy, 93 percent of its population, in Central America. By Clark Kerr's measure of the physical quality of life, Costa Rica ranked far higher than other Central American countries with a rating of 85. In contrast, El Salvador scored 64, Nicaragua and Guatemala 54, and Honduras 51. Even Mexico, a nation with great oil reserves, had reached a level of only 72. By legal mandate, 28 percent of the Costa Rican national budget had to be spent on education and health care.

Although buffeted by external forces, including North American pressure to militarize its North, the incursion of U.S. military "advisers," and a falling world market for its commodities, Costa Rica remained a constitutional democracy dedicated to pacifism. In the aftermath of elections in 1948, a brief but bloody civil war had ravaged Costa Rica. José Figueres, a coffee planter, led guerrilla forces which overthrew a military dictator and, in 1949, he framed a new constitution which abolished the army—dramatically including his own armed forces. Eight months after taking power, Figueres turned the government over to the man who had won the election. In 1953 and again in 1970, Figueres himself was elected president.

Since then, a free press and an independent judiciary flourished. Internal order has been maintained by a lightly armed 9,000-man police force. The National Liberation Party, a group of social democrats and liberals, has peacefully jousted for office with more conservative Catholic parties and a small Marxist opposition. Various governments nationalized major sectors of the economy while allowing large multinationals, such as the old United Fruit, to operate in a capitalist environment. Costa Rica gradually emerged as a mixed economy, heavily devoted to social welfare and committed to change within a constitutional system.

Liberal democracy prevailed in Costa Rica for reasons which were, in some ways, in stark contrast to the "causes" often cited for either the military dominance *or* the peaceful transformation of other Latin countries. Costa Rica, for example, did not possess any great source of natural wealth, such as oil, which would have allowed reformers to "pay off" a landed elite or an army for their acquiescence in socioeconomic changes. "Ironically," as Eduardo Ulibarri has written, "Costa Rica owes much of what it is today to its being isolated and poor during the three hundred years of colonial domination."[4] Lacking precious metals, mineral resources, or a large Indian population, Costa Rica did not offer the opportunities for exploitation which tempted both the Spanish and the North Americans in Guatemala and El Salvador. Colonial officials left the country in isolation and the immigrant residents of this "Switzerland of Central America" cultivated relatively small plots of land, without either displacing the native Indians or importing slaves. Luis Alberto Monge, the president in 1985, argued that the absence of slavery was a critical dimension in Costa Rica's development:

> The long history of institutional stability in Costa Rica is due to the fact that it did not have slaves. From the most humble of colonists to the Spanish governor, everyone had to cultivate the land to make a living. This situation generated an egalitarian consciousness and led to the development of social institutions that laid the foundations upon which a democratic and pacifist culture has developed.[5]

Costa Rica was fortunate too in having political leaders, such as Figueres, who put the cause of forging a liberal democracy ahead of either class or personal interests. Its presidents usually emerged from the ranks of teachers, lawyers, and small plantation owners. Although threatened by invasions, including that of Walker's filibusters, the Costa Ricans depended on a civilian militia rather than a military caste for their defense.

Costa Rica also benefited from an absence of North American interference in her political affairs. While the United States meddled in Nicaragua in the 1920s and 1930s attempting to secure "stability," it succeeded only in establishing the brutal Somoza regime. During the same period in Costa Rica, two men, Ricardo Jiménez and Rleto Gonzales Viquez succeeded each other peacefully in the presidency between 1924 and 1936. Unaided by the United States which preferred to support a rising young class of military elites in the rest of Central America, these leaders carried out land reforms, broadened political freedoms, built schools, and "pursued government programs that would eventually make it possible for Costa Rica to have the only working democracy in Central America."[6]

By 1981, however, Costa Rica could hardly be considered an Eden. Borrowing money to finance social welfare, the country had amassed one of the highest per capita debts in the world. In return for renegotiation of its loans, the Costa Rican government agreed to severe austerity measures imposed by the IMF. Economic development almost halted, the number of families living in poverty increased, while malnutrition and infant mortality—once on a par with industrial nations—started to climb.

In 1982, banana workers struck in a violent episode and in 1983, even doctors, a relatively privileged class, abandoned their hospitals, demanding higher wages. By 1984, many sectors of the public protested against a 300 percent increase in electricity rates demanded by the publicly owned utilities. In each case, the government eventually responded by granting public demands but the economic space for such maneuvers gradually narrowed.

In 1985, United Brands—previously the hated "octopus" of United Fruit—cut its banana production in Costa Rica because of lower costs in Educador. The company offered to sell land and houses to its workers in Costa Rica, but the government could not raise the required $15 million. Pressured by the American government, United Brands sold its properties for a pittance.

Caught in a crisis between the population which expected increasing social benefits and a world economy which demanded belt-tightening austerity, the government was forced to undertake vastly unpopular measures and to depend critically upon North American aid. Nonetheless, the constitutional framework held together in spite of severe economic pressures. "Many feared Costa Rica might yield to the contagion which is prostrating the rest of Central America," President Monge declared in 1984. "Our medicine is bitter, but we have prevented the contagion."[7]

Whether future events would support Monge's optimism depended not only on his ability to control mounting social tensions, but most critically upon North America's willingness to avoid militarizing the country, its flexibility in rescheduling Costa's Rica's debts into long-term bonds, and its generosity in providing a large amount of per capita aid (second only to Israel) to resuscitate the Costa Rican economy.

Whatever the eventual fate of Costa Rica's unique experiment, both optimists and pessimists could reasonably argue that the little country represented a special case: It was, for good or evil, freed from the influence of multinationals; it had a long history of constitutional rule; and it possessed a homogeneous, pacifist, literate, and small population.

One could creditably argue that a Latin nation such as Colombia—almost twice the size of Texas, whose 28 million people had been bloodied by eight civil wars in the nineteenth century and by a perpetual siege of "La Violencia" during much of the twentieth century—represented a far different, more ferocious climate for the flowering of liberal democracy and economic development.

COLOMBIA

> Each Latin American child is born owing $300, while each minute
> this crazy world spends $1 million on deadly arms.

—BELISARIO BETANCUR
President of Colombia, 1982

In 1902, after a vicious "War of the Thousand Days" in which one hundred thousand people perished, Colombia went bankrupt. The government decided on a simple expedient, issuing more money, but it lacked even the paper on which to print it. The Conservative government solved its dilemma by commandeering a load of candy wrappers. The problems simply multiplied:

• After losing the Isthmus of Panama, its richest province, to Teddy Roosevelt, Colombia became dependent on coffee exports to the United States. Its convulsive attempts at land reform had resulted by 1983 in an increase in the concentration of *latifundias* in the hands of the oligarchy. The richest 10 percent of Colombians received 50 percent of the country's wealth while the bottom 10 percent subsisted on 5 percent of national income.

• Between 1946 and 1966, Colombia suffered from *La Violencia,* a mindless battle between Liberals, Conservatives, Marxists, and bandits which killed at least two hundred thousand people. During this tragic era, people wreaked their private revenge, plantation owners dispossessed peasants, the army slaughtered Indians, the government lost control of most of the nation, and every side mounted its own armies. Even by the 1980s, some reporters estimated that as many as 200,000 private citizens remained armed.

• By 1983, illegal drug exports probably constituted Colombia's biggest source of foreign income; the military, officially supported on an annual budget of $217 million, reportedly received $600 million in bribes;

and Colombia's drug mafia assassinated public officials and threatened U.S. Embassy children with death if the United States extradited Colombian drug dealers.

The Republic of Colombia hardly seemed like a model of economic development or "Latin America's oldest and largest Spanish-speaking democracy."[8] Clearly, many facts undermined such assertions. Yet, John F. Kennedy had once chosen Colombia as a "showcase" for his Alliance for Progress and the United States spent $1.5 billion between 1960 and 1975 in loans and grants to the country. Kennedy apparently believed that Colombia offered "a high degree of opportunities and challenges both economic and political which the Alliance was designed to meet."[9] Was this opinion, expressed in a government document of 1977, gravely mistaken? The persistence of corruption and class divisions, the challenge of both Marxist guerrillas and right-wing "death squads," and the growth of a frightening drug empire would seem to lead to the conclusion that Colombia's problems had proven intractable.

Yet, acknowledgment of the darker side of Colombian life should not obscure the country's great achievements. In tangible ways since 1958, Colombia set a remarkably positive example for Latin America.

Until the 1950s, Colombia was a backward agricultural economy, overwhelmingly dependent on the export of coffee to North America. By 1985, however, coffee accounted for only 4 percent of the gross national product and Colombia had evolved into an urban, increasingly industrialized country in which per capita income rose to $1,500 annually.

During the 1960s, the Alliance for Progress encouraged the building of roads, schools, an electrical network and a communications system; counterinsurgency aid helped to cure the plague of *La Violencia.*

By the 1970s, as the mixed economy expanded, Colombia exported chemicals, medicines, machinery, and electrical equipment. In 1970, Colombia had exported only $200 million worth of manufactured goods; by 1980, such exports increased to over $1 billion. Overall, Colombia's diversified economy grew at an annual rate of 7 to 9 percent between 1970 and 1981. Although the country had some oil and coal, it emerged by this period as an energy-importing, export-manufacturing economy.

The world slump in the early 1980s slowed but did not stop the rate of growth. Colombia had to devour much of its accumulated foreign reserves in paying off foreign debts while still importing the capital equipment necessary for the manufacturing sector. Nonetheless, the country weathered the recession in better condition than most of Latin America.

Socially, after 1958 when the two major parties concerned with pragmatic reforms began to alternate peacefully in office, Colombia expended an increasing amount of its revenue (about 10 percent) on education. By 1985, 85 percent of the population, including Indians living in remoter sections of the Andes, could read and write. On the Kerr index of the physical quality of life, Colombia achieved a rating of 71, while its ethnically and geographically similar neighbors, Ecuador, Peru, and Bolivia, ranked 68, 62, and 43 respectively.[10] An intensive birth control campaign reduced the population growth rate to a moderate 2.3 percent annually by 1983. The country suffered from little racial discrimination; a knowledge of Spanish sufficed as a route to social mobility.[11] For the first time in 1958, women received the right to vote and to hold office.

While Colombia progressed in many sectors and the diversification of the economy broke the stranglehold of the coffee oligarchy over the society, some egalitarian critics were disturbed in the 1980s about the new structure of the society. Although sharply debated, some observers argued that the "Colombian economy was becoming increasingly concentrated in fewer hands" and that the rich received a higher proportion of national income than in 1960.[12] One critic, a former Colombian finance minister, argued that ten large corporations dominated the economy and that "the country [was] one step away from the point where four or five people [handled] the main controls of the economy."[13]

Such perceived disparities in wealth, regardless of any consequent benefit to productivity or efficiency, inevitably concerned many elements in Colombia. The Catholic Church, formerly a bastion of the status quo and the Conservative party, split into different ideological camps over the issue of economic inequality. In 1981, a group of Colombian bishops declared that the insecurity of life in the country (Colombia then had the highest murder rate in the world), immorality, and other forms of crime such as the drug trade were caused by inequalities in the socioeconomic sector.

Other sectors of the society—some urban workers and displaced peasants, led by university students—adopted violent revolutionary tactics in order to overthrow the status quo. Among many splinter groups, the two most important guerrilla movements were FARC (Revolutionary Armed Forces of Colombia) and M–19 (The April 19th Movement).

FARC drew its support from the peasantry and its leadership from the Communist party. The organization called for land reform, "armed colonization" of rural areas, and a "prolonged people's war." It sought a vaguely defined socialist society.

In contrast, M–19 was urban-based, stressed an extension of economic and political democracy, the encouragement of small enterprises, and a foreign policy based on nonalignment. Pressed by the army in the early 1980s, M–19 retreated to Caqueta, an inaccessible region located 1,000 kilometers from Bogota. From there, it battled 17,000 government troops who sought vainly to dislodge the guerrillas.

In different ways, FARC and M–19 traced their heritage far back into Colombia's violent history. On paper, Colombia had long been a constitutional democracy with a full panoply of rights. In practice, the country split apart in 1849 between Liberals (who favored centralism, free trade, and secularism) versus Conservatives (who longed for a corporatist and Catholic regime). The parties alternated in power but, when one of them controlled the anarchic state, they allocated privileges only to their own members and did not hesitate to brutally repress their opposition.

The Conservatives and Liberals gradually forgot the issues which divided them. Party identification became a family and village matter, almost an automatic inheritance. By 1930, in an atmosphere of ingrained hatred and an economic depression, the Liberals abandoned their "free trade" platform and sought increased state intervention in the economy while the Conservatives advocated an "organic," corporate state, modeled on Franco and Mussolini's fascism.

Between 1946 and 1966, as each party formed its private armies, *La Violencia* engulfed Colombia. While its roots lay in old political conflicts, peasant grievances, urban class conflict, clumsy Liberal attempts at reform, and a long history of using violence to solve civil conflicts, *La Violencia* soon assumed a sinister life of its own. Bandits, guerrillas of all faiths, undisciplined army units, greedy land holders, Indians who wished for the return of their land, and people with merely personal grievances joined indiscriminately in one of the bloodiest civilian frays of the twentieth century. More than 43,000 people were killed in 1948 alone, 50,000 in 1950 and, by 1960, Colombia had the highest "intentional" death rate in the world. As Ramon Jimeno and Steven Volk have brilliantly described the chaos:

> Violence became permanent. In different regions, for different reasons, by different participants. Pitched battles, small massacres, individual assassinations. And the state was unable to control the bloodletting. In fact, the state's participation in the repression, combined with the virtual absence of state power in some regions, only stimulated the fighting.[14]

Inevitably, the violence destroyed small land-holding peasants, militarized the society by forcing the state to mount a permanent antiinsurgency force (largely instructed by North Americans), divided the nation into rival armed units, and polarized the social classes. In 1954, General Gustavo Rojas Pinella took over as dictator. He cruelly repressed all political critics, armed or civilian, but wisely granted amnesty to 15,000 guerrillas. Rojas's dictatorship pushed the Conservatives and Liberals into an unusual coalition. In 1957, their "National Front" deposed Rojas and replaced him with a unique constitutional arrangement which salved the wounds of the civil war.

The National Front agreed to alternate the presidency every four years between the Liberals and the Conservatives. Each party was also entitled to elect one half of the Congress and to divide the state bureaucracy according to party patronage. This approach was linked to *Plan Lazo,* a serious attempt to combine economic reform with severe counterinsurgency measures. Equipped with North American weapons, Colombia's army decimated various guerrilla bases scattered throughout the country.

While the National Front controlled the cities—and some argued that the oligarchy provided funds to both parties—it did not suppress a free press, abolish trade unions, impose dictatorial restraints on the courts, or destroy political competitors. The Colombian Communist party, attracting some 1 percent of the population, and various socialist parties, about 7 percent of the electorate, continued to operate. Illegally, however, the army arrested or executed people it considered "subversive" while guerrillas dominated the poor, more distant provinces.

In 1982, Belisario Bentancur, a journalist, assumed the presidency and ushered in a new era in Colombian politics. Although officially a Conservative, Betancur knew about the plight of the poor from his own experience. No one considered him either a military man or as a genuine member of Colombia's often vaguely defined "oligarchy." He grew up in a small, poor village. His illiterate parents had twenty-two children. Seventeen died from a disease "known as underdevelopment," as Betancur bitterly described it.

Betancur was a "social Christian," an advocate of Western culture, a defender of representative democracy, and a man who favored an economy mixed between capitalism and socialism. He criticized the role of the United States government in the Dominican Republic and Nicaragua as imperialistic but regarded Cuba as having fallen under the rule of "another imperialist power." In 1983, Betancur gained the leadership of the "Contadora Group" (including Mexico, Venezuela, and Panama) in a positive, independent attempt to bring peace to Central America.

Domestically, Betancur faced five interrelated and extremely serious challenges:

First, he had to free Colombia from the violence unleashed by his own military and police. In their zealot's enthusiasm to crush subversion, the Colombian police and military had far exceeded the limits of fighting a rebellion. Between 1974 and 1982, Colombian authorities had arrested at least 110,000 people without trial, killed forty-eight Indian leaders (who had taken back land legally allocated to them by the federal government), and arrested thirty-six trade union leaders, some of whom "disappeared." In 1980, Amnesty International condemned the government for "prolonged incarceration without trial, torture, the usurpation of civil proceedings by the military, and political assassination."[15]

Betancur (and his immediate predecessor, Julio Turbay Ayala) took swift and generally effective action against the military's attempt to usurp civil power. In 1982, they lifted an official state of seige and freed all political prisoners who had been identified by Amnesty International as prisoners of conscience or possible prisoners of conscience. All trials in progress were transferred to civilian courts where judges usually determined that there were no grounds for prosecution. President Betancur also signed into law a sweeping amnesty freeing all political prisoners who had been convicted by military courts for "rebellion."

These liberalizing actions did not entirely free Colombia from political fear, for Betancur faced a second, even more sinister challenge from the right. Perhaps in response to legal curbs on their power, some elements in the military allegedly joined with the drug mafia in forming a private army of right wing terrorists, MAS (Death to Kidnappers). In 1981, an airplane dropped leaflets over the city of Cali announcing that "mafia chiefs" had created an elite strike force to execute "kidnappers" (opponents of any political persuasion). In the next two years, MAS murdered some 300 people, mainly peasants and trade union leaders. Although the army and police denied collaboration with MAS, Amnesty International declared that it had evidence directly implicating sections of the armed forces with MAS.

Betancur struck back at MAS by ordering the unmasking of its members and their prosecution. Colombian newspapers published descriptions of MAS terrorists, the attorney general's office indicted suspected murderers, and army interrogators who had alledgedly tortured prisoners went on trial in 1982. In 1983, after sending his own family out of the country for their safety, Colombia's attorney general put on trial sixty military officers and soldiers accused of participation in MAS. By

1985, the wave of "private" terrorism had subsided but had not yet disappeared from the Colombian countryside.

The MAS terrorism demonstrated the extent of Betancur's third grave problem, the malignant influence of drugs on Colombian society. By the 1980s, the Colombian export of marijuana, cocaine, and Quaaludes probably exceeded $3 billion a year (or a street value in New York of $80 billion). This lucrative trade inevitably contributed to the endemic corruption of Colombia and a spate of speculation. Top military officials, members of congress, even the head of Colombia's antidrug bureau were implicated in bribery. Profits from the drug trade which could, in theory, wipe out Colombia's foreign debt in one year, remained out of reach of the state or the normal economy. Once laundered, the illegal dollars often entered the economy, contributing to inflation.

By 1985, Betancur's government took two pragmatic steps. The central bank was authorized to accept dollars and exchange them into local currency without questioning their source. This move, which some regarded as hypocrisy, did allow the central bank a higher degree of control over inflationary pressures. Simultaneously, in spite of death threats and several murders, government officials bravely prosecuted the more prominent drug dealers and extradited some of the Colombian mafia leaders to the United States for trial. The army destroyed large drug-producing "plantations," their factories, and air fields in a series of increasingly effective strikes.

Nonetheless, the connection between drugs, the "death squads," and part of the military illustrated a fourth delicate problem plaguing Colombia's liberal democracy: how to control the army? Betancur needed the army to subdue violent rebellion and, since 1958, the military caste had seldom directly intervened in civilian politics. In a time of economic pressure and internal revolt, however, the army had increased its power and audacity. In 1983, for example, the army high command dared to order all of its officers to donate one day's pay to the defense of the sixty MAS collaborators and conferred a decoration on a colonel who was one of the accused.

Betancur chose a compromising—and some critics said, dangerously cynical—approach in dealing with the military. One the one hand, the president denounced military expenditures, tried to play a peaceful role in his region's affairs, and publicly pledged the military to a limited position in keeping internal peace. On the other hand, he sought to appease the army's appetite for higher salaries (as substitutes for bribes) and for the most sophisticated military equipment, including fighter bombers, Seasparrow missiles, and Exocet missiles. Arms dealers in the West welcomed the new orders and the United States government encouraged the construction of a new Colombian base on the island of San Andres, off the coast of Nicaragua. In 1983, Betancur authorized a military budget of $2.6 billion, a huge increase over an annual military budget in the 1970s of about $200 million. By 1985, the civilian government set the course for Colombia but the military establishment ominously increased its potential power and wealth. Betancur apparently counted on army support in his often lonely battles since much of the officer corps came from his own background rather than the aristocracy. Yet, Betancur's one major hope for controlling the military establishment lay in defusing internal violence, the army's prime *raison d'être*.

Betancur's fifth and seemingly impossible problem was to achieve an internal peace with FARC, M-19, and all the other guerrilla forces that virtually controlled large sections of the provinces. As late as 1983, informed observers of Colombia regarded this paramount task as beyond solution. The army still sought military victory, the economy suffered from recession and produced recruits for the guerrillas, and the guerrillas themselves, undefeated on the battlefield, remained dedicated to violent revolution. All of these factors seemed to portend an incessantly violent scenario for the future. "Any thought of reaching a meaningful amnesty with the guerrilla forces combating the government has become all but impossible," Ramon Jimeno and Steven Volk declared authoritatively in June 1982. "The amnesty was dead."[16]

Yet, by 1984, Betancur had proved that the prophets of doom had seriously underestimated the flexibility of Colombia's system and the statecraft of its president. Betancur, once a poor peasant, saw the justice of peasant grievances and the opportunity for his government to play a positive role in solving peasant problems, and he seized it. In 1983, he held secret meetings with the guerrilla leaders in Spain, swiftly reduced official repression, successfully battled the right-wing death squads, and, by shuffling appointments, tightened his personal control over the army.

In 1984, Betancur achieved the impossible. He reached a cease-fire agreement with the principal guerrilla groups, granted a general amnesty, and opened a "national dialogue" on the underlying reasons which had prompted thirty years of rebellion.

To skeptics on the left, he demonstrated that peace with honor and a chance for change was possible. To skeptics in the military and the far right, he showed that his "fourth way" to progress did not require torture and murder.

The path to progress in Colombia was hardly peaceful. In 1985, for example, M–19 abandoned its truce with the government and resumed its kidnapings, bombings, and hostage-taking outrages. The terror group struck again in November, 1985, seizing the Palace of Justice and taking a dozen Supreme Court justices hostage. This time, however, Betancur struck back with a vengeance. The Colombian army assaulted the building and killed all of the guerillas. The attack also involved the death of many innocent and illustrious civilians. Betancur had decided that only a "total war" could end the mindless violence in Bogotá.

Flawed and bloody, Colombia had established a model of rigid opposition to terroism combined with a series of successful negotiations. Its fragile but still functioning democracy deserved all of the political and economic support that its liberal friends in the hemisphere could offer.

VENEZUELA

By importing all the elements of a new society, the Venezuelans have achieved a complete transformation of their world in a generation's time. If self-determination is the measure of authenticity, Venezuela's society is authentically Venezuelan.

—JOHN LOMBARDI, 1982

In 1947, Jaime Lusinchi, a poor young man from an isolated, rural province of Venezuela overcame all of the economic obstacles, and graduated from medical school. He had little time to practice pediatrics for General Marcos Perez Jiménez reimposed a military dictatorship in 1948. Lusinchi, a student politician, immediately joined the underground *Accion Democratica* (AD) and helped to organize clandestine cells of peasants and urban workers.

A young liberal such as Lusinchi faced imposing obstacles in trying to establish a Venezuelan democracy. His nation, once united with Colombia, had experienced numerous military coups while similar Latin countries, such as Bolivia, had run through 158 military revolutions in 150 years. Economically, in spite of large oil resources, Venezuela had stagnated during the last century. Back in 1850, Latin America in general had achieved the same level of development as North America and, in fact, certain countries such as Argentina had surpassed the wealth of Canada. Yet, the elites of Venezuela and other Latin nations had too often allowed their regions to deteriorate.

Lusinshi's personal attempt to transform Venezuela temporarily failed in 1952 when the dictator's police arrested him and tortured him for a month. Like many of his generation, Lusinchi was forced into exile in Chile, Argentina, and, eventually, New York City, where he scratched together a living at Bellevue Hospital. He joined other exiles headed by Romulo Betancourt in a seemingly quixotic effort to overthrow the dictator.

General Jiménez appeared entrenched for his lifetime. With the aid of the army, the assistance of Venezuela's aristocracy, and a comfortable reserve of oil, the caudillo had crushed an interim reformist government which sought sweeping land reforms and nationalization of the oil industry. Jimenez attacked by exiling the civilian government and disbanding all labor unions, "radical" parties, and peasant organizations. After torturing their victims, the military sent *Accion Democratica*'s leaders, including Lusinchi, into a ten-year exile. By this act, the army may have made its fatal mistake, for the exiles learned abroad all of the organizational skills and party tactics that their new homes could offer.

Nonetheless, the dictator commanded obedience within Venezuela and respect in the hemisphere. He seemed poised on the crest of an authoritarian wave that engulfed Brazil, Chile, Peru, Argentina, Bolivia, and Uruguay. As late as 1977, Latin American expert Daniel H. Levine could summarize the prevailing opinion of most observers of his time by commenting that "the political future of Latin America lies with authoritarian regimes of one form or another. . . . Though these countries all are quite different from one another, in each of them military rule is pervasive and seemingly permanent."[17]

Reality soon contradicted such assertions, most brilliantly in Venezuela. By 1983, Venezuelans freely elected Jaime Lusinchi as president. Other military regimes collapsed in Argentina, Peru, Bolivia, and Brazil. In Uruguay, Chile, and even primitive Paraguay, the Stroessners of Latin America trembled on their thrones.

Lusinchi's election was even more remarkable for it marked twenty-five years of Venezuelan democracy and the fourth time in a row that the opposition peacefully defeated an incumbent president. The leader of the Christian Democrats (COPEI) graciously handed over his presidency to the AD candidate. An advocate of land reform, oil nationalisation, and "socialism," the AD had achieved legitimate constitutional status with COPEI, originally a more conservative, Catholic party.

Equally significant, the once dominant military stood at ease in 1983, tolerating the democratic process. From 1821 until 1958, the army had seldom taken this stance. After Bolívar had won Venezuela's independence from Spain, a cabal of war lords ruled the sad country. The various caudillos battled for ascendancy throughout the nineteenth century, perhaps most viciously in the civil war of 1859–64 in which forty thousand people died. After the slaughter, Venezuela was an economic ruin. Dictators temporarily exchanged roles with each other until 1908, when Juan Vincente Goméz established his relatively stable autocracy. Bolstered by the discovery of petroleum reserves in 1921, Goméz ran the nation as his personal "cattle ranch" for twenty-seven years. When he died peacefully in bed, officers again jostled for preeminence, allowing only a brief period of civilian rule. Jiménez reestablished prateorian autocracy from 1948 until 1958.

General Jiménez insouciantly presided over a society in which officers and petroleum workers, airplane mechanics and international lawyers were increasingly absorbed in an oil-based, export economy which demanded "orderly, systematic, predictable, and rational behavior."[18] The capricious authoritarianism of Jiménez conflicted with the requirements of a technologically sophisticated society.

In 1958, Jiménez naively ordered a plebiscite in support of his arbitrary and corrupt rule. His abuses had alienated not only liberal democrats, socialists, and a new middle class but the army elite as well. When the plebiscite failed and the army overthrew him, Jiménez fled to Florida with the wealth he had sequestered from the country.

A temporary military junta, led by one of Venezuela's true heros, Wolfgang Larrazabal, promised to establish a political democracy and repatriate the exiles. In one of those rare incidents in Latin American history, Larrazabal kept his promise, crushed right-wing counterrevolts, held free elections, and handed over authority in January 1959 to Romulo Betancourt. The AD under Betancourt established Venezuela's durable democratic style of government. A deservedly popular man, naval officer Larrazabal resigned his position and disappeared with gallantry and ghostly dispatch from Venezuelan politics.

The next decades of liberal government marked the development of new political parties, a peaceful transfer of power, growing tolerance and extensive modernization.

Courts, labor unions, political parties, and the mass media operated freely. The army retained the right to try people for military rebellion but incidents of possible injustice or brutality at the hands of the army or the police were checked by the independent attorney general's office.

In 1982, for example, the attorney general launched trial proceedings against eleven police officers accused of murdering two bank robbers; and a civilian commission of inquiry was set up to investigate the killings of twenty-three alleged members of a guerrilla band.[19]

When, by 1983, Lusinchi—a rotund, humorous, gentle physician, tempered by torture and exile—assumed the president's mantle, he took over a stable government but a troubled economy. Long dependent on oil exports and enormous public expenditures for development and social welfare, Venezuela had entered "La Crisis," as it was simply called, at the end of the 1970s. Pressured by a world recession, Venezuela's oil income fell, the government had to cancel ambitious projects, while unemployment and inflation rose. Lusinchi had to repay a huge foreign debt of $34 billion by imposing austerity measures on his sixteen million people. In 1978, 29 percent of the people said their standard of living had declined but in 1983, 61 percent believed that their lives were worse.

Yet, in the relative world of Latin American rhetoric and expectations, Lusinchi also inherited unmatched advantages from his democratic predecessors:

Although enveloped by "La Crisis," the Venezuelan economy in 1986 was still the most affluent in South America. Venezuela had generated a per capita income of $3,600 in 1986, twice the level achieved by Mexico or the supposed "economic" miracle of Brazil. The country's growth rate from 1960 to 1980 averaged over 6 percent a year, equaling if not surpassing that achieved in Brazil's military dictatorship. By the early 1980s, due to a drop in world oil prices, the Venezuelan economy hardly grew at all but Brazil actually lost ground, and its army relinquished control. As the austerity measures had their effects, both economies rebounded by 1986.

Venezuela had also diversified its economy by investing oil money in manufacturing ventures which used the nation's iron, bauxite, and other mineral resources. The manufacturing sector of the economy doubled its production between 1960 and 1979. As people fled rural, cattle-growing areas in search of urban prosperity, agricultural production—once the pillar of Venezuela's economy—fell and the nation started to import food. Yet, while severe poverty remained in rural areas and on the outskirts of the cities, Venezuelans generally prospered and the gap between the rich and the poor, although still enormous, relatively narrowed.

At the same time, liberal governments in Venezuela wrought a social transformation. They expended the highest amount per capita on the continent in education and provided free schooling for all from the primary level through university. In 1979, for example, Venezuela spent 20 percent more per capita on education than Cuba, twice as much as Brazil or Chile, and seventy times more than Haiti. As a result, from a base of mass ignorance in 1948, 82 percent of Venezuelans had achieved literacy by 1982. Although this rate was not as high as in some of the Latin military dictatorships (92 per cent of Chile's people could read in 1982), the spread of educational opportunity suddenly put Venezuela in the first rank of Latin countries.

On a mundane but critical level, Venezuela's democratic governments had provided 91 percent of their people with safe water by 1979. In contrast, only 57 percent of Argentinians, 55 percent of Mexicans, and 47 percent of Brazilians could count on hygienic water. Naturally, deaths from diarrhea, typhoid, and cholera plummeted in Venezuela.

Venezuela also led other Latin American countries such as Argentina, Mexico, and Brazil in providing electric lighting to 90 percent of its people.

Thus, from its position as one of the more backward Latin nations in 1948, Venezuela achieved a rating of 79 on Clark Kerr's index of the physical quality of life in 1983, while Brazil fell to 68.

In essence, from the 1940s to the 1980s, Venezuela underwent a remarkable and rapid political, economic, and social evolution. In contrasting life under the old dictatorships with the 1980s, John Lombardi rightly observed:

> Venezuela's economic base was transformed from agriculture and stock raising to mining and industry. The political system was tranformed from Hispanic caudillism to North Atlantic populist democracy, and the social system was transformed from a land-based, family-oriented hierarchy to an income-based, technocratic meritocracy.[20]

How did Venezuelans bring about a quiet but deep and lasting change in their society?

Much of the credit must go to the famous "generation of 1928" led by Romulo Betancourt. Inadvertently, dictator Goméz created his own nemesis, a vigorous group of university students who absorbed a liberal ethic during their years of higher education. Goméz (and later Jiménez) persecuted, tortured, and exiled these intellectuals when they sought a liberal democracy, land reform, and the use of oil revenues for development.

In exile, the "generation of 1928" lived in Chile, Uruguay, and Argentina (all functioning democracies at the time) or the United States. There, the young leaders reaffirmed their dedication to liberal policies and learned the techniques of political mobilization. (One may only speculate on the sad fate of Venezuela if the dictators had been slightly more ruthless and simply executed the new leaders rather than sending them into exile.)

When political fortunes allowed Venezuela's future reformers to return from exile, they believed that the creation of viable liberal institutions and a stable rule of law had to preceed an economic reconstruction of their society. The new statesmen were "convinced that the establishment of a democratic system capable of controlling and channeling conflict must take priority over all development goals."[21]

This emphasis on liberal democracy was apparent in Betancourt's original foreign policy. Under the "Betancourt doctrine," Venezuela cut itself off from all authoritarian regimes, whether of the left (such as Cuba) or the right (such as Brazil). Venezuela's presidents condemned American intervention in the Dominican Republic in 1965 and in Vietnam in 1968 as well as Cuba's intent to export revolution. Internationally, Venezuela took the continental lead in supporting Kennedy's Alliance for Progress, assumed with Saudi Arabia the role of founder (and later mediator) of OPEC, joined with Mexico in hemispheric ventures such as *Sistema Economico Latinamericano,* and became committed to the promotion of other "third world" causes. As Castro dropped Venezuela as his prime target for subversion, and Venezuela gained internal political stability, governments in the 1970s and 1980s increasingly advocated the idea of an "open" pluralistic hemisphere and even supported efforts to include Cuba in promoting regional economic cooperation.

Domestically, the liberals set out on a cautious, compromising, pragmatic course which largely fulfilled their economic programs and placated their potential enemies. In the 1960s, for example, they initiated a large-scale land reform by distributing publicly held land and by compensating the aristocracy for private expropriations. Moreover, the government did not slice up the land into uneconomic plots; large estates, if they were highly productive, were left intact.

By 1975, the government was sufficiently powerful to nationalize the oil industry. Revenues from this socialized enterprise allowed the government in build schools and roads, new industries and utilities systems—thus validating its election promises. Whether AD or COPEI ruled, the democratic governments gave all major interest groups a share in growing prosperity and provided the technical competence needed in managing Venezuela's affairs. These were virtues which the military dictators notoriously lacked.

Thus, people as different as large landowners and the growing urban proletariat, church leaders (a minor factor after anticlerical reforms in the nineteenth century) and the peasants newly endowed with land, industrial entrepreneurs and labor leaders found it advantageous to cooperate in creating a liberal polity. Two important groups, however, potentially threatened liberal democracy; the army and Marxist revolutionaries.

After a century and a half of military rule, there was, of course, a genuine danger that a new *caudillo* might emerge and, indeed, various officers sporadically rebelled. They failed, however, to win large-scale support either within the army or from civilians. Gradually, all sectors of the public came to regard technically competent people, subject to the rule of law, and guided by elected governments as their surest leaders to progress. As conflicts were resolved within a new but stable set of institutions without recourse to violence, even the army cautiously assented to a transition in Venezuelan political style.

Many factors helped Venzuela's civilian leaders in reconciling the armed forces to liberal democracy. Some of the officers had themselves been influenced by "the generation of 1928." Goméz and particularly Jimenez had sent many young officers to the United States for advanced training. The dictators believed that greater military prowess would reinforce their autocracy. Yet, in North America, the officers naturally met their fellow nationals, the political exiles, and they were also taught to view their role in society as "professional."

Once the civilian reformers were elected in 1958, they exhibited unusual talent in purging rebellious officers, adroitly shifting appointments so that no officer could secure a geographical base, and ensuring that only liberal officers achieved high military position. New generations of officers, like their civilian colleagues in the bourgeoning middle classes, also began to accept the proposition that a liberal democracy was the only viable alternative to communism.

The reformers wisely and quite literally "bought off" the army. As in Colombia, the government provided fine equipment, delightful officers' clubs, and lush benefits to its soldiers. In fact, Venezuela expended more public monies on the military than any other Latin nation. In 1982, Venezuela lavished $16,595 annually on each of her soldiers while military dictatorships in Argentina expended $11,256 and in Brazil only $6,004.[22]

The government also gave the army a distinct mission: fighting Marxist rebels, its other prime enemy, first in the countryside and then in cities. Inspired by Castro's Cuba, young university students wished to participate in world revolution and thought that both the AD and COPEI governments were insufficiently socialist. (In fact, these governments had nationalized basic sectors of the economy such as oil, steel, petrochemicals, and electricity, but allowed other parts of the economy to function in a free market.)

In the 1960s, the revolutionaries took to the countryside and ignited a destructive terror campaign. They did not anticipate immediate victory. Rather, they hoped to discredit democratic government and trigger a military coup d'état. Once the repression began, so the convoluted doctrine went, the peasants and workers would awake from their lethargy and rally behind the revolutionary cause.

The scenario failed. In the countryside, the guerrillas launched a number of attacks but the military, now loyal to democratic regimes, crushed them. By the late 1960s, the guerrillas turned to urban terrorism, trying to shoot down political victims while sometimes killing innocent bystanders. By 1969, with convulsive last bursts of violence, the terrorists had ceased to function as a significant, cohesive force.

The stability of the army as well as doctrinal disputes within the Marxist ranks helped to ensure the guerrilla debacle. Perhaps the most decisive factor, however, was the skill of successive elected governments. While the Marxists preached world revolution to an inattentive peasantry, the AD and COPEI actually delivered land, new houses, schools, and health care to the most distant sections of the country. The leftist threat died from ennui; it could not provide a believable alternative to the progressive policies and pragmatic achievements of the government.

In determining its political future—in spite of attempted coups, oil company intervention, a drab history of militarism, and its dependence on world markets for oil—"every critical choice since 1936 . . . has been made by Venezuelans." For good or evil, Venezuelans chose to emulate what has been described as "North Atlantic developmentalism."[23] As John Lombardi has commented,

> Economic orthodoxy, political controversy, and social aspirations arrived with the hydroelectric plants and the automobile and steel industries, the supermarkets and the freeways, the housing projects and the suburban residential neighborhoods.[24]

Venezuela's economic miracle, as profound as its political transformation, could be traced to many sources. The country was fortunate in possessing natural resources which a seemingly unending series of *cau-dillos* had neglected. Although the original Spanish colonialists discovered little gold or silver, they brutally exploited Indian labor to cultivate wheat, cattle, cocoa, and later, coffee. By the twentieth century, great reserves of iron ore, aluminum deposits, manganese, and of course, oil, had been discovered. Slowly, the economy made a transition from its originally agricultural focus to an urbanized society based on mining, extraction, and industry.

In addition to its store of natural wealth, Venezuela benefited from human resources, often migrants from equally poor economies who demonstrated their abilities in the new land as able and energetic entrepreneurs.

Originally, during the colonial period, a small elite of Spaniards ruled. Yet, sexual mixing between whites, the indigenous Indians, and imported slaves soon propagated a new and far larger ethnic group, the "prados," a combination of the other three. In response, the Spanish governors created a unique institution, the "Gracias Al Sacar," which promoted social mobility for the "prados." This legal procedure rewarded energetic and worthy "prados" with all of the rights and privileges of the Spaniards—in effect, it was a "legal whitening" used as a reward for economic achievement.

Other minorities soon flowed into the nation. In the eighteenth and ninteenth centuries, the Basques, a poor immigrant people from Spain, distinguished themselves in commerce. During the late 1930s, exiles from the Spanish civil war influenced Venezuelan life by assuming advanced places in law, medicine, the universities, the arts, and even politics. A third wave of Spaniards, Portuguese, and Italians fled to Venezuela after World War II, seeking economic opportunities. In their adopted country, they took over important positions in business, construction, and transportation. By the 1970s, some one hundred thousand Colombians illegally migrated into Venezuela each year, often finding opportunities in the industrial or commercial sectors. Foreigners of many other breeds, ranging from American oil technicians to French intellectuals, served as mechanics and managers, entrepreneurs and professors.

As in so many "fourth way" countries, this heady mixture of peoples sometimes provided the combustible ingredients for political conflict. Yet, these "marginal men"—whether "prados" or Basques, civil war exiles or flamboyant Yanquis—disproportionately provided the leadership for Venezuela's economic transformation.

The miraculous natural element for wealth generation, Venezuela's petroleum production, developed slowly. Unequipped to deal with its oil bonanza, Venezuela's military in the 1920s and 1930s gave away oil at relatively cheap prices. Oil companies brought in their own technology and technicians, extracted and exported the oil, and—except for the very rich—touched the lives of few Venezuelans. The *caudillos* expended their private oil fortunes by building useless public monuments or fattening their Florida bank accounts.

With the war's ravenous appetite for oil in the 1940s and a continuing demand for energy in the 1950s, Venezuelan society entered a growing, technologically sophisticated world which required broadened education, new elites, and a government able to manage a technical economy. Jiménez failed to cope with the new challenges.

When Betancourt took charge of the government in 1959, he initiated a series of measures which brought oil reserves into the nation's service. In the 1960s, instead of expending oil revenues on the elite of Caracas and the enoblement of the capital, democratic governments used their growing income for building an infrastructure of roads, schools, and clinics. Oil money furnished the funds necessary for Venezuela's peaceful land reform as well as the diversification of the country's industrial base. The autonomous Venezuelan Development Corporation, for example, provided the capital to develop the Orinoco River basin. This great endeavor created hydroelectricity projects, iron ore mines, steel and aluminum plants, chemical industries, consumer enterprises and, by 1966, plants which produced Venezuela's own capital goods.

Politically, Betancourt sought to insure the oil revenue flow by helping to found OPEC and later, by nationalizing the industry.

While the public sector controlled the major means of production, private entrepreneurs were consulted and allowed to implement much of the nation's plans through individual enterprise and commerce. Even with the nationalization of oil in 1975, Venezuela remained a truly mixed economy.

The results were spectacular. Manufacturing production grew by 240 percent between 1960 and 1980, and "Venezuela had finally begun to construct an industrial base intended to sustain the economy once petroleum reserves were exhausted."[25]

Venezuelan liberals had found a way to invigorate their economy without depriving any major segment of the public. In two decades, Venezuelans created dams and highways, automobile and aluminium industries, while engaging in new forms of political debate and encouraging ever higher social aspirations.

Experts in the 1970s thought that the oil boom might last forever. The Orinoco Oil Belt, for example, offered the world's largest source of unconventional crude oil: some 700 billion barrels of high-sulphur petroleum. Although refinement of this oil presented a formidable technical task, Valentin Hernandez, the mines minister, predicted in 1976, "we could produce at the rate of 200,000 barrels per day for centuries."[26] He did not face the question of whether the world would want Venezuela's oil.

The dependence on oil revenue and the consequent economic expansion had its obvious dangers. In 1979, just as world oil prices dipped downward, Venezuela became the most trade-dependent country in Latin America. The visions of everincreasing growth had to be curbed as deep faults, particularly in the agricultural area, appeared in the economy.

While Venezuela had more than enough land to feed its people, the country had to import 60 percent of its food in the 1980s. The ambitious agrarian reform of the 1960s had indeed distributed land to the people, but the petroleum boom increasingly lured peasants to the cities. For the remaining farmers, the government failed to provide adequate instruction in farming techniques, high quality seeds, or proper fertilizers. (In fact, the government promoted petroleum-based fertilizers with a high degree of acid, exactly the wrong nutrient for Venezuela's acid-high soil.) Farmers abandoned the land; by the 1980s, only 20 percent of the labor force worked in agriculture.

At that point, however, ex-peasants in the cities often found themselves redundant. A slowing in industrial growth, high inflation rates, and a fall in oil exports resulted in an urban unemployment rate of 20 percent. Even faced with these problems, Venezuela carried out free elections in 1983, launched another agrarian reform program, and provided even the poorest in its cities with basic necessities and even amenities. "With humble but well-built homes, running water, electricity, and often a television and refrigerator," James Le Moyne observed about Caracas slum dwellers in 1983, "they enjoy a standard of living far above the mud-hut and swollen belly poverty seen elsewhere in Latin America."[27]

Several reasons allowed Venezuela, even during "La Crisis," to end grinding poverty, extend education and health care to all, and create an enduring liberal democracy.

Many Latin experts contended that the discovery of oil provided the prime impetus. The country's escape from autocracy, Gary Wynia has argued, "was made possible by Venezuelans' possession of a valuable resource—petroleum—which generated the income needed to finance development without threatening the wealthy."[28]

When this fickle source of prosperity lost value, Venezuelan Marxists said, it proved that the country's extreme dependence on the world market eventually doomed experiments in reformist democracy. Even those who welcomed Venezuela's "fourth way" questioned how democratic governments, deprived of abundant revenues, could continue to delicately balance the conflicting interests of their people. Something had to give—social services, education, patronage, military expenditure, development investments or special services to the urban unemployed. Not a few observers feared that the eruption of social tensions would hasten the return of a new *caudillo* who would enforce "stability and order."

Nonetheless, reasonable men argued that Venezuela's transformation and its future should not be attributed so cavalierly to the presence or absence of material abundance. Clearly, Venezuelan dictators and the rulers of other oil-rich nations have used oil money solely to finance their ultimately futile attempts to reinforce and glorify autocracy. If, then, the possession of a material treasure did not automatically breed a political and social transformation, was it a necessary ingredient in aiding peaceful evolution? We think not.

Significantly, both Costa Rica and Colombia chartered their own "fourth ways" without the benefit of huge foreign incomes. Thus, oil may have eased Venezuela's transition, but it could hardly be regarded as the sole or even paramount factor.

Rather than emerging automatically as a by-product of affluence, liberal polities in Latin America have prospered when certain social conditions coalesced at historically propitious moments:

First, the reformers contrived ways of curbing or channeling the military's lust for power. In Costa Rica, of course, Figueres chose the dramatic path of simply abolishing the army. In Colombia and Venezuela, civilian reformers "bribed" the army. In return, the military establishment, however reluctantly and fitfully, allowed the emergence of a rule of law, civilian political control and technocratic direction of the economy. As soldiers became citizens over the decades, they found it difficult to overthrow the new institutions. In the long run, as James Chace rightly argued, only a policy aimed at the demilitarization of the region, the strict prosecution of death squads, and imprisonment or exile of rebellious officers would allow these fragile experiments to succeed.

Liberal governments also poured funds into education, creating an informed public that understood its interests and was willing to defend a pluralistic social order. The attitudes which so highly correlated with education—greater rationality, tolerance, empathy, and a willingness to use science in the service of man—obviously contributed to both the political and economic evolution of Costa Rica, Colombia, and Venezuela.

Due to education and particularly during eras of economic improvement, the urban middle classes dramatically expanded in these "fourth way" countries. The training, the interests, and the attitudes of these new middle sectors made them natural opponents of both the capricious *caudillos* and the feudal oligarchies. In mixed economies, it was the new middle classes that produced the lawyers, journalists, teachers—and even the rare military officers—who, in turn, led their countries down the path of peaceful evolution.

The Roman Catholic Church, sometimes guided by priests or even bishops drawn from the middle sectors, often viewed liberal changes in their societies with benevolence. In some rural regions of Costa Rica, priests dedicated to "liberation theology" actively aided in land reform and modernization. In Colombia, some of the higher members of the hierarchy and Christian conservatives such as Betancur sought to aid the poor and to mediate church doctrine concerning birth control. In Venezuela, members of the church lent their support to the social Christianity of COPEI while religious fervor generally decreased to the point where only 10 percent of the people could be considered active churchgoers by 1986. This was a far different situation from 1821 when Thomas Jefferson wrote of the grim future of Latin republics: "History furnishes no example of a priest-ridden people maintaining a free civil government."[29]

New ideas affected not only the Latin church but the economies of the successful countries. Costa Rica, Colombia, and Venezuela all welcomed the talents of migrants and the stimulation afforded by foreign contacts. On the economic level, they used the capital and technology of foreign companies (and yet tamed their lust for profits). They benefited, too, from the direct foreign aid provided to them by the United States. Both Venezuela and Colombia received special attention from the Alliance for Progress while Costa Rica emerged in the 1980s as the largest per capita recipient of U.S. aid funds in the hemisphere. Waves of Basques, Italians, Spanish rebels, "prados," and even Yanquis actively participated in the economic and cultural life of these regions. Meanwhile, the more backward areas, such as Paraguay and Bolivia, closed their doors to foreign contact, except for the sinister influence of ex-Nazis.

While granting the importance of these structural factors, it would be a mistake to underestimate the quality of leadership and the devotion to liberal policies and social reform which pragmatic and cautious individuals repeatedly demonstrated in these regions. Would Costa Rica have built its network of schools without Ricardo Jiménez or abolished its army without José Figueres? Would guerrillas in Colombia have reached an impasse without the negotiating talents and toughness of Belisario Betancur? If naval officer Wolfgang Larrazabal had not kept his word or the "generation of 1928" had been executed, would Venezuela be the same today?

No one can answer these questions definitively. We would do well to remember, however, that it is individual leaders—wise or stupid, tolerant or autocratic, humane or brutal, honest or venal—who create or sustain all social structures. For the liberal reformers in Latin America, "politics does not involve choosing between acquiring enough power to impose one's will on society or resigning oneself to political immobility. Rather it requires living with hosts of dilemmas and accepting imperfect solutions."[30]

Contrary to the wisdom of the North American founding fathers, we must also recognize that the problem in Latin America was not creating a democracy in a barren setting, but rather of reinforcing the original tradition of Bolívar. As James Chace has cogently argued, "We misread history if we conclude that democracy is impossible. . . . Again and again when it has been snuffed out, it reappears."[31]

7

Stumbling Giants: India

When societies first come to birth, it is the leaders who produce the institutions of the republic. Later, it is the institutions which produce the leaders.

—MONTESQUIEU

Two of the greatest leaders of our times, Nehru and Mao, inherited a tremendous opportunity: the chance to mold nearly half of mankind in the image of a new society. Both men died disillusioned. As early as 1953, Nehru confessed that "I am completely out of touch" in the swirling economic throes of India, while Mao told Richard Nixon, "I have changed nothing but a village or two near Peking." Yet, the experiments of Nehru and the Gandhis, of Mao and Zhou and Deng could not be ignored, for their policies—however triumphant or bumbling, however humane or brutal—affected the lives of 1,850 million people.

At the beginning of their historic attempts to launch a forced march to modernity, India and China shared certain basic characteristics. In 1950, 80 percent of their populations engaged in agriculture, both countries had per capita incomes of around $50 annually, and each nation sponsored large-scale development schemes under the banners of "socialism" and "self-reliance." Although India had suffered colonial rule and China had been raped by Japan, both countries also had untapped resources: China had a potential advantage in huge coal and iron reserves, while India had a wider margin in exploiting agricultural cultivation, a better educational system, and more sophisticated transportation.

The scene was set in the late 1940s for a contest between the world's two giants since China and India initially chose quite different political paths to progress. In 1949, Mao dictated a totalitarian course in creating an "empire of the blue ants." In order to destroy the inequalities, starvation, disunity, and exploitation of the past, Mao explicitly announced the creation of an autocracy. "We are told: 'You are setting up a dictatorship!' " Mao said. "Yes, my friend you are right. . . . We are told: 'You are not benevolent!' Exactly. . . . To hostile classes the state apparatus is an instrument of oppression, of coercion and not 'good will.' " By 1953, *The People's Daily* could officially and unsmilingly announce: "Today in the era of Mao Zedung, heaven is here on earth. Once the Party calls, tens of millions of the masses jump into action. . . . It was so in the past; so it is today."[1]

In contrast, Nehru hoped to create an egalitarian, socialist society within the framework of a participatory, parliamentary democracy. He left agriculture in the private sector, primarily to the devices of the large land-holders; he granted untouchables new legal rights but seldom compelled the Hindu majority to observe them; he lightly used the authoritarian powers, such as his ability to dismiss state governments, which the Indian constitution granted him. In the malestrom of caste, class, ethnic, linguistic, and religious conflicts, many observers in 1947 doubted that he could lift the pall of poverty or succeed in governing India's 450 million people. Yet, as Chester Bowles observed in 1963, "If we should suddenly wake up and read that Europe had achieved unity comparable with that of India, with a single Prime Minister, a single Parliament, a single set of internal laws, with a common market and a common constitution, the event would be hailed as a modern political miracle."[2]

If Nehru had achieved a "political miracle," largely by nonviolent means, it seemed apparent during the first decade of independence that China had far outdistanced India in economic productivity and in providing welfare for the masses of people. By 1960, the gross national product in India had increased by only 15 percent, while China doubled her productivity. Chinese steel production soared at a rate seven times greater than India's. China's productivity in certain decisive sectors of the economy—coal, cement, fertilizers, electricity—exceeded that of India by 200 to 700 percent. While India's rate of investment doubled between 1950 and 1960, China's increased five times. During this time, China benefited from Russia's direct foreign aid and strict coordination of the two economies, as well as the use of "free" peasant labor. Nonetheless, China's achievements, particularly in industrialization, an expansion of literacy, and advances in public wealth could not be denied by objective observers.

Dry statistics did not convey the tangible ways in which the fate of the average Chinese peasant (at least temporarily) had improved. In 1961, Felix Green summarized a prevailing opinion concerning the contrast between India and China:

> I know the attitude in the West is that India is going slower because she is accomplishing her revolution through a politically democratic process, more gradually, more humanely. But when we move from political theory to the mathematics of human survival, we face the fact that a Chinese child today has better health, better food, better work-prospects, more education, and greater security than an Indian child.[3]

Thus, by the early 1960s, in spite of Russian disillusionment, Marxists in both the West and developing areas hailed China as a triumph of collectivism. What did the lack of political liberty mean, they argued, to once starving peasants who had now created a cornucopia? In any case, they said, a new and higher form of peasant participation was developing in China. It made "bourgeois" liberties (freedom of the press, the judiciary, and the electoral process) irrelevant formalities. Even liberals, however appalled by the human costs, granted that China had made great economic gains. They harbored the suspicion that development might well require totalitarianism. After all, cultural relativists remarked, the Chinese language in 1900 had not even possessed words for such alien concepts as "liberty," "privacy," or "individualism."

History proved this fashionable judgment—praise of China, despair over India—to be, at best, premature, and at worst, wrong. China's leaders had not yet revealed the devastation wrought by Mao's "great leap forward" or his "cultural revolution." China's famines, the erosion of her scientific base, the bureaucratic stagnation of industry—all went virtually unnoticed by casual visitors. Thus, the exposure of the "Gang of Four" and China's abrupt change of course in 1976 burst upon the world scene as a surprise.

Indians had not yet experienced Indira Gandhi's "emergency rule," a mockery of Nehru's ideals, the bloody massacres in Assam, the riots in Bombay, the Punjabi revolt—or the grand consequences of the "green revolution," the emergence of the world's largest middle class, and the entrance of India into the age of high technology.

Now, after almost four decades of experience, we are in a better position to assess the effects of the "fourth ways" adopted by India and

China. Like their ancient civilizations, the results of these experiments were mixed, and contradictory, and often paradoxical.

INDIA

My legacy to India? Hopefully it is 400,000 million people capable of governing themselves.

—NEHRU, 1962

In 1962, when I first saw an untouchable barred from drinking water from a parched village well, I began to comprehend the challenge which Nehru faced.

"He'll get water someplace," an embarrassed district officer said, turning my attention away. "You'll see," the Westernized official said, "even his lot will improve."

At the time, the prediction seemed grimly doubtful. Although the village lay only twenty miles from New Delhi, the "center's" laws and plans had hardly touched the lives of its 1,800 people. The ruling caste of Gujars, the land-holders, forbad untouchables from using the new well or crossing an invisible line in the village; the harijan women had to carry pails of water for many miles from an "impure" well and the men worked for half of the minimum legal wage. Most of the men, involuntarily idled for 260 days a year, sat around smoking the *hookah* and playing cards. Almost universally, the children ignored the village school; half died before the age of ten. The villagers grew subsistence crops in the same way and with the same tools used by their ancestors. They listened to one village radio. The average mother bore eight children. The men vaguely knew of a personage, possibly a god, called Nehru but they did not bother to vote.

By 1986, the seemingly timeless slumber of this traditional village had ended. The village had entered the market economy, producing milk for New Delhi and sending it by truck down a new road. Per capita income, although still miserly, had increased by 500 percent. Caste lines had blurred a little, particularly because untouchables now owned bicycles and could commute to jobs in nearby towns. Four retail markets, a clinic, electrical lights, a lawyer's office, a bus service, two cars, Western slacks and sweaters, and new schools had arrived in the village. People queued up to use the newly installed telephone, a novelty which they had ordered five years earlier and which usually did not work. Fifty percent of children attended school up to the age of fourteen. Contact with cities, promoted by ex-villagers who had moved, had dramatically increased; community television offered movies and agricultural programs; the youths carried transistor radios; a few bold girls wore jeans; and family size had dropped to an average of three children. Indira Gandhi had once visited the village and, as a consequence, most males voted, particularly in elections for village headman.

The ponderously slow but real pace of change in this village—hobbled by isolation and traditionalism, a corrupt bureaucracy, and caste hostilities—illustrated the development of India as a whole since independence. The village was not necessarily typical (*nothing* was typical in India), but it symbolized the overarching characteristic of evolution in India: the extraordinarily uneven pace of economic advance.

On the one hand, no one could deny the tangible triumphs of the nation since 1947. Per capita income, that elusive measure which lumps together the rich and the poor, increased by 460 percent from 1947 to 1985—but only up to the Dickensian level of $230 a year. Thus, half of the population, largely concentrated in village India where 70 percent of the people still worked, suffered from malnutrition or outright starvation.

By 1986, however, India had emerged as a giant industrial power— a prime producer of steel, automobiles, airplanes, refrigerators, television sets, nuclear missiles, and the INSAT 1–B communications satellite. By 1986, domestic oil production hit nearly 30 million tons and Indian planners expected self-sufficiency in the near future. Between 1977 and 1984 alone, the number of television sets tripled to more than 3 million while another 1 million sets were produced annually. Enticed by the goal of self-sufficiency and blessed with a large internal market, the nation financed 90 percent of its development projects through domestic savings and had a relatively small and manageable foreign debt.

Most importantly, India had achieved self-sufficiency in food. The science-based ''green revolution,'' so stunningly successful in the Punjab, had spread throughout much of India by 1986 when 80 percent of the country's wheat and 50 percent of its rice were grown from hybrid, high-yield seeds. In that same year, India achieved a record harvest of 150 million tons of food grains.

As agriculture blossomed, development of classic and ''information'' industries went hand in hand. The city of Kanpur, with its steel and jute mills belching smoke and its railroads loading bales of steel, symbolized ninteenth-century industrialization. The launching of joint ventures with the Japanese allowed the Indian car industry, mired in the 1950s, to move into the 1980s. At the same time, Chandigarh produced silicon microchips, Bombay created nice copies of Japanese computers, and Calcutta spewed forth television sets which absorbed signals from India's satellite. "To live in India today," William K. Stevens commented in 1984, "is to have a ringside seat at the simultaneous unfolding of the industrial and post-industrial revolutions, telescoped drastically and run at high speed."[4]

Still, in its drive to transform rural feudalism into a modern industrial society, India was hampered by many obstacles. The symbolic contrasts were appalling:

• In 1981, ox-carts carried MG–21 fighters to the Republic Day parade in Delhi.

• In constructing a magnificent site for the 1982 Asian Games in record time, camels were used as the mode of transportation.

• In 1984, scientists redesigned a fertilizer bag traditionally carried by peasants. They attached a modern electric motor. Peasants refused to carry the now useless bag through the fields since it was far too heavy.

• In 1986, in a country which boasted the largest number of technical students in the world, women cleaned temple steps with toothbrushes, untouchables were sold into bondage, and businesses still hired boys whose only job was to open ancient ledgers for clerks who wrote with quill pens.

"The country often clings to obsolete and in some cases ancient ways of doing things," Stevens wrote in 1984.[5] Information processing had yet to be adopted widely, "brown-outs" of the electrical system were common, and the telephones, bereft of the ministrations of skilled technicians, only worked sporadically.

One major bottleneck was a lack of skilled, competent, and honest technicians. The educational system, although vast, had failed to produce enough technically trained people. Bribery, open cheating, skilled rote learning, and sycophancy to one's professors too often resulted in a university degree. Those with the highest levels of education, such as well-trained doctors and engineers, fled the country to work under less appalling conditions. (This exodus had the one advantage of bringing in some $1 billion a year in foreign remittances.)

The unprecedented industrial disaster in Bhopal in 1984 illustrated the risks of importing dangerous high technology into an unprepared social environment. Union Carbide India built a complex pesticide factory which contributed directly to the great surge in food production. Yet, the plant developed a poisonous leak, killing two thousand people and critically injuring two hundred thousand more. Experts traced the catastrophe to mechanical difficulties (outdated machinery, inadequate maintenance, few spare parts) and to a lack of skilled labor, worker training, and close inspection of the hazardous enterprise. Without proper public education or a pool of skilled manpower, the plant was placed in a technologically naive environment. "When we set up this plant," Kamal Pateek, the senior project engineer said, "we used workers just out of the agricultural age."[6] The company had failed to install complex and expensive safeguards which existed in industrialized regions.

In addition to a lapse in educated technicians, India's blend of socialism and capitalism created a bloated, corrupt, and restrictive bureaucracy. The central bureaucracy, in its eagerness to compel equality, set production quotas—but these were designed to compel companies *not* to exceed specified targets of production. Such rules automatically stifled efficiency and initiative. Corruption was so widespread in the once-respected civil service that businesses regularly bribed officials to lift quotas on imports, to curb competition, to ease (or restrict) the ubiquitous "permissions" required for almost any activity. In the countryside, landlords in such regions as Bihar blithely ignored laws on land reform since they had already seduced high officials into complacency.

Beset by patronage (encouraged by a religious system which deemed generosity to one's caste-fellows as a duty), corruption, political interference, and a lack of incentives, the publicly-owned sector of the economy, some 25 percent of all activity, performed less efficiently and had the slowest rate of growth. The private realm, typified by the great Tata and Birla industries, was also hemmed in by licensing requirements, production controls, import restrictions, and a lack of alliance with foreign sources. Only small-scale industries, those capitalized at less than $5 million, were free of direct controls and these grew vigorously. Small bicycle factories, for example, produced sufficient models to satisfy Indian demand and to create an export profit.

Nonetheless, because of blatant tax evasion by the richer classes and the mistakes of a crippled bureaucracy, much of India's effort was channeled through the "black market." Observers estimated that 30 to 50 percent of all economic activity, particularly in consumer goods, flowed through "black" channels.

Agriculture, totally under private control, experienced a miraculous boom but could not quite keep up with population growth. Some 400 million Indians still subsisted on the edge of starvation. Neither urban squatters nor the more impoverished peasantry could afford even the low grades of rice sequestered in government store houses. "Administered" prices for food, governed by the bureaucracy, rose by about 80 percent between 1980 and 1984, while prices for better food in the private sector increased by a relatively moderate 20 percent during the same period.

The government, not nature (in spite of a drought in 1980) was responsible for this disparity. The government could have decided to garner foreign exchange by exporting its surplus food grains, particularly rice, but instead chose to store the unused portion. For the lowest segment of the population, deprived of a cash income, the government might have decided to use stored rice and wheat as barter payment for subsistence peasants, thus increasing rural employment and improving nutrition. By 1986, New Delhi had not made this choice.

Thus, while the middle classes and the rich in the cities prospered and grew, fattening themselves on "black" luxuries, whole sections of the nation stagnated or floated aimlessly into chaos.

The northern state of Bihar, a region which contained two fifths of the country's mineral resources, became the preeminent example of violence, incorrigible corruption, feudalism, and poverty. The great majority of the state's 70 million people worked as agricultural laborers under the thrall of landlords who refused to pay a minimum wage. Police and hired armies of "goondas" blinded criminals and dissenters who objected to the system by putting out their eyes with needles or acid.

Ironically, Bihar was once the home of nonviolent ideals. It was the center of ancient Indian civilization, the abode of Buddha and Asoka, and the incubator of the Vedic agricultural civilization where classes crystalized into castes. The Brahmins and priests still ruled in Bihar, condemning the lower castes to destitution, brutality, and privation.

Sporadic attempts to industrialize Bihar had faltered. Thirty-eight of Bihar's forty publicly-owned enterprises were failing to make a profit in the 1980s. Students rioted for the right to cheat, and won. The landlords used laborers as serfs. Corrupt officials stole half the monthly pension of $2.40 owed to the aged. Doctors routinely paid officials for postings to urban areas where their own bribes were higher; and when doctors went on strike in Bihar, they looted government hospitals of equipment and supplies.

"Bihar had become a symbol of waywardness and dashed hopes," one commentator wrote. "Corruption, gangsterism, intimidation and the rusting of standards in public life had combined to give it a nightmarish quality."[7] Under Mrs. Gandhi, the local government was headed by a rich Brahmin who jailed critical journalists, unleashed the police on his enemies, laughed off charges of taking bribes "with a wave of his heavily beringed fingers" and boasted, "I enjoy the confidence of the electorate as long as I enjoy the confidence of Mrs. Gandhi."[8]

If Bihar was an island of tyranny where the weak struggled for a meager subsistence in a region of potential bounty, it was fortunately not typical of social progress in other parts of the country.

Throughout India, electricity, modern medical clinics, and hygienic water supplies had expanded into many of the villages.

Schools had spread literacy to some 40 percent of the population by 1984, up from 16 percent at the time of independence. Life expectancy had soared from thirty-two years in 1947 to fifty-five by 1985. Large if still inadequate birth control campaigns cut the rate of population growth to about 2 percent a year, largely through laparoscopy and vasectomy. The application of science to agriculture provided an unprecedented Indian level of nutrition; by 1984 "an estimated 350 million to 400 million Indians had a standard of living ranging from nutritionally adequate to materially lavish. That is as many people as lived in the country at independence."[9]

A new middle class, some 70 million people, had emerged as a result of industrialization, urbanization, and an enormous growth in service enterprises. This social vanguard, larger than the entire population of India's former imperial ruler, tried hard to break away from caste boundaries, valued education as essential for their children, and—while often consulting astrologers—believed that they affected their own destiny and were "entitled" to certain rights. "A large proportion of the urban middle class is less than one generation out of the village, so it is linked with the village," said Bashiruddin Ahmed, director of an Indian institute for development in 1984. "The news and views of the middle class are no longer news and views confined to just the urban areas."[10]

In spite of major social changes, India had far to go on the path of modernity—and this gap between reality and aspiration increasingly angered Sikhs who sought autonomy, peasants in Bihar who demonstrated for minimum wages, Assamese who hated the incursion of 4 million Muslim migrants, and armed squads of revolutionaries in the hilly forests of Andhra Pradah who proclaimed, "Lai salam! The world is ours!"[11]

The social disparities in the emerging new India were all too apparent. Half of India's 576,000 villages had no electricity in 1983 and many had no road access or decent drinking water. In the villages, less than one third of the men and one fifth of the women could read. The infant mortality rate reached 129 per 1,000 annually compared with 56 in China and 14 in Great Britain. The 100 million untouchables, although theoretically protected by law, were still sold into bonded labor.

Population growth had been slightly curbed but planners still predicted that one billion people would live in India by the turn of the century. This meant, among many other problems, that population growth alone had created 130 million more illiterates by 1983 than at the time of independence. Illiteracy, in turn, fed the population explosion by, for example, allowing the continuing circulation of myths such as the belief that vasectomy was castration.

As a consequence of all of these failings, India scored a rating of only 43 on Clark Kerr's index of the physical quality of life while China ranked at 69 and the neighboring, troubled island of Sri Lanka achieved a level of 82.

On the political level, James Traub concluded in 1984, "India is falling apart. But then," he added, "India is always falling apart."[12] The fragile union of India, bloodily stripped of Pakistan, achieved independence in 1947 under the democratic socialism and aristocratic tutelage of Nehru. For seventeen years, although he never commanded an electoral majority, Nehru managed to keep the peace and preserve constitutional and legal safeguards over an enormously diverse collection of peoples: 250 million Hindus, 90 million Muslims, 6 million Sikhs, 500 independent maharajahs, 23 language groups with 200 dialects, and 3,000 castes. Enamored of Stalinism, this Cambridge-educated Brahmin nonetheless maintained a fragile parliamentary democracy during his lifetime.

Nehru's daughter, Indira Gandhi, eventually succeeded him in 1966. She claimed many triumphs: pushing India into the age of high technology by exploding an atomic bomb in 1974, the launching of satellites, and the creation of Bangladesh after a brief war with Pakistan.

In 1975, however, a court found her guilty of malfeasances in the 1971 election. Ignoring the supreme court, Mrs. Gandhi declared a "state of emergency," imprisoned 100,000 people without trial, totally censored the press, and denied civil rights both to her critics and to the poor. She sent in 60,000 police to break up the *gherao* of the secular saint, J. P. Narayan. She crushed a rail strike by mass arrests without warrants and submitted their leaders to torture. On June 25, 1975, she jailed all of the opposition leaders—J. P. Narayan, M. Desai, S. Reddy (who died from her experiences), and even the harmless dowager queens of Gwalior and Jaipur who had dared to criticize Mrs. Gandhi.

Mrs. Gandhi also gave great latitude to her son, Sanjay, as the enforcer of her most important domestic program, birth control. A ruthless social engineer inspired by Mao, Sanjay moved slum dwellers out of India's major cities and set up camps where thousands of males were sterilized. The men had been bullied and bribed to enter the camps where they underwent vasectomies under primitive conditions.

With the mass media curbed, Mrs. Gandhi mistook political quiet for submission and called for elections in 1977, assuming that she would win a seal of approval for her emergency. She lost, and temporarily handed over power to an enfeebled *Janatra* coalition. Composed of old men, religious fanatics, and corrupt opportunists, it was merely an alliance of the discontented. The government collapsed in 1979. In 1980, portraying herself as a misunderstood martyr and benefiting from an Indian longing for a royal dynasty, Mrs. Gandhi won an astonishing victory in free elections and returned as prime minister.

Backed by a landslide of votes, Mrs. Gandhi grew increasingly autocratic, demanding obedience as the price for her toadies' advancement. Corruption, amorality, and brutality characterized both her chief ministers and petty bureaucrats. As the more brilliant members of the government drifted into the opposition or political apathy, Mrs. Gandhi surrounded herself with sycophants and increasingly blamed the country's woes on vague foreign enemies. She used her considerable political flairs either to depose opposition leaders from positions of authority (as she did successfully in the Kashmir and Bengal), bribe politicians to join her Congress (Indira) party, or fake local parliamentary elections. When all else failed, she used military power to crush dissidents in Assam, Bombay, and the Punjab.

As her appointment with assassins approached, Mrs. Gandhi tried to tighten her authoritarian grip but met with severe resistance. In Andhra Pradash, India's fifth largest state where 77 percent of the populace was illiterate, the Congress(I) party lost elections to the linguistically based Telegu Desam party, led by former film star N. T. Rama Rao. By issuing transparent excuses and bribing Telegu Desam legislators to change the aisle to her party, Mrs. Gandhi managed to depose Rama Rao as chief minister. She had seriously underestimated his popularity, particularly as a sincere defender of women's rights. Andhra Pradash exploded in mass demonstrations and episodes of violence. Mrs. Gandhi moved in troops but her puppet minister could not muster a majority in the state legislature. A general strike by Rama Rao's ardent supporters crippled the state. The people danced in the streets and threw flowers in the air when Mrs. Gandhi gave up her attempts at manipulation and returned Rama Rao to elected office in September 1984.

Mrs. Gandhi's capricious exercises in power—particularly in regions which had grown used to a measure of autonomy and especially among the new middle classes who could see through her subterfuges and disliked her open appeals to Hindu chauvinism—and her blatant attempts to become "Empress" of India undermined faith in the country's basic institutions. After 1975, the independence of the judiciary remained weakened, Congress(I) politicians led street mobs of Hindus against Muslims and Sikhs, and the once respected police became enemies of the people. "The only things that came to matter were money, muscle and influence," an Indian columnist wrote about her last years.[13]

When sixteen retired Sikh army officers above the rank of colonel condemned her armed intervention in the Punjab, and her Sikh bodyguards killed her in 1984 in retaliation for her raid on the holy temple of Amritsar, Mrs. Gandhi left behind a seriously weakened polity. "Indira Gandhi did not want a strong Parliament, an independent judiciary or a free press," the *Indian Express* observed one week after her death. "The desire for a centralized power system weakened governmental authority itself."[14]

Mrs. Gandhi's murder sparked riots throughout India. Sometimes led by Congress (I) agitators and abetted by police who ignored cries for help, fanatical Hindus slaughtered three thousand Sikhs and burned down the homes of another twenty thousand. Nonetheless, Rajiv Gandhi, her remaining son, was precipitously named as head of the Congress party. Except in the violence-torn states of Assam and the Punjab, Rajiv Gandhi followed the constitution and called for immediate elections. In 1984, he scored a greater electoral victory than either his mother or grandfather had ever achieved.

Even while basking in his grand democratic triumph, Rajiv Gandhi, more than other members of the Nehru dynasty, had to resolve the delicate problem of maintaining a stable liberal democracy and a growing economy in an atmosphere of virulent communal tensions. The cracks in India's polity ran along four separate, but related seams: linguistic divisions, caste hatreds, economic rivalries, and religious hostilities.

Linguistic divisions, often identified with "nationalities," constituted one critical threat. In the Indian heartland, a constituency to which
Mrs. Gandhi pandered in the last years of her life, Hindi ruled but only
37 percent of Indians as a whole spoke the language. The remainder of
the people communicated in their own tongues: 10 percent in Telegu, 8
percent in Marathi, 8 percent in Tamil, and 7 percent in Bengali. A thin
elite of perhaps 3 percent of Indians continued to use in the colonial
language of English.

This diversity in culture and languages posed severe challenges to
political stability and national unity. Politicians in parliament often had
to bring interpreters with them. Higher court judges could not understand decisions rendered in regional languages. Some members of the
universities and the civil services agitated for the dominance of a particular language in their regions. Intellectuals in various areas increasingly
addressed themselves to a pulp culture phrased in regional dialects. Thus,
as Selig Harrison warned, "In each region writers and intellectuals will
be caught in an atmosphere of political ferment that will, in most instances,
emphasize and honor parochial rather than universal values."[15]

Caste hostilities, sometimes intermixed with language, opened more
wounds. The caste system had been woven into the fabric of Indian life
for centuries. While it infiltrated Islam and Christianity, castism served
an indispensable function within the Hindu theodicy of rebirth and pre-
destination. In everyday life, the caste system may have provided order
and integration, but at a cost of a callous ritual of demarcations and
humiliations. In crises, as a study of a cyclone disaster in 1977 indicated, one's caste dictated which victims would be saved (one's caste
fellows) and which would be left to die.

New caste associations and political parties emerged exactly in step
with India's economic progress, for the traditional castes wished to preserve their privileges in a society which theoretically encouraged individual equality of opportunity. The police forces in India too often came
from higher castes and used their power to intimidate those from the
lower castes. In some areas, the "scheduled (lower) castes" resisted,
demanding that landlords raise their wages and stop the completion of
dams that would flood their already miserable lands. The prospect of
change in the old order frightened the resentful higher castes and they
often responded with violence.

Economic tensions mingled with the other sources of political instability. Communal riots between Muslims and Hindus, a constant peril
in India, drew some of their bitterness from the fact that Muslims had
emerged as highly successful small businessmen, increasing the ire of

Hindus. The Bombay riots of 1982, on the other hand, were essentially a battle among have-not migrants recently lured from the countryside. In Bihar, battle lines were drawn between the feudal elite and landless laborers. In the Punjab, part of the terrorism stemmed from a government policy of irrigation which allegedly favored less-productive,but Hindu sections of Haryana. In Assam politicians cried out that "every drop of oil taken from Assam is a drop of Assamese blood"—a slogan that reflected ethnic sensitivities but blocked the rational exploitation of oil reserves.

Mrs. Gandhi's attempts to stifle regional autonomy and centralize all power in New Delhi merely exacerbated local grievances. Weak and corrupt state governments automatically deferred to the center's commands (thus, for example, creating the water shortage in the Punjab), alienated minority groups, and hindered regional enterprise.

Religious differences, illustrated by the terrorism and bloody repression of Sikhism in the Punjab, further contributed to India's political chaos. The dynamic forces which threatened India's disintegration—fears of religious extinction, the setting of caste against caste, economic discrimination, battles for linguistic and religious autonomy—were enough to frustrate the greatest of statesmen. As N. A. Palkhivala, a former ambassador to the U.S., said, "In modern India, Machiavelli would have remained unemployed because of his political naiveté."[16]

In 1984, all of the inflammatory passions plaguing India erupted in the Punjab. Violence in the Punjab presented one of the great paradoxes of modern India. The Punjab was no Bihar: it had experienced the "green revolution," abolished rural poverty, and achieved magnificent levels of education and health. For many leaders in the "third world," the Punjab, rather than Mao's communes, had become the model of real hope for escaping desperate rural poverty.

And yet, in 1984, seething discontent resulted in armed terrorism. Thirty thousand Indian troops, often led by Sikh officers, had to occupy the Punjab.

THE PUNJAB PARADOX

An acre in Middlesex is better than a principality in Utopia.

—THOMAS MACAULEY

"We have been able to prevent people from dying of hunger," Indira Gandhi said in the last interview she gave before her assassination. "Our food production has kept up with the population.'' There had not been a major famine in a decade, she continued, proudly pointing to what she looked upon as her major accomplishment.

Ironically, the Sikhs of the Punjab, the religious minority whose industry was chiefly responsible for ending India's chronic starvation, also produced the bodyguards who shot her. The roots of Sikh discontent were still more ironic: Enterprise made them prosperous; prosperity lessened distinctions among castes and classes, and the trend toward equality generated fanatical opposition to change by those whose status was thus threatened. Indeed, the Punjabi experience contradicted an important belief, quite prevalent in the West, about the relation of politics to economic development. As the wealth of this historically unstable region boomed, the dangers of anarchy steadily mounted, precisely because all groups were enriched. Mrs. Gandhi paid the ultimate penalty for her one great achievement.

It was truly a great achievement, nonetheless. Punjabi Sikh peasants grew two thirds more wheat per acre in 1984 than the agribusinessmen of midwestern America. Although they constituted only 2.5 percent of India's farmers, they contributed 25 percent of its wheat and 45 percent of its rice reserves. Between 1960 and 1980, the area's production of both crops went up four times, while the yields of sugar cane and cotton doubled. Farm income rose twofold and agricultural investment sixfold. Small-scale industries flourished. Led by the Sikhs—52 percent of the state's population—Punjabis sent nine tenths of their output to the rest of India in 1983 and reinvested their earnings at the remarkably high rate of 35 percent annually. This Sikh-dominated domain, ''India's shining example,'' provided the nation's margin of hope.

The Sikhs' material advancement began inauspiciously in 1947. A series of late-19th-century British-built canals and dams had collapsed, Indians and Pakistanis were fighting over the use of the Indus River, and millions of refugees swept back and forth upon the ruins of the economy. Known for four centuries as ''the land of agitations''; tucked away in a volatile triangle formed by Pakistan, Kashmir, and the Himalayas; full of nomads when the rains failed; devoid of natural resources; victimized by partition—the Punjab did not seem at all likely to nurture blossoms in the dust.

Yet by 1960 several factors converged to create a renaissance. First, lacking opportunities at home, Sikh men fled ''abroad''—to commerce in Bombay, to transportation in New Delhi, to the Indian Army (where the percentage of Sikhs was seven times higher than in the population as a whole), and to California and New York City (they maintained a temple in the Borough of Queens). Conscientiously, the Sikh diaspora sent back remittances that provided a pool of local capital.

Meanwhile, after nine years of negotiation, the World Bank persuaded Pakistan and India that joint exploitation of the Indus would benefit both countries. A system of waterworks started to emerge in 1960, particularly on the eastern side of the border. Harvests remained relatively stagnant in Pakistan but began to improve in the Indian Punjab. Long recognized for diligence, willingness to innovate, and receptivity to science, the Sikhs then eagerly adopted the weapons of the green revolution: new kinds of seeds (such as the "dwarfs" originally developed in Mexico and the Philippines), modern irrigation methods, and chemical fertilizers. Encouraged by private and government loans that offered a chance of profit, agricultural extension officers, and price guarantees, Sikh peasants experimented with rice and other crops that were entirely unfamiliar to them. During the years 1966–69 they planted new brands of high-yielding wheat in 70 percent of their fields.

It was the larger Sikh landowners who took the lead. Eventually, tenant farmers and even landless laborers joined in this process that included self-betterment. The typical Punjabi consumed 3,000 calories a day in 1982—a 50 percent improvement on the diet of Indian peasants elsewhere. By 1985 average earnings were three times higher in the Punjab than in the rest of the country's agricultural regions. It boasted more schools, more health facilities, more banks, more tractors, and more television sets per capita than any other Indian state.

Life expectancy and adult literacy doubled between 1965 and 1985. Thanks to prosperity, parents ceased to feel the need to beget large numbers of children: Helped by family-planning campaigns, the Sikhs slashed the state's rate of population growth from 2 percent a year in 1970 to 1 percent in 1984. Full employment was realized, too, with the coming of mini-tractors, thrashers, and a new system of crop rotation. In fact, the laborers of poorer areas flocked to the Punjab until the army sealed it off in 1984 in the wake of the trouble at the Golden Temple, the Sikhs' holy shrine.

The region reaped the benefits not only of a science-based transformation of agriculture but also of marked industrialization in the towns. Twenty thousand credit unions, in a state of 17 million, financed the expansion of the service sector and of small, labor-intensive factories. These, in turn, gave the landless, particularly the untouchables, a chance to move to urban districts, notably Chandigarh, the joint capital of the

Punjab and the neighboring state of Haryana. Consumer industries and little machine shops proliferated in the city, and in 1983 the country's first plant to manufacture silicon chips opened there.

India's government played an important role in promoting this exceptional economic and social advance, partly through what it did and partly through what it did not do. In spite of Mrs. Gandhi's socialist ideology, it did not collectivize the land and instead aided private farmers, providing tube wells, roads, electrification, schools, clinics, and birth control. With financing from the World Bank, New Delhi revitalized colonial-era irrigation systems.

Education was expanded on all levels. Popular television programs directed at peasants spread knowledge of farming techniques, markets and prices to the remotest villages. (India's new satellite made such information still more widely available.) Reversing the urban bias of national policy, Mrs. Gandhi's Finance Minister lifted controls on the cost of food sold in the cities, offered a guaranteed minimum profit to Sikh farmers, and made available low-interest funds to assist them in purchasing fertilizer and seeds.

The government's support of the "Sikh ethic," a local version of Max Weber's famous Protestant Ethic, helped the Punjab escape its dreary cycle of floods and droughts. Soon it emerged as India's development model.

The tragedy was that the Punjab's economic miracle did not generate long-term political stability and may actually have undermined it. Back in 1947, in the last days of the British raj, the state's Akali Dal party demanded the creation of an independent Sikh nation. It did not prevail, and India's constitution did not even recognize the separateness of the Sikh religion, lumping it with Hinduism. During the communal riots of that era, Sikh bandits sided with Hindus, sabotaging trains and murdering Muslim refugees. Notwithstanding the 80 percent illiteracy rate of Punjabi Sikhs and Hindus in 1947, they eventually took part in elections and benefited from the protections of secular Indian law.

But Sikh nationalism refused to die. In 1966, against his deepest inclinations, Jawaharlal Nehru bowed to the Akali Dal and divided the state into a new, Punjabi-speaking, predominantly Sikh Punjab and Hindi-speaking Haryana, with a Hindu majority. To the consternation of the Sikhs, the two shared a common capital, Chandigarh.

Sikh particularists continued to nurse their grievances. At the same time, the coming of affluence under the country's democratic system increased the well-being and political power of the Punjab's most disadvantaged people, the untouchables, a caste that has survived in Sikhism despite the religion's egalitarian ideals. By the 1980s, the typical *harijan* owned a home, bicycled to work, earned cash wages, drank illegal whiskey, watched television, and escaped the worst humiliations of the past. "We're free!" proclaimed one of this group to Richard Critchfield in 1982.

Unhappily, the new freedom contributed to the Punjab's current crisis. Many lower-caste Sikhs backed the Congress (I) Party, so that contrary to the hopes of their upper-caste coreligionists, who tended to support the Akali Dal, it governed the state until 1984. The untouchables feared that autonomy would reinvigorate the caste system: Sikh nationalists craved a return to tradition, and unscrupulous "saints" identified its erosion with the explosion of upward mobility. Younger, rich Sikhs actually joined more radical political formations holding out the heady prospect of a new nation.

In the 1970s, as prosperity started to divide the Sikhs, it also began to estrange them from their fellow Indians. Rightly or wrongly, they believed that they had contributed far more to the country than the government acknowledged in making appropriations, investments and appointments. Unrest spilled over into trivial matters, too: Sikhs composed an astonishing 50 percent of India's Olympic teams, for example, and complained that Olympic finances were being neglected.

The real nature of New Delhi's discrimination toward Sikhs was far more complicated. In a misguided attempt to spread wealth more equally, socialist planners tried to divert investment from the Punjab and even to force local investors to place their money outside the state. On the other hand, 16 percent of the officer corps and 15 percent of the national civil service consisted of Sikhs.

Myths of injustice gathered force regardless of fact. By the 1980s, militant Sikhs were planting bombs, sabotaging railroad trains, and using motorcycles to make hit-and-run attacks on Congress (I) and government officials. Battles among the police, adherents of the Akali Dal, and Hindu and Sikh supporters of Congress (I) exploded throughout the state.

The zealots declared a holy war on New Delhi in 1982. Sikh terrorists stopped buses on the Grand Trunk—an important highway—lined up passengers, demanded to know their religion, and killed Hindus and members of the Nirankari group, a dissident Sikh sect. Sant Jarnail Singh Bhindranwale, the most violent and charismatic Sikh leader, swore that he would "slaughter all Hindus in the Punjab." He and other men of blood hid in the Golden Temple at Amritsar, a traditional sanctuary in addition to being the faith's holiest structure. Under the leadership of a disgraced general of the Indian Army, the insurgents brought automatic weapons inside the temple. Outside, they clashed with Sikhs who adhered to the Congress (I), while some Sikh holymen joined Hindus in days of mourning.

Anarchy forced the president of India, Zail Singh, a Sikh, to dismiss the provincial government in October 1983. Singh's turning out his own Congress (I) party, however, merely resulted in the Akali Dal bemoaning his unwillingness to act more quickly. At this stage, Bhindranwale, backed by wealthy students as well as peasants, took the spotlight away from the more moderate Sikh leaders.

Having been coached and financed at the end of the 1970s by Mrs. Gandhi's younger son, Sanjay, who saw him as an instrument for splitting the Akali Dal, the Sant effectively pushed the party to more and more extreme positions. Its thirty-three demands included recognition of Sikhism as a separate religion and Amritsar as a holy city, the extension of the Punjab's boundaries, greater rights over shared rivers, a larger part of the nation's development funds, regional control of taxation, and political decentralization.

In spite of her rhetoric, Mrs. Gandhi refused to grant even minor, symbolic concessions, prompting Bhindranwale to step up the violence in early 1984. Sikh leaders burned copies of the constitution, and terrorists killed Congress (I) politicians, Sikhs opposed to violence and innocent by-standers. The prime minister responded by giving the Army wide ranging powers of arrest and seizure, imposing censorship and curfews, and using the preventive detention laws to arrest Sikhs. She also appealed to Hindu communalism, thereby exacerbating Sikh fears of domination by others. This, combined with her unwillingness to offer the slightest conciliatory gesture, drove moderate Sikhs to resistance as well. Soon the country was faced with a full-blown insurgency in its agricultural heartland and showpiece.

Finally, on June 6, 1984, Mrs. Gandhi attempted to crush the monster she had helped create. Troops were sent in to clean out the fanatics from the Golden Temple. They killed about a thousand people, including the extremist chieftains. Thereafter, the prime minister basically ignored the religious hatred resulting from the attack, and made no serious attempt to placate the Sikhs or to resolve the Punjab's problems. In this atmosphere she was gunned down.

Indira Gandhi's legacy was a sad one: communal enmity, the weakening of parliamentary democracy, and a steady erosion of capable leadership within her own party. The dangers to India's freedoms, to its fragile if increasing prosperity and to its unity were obvious. Rajiv Gandhi, who followed his mother as prime minister, had to do what Nehru did: defeat the forces of revenge by promoting reason and tolerance.

In a sense, Rajiv's task was more formidable than his grandfather's, for India had been traumatized by 429 racial or religious riots in 1984; Nehru was appalled when a mere 23 broke out in one of the years he held office. At times, this required resorting to force—which meant calling in the army, though, not the police, with their growing reputation as abettors of violence. To be sure, such inevitable dependence on the military could trigger a coup d'état, or at minimum heighten tensions between Sikh and Hindu soldiers, but the risk had to be borne.

Most observers believed that Rajiv Gandhi would prevail—temporarily, at any rate. The splintered opposition, especially the fanatical, corrupt Hindu groups vulnerable to bribes and offers of power, found it very hard to forge a national union.

The outlook for the longer run was more tentative. Nonetheless, several underlying elements of strength—and of weakness—suggested that the country and its liberties will survive further "dangerous decades."

First, Mrs. Gandhi's death stimulated a new political competition in New Delhi that reduced the overconcentration of power she fostered and rectified distorted balances among the states. The consequent curbing of the central government's bureaucratic medling helped neutralize, if not altogether eliminate, demands for regional independence.

Second, India was a significant industrial power. It had a network of mutually dependent factories and industries, transportation and communications facilities, and food suppliers. They interlocked the subcontinent's various parts, so that any real attempt to break up the relationship—say, by creating a Sikh nation called "Khalistan"—would founder. The Punjab, India's breadbasket, could not afford a political divorce from its markets, nor could any conceivable government in New Delhi allow such a development. India's leaders knew this. Even its separatist advocates were simply engaged in a serpentine game whose point was not to dissolve the union but to increase their share of the national power—or in too many cases, to fill their purses.

Third, although India was disunited, oddly enough that disunity itself limited the possibilities of geographical fragmentation. If much as the country as a whole was divided by religious, caste, class, linguistic, and ethnic disparities, so too were its states. The dream of Khalistan—

envisioned as a thin sliver of territory stretching from the Punjab almost to Bombay—could never be a reality, because social hatreds, clashing economic interests and religious minorities would split it apart.

Eventually, the Sikhs and the other discontented peoples of India had to settle for major concessions on taxation, local management of development spending, and symbolic gestures—for instance, recognition of the separateness of the Sikh religion. In fact, what India needed was a return to the traditions of the first Sikh. Five hundred years ago, Guru Nanak chose a Muslim musician, Mardana, and a Hindu peasant, Bala, to travel the countryside with him as he created a new faith. Together they preached, "There is no Hindu; there is no Mussulman; we are all brothers." Only this message, reinforced where necessary by military power, allowed India to preserve its freedoms and build on its economic accomplishments.

India's experience since independence underlined five fundamental lessons about the process of development:

First, as the Punjab brilliantly demonstrated, advances in agriculture complemented industrialization and the modernization of social services, rather than hindered them. The Punjab's small land-holders vastly profited from the "green revolution." They benefited particularly from the scraping of national controls over farm prices, government investments in the rural suprastructure, and the application of science to the poorest plots of land. These measures, in turn, generated a "virtuous cycle" of increasing peasant incomes and a higher demand for both agricultural-related products and consumer goods. Small industries multiplied to meet this need and allowed "wealth to fructify where it can bring the fatest growth."[17] Grandiose five year plans emphasizing heavy industrialization were unnecessary and counterproductive. As the Punjab's peasant agriculture had shown by 1985, "the world's largest and poorest industry is suddenly the one in which productivity can increase fastest."[18]

This lesson of the "virtuous cycle" extended beyond the Punjab to any nation with an unused agricultural potential. During the 1970s, seventeen of the twenty-three fastest growing economies in the world (including Colombia, the Ivory Coast, and Malaysia) also scored agricultural advances of more than 3 percent a year. Conversely, where farmers were not left free to follow their comparative advantage, entire economies stagnated, retrogressed, and often starved. Among the seventeen countries with the least growth in GNP during the 1970s (e.g.,

Ethiopia, Ghana, Guinea, and Zaire), eleven had agricultural growth rates of less than 1 percent a year.

Second, contemporary India illustrated the vital role of education in the quest for progress. In those provinces where education flourished, such as the Punjab, people eagerly grasped the opportunities which nature offered to them. In states where education languished, such as Bihar, economic and political anarchy prevailed. India also illustrated that there was no linear relationship between formal education *per se* and economic, social, or political advances: the state of Kerala had the highest rate of literacy in India and yet suffered from a lack of skilled doctors, technicians, and engineers. The reason was clear: education in Kerala, administered by teachers who had bought their posts with bribes, was of inferior quality and unrelated to the needs of the state or the country.

Third, India and particularly the Punjab, indicated the importance of decentralizing power in ways that engaged the attention, the allegiance, and the participation of the lowliest peasant. On the economic level, the Punjab's farmers—once equipped with a minimum of scientific techniques—were in a far better position than New Delhi's planners to respond productively to new challenges. Freed to pursue their own advantage by price decontrol, the big and little farmers of the Punjab creatively used their intimate knowledge of soils, weather, crops, irrigation, and markets to fill India's breadbasket.

Fourth, the Indian situation showed that national leaders who treated symbolic issues with disdain ran grave risks of inciting revolution. Again and again—in the Kashmir, in Andhra Pradash, in Assam—Mrs. Gandhi refused to grant requests of a purely symbolic nature. Her greatest mistakes were in the Punjab. Moderate Sikh leaders had repeatedly suggested that she modify the Indian constitution to recognize Sikhism as a separate religion, to declare Chandigarh as the sole capitol of the Punjab, to sanctify Amritsar as a holy city, and to make slight modifications in the borders of the Punjab to encompass predominantly Sikh villages. Each of these actions would have cost little money, left the Indian union intact, and engendered only verbal opposition from rightwing Hindus. Yet, unlike the Meiji rulers of early Japan, Mrs. Gandhi failed to compromise on issues which had no importance to the national welfare but were of volatile emotional significance to many people. Her intransigence reaped a whirlwind and left her son Rajiv in a position where moderate Sikh leaders who wished only to preserve their religion's symbols had virtually disappeared.

Fifth, the saga of the world's largest democracy—bloodied and battered though India was—demonstrated that people who had once experienced the raucous politics of a liberal democracy could not long be satisfied with demagogic promises or even by economic growth alone. Mrs. Gandhi's electoral disaster in 1977 after her imposition of emergency rule, her humiliating defeat in Andrha Pradash by Rama Rao, and the Punjab insurrection in 1984 all indicated that Indians did not wish to trade a truly responsive political process for obedient submission, hero worship or even the promise of more bread. The events in India demonstrated, as James Traub observed, that "millions of uneducated Indians have taken seriously the promises of democracy."[19]

8

Stumbling Giants:
China

A society without human rights is a fearful society. Only with respect for human rights can we achieve real modernization for the people.

—Street poster, People's Square,
Shanghai, 1978

In 1949, when Mao began to experiment with one quarter of mankind, many Westerners uncritically praised his regime. Admittedly, Mao had ended the brutal rule of Chiang, who used to bury his enemies alive; Mao distributed land to the starving peasants; and he dispatched "barefoot" doctors and teachers into the hinterland to spread health, literacy, and communism.

If, as Marx once claimed, he "had set Hegel on his head," Mao did the same to Marx. Refuting all of the logic of Marxism, Mao, the son of a kulak, jettisoned the industrial proletariat as the vanguard of revolution and mustered the energies of China's teeming peasantry. Yet ironically, in the Marxist hagiography, Mao ranked just after Marx and Lenin for he had, in the opinion of Jan Myrdal, solved the problem of how "the revolution can be prevented from degenerating." Han Suyin believed that, unlike Stalin, "Mao had an ever-present concern with the practical application of democracy."[1]

Until Mao's death in 1976, many non-Marxists also revered Mao's "pure" brand of Communism. One visitor said that the Chinese model represented "the incarnation of the new civilization of the world." Another described China as "a kind of benign monarchy ruled by an emperor-priest who had won the complete devotion of his subjects."

Simone de Beauvoir discovered that "life in China today is exceptionally pleasant." Even David Rockefeller, a pillar of capitalism, testified
that Mao had produced "national harmony . . . efficient and dedicated
administration . . . and high morale and community of purpose."[2]

In elevating Mao to sainthood (or, at least, to the ranks of superb,
humane administrators) followers of the cult ignored the ravages of
famine, the corruption of the bureaucracy, the repeated failures of Mao's
campaigns, the humiliation of intellectuals, and the stripping of the
countryside to enrich the cities in a quest for industrialization. When
taxed on the horrors of collectivization and the brutal purges which
sporadically swept China, admirers of Mao excused the "benign
emperor's" actions as "necessary" steps in guaranteeing an enthusiastic national consensus and in solving the economic problems of a
huge, backward, and overpopulated country.

The great awakening came only after Mao's death, the defeat of the
"Gang of Four" and the ascension to power of Deng Xiaoping in 1976.
Deng—an old colleague of Mao's who had personally suffered degra-
dation and whose son was paralyzed by Red Guards who threw him
from a roof during the "Cultural Revolution"—set China on a new
"fourth way" to progress and honestly revealed what had really gone
on in such typical provinces as Shanxi.

SHANXI: THE TARNISHED DREAM

In agriculture, learn from Dazhai.

—MAO

In 1948, when William Hinton, an American farmer educated at Harvard, first visited the village of Long Bow in Shanxi province, he found
a land which had been devastated by starvation, rapacious landlords,
and Japanese invaders.[3] The people subsisted on wild berries and corn
cakes. During Hinton's initial voyage, the Communists took over, distributed land to the peasants, executed the more notorious landlords,
and ushered in an era of equality.

Shanxi offered a promising environment for the Communist experiment, although "it was just starting to emerge from centuries of medieval poverty and ignorance."[4] Once an independent kingdom, the
mountainous Shanxi area had maintained verdant, grain-exporting fields
bordering the Yellow River. In China, the "Shanxi man" had gained

fame as independent, stoical, diligent, hard-working, person, skillful in business, not unlike the Sikhs. "He who holds Shanxi, holds the world," an ancient Chinese proverb said of this once prosperous region.

In fact, despite the cruelties of civil war and Kuomintang domination, Shanxi seemed a far better economic gamble than did the Punjab. Because the Indian province and Shanxi resembled each other in many ways—water resources, quality of soil, population size, rates of literacy and health—a comparison of the subsequent histories of these regions offered more enlightenment than a general comparison of the vast and often differing landscapes of China and India as a whole.

At the time of gaining independence, Shanxi enjoyed several economic advantages over the Punjab. Shanxi possessed significant reserves of coal and iron ore while the Punjab was barren of minerals or energy sources. Shanxi lay closer to its capital and had fewer mouths to feed. Its people spoke the same language, had a common culture, and did not suffer from the hobbles of religious hatreds or caste restrictions.

In the early days of the revolution, particularly between 1949 and 1952, Shanxi experienced genuine advances. Hinton, in *Fanshen* and *Shenfan,* documented these changes in one Shanxi village, Long Bow. Although the village could hardly be considered typical (it was partially industrialized and had a significant minority of Catholics), the history of Long Bow presented an unmatched chronicle of alterations since 1948.

Before the Communists came to Long Bow, Hinton observed, the peasants had to give most of their crops to landlords. In times of bad harvests, the tenants starved or sold their children. When the Communists won the civil war, the peasants of Long Bow gained ownership of their land and worked cooperatively to fashion a new way of life. They planted trees and vegetable gardens, created a canal, sent their children to school, worked in new brick-making and cement factories, and benefited from free medical care and some industrialization. By 1971, however, when Hinton again reported on Long Bow, he found that the village had failed to escape the cycle of the seasons and had lost its forward thrust.

Like the rest of Shanxi, Long Bow had staggered through two further stages of the Chinese revolution that resulted in military conflict between different ideological factions.

In 1958, seeking the Great Leap Forward, Peking imposed an essentially Stalinist model on Shanxi. The government collectivized agriculture, purchased food at below-market prices to feed industrial workers, decreed production quotas, paid peasants in equalized work credits, and used peasant labor to construct new enterprises. Basically, the government attempted to exploit the Shanxi peasants in an unrelenting drive toward rapid industrialization. Food production dropped, "backyard" steel furnaces failed, and grand plans issued from Peking ignored local needs, resulting in a decrease in cultivated land in Shanxi. Only later did the authorities admit that some 16.5 million Chinese died from famine and political repression during this period.

In 1962, pragmatic Chinese leaders headed by Zhou En-lai attempted to rectify the excesses of the Great Leap Forward in Shanxi. They allowed a partial return to the cultivation of private land, encouraged trade fairs where produce could be sold for profit, and decentralized decision making. "Teams," essentially the traditional villages, were now allowed to decide local matters of irrigation and technology. Abandoning a strict Stalinist approach, Zhou En-lai called for "agriculture first." Production in Shanxi increased but only barely kept pace with population growth.

The left faction in the party did not condone this hesitant return to "feudal" and "capitalistic" practices. Attempting to reach a purer stage of Communism, Mao unleashed the Cultural Revolution in 1966 which, among other effects, sent hundreds of thousands of urban people to Shanxi "to learn from the peasants" and, not incidentally, relieve pressure on the cities.

In Shanxi—indeed, in China as a whole—the Dazhai commune emerged as the greatest symbol of the Cultural Revolution. A totally collectivized brigade of eighty-three families living on 250 acres of Shanxi land, Dazhai was supposedly an example of self-reliant, highly productive, industrious, happy, and fully socialized farmers. When Mao proclaimed, "In agriculture, learn from Dazhai," millions of posters, gardens, mountain walls, even songs and poems repeated the slogan throughout China. Dazhai became a shrine visited by millions of Chinese and foreigners. According to party publicists, Dazhai peasants had voluntarily relinquished their private plots, spread income equally among families, worked tranquilly with each other, and boosted grain yields to unparalleled levels. The party dispatched a special bureaucracy of "Dazhai Inspectors" throughout China to ensure that all communes lived up to the model's results.

Questioning the Shanxi example, journalist Russ Munro suspected fraud when he found that the self-sacrificing peasants of Dazhai wore new leather shoes as they picked fruit in their model, but muddy orchard.

After Mao's death, Deng Xiaoping admitted that the state bureaucracy had secretly contributed millions of *yuan* and thousands of additional laborers to subsidize the exemplary, but fake commune. The commune leader falsified production figures and, according to *The People's Daily*, killed 141 people during the persecutions of the Cultural Revolution.

Food production in Shanxi stood in stark contrast to the success of the Punjab. There, as we have noted, peasant capitalism aided by wise government policies and infrastructure investments wrought an economic miracle—in spite of the Club of Rome's computers, the supposedly untainted oracles of our time, which had prophesized an Indian megafamine. As late as 1983, such Western idealists as Stephen Spender joined with such Marxists as Paul Sweezy in mythologizing life in Shanxi. Chinese Communism, they once believed, would not only feed the people but would also create a liberated and more harmonious communal life for the peasants.

Reality in Shanxi forced such ardent Maoists to recognize that China went through famine even up to 1981, and that the Cultural Revolution sacrificed millions in the rural areas in exchange for an economic disaster. Scarred, bloodied, but honorable, India, as exemplified even in the turbulent but rich Punjab, came much closer to satisfying the ideal of providing both bread and freedom to the world's peasants.

Perhaps learning from the Punjab (or the even closer illustrations of land reform in Taiwan and South Korea), the new Chinese leadership of 1977–78 radically revised state operations once again in Shanxi. Deng allowed a return to private sales of grain, profit-oriented markets, and restitution of the household as the basic governor of production. The peasants became virtual sharecroppers as the state administration retained control over the land but allowed the peasants to sell their excess produce on the private market.

Peking more or less abandoned its policy of collectivization in Shanxi. The "responsibility system" prevailed, encouraging family farming. The individual household cultivated a plot of land assigned by the commune, turned over the produce to a state purchasing agency, but kept the power to consume or sell any surplus beyond its particular quota. Since 1977, state investment in agriculture grew markedly, agricultural science was freed from ideological restrictions, and new industries produced more products, including chemical fertilizers, and consumer enticements for purchase by the peasantry. Peking reversed its urban bias and allowed food prices to rise with market demand. Except for a lack of political freedom, these policies bore a remarkable resemblance to the Indian model.

The initial results were impressive. In the short time between 1977 and 1979, for example, Shanxi grain production went up by 17 percent, meat increased by 35 percent, and fruit crops soared by 60 percent. By 1980, household incomes in Shanxi, supplemented by private gardens had risen by 15 percent and, by 1986, had almost doubled. The average grain rations allocated by Shanxi communes to the individual rose from 330 pounds a year in 1977 (bare subsistence level) to 720 pounds in 1985.

Nonetheless, the State Statistical Bureau still estimated that the real income of city workers exceeded that of Shanxi peasants by 100 percent, a higher degree of inequality than generally existed in the Punjab. China still had to import significant amounts of grain while India could depend on the Punjab for a surplus.

By 1982, Nicholas Lardy, the foremost American expert on Chinese agriculture, estimated that food production had returned to the levels which existed before the Sino–Japanese War. This represented a modest, real improvement since 1949 but one that hardly matched the Punjabi miracle. By 1985, food in Shanxi was more readily available and the rate of population growth had fallen drastically to 1.3 percent annually, offering substantial hope that Shanxi could defuse the "population bomb." Public health in Shanxi vastly improved: before 1949, the average peasant lived to twenty-five but, by 1985, the peasantry had achieved a life expectancy of sixty-four. As in the Punjab, infant mortality during the same period dropped by about 60 percent and a whole new generation of literate children was created.

In the early 1980s, when William Hinton returned again to Long Bow, he found that an asphalt highway connected the village to other hamlets in Shanxi, new factories had sprung up, and corn production was mechanized. By adding potash, phosphorus, and nitrogen to fertilizer, the peasants doubled the yield of crops and even exceeded the level achieved at Hinton's own farm in Pennsylvania. Almost every family also raised pigs and vegetables which they sold to a nearby industrial city.

A virtuous cycle had begun in Shanxi as it had earlier in the Punjab. Between 1978 and 1985, agricultural income doubled. Led by the richest peasants, twenty thousand farming families invested $840,000 in 1985 in creating 400 industrial and commercial enterprises. These, in turn, provided many of the goods needed by the farmers and 40,000 new jobs which instantly eliminated unemployment in the province.

Problems remained: Shanxi's soil had reached about its highest level of productivity and further increases required new technology. Peasants displaced from the land could not, however, be absorbed in Shanxi's cities and required new jobs in small-scale industry. Although the ranks of starving peasants decreased, the gap between rich and poor peasants increased. (The richest fifth of peasants in China received about 36 percent of per capita income and the poorest fifth, some 9 percent.)[5] Such disparities allowed old Maoists to stir the cauldron of disatisfaction in Shanxi.

Yet, in Shanxi as in the rest of China, it seemed most likely that Deng Xiaoping was correct when he declared in 1984, "We have repudiated the Cultural Revolution in its entirety. Isn't that enough? Do I have to burn joss-sticks and swear an oath before Buddha?"[6] The intensity of Deng's oration indicated the deep hope of China's leaders that they had left the upheavals of Mao's period behind forever.

CHINA UNDER MAO

We have wasted twenty years because of radical leftist nonsense.

—Hu Yao-Bang
Secretary General, Chinese
Communist Party, 1985

Shanxi reflected in microcosm the convulsions China suffered under the despotic rule of Mao. After a promising beginning, as Paul Johnson rightly described the era, "Mao's reign was a lurid melodrama, sometimes degenerating into farce but always, in the deepest sense, a tragedy: for what he caused to be enacted was not theatre but a gigantic series of experiments on hundreds of millions of real, living, suffering people."[7]

During the first years of Mao's regime, few questioned that the nation prospered in material ways. Her economy not only recovered from the privations of invasion and civil war, but bounded ahead at a dramatic forced pace. Between 1949 and 1958, objective observers estimated that energy production went up at an astounding rate of 25 percent annually while steel production increased at almost the same speed. Industrial output in all sectors may have climbed as much as 15 percent annually. Because of an intense emphasis on heavy industry during this period, agriculture relatively lagged and yet, farm production still grew about 33 percent between 1950 and 1957.[8]

Four elements contributed to China's rapid expansion during this brief time:

Confiscation of wealth and a relative restriction on consumption allowed China to quintuple its rate of capital investment between 1950 and 1959.

China mobilized masses of previously idle peasants—who often worked voluntarily, eagerly and cooperatively—in providing a valiant source of substitute capital for building roads and dams, canals and factories.

China closely coordinated her economy with that of Russia. Russia directly contributed $3 billion in aid to China (which often had to be repaid at commercial interest), technical advisers, and advanced machinery. Russia also provided a synchronized market for rudimentary Chinese exports.

Until 1958, China followed pragmatic and flexible economic policies, relatively unconstrained by ideology. In the China of those years, as Wilfred Malenbaum and Wolfgang Stopler observed, "cold and objective appraisals were made of the stages necessary to achieve a state of continuing progress from inadequate starting points. Throughout, they demonstrated flexibility in selecting courses of action."[9]

With some modifications, most of the early Chinese policies would have fitted the economic requirements of a politically free society as much as a totalitarian one. Mao, however, added a degree of regimentation and brutality which, he hoped, ensured discipline. In 1951, in an effort to confiscate more land and to introduce "thought reform," Mao campaigned against "counterrevolutionaries." After mass rallies, cadres tried 800,000 people. In the first six months of 1951, Zhou En-lai later estimated, the government executed 22,500 people each month. Some 2 to 15 million people were killed in Mao's first postwar purge. The killings, particularly of land-holders who, in a somewhat different context, played a constructive part in modernizing agriculture in such other areas as the Punjab and the Ivory Coast, hindered the economy's growth.

In a fit of frustration between 1957 and 1959, Mao brought the Chinese economy to a shuddering halt with his reckless Great Leap Forward. This romantic, cruel attempt to compress history was Mao's effort to attain the stage of pure communism postulated by Marx. The Great Leap Forward vividly illustrated the chronic, fatal flaw of authoritarian regimes. Unchecked by countervailing institutions, uninformed of judgments other than their own calculations and visions, the ruling leaders willfully tore apart the fabric of their society and unintentionally wrecked its economy. In the short span of three years, Mao undid much of the progress achieved in the preceding decade. As he later admitted, "The chaos caused was on a grand scale, and I take responsibility."[10]

Mao ordered 90 percent of the Chinese population to join self-reliant communes. Each commune held eight thousand families and was supposed to produce its own steel, consumer goods, food, and particularly grain. (The emphasis on self-sufficiency in grain led peasants to strip the land of trees and uproot their pastures, thus increasing soil erosion and destroying the fruit and dairy industries.)

Bereft of technicians, steel and related industries collapsed. Appalled at the waste, Russia withdrew her aid and Khrushchev denounced China's leaders as "madmen."

Aggravated by drought in 1959, agriculture failed, and famine swept the nation, killing millions. Temporarily, Mao relented and turned the economy back to technocrats while he brooded over ways to reeducate the "poor and blank" peasants whom, he believed, had been misled by intellectuals and bureaucrats.

Between 1964 and 1966, Mao unleashed a counterattack on dissenters by sponsoring the Cultural Revolution, essentially a rebellion by young, xenophobic, and semiliterate Red Guards against supposed "scholar-tyrants" and inept officials. Encouraged by Mao and his wife, the Red Guards attacked universities, looted and burned libraries, and closed down technical institutes. Deng later said that only four members of the eight hundred technicians of the Metals Research Institute dared to visit their library. Any of the one hundred fifty thousand members of the Academy of Sciences who used their laboratories were denounced as "white specialists." Under these conditions, scientific activity abruptly ceased. Writers and artists were either executed or forced to abandon their work.

The Red Guards also attacked any people whom they identified with decadent foreign influences. Street mobs closed shops which sold cosmetics, dresses, sunglasses, chess sets, jazz records, and works of art. Disdaining mere sentiment, the Red Guards forbad ornate marriages and funerals, itinerant musicians, and the public display of affection.

Illiterate mobs ransacked the homes of doctors, writers, and scientists in search of "polluting" bourgeois culture, forcing them to destroy books and paintings. Surgeons, engineers, and party officials, including Deng himself, were exiled to the countryside.

Over all, according to *The People's Daily*'s eventual estimate, 100 million people suffered from political humiliation, trials, exiles, or executions. The Red Guards charged their victims' families for the cost of bullets used to execute them.

The Cultural Revolution had a corrosive effect on the idealism of the party itself, for it undermined the nation's newly established unity and decimated the morale of young people. As the Red Guards dismantled the schools and 18 million teenagers were shipped from the cities to the communes, a later government reported that 100 million young people ended up illiterate or untrained. Ironically, "the legacy of Mao's utopian venture was a generation of lost and frustrated youth." [11]

With Mao's and Zhou's deaths in 1976, the old order collapsed. [12] Mao's wife and some of her radical colleagues tried to assume power, but they were elbowed aside by a tough, disciplined old man, Deng Xiaoping, who reemerged from obscurity in 1977. Deng had repeatedly denounced the Cultural Revolution and by 1978, he dictated a series of new and pragmatic policies that rang down the curtain on Mao's dynasty. [13]

CHINA UNDER DENG

It doesn't matter whether a cat is black or white so long as it catches the mice.

—DENG XIAOPING

In 1977, a diminutive old man entered the stands at a Beijing football match. Astonished Western diplomats realized that a major event had occurred before their eyes as 80,000 people rose from their seats to cheer Deng Xiaoping's return from exile.

This small, gravelly-voiced man from Sichuan province hardly seemed a charismatic figure and yet, unlike many of his generation, he had survived a turbulent life and emerged as the elder statesman of China.

Born in 1904 as the eldest son of a wealthy landlord, Deng like Zhou had gone to France for his education and absorbed Marx's doctrines. Upon his return, he joined the Chinese Communist party in 1924 and participated in all of its important battles. He fought against warlords, survived the bayonets of the Japanese army, and weathered the fierce civil war against Kuomintang tyranny.

With Mao's rise to power, Deng served the party faithfully but not uncritically. He was identified with the Great Leap Forward and it was not until the early 1960s that his criticisms of this violent episode became known in inner party circles. In 1966, he fell victim to the Cultural Revolution. Mao's Red Guards accused him of advocating a meritocracy and dubbed him "number two capitalist roader." They blamed him for sponsoring rural reforms.

After compelling his family to testify against him, the Red Guards forced Deng to confess his "crimes of thought and action" before his exile to a cowshed. In defending his pragmatic policies, however, Deng quietly added, "My thoughts and ideas are not directed by those of Mao Zedung."

After seven years of exile, Mao allowed Deng to return to political power but, in the struggles accompanying the "great helmsman's" approaching death, Deng went into disgrace again until 1976 when Hua Guofeng temporarily assumed Mao's mantle. Deng gave Hua his support but secretly maneuvered his own protegees into positions of influence.

In 1977, he was strong enough to launch China on its boldest experiment: he turned loose the peasants in a rush for profits, unleashed a million enterprises from central state planning, welcomed technological contacts with the West, and gave qualified support to freedom of expression. In 1980, the extraordinarily resilient Deng could say "I have a clear conscience all my life. I made many mistakes. . . . Except I can say they were mistakes of good intent."[14]

In rapid succession, Deng engineered a series of basic economic reforms in China:

Learning from the Shanxi calamity, Deng first allowed freer economic policies in agriculture. In 1979, he split communes into smaller, family-based units with greater autonomy over what they grew and over prices, telling them "to get rich." Rural households gained the right to subcontract land, to engage in profit-making household industries (such as tractor repair), and to sell their produce privately. This "responsibility system" permitted farmers to specialize, diversify, hire their neighbors, and produce food at market prices for urbanities.

Reality forced Deng to increase food production in China, a country where arable land amounted to only one quarter an acre per person, as opposed to 2.1 acres in the United States. This meant that China had to feed her ever increasing people, 25 percent of the world's population, on 7 percent of the planet's cultivatable land.

Deng's new order reaped enormous benefits for the peasants. Grain yields increased from 2,947 kg a hectare in 1980 to 3,655 kg in 1983. In 1984, China harvested more than 400 million tons of grain, an unprecedented record. Simultaneously, peasants doubled the amount of land devoted to market crops—grapes, cotton, soya beans, and livestock. By 1985, "peasants in China had doubled their wheat production, through increasing productivity per square inch of their tiny plots by an annual average of 12 percent in the past seven years. By retreating from communism, China had almost instantly become the world's greatest wheat producer."[15]

While easing China's eternal food crisis, peasants also turned increasingly to small-scale industry in rural and village enterprises. These enterprises, housed in everything from shacks to brick plants, ranged from food processors to manufacturers of cement, from biogas stations to textile weavers. Owned by families or local corporations, these little industries accounted for 25 percent of village production in 1985.

Between 1979 and 1984, rural per capita incomes more than doubled to $150 a year. Some farmers earned as much as $10,000 a year while a substantial minority of rich peasants became "10,000 *yuan* households," earning $4,000 a year, the benchmark of Chinese affluence at that time. (Some peasant families checked their productivity at this point, fearing that Maoist officials, who still dominated some rural areas, would merely extort more "charitable contributions" from them.) Meanwhile, the numbers of chronically malnourished peasants dropped. In 1978, 280 million of China's peasants earned less than $50 a year; by 1984, that awesome figure declined to 24 million people.

In spite of its splendid achievements, Deng's agricultural policy faced formidable obstacles. Some 70 percent of China's land in 1986 was regarded as "low yield." Only the application of scientific knowledge, which the peasants eagerly sought, and increased mechanization of farming could achieve the projected levels of production in the next century. "We have almost reached the maximum benefits that accrue to the right policies," economist Qian Jiaja said in 1984, "any leap forward will have to come from science and technology."[16] There was indeed great room for improvement since China still lagged behind the productivity of the Punjab and even Taiwan in its yield per acre.

Success in mechanizing agriculture, however, entailed the displacement of peasants from the land into industry. This, in turn, required a further expansion in small-town enterprises in order to absorb surplus labor since, by 2010, some 400 million ex-peasants were expected to live in rapidly growing small towns.

The new Chinese leadership envisaged a major program of rural industrialization, spurred by market forces, which would redeploy peasants into rural industry, while avoiding the costs of urbanization and coerced labor. In fact, the number of self-employed small entrepreneurs

(those who hired seven or less workers) whom Mao had once stigmatized as the "tail of capitalism," jumped from 140,000 in 1978 to more
than 7.5 million in 1984.

Deng's bold experiment also introduced wide ranging economic reforms
in China's cities and urban industries. By 1985, Deng had decentralized
control over China's 390,000 state-owned enterprises. Companies paid
business taxes to the central government but retained profits for reinvestment or bonuses. The state granted a high degree of self-manage-
ment to each factory.

Both managers and workers benefited from an incentive system which
rewarded high-quality production and the ability to surpass quotas specified under the "responsibility system." In many instances, the government allowed companies to break the "iron rice bowl," that policy
which once guaranteed job tenure regardless of the shoddiness of work.
Particularly on the coast, the regime encouraged regional enterprises to
compete against each other and allowed *songbang*—a "loosening of the
ropes"—to devolve decision-making powers from the centre to regions
and individual companies.

The initial results, while not as spectacular as in agriculture, were
impressive. Between 1978 and 1983, industrial production increased by
about 50 percent, construction activities went up 60 percent, and transport grew by about 61 percent.

Certain enterprises boasted particular success stories:

In 1975, the Zigong steel-casing plant, once paralyzed by the Cultural Revolution, tried to resume production. Initially, its management
could not even afford to buy bamboo sleeping mats for the workers.
After a period of recuperation, the new management introduced Deng's
reforms on a trial basis in 1979. Within a year, the value of the plant's
production of steel valves quadrupled. As wage incentives motivated
the workers, production of steel casings jumped from 1,500 units a year
in 1979 to 10,000 in 1984. The wages for workers doubled since 1979
to $600 a year in 1984. The director of the factory, a party member,
said that "we tell the workers to love their country and factory and to
work hard." But he added, "we also teach them that they should become
wealthy."[17]

In the booming Shenzhen economic zone near Hong Kong, China
Excelsior Aluminum Company enjoyed a similar success. This factory
illustrated another aspect of Dengist policies; the launching of joint
enterprises with foreign interests and technology. A Hong Kong private
investor advanced most of the capital. Australia furnished the ingots.

Katagi Aluminum Company of Japan supplied much of the machinery and a corps of technicians to instruct the Chinese laborers. The factory produced three times as many aluminum sheets as other Chinese enterprises.

Beyond improving the production of traditional heavy industries, China moved into the realm of high technology. By 1985, China exported computer software to Japan and the United States. The Tianjin Research Institute manufactured the first Chinese fiber optics in 1979, those miraculous filaments which automatically controlled Peking's new subway. Innovative industries were created under Deng's guidance for lasers, biotechnology, and aquaculture (a booming industry in a nation which had 8 billion hectares of fishing grounds).

Chinese planners pinned much of their hopes for the future on the development of nineteen free economic zones and cities located along the country's coastal rim. Modeled after Singapore and Hong Kong, these areas offered an "open door" to Western technology with such inducements as low taxes, cheap labor, and reduced bureaucratic controls. In return, they benefited from the import of foreign capital, technology, and efficient management. Chinese economists predicted a "three step technical transfer": a movement of technology from industrial countries to China's rim, then from the coastal areas to the interior's large cities, and thence from the cities to the small towns and villages.

The surge in industrial production and in agriculture greatly improved the welfare of the average citizen. On all the key measures used in Clark Kerr's index, China made notable progress under Deng. Between 1977 and 1985, literacy rates went up from 55 to 75 percent of the population, life expectancy increased by four years, and infant mortality dropped by 15 percent. At a rating of 69 on the Kerr index, however, China still lagged behind other countries with a dominant Chinese population. Supposedly infused with a "Confucian ethic" but ruled under different political systems, South Korea scored 82, Singapore 83, and Hong Kong 86.[18]

By certain measures, urbanites in China did particularly well. "Consumerism," encouraged by a Dengist government which told people to spend their savings, a policy deplored by Maoists, spread wildly in China's cities. Items considered as luxury goods in 1978 became universally available by 1985. A survey of urban households in 1983 revealed that 76 percent had sewing machines, 83 percent had televisions, and all had radios. Possession of bicycles more than doubled since 1978 and ownership of watches had almost tripled. Color TV sets and video cassette players became treasured items of conspicuous consumption.

Yet the gap between the privileged urbanites and the great rural majority had actually lessened since Mao's time. Under Mao, in spite of an ideology of egalitarianism, great disparities existed between urbanites and peasants, party officials and ordinary citizens. Party cadres were paid at highly unequal rates under Mao, strictly according to their position in the bureaucracy. Thus, in the late 1970s, the lowest party official in a system of twenty-four ranks received 40 *yuan* a month while those at the top got at least ten times as much.

Before Mao disappeared from the scene, the countryside particularly suffered from deprivation since the party squeezed the peasantry in order to finance urban industrialization. In the cities, people received free education and health care while in the communes, peasants had to pay for these services. Urban families earned five times the pay of peasants who actually received less income than villagers in any other part of Asia.

Under Deng, that pattern began to change. Between 1978 and 1983, as the system of private incentives paid its bonuses, the real income of peasants increased at twice the pace of urbanites. While peasant income still lagged about 40 percent behind city dwellers in 1983, the peasants, fed by their own produce, could afford about the same expenditure on manufactured consumer goods (sewing machines, bicycles, radios) as did urbanities. Perhaps more importantly, the peasants invested in their private housing. By 1985, almost 50 percent of peasant homes had been built in the years after 1980.

When Mao ruled, the party condemned such private initiatives by peasants and the materialism of urbanites. As a result of the freer economy sponsored by Deng, the official line changed. In 1985, *The China Daily* hailed the fact that young women wore cosmetics and colorful dresses, families crowded into new restaurants, and that the production of washing machines, refrigerators, and color TV sets had increased by as much as 62 percent since 1978. "Leftist thinking ignored the simple fact that consumption helps to determine production," *The China Daily* editorialized in a tortured reinterpretation of Marxism. "Some social aspirations that were once wrongly labeled bourgeois are actually the force driving modern society."[19]

While the peasantry put much of their new income into building houses, most urban residents, forced into rented government quarters, continued to live in cheap but extremely crowded conditions. In 1984, the average city dweller had only 3.7 sq meters of housing and, more often than not, three generations lived under the same roof.

Such congested living conditions bred corruption. Since the Cultural Revolution, more than 20,000 party members were found guilty of abusing their power to obtain special housing. To alleviate the crowding, Deng's regime continued to hinder urban migration but almost tripled the pace of apartment construction. On a national level, the government provided a major subvention for rentals ($8 billion in 1983) and allowed private corporations in the experimental economic zones to enter the real estate industry and build new apartment blocks.

In the long run, as the Dengists knew, neither China's crowded housing nor many of its other problems could appreciably change without severe curbs on population growth. Reluctantly under Mao and vigorously under Deng, the government took steps to alleviate the pressure.

China's population problem had deep roots. In A.D. 2, when China took its first census, 59.6 million people lived in the country. By 1949, the numbers had multiplied tenfold. Since Communist rule, the population almost doubled once again. Yet, during Mao's time, the government took little action to control population growth, both because such policies contradicted Marxist orthodoxy and because Mao thought China could afford to lose 300 million of its people in a nuclear holocaust.

In the 1970s, however, the Communists recognized the gravity of the problem and introduced stern measures to control the population expansion. Party cells received the right to decide which couples should have children. Families which agreed to limit their children to one gained special privileges.

Cadres were assigned to keep track of each woman's menstrual cycle. If a woman missed her period, she was ordered to have an abortion. By the 1980s, abortions may have outnumbered live births. Women widely adopted interuterine devices and sterilization. These measures reduced China's growth rate to 1.3 percent by 1985 but, even if people accepted the one-child family, China's population would still grow to 1.2 billion by the turn of the century.

The employment and education of these new generations presented a formidable problem to the Chinese leadership. In thrall to his anti-intellectual vision, Mao had humiliated teachers, closed down schools, shuttered the universities, and allowed mobs to loot libraries.

Even when denouncing the "spiritual pollution" of young minds and pursuing its mania for secrecy, the Deng regime tried to rectify the educational gap. By 1984, China enrolled about 2 million university students, more than triple the 1977 figure of 620,000. The quality of their education was, however, questionable.

Superannuated professors had reached an average age of sixty-five. They taught by the rote method and submitted themselves to political control. A professor who wished to conduct research had to secure the permission not only of the university's president and various other officers, but also his party committee. Denuded by the Cultural Revolution, libraries limited student access to books and journals. Within the universities, political authorities determined what was read, how the professor presented his material, and the interpretation of both facts and theories.

While the impediments were great, several developments indicated that intellectuals and scientists, like peasants and factory managers, were gaining the autonomy to do what they knew best.

Students once again began studying controversial subjects such as economics and political science, rather than Marxist theology. Government research projects were opened to competitive international standards and bidding. In some universities, such as Nankai, department heads were popularly elected for three year terms, rather than appointed because of their political reliability. Autonomous factories began to sponsor their own research projects within the universities. Groups of professors banded together to found private colleges. Healthy as such advances were, most observers questioned whether China's sclerotic universities would be allowed sufficient freedom to contribute significantly to national development.

In general, in the universities and throughout the society, stifling bureaucracy and the threat of a return to absolute dictatorship was a bottleneck to further economic and social advances.

Clearly, the people who ran Deng's pragmatic system had progressed markedly over the time of Chiang and Mao in building a framework for protecting basic individual liberties. Indeed, observers could argue that the Chinese enjoyed more freedoms, even within the bonds imposed by the bureaucracy and their grinding daily lives, than ever before in history. In certain key arenas, Deng and his fellow pragmatists dramatically reshaped Chinese politics.

On December 7, 1984—a date which may well go down in history as an important landmark in Chinese evolution—the Communist party declared its independence from doctrinaire Marxism. *The People's Daily* announced that "Marx died 101 years ago and his works are more than a century old. Some were his visions of that time, after which the situation changed greatly . . . some of his ideas are not necessarily appropriate to his time. . . . We cannot depend on the works of Marx and Lenin to solve our modern questions.'' The front-page article warned that ''to frame actual life in all its rich variety within the context of certain theses of Marxism-Leninism can only impede historical progress.'' The editorialist said that unless China adopted its own brand of socialism, it would ''lose touch with reality and be left behind'' in the race of developing nations for material advance.[20]

Marx was hardly dead in China. On December 8, in a small box, *The People's Daily* said that the original text should be altered to read, ''We cannot expect the works of Marx and Lenin at that time to solve *all of* our problems.''[21] Students and professors still had to spend one sixth of their time memorizing Marx, party theorists still labored over the problems of how to inject the law of supply and demand as well as capital's ability to generate value into standard Marxist doctrine. The Dengist spokesmen still insisted that Communism was their eventual ideal.

Yet, most analysts (including Russian and Vietnamese) agreed that Marxist doctrine was losing its grip over China's grand search for modernization. Other official news releases had presaged China's change in ideology. In 1983, Shanghai's *Social Sciences* journal first criticized Marx's *Das Kapital*. *The Red Flag* called for a search for truth ''on our own,'' unaided by Marxism. And *The People's Daily* argued that Chinese scholars would greatly benefit from access to non-Marxist theories.[22]

Without totally abandoning the rhetoric of Marxism and the ideological unity it offered to China, these announcements were ways of warning the old guard that new ideas, even ''heresy,'' were welcome in fulfilling China's goals of ''the four modernizations.''

The Dengists' first steps in changing the political structure were attempts to replace governance by the cult of personality and bureaucratic dictates with a consciously molded system of stable institutions (or *zhidu*). In his own self-depreciating way, Deng granted greater autonomy to regions, localities, enterprises, and factories. The government set up rudimentary mechanisms for consulting public opinion. In some factories, as Deng pruned the party's central powers, workers held free and secret elections of their managers.

Most important, as a system of checks and balances began to emerge, the Dengists tried to create a rule of law. Summary decisions by local lords, drumhead trials, and mass rallies of ''self-criticism'' gave way to objective courtroom procedures. A revitalized National People's Congress issued a series of new laws while universities began once again to train lawyers in their interpretation. More strictly than ever before, both the party and the government had to abide by the letter of the constitution and of the new system of laws. In an attempt to stop a new wave of corruption and crime, the police enforced the laws stridently and severely. According to Amnesty International, Chinese courts imposed about half of the world's official death penalties (for ordinary crimes) in 1985.

In addition to establishing a new system of harsh but universally applied laws, the Dengists particularly attacked bureaucratic inertia and privilege by purging the party itself and by decentralizing decision making to the lowest possible level. As early as 1981, Deng condemned the "bureaucratic phenomenon" as "the most serious problem for our nation." He bitterly criticized bureaucrats who were "sticking to ossified ideology, blindly observing absurd regulations, creating redundant organizations, employing more people than needed and avoiding decision making."[23] By 1985, the party had slashed the number of cadres under central government control by two thirds and handed over their powers to provinces, country administrators, and local entrepreneurs. These people executed decisions without first reporting to the central government.

The winds of change also affected China's intellectuals. In 1983, Deng himself apparently endorsed freedom of expression when he declared, "In mental endeavors as complicated as literature and art, it is absolutely essential for writers and artists to utilize totally their individual creative spirit. Writers and artists must have freedom. . . . No interference in this regard is permitted."[24]

Further, in 1985, the National Writers Congress met for the first time after Mao's demise and called for freedom of thought, literary expression, and the abandonment of workers' and soldiers' stereotypes. Speakers publicly condemned the purges of the Great Leap Forward and the Cultural Revolution. Hu Qili, the overseer of cultural affairs for the party secretariate, officially assured the delegates that "literary creation must be free."[25]

The People's Daily again stressed the new status of intellectuals by abandoning the Marxist position that the working masses were the key to all historical developments. It was "inaccurate," the party organ said, to view "the masses as the makers of history." Rather, scientists, thinkers and artists "are the real makers of all advanced scientific, cultural and artistic works."[26]

Whether the party leaders meant these words, however, was dangerously uncertain. In the same speech where he praised freedom of expression, Deng still maintained that the sole criterion for judging "the correctness" of literary work was whether it helped modernize the country. And, in 1983, the party sanctioned a bizarre "anti–spiritual pollution campaign" which condemned Western art forms and "bourgeois" liberalism. Ideologues declaimed that Western-style democracy was a "poisonous weed." In a highly contradictory fashion, then, the party moved toward a more open economy, a rule of law, and a degree of citizen participation while simultaneously it issued mixed signals concerning its willingness to allow artistic freedom or political liberties.

In a society which had undergone rapid, crippling changes in policy—ranging from 1957 when Mao briefly allowed "a hundred flowers to bloom" (perhaps in order to lure dissenters to their death) to the mindless repression of the Cultural Revolution—it seemed the wisest course for intellectuals to maintain a cautious silence on controversial issues.

According to Amnesty International, Deng's government still held many prisoners of conscience. The organization could give no reliable figures on the total number of people who were imprisoned in 1985, but officials estimated that perhaps 2 percent of the prison population were political offenders. The head of Peking's No. 1 Prison claimed that this figure represented a sharp decline in political prisoners since the height of Mao's terrorism when 70 percent of all convicts had supposedly committed political crimes. The government still endorsed "mass-sentencing rallies"—directly contravening its own, new criminal code—and increased the number of executions since 1982.[27]

The political prisoners included students who had participated in the "Democracy Wall" campaign of 1978, protestors against human rights violations, Catholic priests who refused to join the state church, Tibetan nationalists, and even lawyers who dared to defend their clients against the government. The prisons also confined former party cadres who had been stigmatized as supporters of the "Gang of Four."

The imprisonment of this last group, the "leftists," twisted justice ironically, for the old adherents of Mao who were still free continued to urge more repression—against, of course, those who had abandoned the "true belief." Certain areas of China, such as Shanxi and Hunan, the home of Mao, remained Maoist strongholds. Some elements in the army, disaffected by Deng's miserly appropriations, contained dangerous factions of unrepentent Maoists who did not hesitate to announce their faith in army journals. Traditional xenophobes in many regions decried the growth in Western investment, the move toward "capitalism,'' and the erosion of egalitarian ideals by ''foreign'' cultural influences.

These groups united in their opposition to such Dengist policies as creating free economic zones, allowing the growth of a new class of relatively rich peasants, favoring university graduates rather than party regulars for promotion, and purges of ultraleftists within the army.

Changes on the scale that Peking introduced, even when the swarming peasant majority welcomed them, disturbed the comfortable order for a few. Perhaps the single class within China which ''suffered'' the most was the lower rank of the 40 million member party hierarchy itself. Although the Dengists had fired one tenth of 1 percent (40,000 people) of the party bureaucarcy, unrepentant Maoists grudgingly resisted many reforms.

Technically, party officials could not engage in profit-making businesses, a galling restriction in a society where the lowliest of 800 million peasants could pursue private enterprise. Together with other members of the salaried classes, party officials bore the burden of increasing urban food prices and other forms of inflation—without getting the benefits of bonuses given to factory workers or the profits taken in by peasants.

Lacking legitimate ways for personal enrichment, a mounting number of party officials resorted to blatant corruption. According to *The People's Daily,* party members on Hainan Island imported duty-free cars, supposedly to support modernization efforts, and then sold them for a large profit to private buyers. Army officers in Fuzhou province created ''shell'' companies to scam foreign imports. Fake enterprises in Anshan, ostensibly run by the party, bought steel at low prices and fraudulently resold it to cooperatives.

Corruption not only weakened the edifice of modernization but it gave Maoists a ready-made argument for tightening the party's discipline. Rightly, Deng railed against swindlers in 1985 but ''leftists'' seized the occasion to warn again against ''decadent bourgeois thinking,'' including such irrelevant happenings as rock concerts and disco dancing.

The Dengists fought back against their ''leftist'' internal opponents on several levels. The government encouraged courts to prosecute party members, particularly those involved in speculation in foreign currency and those engaging in profit-making business. The Dengists also sponsored a severe crackdown on ordinary crime which had, in fact, increased since 1978.

In addition, the government began a systematic search for young, educated, and incorrupt leaders to infuse new blood into the body politic. This very important effort to regenerate the party was in heartening contrast to the perpetuation of "The New Class" in many Communist nations, those who blithely settled into their privileges as senility approached.

In the early 1980s, the Dengists began to transform the bureaucracy by announcing that only "young, knowledgeable, professional, and revolutionary people" would be promoted to high office. The government introduced the *zhaopin* system, actually a reincarnation of the Ming dynasty's approach, whereby middle-level cadres were selected by public advertisement and examinations open to all. As a result by 1985, the government slashed the total number of party functionaries by 34 percent, lowered their average age by seven years, and doubled the number of university graduates in official ranks to 43 percent.

Similarly, in the country's three thousand largest industrial concerns, the number of executives was cut by 25 percent and their mean age reduced by five years. Half of the managers, double the proportion of 1979, had post-secondary degrees. Although "connections" *(quanxi)* still counted heavily, as they had under Mao, and educated people still faced discrimination, the reigning pragmatists had taken major steps to establish a genuine meritocracy.

A RED REFORMATION?

China cannot develop in isolation from the world.

—DENG XIAOPING

In a nation historically plagued by violence and authoritarianism, privation and unfair privilege, it would be ingenuous to expect that reformers could abruptly sever ties with the past, overthrow tradition, and build a new society in one decade—or for that matter, in one century.

Mao tried and bloodily failed. According to to some Western estimates, Mao's quest for an egalitarian utopia, with its consequent famines and purges, cost more than 40 million lives.

Indeed, one could reasonably argue that continuity with the past rather than change was the hallmark of modern China. The spartan peasants still labored in the fields as they always had, the bureaucracy selected its madarins in traditional fashion, and Deng compared himself to Li Hongzhang, a great reformer who wished to push the backward Qing dynasty into the modern world. Candid about Chinese realities, Deng publically admitted that even Li had failed and said that he did not wish to be remembered as simply another leader of this ilk.

Would Deng's attempts to modernize China fulfill his dream of quadrupling the country's wealth by the end of the century? The fate of Mao and Li, the strains imposed by population pressures, the exhausted quality of China's poor earth, the resistance of a rigid bureaucracy—all gave reason for skepticism.

Yet there was substantial hope that the reformers might eventually succeed in the herculean task of transforming China's economy and cleaning up its Augean political household.

By dismantling 54,000 communes, the Dengists initiated a virtuous cycle in the countryside akin to other "fourth way" nations. The rich harvests created a demand for new industrial goods and services produced by rural industry, while the ranks of absolutely poor peasants dwindled.

Heavy industry, stimulated by a decentralization of management and an incentive system for workers, grew at 10.2 percent a year in the early 1980s while export trade jumped to $41 billion in 1984. The xenophobia trumpeted by Mao went into a precipitous decline as Deng admitted, "We need the financial and technological assistance of other countries."[28]

The Dengist social policies—a strict curb on population growth, an opening of housing construction to private groups, and a regeneration of education—measurably improved the peoples' welfare.

Ideologically, Deng affirmed his allegiance to socialism, declaring that "the aim of socialism is to allow all the people to become rich together, not to produce two classes."[29]

In practice, however, the Dengist apostasy created a mixed market economy, plugged into international trade, gingerly allowed a new degree of cultural freedom, tried to establish a rule of law, and cautiously dismantled the party bureaucracy.

As peasant incomes and productivity doubled in seven years, university graduates tripled, and life expectancy increased, few Chinese appeared to question that Deng's "fourth way"—whether it was called "commodity socialism" or "the tail of capitalism"—had materially improved their lives.

The reasons behind this success were clear and simple:

Deng's policies invigorated a dormant peasantry, once quiescent under Chiang's landlords and Mao's communes. As in the Punjab, the rise of the peasantry gave the initial impetus to economic growth.

By breaking the "iron rice bowl," devolving authority on enterprise managers, and rewarding good workers, the pragmatists introduced new incentives and freedoms into a command economy. While paying service to the ideals of Marxism–Leninism, the Dengists actually began to transform parts of China into new Hong Kongs and Singapores.

The government struggled to end China's hatred for the outside world and welcomed foreign capital, export links, new technology, and managerial skills along the coastal rim. Like Japan during the Meiji restoration or the Ivory Coast, Venezuela, Malaysia, and Singapore in the twentieth century, China opened its doors to the world.

The pragmatists developed their nation's human resources by rescuing a generation of young people from their rural exile, rejuvenating universities and research institutes, and cutting the powers of the bureaucracy. By paring the bureaucracy, perhaps the single greatest impediment to change, infusing the party with young technocrats, and taking the first steps towards establishing a rule of law, Deng attempted to institutionalize his reforms.

Each of these policies had in fact been adopted in other successful regions. The Dengist reforms could offer genuine options for all developing areas. There was nothing unique in the Dengist reformation, no particular policy which could be traced to a doctrinaire ideological position or even to the ineffable "Confucian ethic."

Many scholars have explained the country's success—as well as the economic achievements of Hong Kong, Taiwan, and South Korea—by reference to the values of the Chinese themselves: diligent, thrifty, family-oriented, eager for education, and willing to innovate. These qualities, as we have stressed, are indeed important and may help to explain the original impetus behind a drive to economic growth. Clearly, too, the Chinese element in other societies—Malaysia, Singapore, Indonesia—has achieved much greater material success than other segments of the population.

To ascribe China's progress solely to the people's basic ethics, however, too easily dismissed the country's dismal record under Mao and Chiang. Such a theory also overlooked the case of Taiwan, where specific policies, not a "Chinese character," accounted for the country's erratic economic history.

In the 1950s, Taiwan, like China, undertook land reform, an import substitution policy, suppression of dissent, as well as huge investments in an army and the bureaucracy. Like China, Taiwan stumbled along until the 1960s when economist K. Y. Yin launched the country on a new path. Stimulated by the creation of free economic zones, a retrenchment in government spending, and favored treatment of foreign investment, Taiwan surged for ahead of mainland China in economic growth and the provision of social welfare. The Taiwanese succeeded because "they invented ways to stimulate exports and to derive the benefits of world price competition, while still shielding sections of the domestic economy."[30] By the 1980s, China had more or less adopted the Taiwanese (and Punjabi) blueprint for the development of vastly greater resources.

No one knew whether the mainland's reforms could be maintained or even expanded in the China of tomorrow. Pessimists pointed to "leftist" strength, the lack of certain economic prerequisites (particularly, shortages in energy and transportation), the opposition of an entrenched bureaucracy, and the lack of a tradition of independent reasoning as preeminent obstacles to continued progress.

We dissent from such long-range forecasts of a return to misery. The unleashing of economic growth has created a series of new interest groups—technocrats, local enterprise managers, "rich" peasants, young party members—who have developed a vested interest in maintaining the reform process. These increasingly powerful groups would be loath to retreat to Maoist times. Further, China's 800 million peasants, the first beneficiaries of reform, seemed enthusiastic about a system that encouraged them to enjoy the fruits of their labor. They had no tangible reason, as they did under Chiang, to join a new revolution. Thus, "even as they taste a measure of the good life after three decades of tumult and austerity, China's citizens are daily making it more difficult for their leaders to turn the clock back on their economics-first policies."[31]

Will economic modernization lead to greater political and intellectual freedom? To some degree, Chinese pragmatism and the drive to modernity may, in themselves, have generated some impetus toward greater freedom since, as Kent Morrison argued in 1984, "it is possible that the liberalizing efforts of scientific and technological advancement will win [Chinese thinkers] a greater measure of intellectual freedom."[32]

After all, the government required certain types of intellectuals for its own purposes and had to grant them freedom, at least within their own realms of inquiry, if it was to achieve its economic goals. Further, under Deng, China rapidly adopted the economic techniques of Western nations and "it is no coincidence that those societies that serve as models of modernity for the Chinese today are the same liberal democracies that have carefully nurtured and zealously guarded independent thought.''[33]

Just possibly, the changes in China (and Eastern Europe) may have also shaken the political realm for, as Flora Lewis observed in 1985, ''the impulse to seek 'truth from facts,' which the Chinese have admitted, is at work throughout the Communist world. For the long term it presages some transformations that can sweep the global political landscape.''[34]

Tragically, however, one must conceed that history offered no guarantees that such predictions would come true. On a world basis, as we have remarked, economic modernization has not inevitably brought with it political liberation. There is no juggernaut which automatically advances the cause of freedom—only the lonely, difficult choices of a country's leaders.

In China, the Confucian tradition, historical inexperience with democracy, and Marxist orthodoxy all militated against the development of liberal institutions and truly independent thought.

Those who sought political freedom in China took heart from the words of Wei Jingsheng who wrote in the underground journal *Tansuo* in March 1979: ''Furthering reforms within the social system and moving Chinese politics towards democracy are the prerequisites necessary to solve all the social and economic problems which confront China today.''[35]

Sadly, however, the few brave liberals in China also had to contemplate Wei Jingshen's fate. In 1986, Wei was still serving a fifteen-year prison term for writing those words.

9

A Tale of Two Cities:
I. Hong Kong

One country, two systems. . .

—Deng Xiaoping

I n 1841, Her Britannic Majesty's servant, Capt. Charles Eliot, won
a minor skirmish with China, the "First Opium War." He seized
Hong Kong "in perpetuity" at the behest of merchant-adventurers who
wished to use the port as a center for exchanging India's opium for
Chinese tea and silk.

Captain Eliot, a gracious if unabashed colonialist, promised the four
thousand fishermen on the island that they would be secure "in the
free exercise of their religious rites, ceremonies, social customs . . .
and in the enjoyment of their private interests."[1]

Unimpressed by the acquisition of "a barren island with hardly a
house on it," Lord Palmerston, the foreign secretary, recalled the officer to England in disgrace for accepting such a miserly prize.

In 1984, Communist China signed a draft agreement with Britain
returning the crown colony—now a major exporter of textiles and
computers, crowded with 5.6 million people, and boasting a per capita
income of $5,000 annually—back to mainland control in 1997. China,
too, promised to preserve "all the rights and freedoms which the people of Hong Kong now enjoy" for at least half a century after the
reunion.

Peking had good reason to covet Hong Kong. In 1985 alone, Hong

Kong purchased over $4 billion worth of Chinese exports (usually for shipment elsewhere) while China imported $1 billion in goods from the colony. The colonial enclave, slightly over 1,000 square kilometers in size, was an economic jewel, an eminently successful experiment in "pure" capitalism. From 1945, when Hong Kong had a population of only 600,000 people, this crown colony enjoyed the freedoms and protections of British rule and grew economically at an average rate of 9 percent a year—far ahead of China's capricious record and thrice the real growth of Western nations.

In 1983, hardly the most propitious of years in world economics, exports rose again by 10 percent and accounted for 90 percent of Hong Kong's production. In one year, 1984 to 1985, Hong Kong's trade with China (second only to that with the United States) soared by 111 percent.

Significantly, Hong Kong—a distinctly Asian city whose population was 98 percent Chinese—had achieved twice the rate of growth and a far higher per capita income than her "sister" cities, Canton and Shanghai. Hong Kong still had hoards of poor people but the disparities between the rich and poor had steadily decreased since 1945. Canton and Shanghai, in contrast, commanded a vast supply of resources, oil, and food. They had comparable histories of Western contact (and exploitation) up until 1948, and their citizens participated in a common traditional culture. Shanghai had a much better developed industrial base. Yet, under Mao, the mainland cities with all of their advantages had lagged behind Hong Kong, a bastion of capitalism in the immediate shadow of the world's greatest experiment in collectivism.

The record of these three Chinese cities provides the best natural experiment we have for evaluating the relative advantages of capitalism and communism in Asia. As one of the last remaining examples of genuine laissez-faire practices, Hong Kong had clearly surpassed her neighbors.

Next to Japan and Singapore, Hong Kong's citizens had the highest per capita income in Asia. Its people lived longer, ate more, and had a higher rate of literacy than those of Canton and Shanghai. They read what they wished, traveled freely, and did not fear the midnight call of the local commissar.

Life was hardly perfect in Hong Kong. Until 1982, as colonial subjects, its people did not vote. As capitalist "lackeys," the great majority worked very hard, lacked the total security which the workers once possessed in nearby Canton, and at times, suffered from brutal factory conditions.

Housing was particularly shocking because Hong Kong had no zoning laws and refugees from the mainland had to subsist in squatters' huts, often abutting luxurious apartment buildings on Hong Kong's hills. Since the government did not use deficit financing or issue bonds, it relied heavily on the sale of public lands to unscrupulous bidders who had no concern for the general welfare. As a result, an unsavory mass of tin shacks, often "protected" by extortionists from secret societies, rose above one of the world's most spectacular harbours. Expatriate businessmen, for example, paid HK$ 25,000 a month for beautiful apartments in 1985—ten times the total wage of an average Chinese who lived in crude shanties next door to them.

Yet millions of mainland Chinese, particularly from Canton and Shanghai, made the illegal and often dangerous trek to Hong Kong where real incomes were much higher. According to public opinion polls, they came for two tangible reasons: first, attracted by Hong Kong's glitter and bustle, they sought the often elusive goal of "opportunity"; second, and of almost equal importance, they wanted "personal freedom." By 1985, more than half of Hong Kong's population was made up of people who were born in China.

The refugees often found what they sought, for Hong Kong's annual per capita income in the 1980s was more than twice as high as Shanghai, China's richest city, and at least three times that of adjoining Canton, its linguistic and cultural twin. While such per capita figures hid a great gulf between the wealthy and the rickshaw drivers of Hong Kong, the fact remained that the real quality of life had improved for even the poorest.

On Kerr's combined measure of infant mortality, life expectancy, and adult literacy, China scored 69 and Hong Kong rated 86 (while Japan stood at 96).[2] Life expectancy in Hong Kong reached an astonishing seventy-six years in 1985. Since a high score on this physical quality of life index required broad educational opportunity, excellent health care, and good nutrition for the entire population, it was clear that Hong Kong had achieved an advanced level of welfare for its people—higher than nations such as Argentina, Yugoslavia, and Portugal which had comparable per capita incomes.

Politically, Hong Kong's people enjoyed liberties and protections absent in China, South Korea, or Taiwan. Its citizens benefited from extensive educational and public services. Fifty percent lived in heavily subsidized, if still inadequate housing. Hong Kong had a free and vociferous press, a legal system based on English precedent, an untrammeled television network (often secretly watched in China itself), and complete freedom of speech. Clan, religious, political, and provincial associations operated freely.

Even in times of violent crisis—such as the Cultural Revolution in 1967 when Maoists rioted or the sporadic street battles between Maoists and Kuomintang supporters—the police "adopted passive and humane crowd control techniques."[3]

Trade unions, usually dominated by Communist Chinese, organized freely but seldom exercised their right to strike. This relative passivity was not due to government dictation but rather to mainland politicians who had ordered union leaders to maintain an atmosphere of economic tranquility during the critical transition period up to 1997. Like the most doctrinaire of capitalists, the Dengists feared that overt manifestations of labor unrest might lead to a flood of capital from Hong Kong.

While Hong Kong was strong in protecting individual liberties, it was hardly a democracy before 1982. Until that year, only minor local council members were elected, while the British governor appointed members of the colony's Executive and Legislative Councils. Hong Kong's elite of British and Chinese businessmen traditionally dominated the political order and provided basic social welfare services.[4] At the insistence of Peking, the British colonialists did not even hold a referendum to inquire what Hong Kong's people really wanted for their future.

Church, labor, and social agency leaders vigorously advocated direct democracy. Yet, a strange melange of other groups wished to continue a system which they euphemistically described as "consultative democracy." Communists rightly feared that they would lose elections and that a bad precedent would be set for Hong Kong's future in 1997. Businessmen and communists alike did not wish to disturb Hong Kong's astounding economic growth by introducing a system that might produce "demagogues" who would demand uneconomic forms of social welfare. Kuomintang partisans feared confrontation with communists.

About the only powerful group that verbally advocated a move toward democratization was the higher government officials themselves, including the British governor, Edward Youde. In 1984, a British "green paper" provided for elections to major political councils and a gradual transition to the election of the Governor. With this action, Youde placed himself in the honorable tradition of Sir John Pope Henessey, Hong

Kong's Irish governor from 1877 to 1882 who personally overthrew a despised oligarchy of Englishmen who then ran Hong Kong. Henessey first gave the Chinese community a share in the management of public affairs.

Even the limited reforms of the green paper did not secure enthusiastic popular support. The communists described it as a sneaky way of undermining Peking's eventual "miniconstitution" for Hong Kong while some conservatives feared that the society might lose its liberal institutions by introducing mass participation.

In reality, the average people of Hong Kong wished to preserve their real freedoms—political, legal, and economic—rather than tampering with the system. Public opinion polls in 1982 indicated that 95 percent of Hong Kong's population simply wanted to maintain the status quo. By this, they meant specifically that they desired continued assurances, whether under British or Chinese rule, that they would enjoy "freedom of speech," "a comfortable living environment," "freedom of choice," and "economic freedom." Interestingly, in an intensely materialistic society, they rated an intangible benefit, "freedom of speech," as *the* most important value which any government should conserve.

This reluctance to change the political order also had solid economic roots, for Hong Kong had leaped ahead of urban areas on the mainland without marked inflation, unemployment, a forced accumulation of savings, political killings, or the imposition of Maoist totalitarianism.

The city-state's startling growth took place in an atmosphere of unbridled capitalism.[5] Its elite of 40,000 Chinese and British businessmen advocated complete freedom of imports, foreign exchange, prices, wages, and foreign investments. Private corporations controlled both the economic and social life of the colony. "The Bank" (The Hong Kong and Shanghai Banking Corporation) alone had assets twice as large as the annual GNP. The income gap between rich and poor had lessened over the decades while the real income of all greatly increased.

Moreover, Hong Kong prospered in spite of a total lack of resources, the energy crisis, and an influx of 40,000 illegal Chinese migrants annually over a period of thirty-five years. As a trading center, it survived the time when the United States banned all imports of goods which originated in mainland China and it equally prospered when Mao tried to cut all ties with the West.

No one, least of all the original British colonialists, predicted that Hong Kong would effect such an economic miracle. When Hong Kong was founded in 1841 by the luckless Capt. Elliot and opium traders, the colony's first British governor, depressed by his lowly assignment, harshly dismissed Hong Kong as "a pile of barren rocks."

Indeed Hong Kong never had timber, iron ore, rubber, minerals, precious metals, or energy resources. It had to import half of its food—and even its water—from the mainland.

Further, Hong Kong became the single most densely populated place in the world. Since 1945, Hong Kong's population grew tenfold. In spite of government efforts to slow migration, the population continued to increase at the fast clip of 3.4 percent a year as late as 1984. The downtown area of the Kowloon district contained more than 150,000 people per square kilometer. Land prices predictably soared to astronomical levels: a square foot of land in North Point cost no more than HK$ 10 in 1948 while in 1985, the same tiny parcel of land went for HK$ 4,000.

The outside world paid little heed to Hong Kong and, unlike its generosity to places such as Tanzania, did not provide aid or gifts to the colony. Like the rest of Asia, Hong Kong suffered invasion by the Japanese. It did not, however, benefit from postwar infusions of foreign aid as did Taiwan, South Korea, Japan itself, or even China during its period of Russian collaboration.

Governed by outlanders and lacking the supposed prerequisites for industrialization, the 5.6 million strivers who lived in Hong Kong nonetheless did what most so-called developing nations have utterly failed to do. Conservative economists P. T. Bauer and Alvin Rabushka credited old-fashioned virtues—fiscal responsibility, low taxes, free trade, the absence of wage and price controls and of barriers (or bureaucratic incentives) to investment, and the ability to remove profits at will. Others pointed to the availability of unlimited cheap labor, to the superior port, and to the abundance of technical skills. Roy Hofheinz and Kent Calder stressed the contribution of Confucianism, with its emphasis on savings, frugality, diligence, planning for the future, the maintenance of the family, and a stable social order.[6]

Taken individually, each of these explanations was flawed. Free enterprise failed miserably, for example, in resource-rich Zaire. Various Asian ports have withered. China exploited its millions without the same results. Nor did Confucianism have a corresponding effect in nearby Canton, despite its virtually identical cultural background.

Taken together, though, the different theories put forward helped to account for Hong Kong's fabled progress. To begin with, capitalism worked because of the stable investment climate provided under the Union Jack. Yet, absent a first-rate harbor, the colony could not have participated fully in export markets. Moreover, as George Brockway has pointed out, laissez-faire would have fallen on its face without exploiting poorly paid workers.[7] (Interestingly, China's rulers established industrial estates in neighboring Guangdong Province to sell labor at one half its Hong Kong price.) As for the "Confucian ethic," it played a role resembling that of the Protestant Ethic in Europe and North America—but only because Hong Kong's policies, unlike Mao's, allowed such values to flourish.

Whatever its components, the miracle wrought by Asian capitalism became all the more impressive when Hong Kong was contrasted with mainland urban areas possessing comparable characteristics—plus assets like iron ore, coal, and farmland. To be sure, as we have noted, communist rulers from Mao to Deng could make a few boasts of their own: much improved health services, the creation of a manufacturing base, the spread of literacy, and agricultural productivity that kept pace with demographic pressures. But no one, including Deng, denied the colony's superior performance.

Some specialists attributed China's relative backwardness to the problems engendered by sheer size. Feeding and ruling 1 billion men, women, and children, only 20 percent of them urbanized, was certainly a greater burden than administering a territory of 399 square miles. Deng reportedly commented that he could have reproduced Hong Kong's prosperity "if I had to deal merely with Shanghai."

Be that as it may, Fox Butterfield has shown that contrary to myth, prior to 1977 Mao's regime invested twice as heavily in urban areas as in the countryside, where peasants received one fifth of a city dweller's income.[8] As late as 1980, when grain imports reached an all-time high of almost 14 million tons, the government shipped most of its food purchases to the towns.

This unexpected bias added to the validity of comparing communism in China with capitalism in Hong Kong by focusing on Canton and the mainland's most advanced port city, Shanghai. The yardstick also offered clues to the impact of reunification on the country as a whole.

Besides a common language, the Cantonese and the majority of Hong Kong's people shared a commercial background and a memory of foreign domination. Canton was an important industrial center, contributing to China's position as the world's largest textile manufacturer, to its number two ranking as a producer of radios, and to such high-tech undertakings as computers, electronic microscopes, and missiles.

Conditions were better than they were before the coming of the People's Republic. According to the State Statistical Bureau, $351 in public services, as well as free education, medical care, and old-age pensions, supplemented a per capita income of $276 in 1984. The official apparatus provided jobs and inexpensive housing.[9]

The security notwithstanding, life was drab and dreary by "bourgeois" standards; thus the liveliness and consumerism of Hong Kong were constant temptations. Virtually everyone in Canton had relatives who had escaped, often by swimming the treacherous currents that separated the two cities. Migrants frequently visited with tales of good fortune and bearing such gifts as shoes, Walkmen, wristwatches, television sets (which could be connected, illegally, to the colony's TV stations), and even baskets of food originally exported from Canton.

These visits, encouraging dreams of wealth, change, and liberation, generated a daily flow of illegal immigration that neither the Chinese nor the British were able to stem completely. There is no reason to doubt that after 1997, as before it, Hong Kong will continue to cast a spell over the men and women of south China, perhaps eventually altering Canton's lifestyle.

Shanghai had its own lures. The once thriving industrial center and port had a formidable reputation for enterprise that went hand in hand with a per capita income six times greater than the rest of China's. Add to this a suffocatingly crowded agglomeration of 11 million human beings and you had what was probably the fairest mainland comparison with Hong Kong.

Shanghai factories, the most productive in the land, turned out one eighth of all goods and a fourth of all exports in the 1980s. Strong Western influences in the past, a high level of schooling, and skilled management accounted for a good deal of this relative wealth. As in Canton, workers had medical insurance, factory-subsidized apartments, recreation facilities, and lifetime jobs—that in Shanghai they could sometimes pass on to their children. (Deng, consciously emulating Hong Kong, tried to end the practice.) Clothing was better and more colorful than in the south, and many workers owned TV sets. Food was so abundant that some restaurants stayed open twenty-four hours a day.

Pure Maoists viewed Shanghai as a seedbed of problems, starting with its origin as a half-breed offspring of traditional China and dynamic nineteenth-century capitalism. The match, reflected in an exciting string of skyscrapers built on mud flats, produced a vibrant political, economic, and intellectual atmosphere—encouraging a reputation for urbane, modern, conniving ways and attracting the country's most talented, if opportunistic, people. Mao preferred to divert investment elsewhere, yet productivity grew more quickly in the "decadent," "sinful," metropolis than in the urban centers favored by revolutionary zealots. Shanghai continued to hold out unusual opportunities for personal initiative and innovation.

More dangerously, it had been a haven for liberalism and rebellion. During the Cultural Revolution it proclaimed a "People's Commune" that sought to open up civic institutions and decentralize the bureaucracy. That threat to the established order lasted only seventeen days. The "Gang of Four," which tried to seize power in Peking after Mao's death, all came from Shanghai. When Deng triumphed, the city sprouted posters demanding the "Fifth Modernization" (constitutional democracy), further economic reforms, and the granting of civil liberties.

Thanks largely to a flood of jobless, educated young people who escaped from the peasant communes where they had been forced to work until 1976, Shanghai was still restless. The returnees sought secure, well-paying positions, ration coupons, and residence permits. Alarmed by the emergence of a class of unemployed (who sporadically staged riots and sit-ins), the Deng regime imitated Hong Kong in setting up a number of "urban collectives." These neighborhood workshops, in effect experiments in private enterprise, produced much of the local goods and services. They were exempt from the central plan, were run by young entrepreneurs, and absorbed nearly half of Shanghai's high school graduates in the 1980s. Nonetheless, Hong Kong retained an irresistible attraction for budding capitalists, political dissidents, individuals pursuing wider opportunities, and talented people generally, strengthening Peking's conviction that reunion was imperative.

What will that mean in practical terms after Hong Kong's master changes in 1997? Judging from the fact that it rapidly exported capital and already had spent roughly $1 billion on New York real estate by 1984, the enclave's elite seemed pessimistic about the future. So were a number of old China hands, including Chalmers Johnson, who predicted the collapse of the local economy, a new wave of refugees and a "vast tragedy." But others, among them David Bonavia, foresaw the boldest experiment in any country in the world.

Western commentators generally inclined toward the negative assessment. London's *Economist* expected Hong Kong to become merely another "Party-run slum." The New York *Times* suggested that the regime could not permit the island to be more free than the mainland. *Foreign Affairs* was unable to find a "truly just" resolution of the colony's predicament. And *World University Times* argued that "the social mobility that an unchanged Hong Kong would generate once it becomes part of mainland China, and underlies its success, could form an intolerable threat to Chinese leadership. Money is power, and can pay for coup d'états."[10]

Possibly, just possibly, the doom-sayers were wrong, and common interests will bring about a peaceful and profitable relationship. Anticipating a marriage of yin and yang, Communist officials publicly declared their intention of preserving Hong Kong as an autonomous and capitalistic region. They promised to let it keep its own currency, legal system, free port, and free-wheeling economy. They even said that they would not attempt to shackle the press or curb public debate.

There were very solid reasons for Peking to make such dangerous commitments. The entrepôt provided one third of China's foreign exchange, helping to offset a huge imbalance with Japan, the mainland's major trading partner, and was the source of substantial direct revenues. Peking's stake in Hong Kong's shipping, real estate, cold storage, and oil-supply industries, to cite a partial list, brought in an annual income of $400 million in the 1980s. Prime Minister Zhao Ziyang went so far as to claim that mainland investments in the colony exceeded its outflow. The Communists were cautious about taking radical steps that could threaten these various sources of money.

They also wanted to take advantage of—and therefore protect—Hong Kong's abundance of technical expertise and its extensive foreign contacts. Oil exploration in the South China Sea made these assets especially important, for the country lacked the ability to develop its petroleum deposits alone—a point illustrated in 1984 by the sinking of a costly oil rig that its Navy had been towing from Japan. The colony's Western trading partners—notably the United States, the recipient of 40 percent of its exports and the largest overseas investor—pressed the mainland government to respect the legal and economic status quo.

In sum, it was not surprising that the practical Deng appeared quite willing to allow pecuniary interests to prevail over ideology. Nor was militant nationalism likely to get in the way: In 1977, when Portugal offered to return Macao—the adjacent but smaller, less prosperous territory—Peking politely refused to take it back, apparently fearing that if it did, skilled workers, investors, and traders might be frightened away from Hong Kong.

Of course, given China's history of sudden convulsions, it was always possible that a new leftist cabal could cancel any Sino–British agreement that guaranteed this city's Western institutions. Mao Zedung often sacrificed modernization to revolutionary goals, and some future Party boss might be disposed to follow his example.

On the other hand, barring a development of that kind, Hong Kong may be the stage for a unique union of political and economic opposites that ultimately could have a startling impact on China. David Bonavia even envisioned the whole mainland becoming a mere "hinterland" to Hong Kong—increasingly oriented to the profit motive, more adept at using modern methods, and less insistent upon intellectual and moral conformity.

The colony's inhabitants had little choice except to seek a reconciliation with the land of their ancestors, since the British Nationality Act of 1982 denied them residence in the United Kingdom despite the British passports they held. Public opinion polls indicated that 95 percent of them would stay on if China respected their civil and economic rights. Once reunion is accomplished, the city's technocrats could well spread out through south China, assuming positions of trust and power.

Reared in an atmosphere where the press was not only free but disputatious, the people of Hong Kong will distrust official propaganda. Accustomed to the protections of British law, they will view the activities of the secret police with resentment, perhaps resistance. Westernized and educated, they will add a leaven of disturbing individualism and dissonance to collectivist uniformity and complacency. Yet any Chinese regime bent on modernization will need their skills—as well as their leadership—and will have to treat them with caution if not tenderness.

Consequently, 1997 could mark the merging of two quite diverse ways of life, two forms of economic enterprise and two different political orders, Outside the wealthiest class, most Hong Kong Chinese believed that the mainlanders will become more and more like them. They particularly looked to China's coastal rim as a key to the future.

It was precisely the development of the nineteen cities and free trade zones in China—inspired by the Dengist vision that they would ultimately transform the interior—that gave Hong Kong a pivotal role in Asia's future. Some of these "special economic zones," the number of which constantly grew, closely adjoined Hong Kong. All of them had, ironically, once been "treaty ports," forcibly opened up to foreign trade and dominance during the colonial period.

One such zone, Shenzen, lay just across the border from Hong Kong, intimately affected by the colony's example. Already by 1985—when Hong Kong had emerged as the biggest investor in the zones, had helped to build a common transport system, and had provided the expertise for constructing and running everything from factories and power plants to hotels—it had become apparent that Hong Kong would serve as a vital pipeline of technology, a major source of capital, and a powerful example to the mainland.

HONG KONG AND THE OPENING OF CHINA'S CITIES

Whatever Hong Kong can do, we in Shenzhen can do as well or better.

—The People's Daily, 1983

In 1982, the Chinese put up a barbed wire fence around Shenzhen, a 126 square mile enclave that stretched across the northern border of Hong Kong. Ostensibly, the government built the fence to keep out smugglers. Actually, Louis Kraar suggested in 1983 that "the place is becoming so bourgeois" that the Chinese authorities wished "to seal it off from the rest of the country."[11]

Shenzhen, perhaps the most prosperous of China's free economic zones, decentralized decision making, offered incentives to foreign investment, exported its wares not only to Hong Kong but to the interior, and imported well-educated workers paid on the basis of their performance.

The results were obvious: factories, mills, office towers (including a 55-story skyscraper, the tallest in China) and sprawling housing developments sprang up. Free city markets and vendors offered refrigerators and color TV sets to consumers with friendly open smiles. The provincial leaders even envisaged the establishment of a French-run Club Med in this major new exporting center. The population of Shenzhen increased ten times between 1980 and 1985 and its people were among the few Chinese who could legally watch Hong Kong television on their imported sets.

The scope of Shenzhen's boom was so visible that one group of Chinese officials visiting the zone gleefully thought that they had wandered over the border into Hong Kong. (Other, more dour Maoists on the tour recognized where they were and decried the enticing evils of "raw capitalism," Hong Kong-style.)

Deng Xiaoping acknowledged the risks and denounced corruption in Shenzhen and other economic zones. Nonetheless, he stuck by his initial resolve and announced in December 1984, "We are embarking on another ambitious program. We regard it as a kind of revolution."

Shenzhen (as well, to a lesser extent, such neighboring areas as Zuhai, Shantou, and Xiamen) had become a laboratory for testing the economic and political symbiosis between Hong Kong and China. In a vigorous effort to attract foreign technology and investment, the government promised cheap labour, virtually free land, low or nonexistent taxes, and autonomy to completely foreign-owned companies or joint ventures. By 1985, one hundred foreign industries made deals worth $2 billion in Shenzhen.

Meanwhile, a consortium of Hong Kong and Chinese contractors began building a 240-km superhighway linking Hong Kong, Shenzhen, several other special economic areas, and Canton. Shenzhen also started construction of a new international airport, a deliberate substitute for creating a second airport in Hong Kong. Joining with the Canton–Peking and Canton–Hong Kong railways, as well as Pearl River marine transport, the transit system opened up trade and industry for a still-poor but developing regional population of 320 million people.

Across the Pearl estuary from Hong Kong, another free region, Zuhai, exempted all imports of technology and capital from customs and reduced income tax to a uniform 15 percent. Zuhai also tripled its expenditures from 1983 to 1984 in an attempt to improve roads, factory buildings, power supplies, and telephone services. A variety of companies from steelmakers to yacht manufacturers rushed in to exploit Zuhai's possibilities, and its economy blossomed. Hong Kong investors (followed by Americans and Japanese) topped all others in building new factories.

In 1985, the government joined together Zuhai, Shenzhen, Shantou (Swatow), Canton, and the primitive Hainan Island to form an "Open Coastal Economic Zone," an even greater free trade region to encourage further development. This huge new configuration, lying near Hong Kong, made the area the largest and most "open" section in China. The zone concentrated on light industry, shipbuilding, plant construction, farm implements, machinery, and electrical products. Hong Kong expertise and money poured into these industries as well as off-shore oil concessions which sprouted up on the coast of the new region.

Such areas absorbed large amounts of foreign investment, although not quite as much as China wished. Between 1980 and 1985, China took in $3.3 billion in direct foreign investment in its free trade zones. The highest proportion of money came from Hong Kong. The new investments—plus the opening of China's untapped market and its bourgeoning export industries—resulted in a healthy foreign exchange reserve of $16.5 billion in 1984.

The creation of free economic zones near Hong Kong not only aided in the economic modernization of China but also offered non-material benefits. Officials in Shenzhen, for example, argued that their experiences in that area set "positive examples" for the hinterland. As Chinese staff became acquainted with new technology and modern management, the officials said, a higher level of skills spread throughout China.

Because of a lack of university-trained managers in the new areas' commercial and financial sectors (fewer than four percent of China's 2 million managers held university degrees), the Guandong free zone established a personnel service of its own in conjunction with Hong Kong. The agency provided counseling for applicants to foreign universities, English-language testing, and supplies of educational equipment. Guandong also tried to woo 30 million overseas Chinese, many of whom passed remittances through Hong Kong, to return home and serve the goal of modernization.

While the free regions helped to augment China's "human capital," they also demanded other social changes, most importantly, a streamlining of China's bureaucracy and its laws. The intrusion of foreign influences, for example, required China to establish a completely new set of tort laws which secured property and reduced arbitrary incursions by the central bureaucracy.

China's cumbersome bureaucracy, with its conflicting and overlapping system of jurisdictions, constituted the single greatest human obstacle to a further expansion of Hong Kong along China's coastal rim. Some of the "free" regions took exceptional steps to reduce the bureaucracy's powers.

Shekou, an industrial enclave within the larger Shenzhen zone, showed the way to break through the bureaucratic barriers. Shekou radically and perhaps uniquely carried out the decentralization program advocated by Dengists. "China Merchants," an innovative corporation, controlled Shekou and turned it into a virtually independent little kingdom outside of the control of either provincial or central authorities.

Based in Hong Kong, China Merchants, a pragmatic joint venture company, ran Shekou as a truly autonomous venture. Zhang Shi Xiang, a company official, said in 1983, "We have the full right to decide what will be done in Shekou."[12] As a result, China merchants dealt with foreign investors as a single organization with the power to make all basic decisions—a drastic simplification of China's bureaucracy and proliferation of rules.

China Merchants established its own Hovercraft service to Hong Kong, a mere forty-five minutes away, and began issuing visas to tourists immediately upon entrance. Various international companies took advantage of the open atmosphere of Shekou. East Asiatic, Denmark's largest private company, engaged in a successful venture building steel containers. China Excelsior Aluminum, a joint Hong Kong–China enterprise, started production in 1982. Another Hong Kong firm joined with China Merchants in building a large steel factory while a mutual venture, Radofin Electronics, started to produce small computers. Shekou showed that Hong Kong's economic magic could vitalize China, benefiting not only the government but the workers.

By Chinese standards, Shekou's workers received a high standard of living, including subsidized food, very inexpensive housing, and foreign exchange certificates which they used in special shops to buy everything from cameras to fashionable dresses. The workers earned a starting salary of $60 a month in 1983, a minimal wage but twice that of other urban workers in China. In return, the workers were judged by their ability, gave up a traditional two-hour siesta, and could be fired by company managers. By 1985, their productivity approached the standards achieved in Hong Kong, England, and Denmark, the homelands of their parent companies.

In spite of a lack of skilled labor, vagaries in the export market and, initially, galling governmental restrictions, Shekou become a brilliant model of linking Hong Kong's vibrancy to the mainland's potential. Gradually, Canton, as the capitol of the Southern Economic Zone, began to adapt the lessons of Shekou.

Farther north on the coast, even Shanghai—plagued by urban decay, overcrowding, and the aging infrastructure put in place in pre-Communist days—showed signs of recovering its original status as China's industrial "beach head." Shanghai moved somewhat more slowly than the south, not least because some of Shanghai's businessmen remembered that the Maoists in 1949 had reneged on their promises to maintain the freedom of Shanghai's industries.

Nonetheless, Shanghai possessed a port which once matched Hong Kong's; it had plenty of energy resources and minerals. According to the central government, Shanghai also had 1.27 million researchers in the natural sciences and 169 institutions of higher learning. In the 1980s, an increasing stream of distinguished visitors from Hong Kong (as well as Japan and America) enlivened the more advanced institutes in the region.

In 1984, the government decided to enlarge the Shanghai economic development zone to include tax-exempt foreign enterprises, 100,000 indigenous industries, 49 cities, 301 counties, and a potential market of 210 million people. As Mary Lee observed in 1985, Shanghai might "regain its pre-Liberation status of China's most bustling and sophisticated city . . . it could even prove in time to be a rival to the future Hong Kong."[13]

Although no one could predict what China's rulers in the twenty-first century might do, it seemed probable that China's new technocrats and even its peasants who increasingly watched television would turn to Hong Kong as a model of their future. With its driving capitalist spirit and liberal institutions, its well-educated and ambitions population, even with its urban blemishes and limited democracy—Hong Kong seemed destined to emerge as one of China's "engines of development," particularly in such comparable areas as Canton and Shanghai.

The trade zones in Guandong, the free-enterprise collectives in Canton, the fleeting yet persisting appearance of posters on the "democracy walls" of Shanghai—those pleas for individual freedom that kept reappearing no matter how often the authorities scrubbed out "subversion"—all indicated that China was already learning from its most important window on the West.

Indeed, anticipating Hong Kong's reentry into China, some observers such as Joseph Chai argued in 1984 that "China appears to have few options other than comprehensive economic reform throughout the country."[14] And Audrey Donnithorne even portrayed a time when China would adopt the English-style laws and limited government of Hong Kong.[15]

Behind the play of events and personalities, then, the real issue was not China's influence on Hong Kong. It was Hong Kong's influence on China. No one expected Hong Kong, a city devoted to making money, to exert the cultural force of an Athens or a Rome.

Yet, in the economic realm, it is worth remembering that Venice, Amsterdam, and the Hanseatic League have already shown that small city-states can change the destiny of continents.

A Tale of Two Cities:
II. Singapore

You have to learn how to succeed to see who performs better, and then copy them . . . there will be no distinctive life forms in the future, it will be one inter-related and integrated world.

—LEE KUAN YEW

In the 1980s, rows of orderly terraced houses and majestic high-rise buildings, interspersed with manicured lawns and splashes of red and purple flowering plants impressed even the most casual visitor to Singapore. The movement of long lines of automobiles at rush hour, the sounds of construction, and the briskness in the walk of pedestrians along the sidewalks of Orchard Road or Shenton Way, the hundreds of factories in Jurong and Woodlands, reflected a purposefulness and modernity that only a few envisaged one hundred fifty years ago.

Singapore, then a jungle with about one hundred inhabitants, was founded in 1819 by Sir Stamford Raffles in his search for a new British commercial center in the East. He established a base on behalf of the British East India Company, which in 1867, together with Penang and Malacca (Malaysia) became a British crown colony. Singapore had no mineral resources, inadequate food and water, an inhospitable climate, a rash of tropical diseases and only one potential asset: a deep water harbor.

The opening of the Suez Canal in 1869 increased Singapore's prosperity and progress attracting a flood of immigrants from China and India.

For three and a half years (1942–45) Singapore was occupied and administered by the Japanese military, returning to British governance on September 1945.

Wary of opposition from Malayan leaders to the creation of a union originally planned to include Singapore and eventually Sarawak, North Borneo, and Brunei, the British colonial office separated the administration of Singapore from that of Malaya and accorded it a new status as a separate crown colony in 1946.

Singapore is situated between the Malayan Peninsula to the north and the east, and Indonesia to the south, barely 1° north of the equator. By 1985 the Republic of Singapore consisted of the Island of Singapore (with a land area of approximately 224 square miles), fifty seven islets and a multiethnic population of 2.5 million people.

The United Nations christened the 1960s as The Decade of Development, but in Singapore it was appropriately described as the Turbulent Decade by her former Minister of Finance, and one of the key political and economic architects, Goh Keng Swee.[1]

At the dawn of the 1960s, Singapore was still a British colony, albeit with self-governing powers in domestic affairs. Political events, however, moved swiftly. Singapore joined in a short-lived merger with Malaysia (1961–63), which Lee Kuan Yew, Singapore's prime minister, had worked assiduously to attain. The earnestness of the leader's conviction of the importance of linking Singapore's future to that of the peninsula state lying to her north in a federation was concretely evidenced in Lee's appointment of Yusof Ishoh (a Malay), as *Yan Di-Pertuan Negara* (Constitutional Head of State). Malay was to be the national language.

Within two years of the formation of the federation, however, tensions between Malayans and Singaporean leaders reached a breaking point. Basic differences in the conception and functioning of the federation, and ethnic conflict—both between Malays and Chinese, as well as divisions between Malay Chinese and Singaporean Chinese—promoted the expulsion of Singapore from the fledgling union.

On August 9, 1965, teary-eyed Lee Kuan Yew announced the creation of an independent Republic of Singapore.

Peace and prosperity were not to be the immediate companions of political independence. In fact, even foreign observers were divided in their opinion as to the future and even viability of an independent Singapore. Dr. Albert Winsemius, a Dutch industrial economist who had visited Singapore with a United Nations Industrial Survey team, reacted to her independence with optimism and enthusiasm. He reminded Singaporeans of this on the occasion of their twenty-fifth anniversary by quoting from the 1961 United Nations Team report which he had helped to compose:

> . . . . we do not see any reason why Singapore should not be able to industrialize, provided that it is determined to do so.[2]

In view of the failure of so many other newly independent nations, these were indeed optimistic sentiments, not shared by other commentators of the time. David Bonavia, for example, declared that Singapore had no future outside a "fresh accomodation with Malaysia to restore the natural economic relationship."[3] Author and scholar Ianin Buchanan predicted a resurgence of civil unrest which would be fought in all segments of the society by a disgruntled mass of people who would soon decide that "domestic well-being was more important than a foreign strategic state in South East Asia."[4]

After all, the year preceeding the independence marked the worst race riots in Singapore's history. On July 21, 1964, misunderstandings between participants and observers of a procession celebrating Mohammed's birthday set off racial and religious riots which continued sporadically for more than two weeks. They were reignited again in September following the murder of a Malay trishaw driver. The final count of 35 dead, and 563 injured indicated the tenseness of the communal situation.

For a time after independence in 1965, events supported the more pessimistic observers.

An immediate problem confronting Singapore's leaders was the continued presence of Malaysia's armed forces. Malaysia's leaders proclaimed responsibility for the defense of the island and asserted their "right" to the continued stationing of troops. Suspicious of political intent, the presence of the unwanted military exacerbated an already unhappy situation for the new government. Clearly, an indigenous military force had to be created, as a successor to the Singapore Volunteer Corps and an adjunct to the two infantry regiments which comprised, in toto, the Singapore Armed Forces of 1965.

To add to the problems, Singapore's students, as they had in the preceding decade, strongly voiced their discontent. Banding together as the "Nantah Students for University Autonomy and Students' Rights Committee," students participated in sit-ins, delivered a petition smeared with blood, and attacked policemen with bottles, glasses, and tin cans.

Their grievances involved a bid for higher status by one group of students, and a protest against the introduction of "suitability certificates" designed to deter students from involvement in communist activities.

On the heels of the student rebellion, the *Barisan Socialis,* a radical splinter group of the ruling People's Action Party (PAP) organized labor unrest through demonstrations, called for a general strike, and staged a "sit down" campaign outside of Changi prison. The government arrested hundreds and both police and demonstrators were injured.

On July 18, 1967, still another event, initially perceived as catastrophic, pummeled Singaporeans. The British government announced an intention to withdraw their military base from Singapore by the mid-1970s. Revising their plans six months after their original announcement, the British brought their withdrawal date forward by three years.

Based on estimates of unemployed workers and school graduates, Goh Keng Swee, minister of finance, reported that 43,000 new jobs would have to be created each year until the withdrawal. This was a truly formidable task.

The latter half of the 1960s, however, turned out to be a decade of Singaporean achievement. Comparing her economic position in 1959, when the People's Action Party (PAP) assumed control of government, to that of 1969, Goh Keng Swee reported that Singapore's Gross Domestic Product (GDP) had increased by nearly two and a half times. The GDP in 1959 was $1,968 million; ten years later, in 1969, it was S$4,833 million. Surpassing the targeted five percent growth set by the United Nations, the 1969 figure represented a compounded growth rate of 9.4 percent a year through the decade. Manufacturing grew by 17.1 percent a year; construction at 17.9 percent; and public utilities at 10.2 percent. Entrepôt trade increased from 14.2 million freight tons in 1959 to 37.7 million freight tons in 1969.

The post-Malaysian surge was due to external as well as internal factors. Externally, the United States, Japan, and Europe had experienced an economic boom. At the same time employment conditions in Hong Kong, which had for some time provided cheap labor to foreign investors, tightened. Trade with Indonesia was restored.

Internally, the introduction of the Industrial Relations Act (1968) provided a milestone in new management-labor relations. With an eye toward inducing increased foreign investments, the Employment Act included new provisions such as regulation of the rights and duties of employees, the number of holidays, rest and leave days, and the setting of the standard work week at forty-four hours. The act also gave greater bargaining power to managers, excluding issues such as promotion, transfer, retirement, retrenchment, dismissal and work assignment from collective bargaining. The frequency of negotiation was extended from a minimum of one and a half years to three years with the hope that this would enhance a sense of certainty encouraging foreign investors.[5]

In addition, the government established an Economic Development Board (EDB) in 1961. Armed with its own capital, tax incentives, and a pool of relatively cheap labor, the EDB enticed foreign investors to work with local businesses and cooperatives in order to build new factories and create more jobs. One major ingredient of the development plan for this period was the establishment of an industrial estate (Jurong) and the simultaneous building of housing on contiguous land in order to tap workers from established and planned population centers.

The economic performance of the 1970s marked uneven, but dramatic, growth of Singapore's economy. For the decade as a whole, the Gross Domestic Product grew at an average rate of 9.4 percent per annum. Progress in diversification and a shift away from the entrepôt economy helped to cushion the impact of the world recession triggered by the oil cartel. Manufacturing grew by 14 percent (annually) and accounted for 31 percent of the growth in real GDP, displacing transportation and the communication sectors as the prime mover of the economy. Construction, tourism, and private investment in plants and machinery continued unabated.

Goh Chok Toy, the minister for trade and industry noted:

> Economic expansion was achieved through a quantitative input of workers rather than through productivity increases. Employment increased by 6.6 percent in 1979, while productivity growth fell to 2.6 percent from 4 percent in 1978.[6]

The demand for workers over the 1970s led to an inflow of foreign workers, many of whom were unskilled. In the latter part of this decade, the government again moved to restructure industry and services to produce higher value-added products. The development of high-technology industries became the rallying directive and objective of the next decade.

By the 1980s government policy encouraged a shift away from labor-intensive enterprises. Wage increases in the area of 20 percent a year were recommended in some sectors as a way of inducing employers to mechanize, automate, and computerize. At the same time, skill upgrading of new and redundant workers was promoted through the Vocational and Industrial Training Board (VITB), technological institutes, and the National University of Singapore.

Cooperative government efforts with large multinational corporations—like Tata of India, Phillips of the Netherlands, and BBC Brown Boven of Germany—in addition to the French, German, and Japanese governments, created seven institutes specializing in the training of machinists, tool and die workers, production engineers, computer software and systems analysts, and experts in robotics and computer assisted design and manufacturing (CAD / CAM).

Within two decades, the Republic of Singapore had moved from an entrepôt economy through labor intensive industrialization to an economy focused on computers, robots, biotechnology, information and communication, and sophisticated financial institutions. Between 1961 and 1976, people employed in manufacturing increased by 650 percent. There was work for everyone to do: buildings and offices were erected, electricity, gas, water, postal and telephone–telex services, roads and transportation facilities had to be built.

By the 1980s Singapore had a new problem: a shortage of unskilled workers. Precisely because it had modernized, Singapore no longer had the "competitive edge" of cheap labor. Its own workers engaged in semiskilled and skilled vocations: foreign migrants took the less appealing jobs.

In spurring development, the government called on three types of enterprises: public corporations, local and joint ventures, and foreign multinationals.[7] Airlines, ship repair, and ship-building were the responsibility of the government; supermarkets, department stores, insurance companies and those which provided subcontracting services to manufacturing firms tended to be the province of joint ventures. Foreign multinationals were used to provide capital for large industrial efforts. In addition to the capital inflow, these foreign multinationals were hosted on the basis of established markets which they could provide, as well as the skills and technology which they already had and could transfer to their local Singapore operation.

Indeed, the optimism expressed by Winsemius was not misplaced. Singapore had succeeded in attaining a growth level which ranked her in 1984 as the twenty-seventh richest (in per capita income) of 171 independent countries in the world. Outside of Japan, she attained the highest per capita gross national product in Asia.

In 1984, projections based on current growth rates showed that Singaporeans would be the richest people on this planet by the twenty-first century: surpassing the United States in sixteen years, and Switzerland in nineteen years.[8] Singapore's pace—or Switzerland's—might flag, but the record suggested reasonably that it would continue to grow.

A survey of 93 countries between 1974 and 1984 rated Singapore as the fastest-growing economy in the world, and the country with the most outstanding export growth over that decade. Moreover, the inflation rate (2.6 percent annually) was second lowest among the 93 nations, following Switzerland.

One part of the explanation for Singapore's rapid growth was that Singaporeans were among the world's top savers. In 1982 they saved 28.4 percent of their income: a higher proportion than Japan or China. In 1984, Singapore ranked sixth in the world in the number of savings banks. In addition to private savings, the Central Provident Fund (CPF) poured investment capital into government coffers. All working citizens and residents contributed 25 percent of their salary to this government-managed trust fund. Employers matched the worker's contribution and the government paid the prevailing rate of interest on the contributions. Adding CPF contributions to per capita savings in 1983 placed Singaporeans within a few dollars of Switzerland, the world's greatest saver.

In aggregate terms, the CPF in 1985 held more than S$2 billion; more than S$8,000 for every man, woman, and child in the republic. The fund allowed contributors to withdraw their savings at the age of fifty-five, or earlier to buy a home or shares in specified enterprises with a proportion of their savings. Balances were paid out to appropriate beneficiaries in the event of death or incapacitation.

The foreign reserve, $22.7 billion in 1985, cushioned the overall economy. This reserve kept the Singapore dollar one of the most stable in the world. In terms of reserve, Singapore by 1985 had attained the position of the eleventh richest country in the world. Computed in terms of per capita reserves, only the oil rich ministates with a population smaller than Singapores surpassed the republic's level.

In discussing the role of government in effecting economic change, Goh Keng Swee noted: "We see the modernization process in terms of creating increased material well being for our citizens. This means more jobs, higher incomes, better career prospects, better homes: in short, a better life, materially."[9]

Singapore's leaders were frank materialists, but they carefully linked economic progress with social welfare. Indeed, the average Singaporean experienced many benefits from rapid industrialization.

In the 1950s, when the average Singaporean family earned S$332, the people of Singapore's Chinatown typically lived in windowless cubicles, 1,800 inhabitants to a block. They cooked on fire buckets; large numbers of people shared open bucket lavatories. The wretchedly crowded cubicles spawned disease and early death.

In 1960, when the Housing and Development Board (HDB) was established, more than half of the total population of 1.6 million people lived in squatter huts made of discarded planks, linoleum flooring, without adequate water, electricity, or sewage facilities. The success and exceptional organizing and planning skills of the HDB staff can best be relayed through statistics.

Whereas their predecessors, the Singapore Improvement Trust, built an average of under 2,000 units annually between 1950 and 1959; the HDB constructed 7,320 units in 1961 alone. Between 1962 and 1969, ten to thirteen thousand units were built each year. At that time, (1969) 32 percent of the population were housed in public apartments.

The pace of construction was accelerated. Between 1971 and 1975, 113,819 units of apartments and shops were constructed; more than 126,000 units were built between 1976 and 1980. By 1985, fully 81 percent of the population lived in HDB housing.

The government, wanting to provide an opportunity for the citizens to form a permanent stake in society, created a plan whereby residents of public housing could buy their apartments. Approximately 65 percent of the total number of HDB apartments were sold to the residents under the Home Ownership Scheme begun in 1964. The target was to have 100 percent home ownership by the end of the 1980s.

Using their Central Provident Fund savings (akin to social security in the United States) home owners were required to make a twenty percent down payment on the cost of their apartment, repaying the balance over a twenty year mortgage period at the low annual interest rate of 6¼ percent (1985).

Just as housing was improved so were many other facets of a Singapore citizen's life.

New public clinics and health insurance services proved so efficient that infant mortality rates in the republic dropped lower than that of the United States in 1985. In 1974 infant mortality was 16.8 per thousand births; by 1984 it had decreased to 9.4 per thousand births. Life expectancy for infants born in the 1980s was sixty-eight for males and seventy-two for females; a decade longer than for their neighbors in the Philippines. As major hospitals appeared, new techniques were adopted such as "laser beam" surgery; tropical diseases were eradicated and doctors trained jointly at the National University and at Edinborough entered practice, Singapore emerged as a major medical center for Eastern Asia.

The government subsidized readily available health care. A visit to one of the numerous health clinics or dispensaries cost the patient S$2.50 (a little more than an American dollar); medicine cost S$1.00 per visit. The nominal charge was retained in order to discourage abuse of the system.

The government also became deeply concerned with population control. In the first half of the 1970s, there were five times as many citizens under fifteen years of age as there were over sixty-five. A rapidly falling birthrate, however, strongly encouraged by the government, matured the nation rapidly. In 1984 a cash grant of S$10,000 was made to each low-income mother under thirty years of age who elected to undergo sterilization after the first or second child. More than 100,000 women were sterilized between 1970 and 1984. In addition, hospital charges for those having more than three children were increased in 1985 as a way of discouraging large families. The lowest hospital ward charge for the first and second children was kept at S$100 and S$150; the costs for the third, fourth, and fifth children were increased to S$400, S$600, and S$1,000 respectively.

In 1957, the population (excluding immigrants) grew each year at the explosive rate of 4.4 percent. By 1974, vigorous birth control programs had brought the rate down to 1.6 percent a year. Singapore became the first developing nation to achieve a growth rate which approximated zero by 1985; a necessity for a nation where thousands of skyscrapers already covered its land space.

Education, though not compulsory, was universal among primary age children. Since 1980 and the implementation of the "New Educational System," concentrated effort was placed on the acquisition of languages rather than the learning of factual information during the first three years of primary school. All pupils were required to study two of the four official languages: Malay, Chinese, Tamil, and English. English was the language of instruction since 1984, even for the teaching of Confucianism. Based on their performance in the acquisition of these languages, students were "streamed" into bilingual (normal or extended) and monolingual courses of study. Bilingual students continued their primary education for six to eight years and then proceeded to the secondary stage of their education based on the results of an examination.

Although primary school was free, parents were required to bear a small part of the costs for secondary education: about S$54 a year.

After four years of secondary school, studends were again examined, and sorted into different categories of preuniversity education; two-year junior college or three year school center courses.

Youngsters who were set on a monolingual stream after the third grade continued their education for five years, and if they were successful, went to vocational training centers run by the Vocational and Industrial Training Board (VITB).

Operating sixteen training centers, the VITB offered sixty-one different areas of study, ranging from training in the applied arts, to commercial, industrial, and service skills.

The elaboration and emphasis on skilled work training was markedly evident in the number of large cooperative training centers, as well as in the more highly specialized technological institutes directed by the manpower division of the Economic Development Board and operated in conjunction with foreign governments and foreign multinational corporations.

General literacy rates provided a strong indicator of the rapid advances which were made. In 1957, only slightly more than one half (52%) of the population was able to read or write. By 1983, the overall literacy rate was estimated to be 85 percent: 92 percent for males and 77.5 percent for females. About 40 percent of the literate population in 1983 were fluent in two languages. Among those aged ten to nineteen years, English literacy was 70 percent, according to the 1980 census. English, since 1980, became the primary language of instruction for 90 percent of all students, and since 1984 for all students.

The number of students at the National University of Singapore quadrupled between 1960 and 1985: from 3,500 to more than 14,000. Slightly more than one half of the students in 1985 were female, outnumbering male students in five of the eight specialties offered: arts and social science, sciences, law, business administration, and accounting. Male students predominated in architecture, building and estate management, engineering, medicine, and dentistry. Well prepared by their educational system, few Singaporeans failed to find work.

In June of 1984 only 0.6 percent of the workforce was officially registered as unemployed and actively seeking work. In that same month more than 2,700 job vacancies were recorded by the ministry of labor.

Roy Hofheinz and Kent Calder, in 1982,[10] noted that the omnipresent multinationals in Singapore created a relatively rich class of managers with incomes above the national average. This, together with the free market import policies which tended to depress the wage of unskilled labor, resulted in an income and wealth distribution somewhat less equal than elsewhere in East Asia. Nonetheless, contrary to the pattern in many industrializing nations, substantial increases in all sectors were granted in the 1980s as a stimulus for industries to upgrade their technology. All Singaporeans experienced a real increase in income between 1959 and 1985; the relative gap between the rich and poor did not widen.

Average earnings in 1984 were estimated by the government at a little more than S\$1,000 a month; rising from the 1972 estimate of S\$327 (related in 1983 dollars as S\$673) per month. In addition to income, the amount of money available to people may also be examined in terms of how money was spent and how much was saved. Private consumption expenditures increased at an annual rate of 6 percent during the period 1960–1985. As a share of their GDP, however, private consumption expenditures fell from that of a typical low income country level in 1960 91 percent of GDP (close to that of Bangladesh in the 1980s); to that of a healthy 53 percent of GDP by 1983, which brought Singapore close to that of Sweden. Moreover, Singaporeans spent proportionately more on recreation and travel: 2 percent in 1960 and 5 percent in 1983. They spent proportionately less on necessities, like food and beverages: from 41 percent in 1960, to 30 percent in 1983.

Television sets, nonexistent in 1963, were commonplace by 1985; as were Sony Walkman, video players (found in every fifth home), and telephones (increased from 36 per thousand population in 1960, to 369 per thousand population in 1985). The quality of consumer services was excellent. In 1985, for example, Singapore became the first of the world's nations to have eliminated dial phones and had installed a fully operational fiber-optic cable. The multifunctional digital phone was usable as a terminal for electronic data transmission. The basis for video phone books, video-texts (relaying anything from the prime minister's address to air flight schedules), and banking (cashless paydays), as well as meter reading (water and electricity), and home facsimilies had already been laid.

In other ways, Singapore's government enriched the people's lives by providing seaside vacation chalets for workers at a nominal S\$30 a month; more museums per capita than New York, more public parks than Great Britain, more miles of tree shaded boulevards than Paris, and public housing for a large proportion of the population at the average monthly rental of S\$80.

All of these measures resulted in Singapore's achievement of a rating of 83 on Kerr's index of the quality of life. The island nation exceeded all of her Southeast Asian neighbors, even with their much greater natural resources: the Philippines scored 71, Thailand 68, Malaysia 66, Burma 51, and Indonesia 48. Naturally, Singapore rated higher than other close neighbors such as Vietnam (54) and Kampuchea (40), which had been ravaged by war. Significantly, the small republic also outranked China (69), the ancestral home of most of her inhabitants.[11]

Singapore's marked improvement in the standard of living was sponsored by an exceptionally honest political leadership which conceived of public service as a moral responsibility. Singapore's success, as Ian M. D. Little observed, was "almost entirely due to good policies and the abilities of the people—scarcely at all to favorable circumstances or a good start."[12]

Fashioned after the English model, Singapore's government was theoretically a parliamentary democracy. Effective power lay in the hands of the prime minister, while the president played a ceremonial role. Dutifully receiving visiting foreign dignitaries and new ambassadors, the president was restricted in political participation to signing bills passed by parliament and formally appointing officers of state chosen by the cabinet.

Voting was compulsory: 1.54 million people were eligible to vote in 1985. The people exercised their choice or risked losing their vote in the future.

Since 1959, the People's Action Party (PAP) had won dominance in the parliament under the leadership of its Prime Minister Lee Kuan Yew, his long-time associates Goh Keng Swee (retired in 1984) and Sennathamby Rajaratnam, (Foreign Secretary). The party originated out of a group of intellectuals and students who organized the Malayan Forum in London. Upon their return to Singapore, the young lawyers, journalists, educators, and unionists formed a new, left wing, mass-based political party. In a 1950 address to the Malayan Forum, Lee had focused on the two issues which were to serve as the basis of his political philosophy: the imperative of communal equality and the threatening reality of Communism.

In 1954, many political parties—such as the Malayan Democratic Union, the *Parti Negara,* the *Anghatan Permuda Insof,* the Labor Party, and the Malayan Communist Party—abounded in spite of harrassment by the British. Others, conservative groups such as the Progressive Party and the Democratic Party, were encouraged and expected to inherit the mantle of power protecting British interests in the event independence became inevitable.

Wishing to use constitutional means of securing power, the PAP prepared their inaugural meeting in November 1954. Lee Kuan Yew, speaking in his capacity as one of the conveners of the party stated their objectives as an end to colonialism, the creation of a Malayan democratic government, and an attack on unjust inequalities. At its inception, PAP was a democratic socialist party, modeled on England's Labour Party.

The founding of the PAP was met with amusement and was the subject of derisive editorials. The *Sunday Times,* for example, in reporting the inaugural meeting of the PAP at Victoria Memorial Hall noted:

> I hope the talks at the Hall were not too difficult for many of the audience were very young. Judging from the photographs, a fair proportion will have a number of years to wait to vote. It was sad to see a socialistic movement kicking off in such middle-class conditions.[13]

The PAP's first opportunity for a display of commitment came when floods in December 1954 wrought havoc to more than five thousand residents of low-lying areas. The PAP immediately gave assistance to the victims through organized flood relief committees. This unhappy occasion provided an opportunity for the first collective action of the party after its formation.

Just weeks prior to the 1955 General Election, however, the PAP still found itself the butt of jokes and criticism. Criticism centered mainly on the allegation that the PAP was a Communist-front organization: a serious accusation in view of the British government's power of arbitrary arrest and detention.

Lee categorically denied these charges, although he had as a lawyer defended and befriended persons whose political leanings, if not affiliations, were Communist. In time, an internal struggle for control of the PAP was to be fought between pro-Communist and other members of the PAP with a resulting purge of the former group.

The 1955 electorate saw only four candidates fielded from the PAP; three were successful in their bid for office. Six other political parties led by the Labour Party won a majority of the other seats. Nonetheless, the PAP in its maiden election proved itself a potential force in the country since it had drawn the largest number of votes per candidate.

By 1959 the PAP challenged all fifty-one seats in parliament. Voting had just been made compulsory; campaigning was intense. The platform for this election emphasized independence, union with Malaya, and the need for development without mention of socialist or Communist slogans. When the election results were announced, the PAP found itself in power with a landslide victory of forty-three of the fifty-one contested seats. The party captured 53.4 percent of the total vote. The PAP, however, refused to take office—in accord with their campaign pledge—until the British released political detainees. Reacting to the execution of European rubber estate managers by Communist guerrillas, the British had instituted Emergency Regulations in 1948 which lasted for eighteen years. The most important aspect of this regulation was the power to detain suspects without trial.

Eight detainees were released on June 4, 1959, four of whom were appointed political secretaries to the PAP government when it took office. Two of the four were to be re-arrested years later by the PAP government for their participation in the Communist United Front.

Ironically, in 1963, the PAP government, citing Communist-inspired riots and other violent threats to internal stability initiated its controversial "Operation Cold Storage." Detained under the old and disdained British law, most of the more than one hundred persons who were arrested at this time were leaders and functionaries of the SATU (a trade union), *Barisan Socialis* (a radical splinter group of the PAP), pro-Communist civic organizations (such as the Rural Residents' Association), and undergraduates at Nanyang University. Dr. Lim Hock Sieu, former Secretary General of the *Barisan Socialis,* was arrested in 1963 and detained without trial until 1978.

Derived from British precedent, The Internal Security Act of 1963 was the basis for the political detention of scores of those who were thought to be working to overthrow the government. In 1982, Amnesty International[14] reported that there were seventeen people in detention: eleven for five years, four persons for ten years, and two persons for fifteen years. In a 1985 U.S. State Depattment report to the Congress of Human Rights, however, no known instances of political killings or disappearances in Singapore were noted. Unofficial, but reliable sources in Singapore indicated that in 1985 there were no longer any political prisoners.

In confronting political opposition, the PAP tactics were not unlike those of the most efficient political machines in the United States earlier in the twentieth century: gerrymandering, exclusion from important committees, libel suits, and the issuance of permits for rallies (except during election time). The PAP organized community centers throughout the country to dispense privileges and to cut governmental red tape, while recognizing the right of others (i.e., nonviolent opposition groups) to organize. They held scrupulously fair elections. Their strategy took away the fire of their actual and potential rivals.

For nine years of the early history of the PAP in power (1959–68), the Central Executive Committee of the PAP attacked, outmaneuvered and outlasted their opponents. In 1968, they took all fifty-eight seats in parliament, winning seven contested divisions over the Workers' Party and the Independents. The *Barisan Socialis* boycotted this election, reiterating their threat to persist in a policy of continued "street fighting." The PAP won all seats in the general elections of 1972, 1976 and 1980 with increasing shares of the general vote: 69 percent, 72 percent, and 76 percent respectively.

In 1982, a lone opponent—J. B. Jeyaretnam (Worker's Party)—was elected. In the general election of 1984 he was returned to office and joined by a second duly elected opposition member, Chiam See Tang (Singapore Democratic Party). The PAP in this election received 62.9 percent of the total votes cast. The increase in opposition votes—hardly a major challenge in other democratic countries—worried the PAP leadership and led them to consider ways of encouraging greater citizen participation in government.

The political machine of the PAP operated on the base of an intricate, tightly integrated system of grassroots organizations. The Citizen's Consultative Committee (CCC), the most influential of the local committees, was handpicked by the local MP of the district and screened by the prime minister's office. Participants were responsible for gauging public sentiment, receiving feedback on governmental policies ranging from encouraging courtesy to speaking Mandarin rather than one of the many other Chinese dialects.

As increased numbers of citizens moved into high-rise apartments, residents' committees (RC) were organized as part of the PAP system. In 1984 there were 260 such committees with more than 4,000 members. As the CCC, the officials of the RCs were also carefully screened by the prime minister's office. Confining themselves to local matters, such as involving people in "cleanliness" campaigns, resolving family and neighborhood quarrels, and organizing picnics and outings, the RCs worked closely with the CCC in serving as "the eyes and ears" of government and party. They also maintained a close rapport with local police to help in crime prevention.

Encouraged by the success of these two committees, other peoples'

organizations were developed. Among the more effective of these organizations were the management committees of the more than one hundred
sixty community centers which served the public. The community centers provided kindergartens in the morning, sports facilities for older
children in the afternoon, and cultural activities and quiet reading rooms
for adults and students in the evening.

Although not officially censored, the role of the local press in Singapore has been circumscribed by the government. In a 1984 television
interview, Prime Minister Lee argued his point for maintaining this control: differences within the government should not be aired publicly, it
would only serve to confuse the public.

Letters to the editor in the local press openly criticized specific government policy; journalists, however, engaged in "self-censorship."
Foreign political material openly circulated through the country, at times
irritating Lee and his colleagues into sarocastic comment. Reflecting the
moralistic tone of the society, the government closely monitored television, movies and video tapes to exclude pornography and violence.
Thus, Singaporeans could easily purchase *Le Point* and *L'Express,* but
not *Playboy* or even *Cosmopolitan.*

Order and discipline in the management of all of the society's major
institutions were the PAP's cornerstone policies. Singapore's Anglo-
Indian judicial system dispensed a form of justice which reflected its
colonial past. Without jury trial, appointed judges arbitrated and passed
sentence: caning, fines, and incarceration for crimes such as robbery,
homosexuality, or "outraging of modesty"; death for the possession of
more than fifteen grams of narcotics. Twelve persons, including one
woman, have been hung since 1975 for drug offenses. The lattitude of
dispensing sentences was increasingly narrowed as uniform sentences
were required for the various crimes. Armed robbery by day, for example, was punishable by a jail sentence of no less than two years; robbery
at night, three years; and if a victim was hurt in the perpetration of the
crime, five years.

By world standards, Singapore's crime rate was extremely low. In
1983, fifty-seven persons were murdered and fifty-eight rapes were
reported to the police. This represented one homicide or rape per 44,000
people. Comparatively, in New York City, the possibility of being killed
was one in 4,000; falling victim to a crime of violence (including rape)
was one for every 47 people. The director of the Central Narcotics Bureau
of Singapore estimated that there were 6,000 heroin addicts in Singapore; more than one half were undergoing rehabilitation treatment. The

number of hard-core addicts represented a dramatic decrease from the 10,000 people arrested for drug abuse during "Operation Ferret" in 1974 and thousands of opium addicts who once frequented the streets of Singapore earlier in the century.

Using special dog patrols, strict surveillance of boundaries, urine tests for known, "reformed" addicts, and other efficient methods of enforcement, the government had almost wiped out drug trafficking by 1985. Youthful offenders were a rarity.

With equal severity, the police had virtually eliminated Chinese secret societies, extortionist gangs that had once commanded the allegiance of more than 68,000 members. The introduction of the "Koban," Japanese-style police posts through some of the Singapore's neighborhoods, also helped to hold in check the increased crime rate otherwise commonly associated with rapid modernization and urbanization. Order was maintained by a relatively small force of 6,750 police officers, supported by over a thousand volunteers called Special Constabulary.

Trade unions, another major social institution in Singapore, were strongly pro-Communist when the PAP assumed power in 1959. Restructured under an umbrella organization (National Trade Union Congress) by Devan Nair (former president of Singapore) and other trade unionists, they found themselves soon working cooperatively with the government for the benefit of their workers.

The trade unions were reined in by two pieces of legislation enacted in 1968: the Employment Act, and the Industrial Relations (Amendment) Act. The former rationalized the pay structures, and the latter clearly defined the rights and responsibilities of unions and management. The number of man-days lost in strikes, following these two acts fell to below 10,000 per year as opposed to a previous average of 300,000 man-days. A tripartite National Wages Council handed down its first collective wage increase in 1972; it served as the key instrument of deliberate high wages policy as the economy was being moved into its next phase of development in the 1980s.

The 1984 Employment Bill paved the way for more flexible working hours to accomodate increased use of automated processes and robotization. The 44-hour work week was retained. Greater flexibility in maternity leave arrangements was also introduced to accomodate the increased numbers of women employed in the work force.

In 1984, the government-appointed head of the National Trade Union Congress (NTUC) called for the formation of house, rather than occupation or industry-based unions. Inspired by the union organization in

Japan, this move was supposed to forge an even closer tie between workers and firms. After all, they reasoned, management would be more likely to disclose plans and financial information about profits and operating costs if their association was restricted to the firm.

Legislation in 1984 also forced union leaders to be more responsive to their constituency. Under the previous system, union presidents, general secretaries, and treasurers were elected by rank-and-file members. They were, therefore, not directly responsible to other members of their own executive committee. They could not even be removed for misdeeds such as misuse of union funds. The legislation required union leaders to be elected by the executive committee from among its own members. Under the new legislation, the officers were required to win the support of most, if not all members of this committee and could be removed by them with a vote of no confidence.

In the realm of higher education, the government provided generous funds to the National University of Singapore and closely coordinated the production of graduates in various fields to insure that the University would serve the manpower needs of projected economic development. The vice chancellor of the university, in fact, reported to minister of trade and development.

Established in 1980 through a merger of the University of Singapore and Nanyang University (which was Mandarin-speaking), this unit provided advanced education to about 14,000 undergraduates and graduate students.

The operation of the university was based on models of British and American education. Unlike their models, however, the relationship between instructors and administrators and students and staff was highly circumscribed. Students were subjected to many ambiguities through a system of examinations and secrecy in evaluation. Student activity was restricted to ''nonpolitical'' areas. When a student body organization (the Political Association), for example, brought out a periodical to air its views on current local issues, authorities did not look kindly on this project. The publication was transferred to the official student union whose activities and finances were supervised by the university administration. Even the sale of student T-shirts protesting the priority given to college-educated mothers was quickly stopped. Yet, in contrast to the Chinese system of education, both students and faculty enjoyed freedom of speech; administrators did not attempt to prescribe the presentation or interpretation of facts; and the university libraries were sanctuaries of all forms of literature, political journals, and government documents.

While maintaining a high degree of centralization, the PAP government lacked a committment to any particular ideology, pragmatically choosing to focus on their own achievements and frequently pointing to the faults of other systems of governance.

The pragmatic attitude was revealed in the ruling document of Singapore's government: her constitution. The constitution has been described by the prime minister himself as a hodgepodge compendium of amendments and re-amendments of legislation dating through the various phases of Singapore's history. Even an important reminder of her colonial past was retained in one article. Article 100 of the Constitution allowed appeals from Singapore's Supreme Court to be directed to the British Privy Council. Strange to other, perhaps less confident newly independent nations, Singapore maintained its access to one of the finest judiciaries in the world.

The constitution, together with the long rule of the PAP, guaranteed political stability. Stability, in this instance, did not imply rigidity. In fact, more frequently than other democracies, changes in the constitution itself have been used as an important instrument of governing. Except for Article 3 which declared the sovereignty of the republic, the twenty-nine-year-old constitution was easily alterable by a two-thirds majority vote of parliament.

With a confidence buoyed by past economic success, the 1980s was a time when leaders and other thoughtful citizens reflected on identifying their own "unique Singaporean style" of conducting the business of government and life. There was, however, little doubt that their prime minister, Lee Kuan Yew, had left an indelible mark on the direction of the nation.

The prime minister was the subject of both extravagant praise and harsh criticism. He was long recognized as an intellectual genius from the time he secured the top scores as a Malayan student at ages thirteen and sixteen, to the awarding of a starred, "Double First" law degree at Cambridge.

Lee, however, remained firm in his committments to the common people of the island, leading the government and the citizenry through a political, economic, and social restructuring which has been aptly labeled "nation building."

Lee provided a strong sense of pride to the dominant Chinese population who had been disenfranchized for the most part until 1959. English-educated and "alien" Chinese were placed on equal footing at that time, to compete for privileges which had been open previously only to the English-educated under British rule. Lee, himself, learned Mandarin only in his later years.

Consistant with his early pronouncements, Lee peacefully maintained ethnic and religious diversity. In 1983, the Chinese constituted more than 77 percent of the population; Malays were 15 percent, Indians 6 percent, and all others, 2 percent. In a conscious effort to decrease ethnic hostilities the people were dispersed throughout HDB dwellings. Tiny enclaves (Chinatown, the Indian Seragoon Road) were left as landmark communities and tourist attraction centers. With government subsidies, Malays operated their own social welfare and educational programs as well as Islamic courts. The amenities of modern life—postal boxes, electricity, street lights, and public phones—were extended to the most remote Malay "kampoungs."

Religious freedom was evidenced in the variety of temples (Taoist, Buddhist, Hindu, and Sikh), churches (Catholic, Anglican, Syrian, Methodist, Presbyterian, and Adventist), mosques, and two synagogues.

Respect for law and government were not the result of mere moral exhortation. The PAP attained a high level of civic probity by revamping the civil service very soon after gaining control of the government. The reorganization involved rewarding public officials and bureaucrats for excellence and efficiency through upgrading and financial rewards; and transfering, demoting, or firing those found to be incompetent.

Two organs, the Public Service Commission (PSC) and the Corrupt Practices Investigation Bureau (CPIB), were set up to assure that the system of government operated as desired. The former unit (PSC) dealt with issues such as absenteeism, insubordination, and other offenses specifically related to a job. The CPIB functioned to eradicate corruption. Simultaneously, the government provided an exceptional level of reward for high civil servants. In 1985, the most senior administrators received S$24,366 a month.

Just as bureaucrats in the civil service underwent highly selective recruitment processes, induction into the PAP was as rigorous as anywhere in the world. The initial pool of talent was scouted by a committee headed by the party secretary. Recommendations for parliamentary candidates were then screened with testimonials of character, work ethic, and family background from personal contacts and friends. An informal interview was held. If the candidate was found suitable, then a more formal interview was scheduled with committee members. If successful, the candidate's name was forwarded to a second committee headed by the PAP first assistant secretary general. Again, the candidate was questioned to determine his or her motives, and to ascertain opinions on a variety of topics. A security agency was called on to thoroughly screen the candidate's family, career record, and character.

By the time the prospective candidate passed through the second committee's scrutiny, only the most serious remained. A final interview session headed by the PAP secretary general (the prime minister) was conducted and candidates were accepted or rejected.

The efficiency in marshalling the forces of government and the effectiveness of its operation have led some foreign observers to label the prime minister "The Mr. Clean of Southeast Asia." Eloquent and scholarly, the dynamic prime minister has been both moralistic and direct in his oratory. Voters for an opposition party, he has threatened, cannot expect to have the privileges of PAP organizations and services. He admonished his party membership to work hard and avoid the "soft options." In all of Lee's comments there was one very clear message: leaders know best.

Just as Lee was acclaimed for his role in setting Singapore's course to successful modernization, critics attacked him for the "paternalistic" nature of his moralistic and orderly society.

Pride in national accomplishment pervaded the responses by Singaporeans to the negative comments by such critics. Citing the advances which had been made, the citizens of Singapore reminded them that although Lee was not a perfect being, Singapore was one of the best managed countries in the world. "Many Singaporeans," one respondent retorted, "could possibly be working in the paddy fields at Bukit Timah, or living in communes or attap huts, were it not for the government and Lee himself."[15]

There may have been, from the perspective of the citizenry, a major difference in state directives which encouraged thrift and diligence at work, and those policies which intruded on the most private areas of life. Reflecting on the "success" of the family planning campaign, Prime Minister Lee put forth a policy of selective birth control aimed at "improving the pool of talent" in the nation in 1983. Fifteen months later, strong opposition from many sectors of the society forced the government to abandon its policy of favoring female university graduates. This swift abandonment of an unpopular approach illustrated again the responsiveness of the government. Nonetheless, in March 1985, the Social Development Unit reported spending S$295,000 in its attempts to facilitate meetings and marriage of "appropriate" people through counseling and the use of computer dating, arranged social affairs, such as teas, barbecues, photography and calligraphy courses, and subsidized cruises. An indication of the success of this attempted social engineering was that the unit reported only two marriages occuring after more than nine months of effort and expenditure.

Lee may have failed as a cupid, but he was well aware of his own mortality. In 1984, at age sixty-four, he implemented a successor generation within the PAP itself. All but three of the veterans of the party were retired from the twelve executive seats of the party's Central Executive Committee. Goh Keng Swee, for example, the architect for the economic success of the nation, retired at age sixty-six. China immediately invited him to coordinate the economic development of its nineteen coastal regions at a salary of $500,000 a year. Lee indicated that he too, would retire at sixty-five, saying, "I have a duty to do so for Singapore."

Prime Minister Lee, however, proved himself to be unwilling to leave the business of governing in the hands of unknown or unproven men and women. After a severe review, many new candidates for parliament were drawn from trade unions, and the public and private sectors. In the 1984 elections twenty-four of the new generation, including Lee Hsien Loong, eldest son of the prime minister, won seats in the seventy-nine-member parliament.

The process of "renewal" began in the 1970s. Tested in positions as minister or parliamentary secretaries, the attrition rate of the "new" people was high. From the ranks of fifty younger people introduced between the early seventies and the eighties, twenty were promoted and less than half survived the exacting standards set by the Executive Committee.

In its concern for future generations and its justifiable pride in the immediate past, Singapore adopted an immensely successful "fourth way" to progress. There were a number of factors which can be cited for this phenomenal achievement:

Foremost among them was the thoughtful planning and consideration given to the possible and probable contingencies of economic development. The PAP government guided the city-state through various phases in the development of its hybrid economy, with the willingness and capability of setting into motion long-range policies beyond those of many other democracies.

While maintaining its comparative advantage as a world trading center and its established status in entrepôt trade, Singapore simultaneously encouraged the growth of new industries through import substitution during the early years of the 1960s. Taking advantage of its status as an entrepôt center, Singapore quickly courted Saudi Arabia and the Gulf Emirates, in addition to Indonesia and Malaysia, to process their raw materials. Singapore soon emerged as one of the world's largest petrochemical centers, second only to Rotterdam and Houston.

As the threat posed by the building of petrochemical processing plants developed in the Middle East, Malaysia, and Indonesia, Singapore turned to the exploration of offshore Chinese oil reserves. She joined with other countries in creating joint ventures in manufacturing such equipment as helicopters, oil rigs, and seismic meters to aid in the opening of China.

Import substitution helped to stimulate Singapore's initial growth, but it was not conducive to further advances in technology or management skills. The prosperity and very survival of Singapore's industry depended not only on the upgrading of technology, but also the expansion of markets. Hence, Singapore's government moved to orient the economy to export. Economic development was carried forth through the use of state-sponsored enterprises such as Keppel Shipyards; joint ventures, such as Singapore Petro-Chemical; and multinationals including Phillips and IBM.

The groundwork for the development of indigenous technology was laid during the period of World War II when the Japanese occupation cut off imports. Backyard industries ranging from a paper industry employing ex-clerks to soap factories (set up by secondary school chemistry teachers) and food processing operations were started with little capital, but immense ingenuity.

Simultaneously, following the principle of comparative advantage, Singapore phased out many of its labour-intensive industries and its small agricultural sector. By the 1970s and the 1980s, Singapore's government took concrete steps to develop a new industrial perspective and an "information" society. Assessing the various options and the human resources available, the government specifically encouraged computer services, biogenetics, telecommunications, robotics, aerospace, and "brain services" (i.e., financial, legal, scientific, and technical advice).

Centrally poised in the ASEAN (Association of South East Asian Nations) region and closely linked to Japan, Singapore's leaders recognized the need for advice, software skills, a clearing and routing center in the transmission of electronic data, in addition to research on engineered horticultural and agricultural strains, the installation and manufacturing of robots, and the servicing of helicopters and aircraft.

The rapidity in the implementation of new policies was itself due to historical and social factors. At its independence, Singapore was already a bustling society of migrants. Not weighted down by historical baggage—myths and a host of heroes—or a terribly impoverished rural hinterland, common to some other modernizing nations, the people moved forward with an entrepeneurial spirt, pragmatically taking advantage of the successes and mistakes of others.

The success which Singapore experienced was not automatic or inevitable. Other great ports—Manila, Rangoon, Calcutta—could have made the same progress calling upon major resources within their own control. Instead, they delayed, while Singapore moved ahead as a premier port. It was the rationality and calculated flexibility of Singapore's leaders and its entrepeneurs which allowed the nation to move so successfully through its various phases of development.

The rationality in planning, implementation, and the refocusing of the economy was not based on force. Through consciously meeting the needs of the population in housing and jobs, and eliminating corruption in government, the PAP built up a reserve of legitimacy. Committed to rule by law, a charismatic group led by an austere and brilliant leader moved the society forward without resorting to forced labor, political executions, or the total elimination of dissent. Without using power for power's sake, Lee and his company of equally brilliant advisers, friends, and fellow travelers, were models for the people in the effort and care which they demonstrated for the collective welfare. Consistant with a Confucian ethic and pervasive moralism, Singaporeans accepted the importance of "productivity" as a key to increased wealth and the necessity for retraining in skills as valid options for personal and social growth.

The concentration of the population and size of the nation may also have facilitated the rapidity of change. Campaigns, through printed and electronic media, continued to inform and educate the public about almost every issue from birth control to drug abuse, from the desirability of frozen rather than fresh pork to the advantages of cashless paydays. People were induced to adopt new ways through persuasion rather than brutality.

An ethic which emphasized "proper" behavior, sacrifice of the present for future enjoyment, and the importance of family relations also supported social harmony and cooperation between workers and employers and government. But the country's own history—its ancient legacy of piracy, and student, labor, and ethnic uprisings in past decades hardly testified to the existance of a docile population blindly complying with authority. Even in its era of prosperity, there existed small numbers of school dropouts, criminals and faddists, in addition to the estimated 5 percent of urbanized professionals who have been labeled "yuppies." The latter have described the PAP as autocratic, repressive, high-handed, smug, patronizing, and intolerably harsh toward opponents.

The majority of young professionals, more frequently than not, joined the ranks of business, banks, and bureaucracies with pride in their national achievements and a resolve to maintain growth and opportunity.

The second-generation leaders were mindful of the appeal of opposition perspectives on issues close to the purse and daily lives of the citizenry: the cost of HDB housing, the use and condition of CPF savings, or wage policies. Other critics of the government raised more abstract issues. Did the government, for example, contradict its espoused values—such as an emphasis on "meritocracy"—with its actual practice, such as giving Malays free tuition in college? Did the government step outside its proper boundaries by promoting discredited genetic theories? Was this really a reflection of class or ethnic oppression?

Dissenters, whether within the ranks of the party or oppositionists, were given an opportunity to air their views. The criticisms and attacks, however, were commonly met by PAP leaders with derision or even ridicule. With publicly aired parliamentary sessions on television during prime time, however, the PAP was not able to completely disregard these voices. As one viewer noted in a letter to the *Straits Times,* "You have tried to make a fool of Mr. Chiam (Singapore Democratic Party), but have you paused to think that what he said . . . could be a reflection of what the people in Singapore wanted to ask?"[16]

Less in the forefront of the citizen's mind in the 1980s was a possible slowdown in the economy. With its infrastructure in place, long-term (12–15-year) investment in China, and internal economic adjustments being made within Europe and the United States, the republic faced a new series of challenges.

Whether Singapore can reach the "cutting edge" of scientific and technological progress was a particular concern of scientists and intellectuals. The government was supportive of creativity in the arts, in the fashion and clothing industry and, at least financially, in higher education. The government also provided generous matching grants to entrepeneurs developing new industries or inventions and cautiously allowed an important role to private economic enterprise. Yet, breakthroughs in innovation and creativity required an ambience which included toleration of the "odd-ball" and support for dissent from established practice. Some critics doubted that the organization of the society and its moral climate provided the environment required for creative thought, major technological advances, and innovation either in business or higher education.

Can Singapore be used as a model for other developing nations?

To believe that a given society can be directly copied by another, as we have emphasized, is an exercise in futility. The various combinations of factors responsible for the surge to modernity were rooted in the fibers of Singapore's sociohistorical institutional patterning, the values and norms of the population, and the fortunate convergence of people and events.

Rule by law and efficient bureaucratic organization was strong in Singapore because of the basic respect and expectation of the population. Policies have been carried through because of intelligent planning and stability in the government. Industrial development was shaped by Singaporeans through efficient use of the only resources available: an excellent natural harbor, recognized early by Raffles, and her people.

As delegations from countries as diverse as China and Colombia have learned during the 1980s, however, certain significant policies could be used by other "third world" nations:

• Singapore's encouragement, through the CPF, of an exceptionally high rate of savings and investment.

• The country's flexible and pragmatic program of encouraging appropriate industrialization at different stages of development.

• The republic's large investment in the basic infrastructure and particularly the human capital of the region.

• Singapore's use of the skills, managerial abilities, markets, capital, and technology provided by multinationals.

• The nation's export orientation, encouraged by tax incentives and the building of industrial estates.

• The republic's combination of education, economic incentives, and persuasion as an effective way of controlling population expansion.

• The government's housing policy which not only provided excellent shelter for the population, but also helped to ease ethnic and religious tensions.

• Singapore's mechanisms for establishing and maintaining a stable, uncorrupt, liberal government.

Cumulatively, these policies created one more example of a virtuous cycle: increase in foreign trade yielded income and a high rate of savings; extra monies provided the finances for providing essential services to the population such as education and health care, and the building of an infrastructure for industrial development; upgrading the work force led to a greater variety and quality of products which resulted in further income rises; skilled workers and excellent facilities, in turn, attracted more foreign capital which allowed Singapore to move into the "information age."

It must be remembered that Singapore achieved its advances in the face of exceptional obstacles: a lack of natural resources, no foreign aid, a British withdrawal from the area, deep ethnic diversity and hostilities, the oil crisis, and threats of confrontation from other nations.

There was, of course, no guarantee that Lee's successors would continue his triumphal course. The small republic faced two major obstacles:

First, Singapore was exceptionally dependent on the world economy. Down-turns in world trade drastically affected the country's export-oriented economy. (In 1986, for example, a drop in world demand for computers and other electronic goods resulted in zero economic growth for Singapore.) Singapore's emphasis on "high-tech" industries, particularly in biogenetics and robotics, offered hope that the island republic could once again adjust to changes in economic conditions.

Second, more threatening, some elements in the PAP began in 1986 to demand a one-party government and the suppression of intellectual opposition. For a nation so uniquely dependent on a free flow of information, the triumph of dictatorially inclined people would entail economic disaster. Fortunately, Singapore's scientists, intellectuals, and journalists banded together to oppose such repression.

The really significant question which this equatorial, once barren republic poses to other nations is: If Singapore—a haven for the poor and the humble and bonded of other times—can make such significant advances, why can not other countries learn lessons from her policies and practices?

PART III

THE ADVANCE
OF FREEDOM:
VIRTUOUS
CYCLES

Cautious Reflections

All day long, we worked in the hot sun. . . . Our bodies were tired, but we were happy to be in this new land where there was work . . . and every hope of a good future.

—A Cantonese laborer in Singapore

"There lies a rough quadrilateral with its corners at Tangier, Brazzaville, Darwin, and Hong Kong," George Orwell observed in his classic *1984*. "Whichever power controls [it]," Orwell predicted, "disposes also of the bodies of hundreds of millions of ill-paid and hardworking coolies, expended by their conquerers like so much coal or oil in the race to turn out more armaments, to capture more territory, to control more labour, to turn out more armaments to capture more territory, to control. . . ."[1]

On many counts, George Orwell's prescience did not fail him: in the grim reality of 1984, many in equatorial Africa starved; the world—not least the newly independent nations within the "quadrilateral"—still squandered money on weapons; and the scramble for resources, human and material, continued.

Yet Orwell, in his consideration of underdeveloped areas, failed to envision the future in its fullest terms:

He did not foresee that the world's food supply for every major population group except Sahelian Africa would steadily increase since his time or that the "world has enough resources—technical, scientific, and material—to eliminate poverty, disease, and early death for the whole human race."[2]

An ex-colonial officer in Burma, Orwell erred too in not anticipating the growth of nationalism in Asia and India, Africa and Indonesia. For good or evil, this vehement surge in political self-assertion, the most dynamic and some would argue, dangerously virulent, force in the twentieth century produced a spate of new nations, some benevolent and pacific; others, more cruel and exploitative than their old masters.

Orwell did not predict that a once humbled China would open its bamboo curtain and confidently declare itself ready to learn from and to compete with the outside world; that OPEC nations from Venezuela to Saudi Arabia would try, with a degree of success, to dictate world energy prices; that the Punjab, Dengist Shanxi, and the Ivory Coast would outstrip the agricultural productivity of the American midwest; or that the peoples of Hong King would ''flood'' the markets of Europe and America with their products. In an interdependent global economy where Singapore threatened to overtake Switzerland as the richest country in the world, the former ''coolies'' had clearly begun to exert their latent power.

Most critically, Orwell—as well as many observers of the ''third world''—failed to acknowledge that some regions, inspired by a liberal conscience, had the will and capacity to launch a successful crusade against desperate poverty. The ''fourth way'' areas won their critical economic battles without resorting to cruel dictatorship or the continuing exploitation of a ''bottomless reserve'' of cheap, ignorant, and expendable human beings.

Quite often, the fourth way regions forged ahead of other, comparable areas which originally commanded more material advantages, greater resources, and more ''charismatic'' leaders. Thus—on measures of economic growth, social equity, and the creation of liberal, mediating institutions—the ''gradualist'' Ivory Coast surpassed Ghana, ''infidels'' in Malaysia moved ahead of Sukarno or Suharto's Indonesia, peasant capitalists in the Punjab produced more than the fabled commune of Dazhai, and Asia's city-states accomplished far more than Maoist Shanghai or Canton.

The general significance of these more successful areas lay precisely in the fact that they did not fit many of the more popular theories of economic growth or political development.

Economically, the fourth way regions did not support the contentions of those who believed that great natural resources or large sums of capital were necessary at the first stage of growth. They did not suggest that independence from the world market or self-sufficiency were necessary, or even useful, stimuli for economic expansion. They did not offer much sustenance to those who believed that the symbols of old cultures must be dismembered, their populations held in check, or their old social structures revolutionized before the first groping steps towards affluence could be made. And certainly, their very diversity suggested that many different cultures, under the right political and economic conditions, could sustain values emphasizing science, rationality, planning, tolerance, innovation, and a belief that man influences his fate.

Politically, the fourth way regions indicated that relatively open, even pristinely democratic regimes could stimulate economic growth at least as well and as rapidly as dictatorships; that economic development did not require extermination of the rich or increased exploitation of the poor; and that a tolerance for diversity, cultural pluralism, and dissent could accompany and actually stimulate economic growth. Clearly, the poverty of these areas in the 1950s demonstrated that the creation of liberal, peaceful, and lawful institutions need not await an economic boom and may, in fact, initiate one.

Admittedly, each of the fourth way regions or countries had its own unique history. Each faced severe internal and external challenges, peculiar to its situation in the world. Leaders had to overcome each problem idiosyncratically, using the opportunities which destiny offered them.

Yet, out of the rich tapestries of their histories, the experience of these successful regions suggested a few common ways which the peoples of the world—from the William Tells of Switzerland, to the Meiji nobility of Japan, to the Baoulé, the Sikhs, and the Hokkiens of the twentieth century—used to escape the quagmire of poverty, ill-health, and despotism which still engulfed much of the world.

These common "lessons" did not emerge deductively from some preconceived theory. Obviously, we embarked on our inquiry with specific criteria in mind: we wished to investigate those regions which had grown economically, distributed their new wealth with a degree of equity, *and* had done so, perhaps in the face of violent opposition, in a relatively free and humane political manner. From the disparate histories of these regions, a few common patterns—rising above their greatly different cultural, religious, and geographic lineaments—inductively appeared and helped to explain their success.

THE ESCAPE FROM POVERTY

We have the ability, we have the means, and we have the capacity
to eliminate hunger from the face of the earth. We need only the
will.

—JOHN F. KENNEDY

"The whole family lived in terror, day by day, month by month,"
Tan Kok Seng, a Chinese coolie, remembered about his childhood under
Japanese occupation.[3] Like most Singaporean Chinese, Tan's father had
arrived from his homeland penniless. He eked out a living as a Singaporean peasant farmer, married, and fathered eleven children. In the
1940s, the family ate tapioca twice a day, and little else.

In its essentials, Tan's life as a child did not differ from that of hundreds
of millions of other "coolies" throughout the world. He nearly starved,
received only a slight missionary education, and never left his village
until early manhood: "The only university I would ever go to was the
university of the world."[4]

Yet, Tan had the good fortune to live in Singapore and Malaysia. He
prospered as did others in these regions. Thirty years later, he was an
entrepreneur, conversant in six languages, enjoyed television, had
formed his own political philosophy, and voted in free elections. Unlike
other anonymous millions, he dictated a moving autobiography which
portrayed not only his life but the spirit of these fast-moving countries.
"To anyone who thinks a coolie works as he does because he can do
nothing better, this simple book came as a shock to the human conscience . . . one might be listening to one's own brother."[5]

At fifteen, Tan left his father's farm to work as a food-market coolie
in urban Singapore, a city he had rarely visited before. He labored as a
delivery boy and stock clerk in a freezing storage bin from 6 A.M. to 8
P.M. every day. In the Singapore of 1955, still stricken with poverty,
Tan received $15 a month for his ordeal. It was generous for those days
and, after feeding himself on rice, he gave half the money to his aging
parents.

He worked hard, studied languages, acquired new skills, secured a
temporary job driving for the "Red Hairs" (Englishmen), and then lost
it when his patron left the colony. His new wife got a lowly position as
an "amah" (maid) while Tan struggled to keep his infant son alive. As
the economy went up and down, Tan found temporary jobs in Malay
Kampongs, remote fishing villages, and tin mines. He would return to

his father's farm as a last refuge. For all of his travels and labors, if his society had not been transformed, Tan would have essentially repeated his father's life.

"Then", in 1959, "politics hit us."[6] As Tan recalled Singapore's first general election, "Those were times of great change, and they were changes which have gone on ever since, often at increased speed, and nearly always for the better."[7] Tan witnessed the PAP's innovations—the expansion in economic opportunity, the erection of low-cost housing, campaigns for birth control, the opening of education—and he approved. In 1964, he feared for his son's life in the brutal interracial riots of that time but, "luckily, the Singapore leadership moved with extreme speed, calmed the people, and brought them back to harmony."[8]

Tan recognized that politics came first in Singapore's transformation but, like most others, he personally prospered. By 1968, he had formed a wholesale cooperative, financed partly by a government loan, supplied by his father's and neighbors' farms, and invigorated by his entreprenurial talents. He worked as hard as ever, sometimes as much as twenty-three hours a day. But now, during the propitious time of the Chinese New Year, his new company sold ducks, chickens, and more than 7,000 eggs a day to a burgeoning market. In the best of times, Tan earned $150 a day.

He feared turning into a materialist, "money cannot buy back life."[9] Yet he, as perhaps only a once poverty-stricken person could know, realized that money bought opportunity, freedom—and dignity.

In the last passage of his biography, Tan boarded an airplane for the first time and took off for Hong Kong. He thought, "Let me be free and flying about, wherever I wish to be."

> A hostess passed by and inquired:
> "Sir, a glass of champagne?"
> *SIR!*
> The word was stunning. She meant me. Trying not show my surprise, I smiled, and hastily answered:
> "Yes, please! . . ."
> I don't know how many glasses I had. But I melted into those clouds.[10]

Tan Kok Seng may well have been one of the first coolies to record his own life story for others to read but, with variations in detail, millions of voiceless others from Amritsar to Abdijan have experienced a similar exhiliration during the last decades.

What factors made possible their liberation from poverty and humiliation?

Freedom From Hunger

In many of the fourth way regions—the Ivory Coast, Malaysia, Colombia, the Punjab, Haryana, Dengist China (as well as eighteenth-century Denmark and Meiji Japan)—advances in both domestic and export agriculture were the spearhead for progress.* Those areas which eased price controls over food, allowed small land-holders or cooperatives a high degree of latitude, spread the ownership of land widely, disseminated technical knowledge, and invested in the agricultural infrastructure—dams, roads, seeds, credit unions, schools, and irrigation—were exactly the ones which made great economic progress, not only in commodity production but in all sectors of their economies.

Bumper crops in the Ivory Coast, oriented for export to Europe, augmented peasant income by eleven times in two decades. The Punjab, by judicious investments in the "green revolution," fed much of India and freed its untouchables for work in rural industries. By the simple expedient of increasing prices guaranteed to farmers and allowing them to cultivate private plots, Dengist reformers increased food grain output at 12 percent a year between 1977 and 1985.

These successes contradicted several myths. Famines were no longer inevitable in China and India. Huge investments in big projects or collectivized communes were unnecessary conditions for change to occur. Market incentives alone, supplemented by scientific knowledge and a reasonable infrastructure, started a virtuous cycle in many countries which had long suffered from hunger. Increasing rural incomes stimulated productivity (perhaps for export) and provided still more income for investments in rural industries. These, in turn, opened more jobs, absorbed

---

*There were, as we have noted, prominent exceptions among the successful fourth way regions. Singapore and Hong Kong advanced remarkably but almost totally lacked agricultural resources. In such areas, existing farms were actually phased out as economic growth proceeded for it proved cheaper to import food than to grow it under bad conditions. (This policy led the U.N. to list Singapore among potential "famine" areas in the world. Such a misleading label would apply equally to New York and Paris.) Venezuela used oil reserves as its initial stimulus, dangerously neglecting agriculture. Costa Rica, painfully caught in the dilemma of meeting its debt obligations in a world market where its prime agricultural exports declined, had not yet diversified its economic base.

excess population, and served the needs of peasants who could now purchase what they wanted.

As agriculture progressed, certain social changes—a reduced desire for children as field hands, greater freedom for women, a heightened interest in education—went along spontaneously. For the proprietor efficiently reaping the profits from his own land, the lures (and potential disillusionments) of city life as well as the temptations of violent revolution largely dissipated.

Agricultural advance, of course, required investment. Governments or private sources had to provide transportation facilities, fertilizer plants, ports, and even televisions as ways to encourage production.

Experience also showed that stolid, supposedly conservative peasantry would respond to new, even revolutionary ideas about planting, seeds and irrigation spread by government agents, private organizations, or multinationals. They had first to be shown that the ideas worked and brought profit. The ideology of the educators mattered little, if at all.

Perhaps most critically, as John Kenneth Galbraith argued, history indicated that the most efficient and stable argricultural instrument, privately or cooperatively owned, was "the cultivator-operated land holding: the farm unit for which responsibility lies with the woman or man who works it, one which in scale is related to what the operator can accomplish with her or his own labor and intelligence."[11]

In the Ivory Coast and Malaysia, multinationals served as the initiators of advance by rewarding and stimulating the export of agricultural goods such as palm oil, rubber, cocoa, coffee, timber, and sugar. In other parts of the world, less richly endowed with export possibilities, farmers turned to production for domestic markets. In these cases, the innovators were not the owners of giant plantations; rather, as *The Economist* observed in 1984, "the heroes of these farming revolutions in China, Punjab, and other parts of the third world are smallholders. While skeletal Ethiopians haunt the television screens, a way of avoiding future Ethiopias is being taught."[12]

Even in the Soviet bloc, while Poland and Russia struggled to survive the Stalinist debacle, a few areas learned the lessons of agricultural advance. As a prime example, Hungary not only fed its own people abundantly but earned most of its foreign exchange by exporting meat, wine, fruit, vegetables, and poultry to countries as diverse as Russia and Sweden. In Hungary, peasant cooperatives, ranging in size from 50 acres to 60,000, tilled 70 percent of the land. Each peasant owned a share of the common land as well as his private plot. Simultaneously, the cooperatives established complementary small industries which provided money for agricultural advancement and insurance against poor harvests. Each peasant drew a salary from the cooperative, pocketed his private profits, and shared in any general earnings which the cooperative made. It was a good system, one farm manager said, "not only because it satisfies a man's pride" but because it results in "more and cheaper and better farm goods."[13]

Pioneers in agriculture, while critical in most parts of Africa, East Europe, Asia, and Latin America were not usually sufficient in explaining economic growth.

The majority of the fourth way regions also moved flexibly toward the creation of light industrialization—attuned to their comparative advantages, their human capital, the changing demands for diversification, and the possible advantages offered by international cooperation.

Industrialization

On the road to achieving sustained, compounded industrial growth, each region left its imprint, but four experiences stood out clearly:

Some countries which were rich with resources started on the path by exploiting them. Venezuela and Malaysia, blessed with commodities which the world demanded, showed that the revenues derived from exporting such resources could be used to create a new industrial base producing everything from refrigerators to automobiles. As Venezuela's history since 1921 illustrated, such unusual advantages in themselves did not always prompt the industrialization process. Dictators or corrupt *compradores,* as well as charismatic leaders in a Ghana or Guinea wasted their advantages. In Venezuela, three decades elapsed before an enlightened leadership used its oil revenues to build both industries and schools.

Other areas, not so well-endowed by nature, showed that the development of light industries could form one of the first bases for industrialization. The Punjab, Dengist China, the Ivory Coast, as well as early Switzerland, Denmark, and Japan used small-scale, labor-intensive enterprises as a critical element in initial industrialization. Usually, these were oriented to immediate consumer demands but in some instances, such as the development of the silk industry in Meiji Japan, watch production in Switzerland, and bicycle assemblies in India, the small industries brought in significant amounts of export revenue.

At the beginning stages, a policy which favored "cottage industries" over automated steel plants had many advantages: it offered more jobs; it conserved precious capital; it allowed indigenous industries to exploit local opportunities; it furnished consumer goods to a rural population; it provided the skills and experience needed for further modernization; and it avoided the social and political unheavels often engendered by unchecked urbanization.

India provided a natural experiment in the virtues of various approaches to industrialization. In different regions and different periods, the government experimented with state-owned large industries, privately owned but severely restricted heavy industries, and privately controlled light enterprises. By 1986, the small-scale industries had proven the most profitable while the state-owned enterprises, particularly in Bihar, languished under bureaucratic control and corrupt practices.

Many of the fourth way areas showed that they could profit from association with multinational companies. Singapore and Hong Kong, devoid of natural resources or agricultural possibilities, demonstrated that even the originally poorest and weakest regions could use multinational companies to their advantage. Singapore, for example, provided tax incentives and an infrastructure which attracted corporations which had the capital, technology, and markets which the island republic needed. Singapore's economic leaders transformed the swamps of Jurong into 14,000 acres of roads, building, railways sidings, electrical stations, and a port to handle the needs of the companies. Jurong offered cheap but willing labor as a major incentive. (As the economy grew, wages were increased and that advantage disappeared to be replaced by another: by 1986, Singapore had one of the most productive, if expensive labor forces in the world.) In a mere twenty years, Jurong blossomed, and the "free economic zones" of Dengist China soon followed its example.

The fourth way regions also demonstrated the important lesson that industrialization required constant flexibility in economic policies within the framework of a stable polity. To use Singapore again as an example, the nation shifted rapidly from policies encouraging entrepôt activities, to labor-intensive enterprises, to assembly plants staffed with newly skilled labor, to a high technology service economy—all within the short span of twenty-five years. These changes, unlike those in Mao's China, were not capricious decisions but rather reflected a calculated vigilance to world market trends. This refusal to harness the country to a particular economic doctrine provided one of the keys to Singapore's economic success.

Again, as in agriculture, a virtuous cycle of industrialization accounted for much of the progress in the successful regions. The governments supplied a basic infrastructure, fiscal incentives encouraged light industries or multinational ventures, an increasingly skilled and stable labor force moved into the industrial sector, and the savings garnered by such policies were reinvested in a flexible, continuously changing program for taking advantage of world market conditions. The progress of Hong Kong and the Punjab, Singapore and Malaysia moved along in approximately that sequence.

Interestingly, both in Venezuela and on the Ivory Coast, an infusion of capital sometimes came first in the cycle but just as often, as with Singapore's Central Provident Fund, a large accumulation of savings was an outcome of progress, the last rather than the first step in the process.

Realistic decisions—using nationalized oil in Venezuela as a source of capital for industrialization, encouraging light industry in the Punjab, allowing the French a role in the Ivory Coast, enticing investments from multinationals in Dengist China—depended ultimately on a region's human resources and political will. As Albert Winsemius commented about Singapore's annual economic growth of 8 to 12 percent between 1959 and 1985: "It was no miracle. It was realistic policy and intelligent work in a positive atmosphere of social, political, ethnic and religious harmony. . . . A nation's wealth is not made up of its natural resources. In the long run, the decisive factors are the quality of its human resources and its government."[14]

Human Resources

Like Singapore, other fourth way governments generally recognized the importance of human resources and placed exceptional emphasis on their development. In Africa, the Ivory Coast spent the highest proportion of its budget on education (perhaps ten times higher per capita than in America) and prospered as its initially richer neighbors withered. Fanatically dedicated to education, Costa Rica built schools while the rest of Central America pandered to its armies. Venezuela spent more money on education than any other land in South America and eventually emerged as the richest and freet. While trying desperately to overcome the anti-intellectualism of Maoism, the Dengist regime rebuilt its schools, allowing teachers and researchers a new, if still limited amount of autonomy.

Early in their histories, the highly developed nations of the contemporary world, particularly Meiji Japan and Denmark, had recognized the critical role of education. In the eighteenth and nineteenth centuries, when scholars considered the sources of economic growth, "it was education that came immediately to mind. Not steel mills but schools."[15] During the twentieth century in the mature industrial countries, Barbara Ward estimated that at least 60 percent of economic progress derived from investment in education and research.

Too often the Maos and Tourés of the world forgot this lesson, as did their advisers from either Russia or America. As Galbraith noted, "No error in the advice given to new countries in recent decades rivals that which places investment in industrial capital ahead of investment in human capital."[16]

Yet, while asserting the crucial importance of education at all levels—from informing the farmers of the Punjab about hybrid seeds to creating new industrial managers along China's coastal rim—three qualifications must be kept in mind.

To be effective, education must have relevance to a country's needs. In Malaysia, many of the Malay students concentrated in Islamic studies and, later, could find jobs only as petty bureaucrats. In starving Africa, few universities offered training in agricultural research. In India, three quarters of university graduates became government employees since they lacked technical skills; while lawyers, grossly overproduced in India, ended up doing nothing. Throughout the developing regions, as Thomas Sowell found in 1983, "Desperately needed technological, organizational, and entrepreneurial skills tend to be neglected in favor of literacy education."[17]

To render genuine service, education had to be of high quality. Kerala in India devoted a large proportion of its state budget to "education" yet the teachers were incompetent and the students failed. Guinea proclaimed its devotion to education but taught only political propaganda as its literacy rate fell. Pakistan forced many students to memorize the Koran and to recite it blindly, ignoring the country's silted rivers and salt-corroded land.

To enlighten young minds, education had to be open, critical, accepting of world canons of evidence and truth, and cooperative. In this instance, the International Centre for Theoretical Physics at Trieste provided a model. Every year, five hundred of the brightest young scientists from the "third world," often starving for a free intellectual atmosphere, lived at the center, exchanged ideas openly, and freely criticized each others' work. Many came from isolated or dictatorial areas which did not encourage experimentation, change, or criticism. Abdus Salem, the center's director and a Nobel Prize–winner, had to leave his native Pakistan for lack of intellectual camaraderie; Paul Vitta, a physicist in Tanzania, said that without Trieste, "I am in perfect isolation"; Omar El Amin, whose father was a crewman on a Nile steamer, left the Sudan periodically for stimulation; and Toshar Gujadhur, the only physicist in Mauritius, treasured the Trieste meeting ground because "learning to me is like food. I need it."[18]

In reflecting upon the importance of open centers for learning like Trieste—as well as the pressing need for relevant, competent, and critical education throughout the world—Abdus Salam aptly quoted the Koran's injunction: "The Lord changeth not what is with a people until the people change what is in themselves."

"Alien Influences"

The xenophobes of the world, those who pleaded for the "purity" of their race or the unique "authenticity" of their cultures, seriously misread one of the more important economic lessons of the fourth way regions: those countries which welcomed the disturbing influence of a foreign catalyst achieved the highest rates of economic growth.

Without the French presence, the Ivory Coast would have moldered like isolationist Guinea. Malaysia might have stagnated or turned to dictatorship, as did Indonesia, if its Chinese minority had been as persecuted. Waves of Basques, Italians, and Spanish rebels invigorated Colombia, Venezuela, and Costa Rica while a Paraguay remained in splendid, starving isolation. The success of Singapore was not just its pell-mell rate of economic progress; "Singapore's real marvel is that it exists at all," for it was created by people "once wrenched every which way by ethnic and sub-ethnic loyalties and driven by a Babel of tongues."[19]

Other areas, originally richer and more promising than the fourth way regions, chose an exclusionist approach which cost them dearly in human resources. Nigeria slaughtered its Ibos and exiled Ghanaians, Pakistan threw out its Sikhs, Uganda ejected skilled Indians, and Maoist China tried to extinguish all sources of foreign "spiritual pollution."

Indeed, much of the poverty found in "third world" countries could well be traced to policies which consisted of "repressing, impeding, or even driving out of the country those who possess the human capital to develop it."[20]

The truth was that an "immigrant vitality" rather than a particular ethic—Protestant, Confucian, or Jewish—played an important role in economic progress. Cantonese migrants enlivened Malaysia, Singapore, and Hong Kong while their mother city starved under Chiang and Mao; Lebanese took a leading role in West and East Africa as their brothers destroyed each other in the Middle East; Basques and Southern Italians exploited opportunities in Venezuela and Colombia while the economies of their homelands slumbered; Tamils prospered in Malaysia and Singapore while South India and Sri Lanka stagnated or killed off their religious opponents.

What did these diverse migrant peoples have in common? Certainly not riches or exceptional education. Many came to their new lands, as did Tan Kok Seng's father, with neither sandals nor extra clothes.

We suggest, however, that these immigrants possessed a willingness to take risks—indeed poverty often forced them to take risks. They had an entrepreneurial spirit, an openness to new experiences, and a raging desire for change—often created by the oppression of their homelands—that together helped to create an immigrant vitality. Without it, many of the fourth way nations—certainly Hong Kong and Singapore, Malaysia and the Ivory Coast—would never have escaped the "vicious cycle" of poverty.

The foreign catalyst to growth may not always have taken the form of an actual intrusion of adventurers, exiles or "exploiters" who then took the innovative lead.

At times, the agent of change was "spiritual" or symbolic in nature, an intrusion of fresh ideas which were sometimes welcomed, sometimes feared. Denmark and Switzerland would not have changed so rapidly (and yet peacefully) without the spread of ideas generated by the Enlightenment and the French Revolution. Japan might have remained insulated except for the sudden appearance of "black" boats off her coasts, symbolizing the preeminence of foreign technology.

In contemporary lands, the foreign catalyst took many forms. The ideas of scientific agriculture carried over Indian television played an important role in transforming the Punjab, Haryana, and Uttar Pradash. The technological requirements of the oil industry revolutionized the economic mentality of Venezulans. The lures of modernization prompted both Dengist China and Malaysia to "look east" towards Japan.

The leaders of Asia would hardly have been the same without exposure to foreign influences. At Cambridge, Nehru, Lee Kuan Yew, and the Tunku of Malaysia absorbed liberating ideals. In France, Ho Chi Minh, Zhou En-lai, and Deng Xiaoping learned of Marxism. In Southeast Asia, Japanese propagandists taught Sukarno and Suharto the ideals of a "co-prosperity sphere."

Just as Rome once brought law and advanced technology to Europeans who lived in caves, and ancient China spread civilization throughout the world, the prime catalysts of change in the twentieth century were the economic, scientific, medical, and political ideas originally produced in the West. As Sowell rightly commented, "Those parts of the Third World that have had the most extensive, pervasive, and diversified contacts with the Western world have generally achieved much higher standards of living than those regions that have remained relatively untouched by Western civilization."[21]

Hybrid Economies

While its benefits were often accompanied by arrogance, duplicity, and exploitation, this contact with the wider world enabled leaders in the fourth way countries to lift the restrictions on economic potential imposed by ignorance and insularity. While they gave their systems different titles—"commodity socialism," "democratic socialism," "laissez-faire capitalism"—the successful regions in fact created mixed economies which synthesized elements from classical socialism and traditional capitalism.

These hybrid economies usually included four ingredients: they encouraged a strong, private, market-oriented, often multinational sector in agriculture and productive industry; they allotted government a prime role in creating an infrastructure, including a major educational system, to support development; they often emphasized an export orientation in an interdependent world economy; and they encouraged a high rate of savings for further investment.

First, although the precise mixture differed, the fourth way nations generally allowed the private sector, including multinationals and small land-holders, a major role in creating and distributing products on the free market.

In the more progressive regions of India, Malaysia, and China, small farmers took advantage of free market activities. In the Ivory Coast, large multinational plantations accounted for more than half of modernized agricultural production. In Venezuela, except for the oil industry, private companies took the lead in creating manufacturing units. On China's coastal rim, autonomously run enterprises joined with private multinationals in establishing new productive units. In Hong Kong, except for heavy involvement in building construction, the government allowed a very broad role for private enterprise, allowing complete freedom in capital exports and imports.

In these mixed economies, labels did not reveal much about reality. At one extreme, Singapore announced its devotion to the free market and yet the government engaged in directly productive activities ranging from shipbuilding to housing development. At the other extreme, Dengist China proclaimed its dedication to socialist principles but, along the coastal rim, encouraged foreign investments, allowed managers to run their companies for profit, and told workers they must produce or lose their wages (if not their jobs).

The tolerance of multinationals, whether in China or the Ivory Coast, had its benefits but also its costs. The multinationals generally paid higher wages, introduced advanced technologies, offered more sophisticated management, invested capital, and often filled a vacuum in local consumer needs.

Yet, whatever their altruistic statements, companies such as Unilever and Exxon, Phillips and Companie Française, naturally extracted profits from these regions. In bad years, when poor judgments prevailed or world demand declined, even the more prosperous fourth way nations suffered. Thus, in 1983, after the government invested in unprofitable sugar plantations, the Ivory Coast lost $1.5 billion in "invisible" outflows of foreign profits and hefty payments on loans. A drop in commodity prices virtually crippled Costa Rica and forced multinationals to flee the country. A world glut of oil imposed a huge burden on Venezuela in paying its debt to foreign banks.

On the whole, however, a carefully nurtured and monitered relationship between multinationals and most of the fourth way regions proved a useful supplement to their indigeneous private sectors. This relationship depended critically on the flow of world trade and a diversification of exports. Singapore, for example, traditionally purchased more from abroad that it produced in manufactured exports. Yet, each year, by providing financial, medical, and computer services, Singapore achieved a balanced budget and attracted an average of $1 billion annually in new multinational investments. Its immense reserves, larger than those of

Australia or Canada, cushioned Singapore against swings in world trade and allowed it to engage in mutually profitable operations with a diverse set of multinationals.

Investment in the public infrastructure was a second critical element in the growth of the successful regions. Whether in the Punjab or in the free economic zones of China, the government provided irrigation, transportation facilities, roads, and an educational system at public expense which complemented and stimulated the private and multinational sector. Investments in such public facilities may have exceeded the capacities of any private investor and may not have returned quick, visible profits but they laid the basis for an expansion in individual initiative and productivity.

Third, the more prosperous regions catered not only to their local markets but exploited their comparative advantage on the world market by exporting goods which the world wanted.

Punjabi and Shanxi peasants "exported" food grains to their own vast markets to meet a critical need for good. Malaysia prospered by meeting the world's changing demands for tin, rubber, and palm oil. Venezuela sold its oil and then ploughed the revenues back into modernizing its home economy. These nations' successes, as well as the triumphs of postwar Japan, came from an export orientation.

The opposite approach, a quest for self-sufficiency and import substitution, had its obvious appeals. Theoretically, planners could achieve a heady sense of national pride in creating home industries, new jobs could be opened up, and foreign debt could be reduced if not eliminated.

The difficulties of import substitution, however, usually outweighed its advantages. The automobile industry offered a prime example. In the 1950s, Japan reestablished its motor industries (which gradually became major sources of export income). In the 1960s, encouraged by the Japanese example and the fact that they had much larger internal markets, India and Maoist China embarked on import substitution of cars. Using old English and Russian patents, they produced their own cars and trucks. The cost proved prohibitive even in these nations with potentially great markets (China had only one passenger car for every 14,420 people in 1984 while the United States had one for each of 1.8). The expense of the vehicles remained out of reach for most people. Facing no competition, the car industries did not have to upgrade quality and the cars became increasingly obsolete. Few new jobs were created. Foreign debt for the purchase of, say, Japanese cars declined but the import bills for the replacement of automotive machinery increased.

By 1986, India cautiously engaged in mutual ventures with Japanese car makers while China joined up with American Motors, VW, and Peugeot in new enterprises. In Malaysia, the government's Heavy Industries Corporation allied with Mitsubishi to build a subcompact car. To allow the production of this new car, the Saga, however, possibly required the erection of barriers against other Japanese cars and risked that Japan might retaliate with her own protectionist measures. No one gained in that kind of closed world.

Rather, in the long run, each region benefited most from an export orientation concentrating on its particular comparative advantage.

An export orientation had, of cause, its own dangers, and required, above all, flexibility and foresight. When the world no longer demanded exports of cheap clothing or shoes, Singapore shifted rapidly to computers, biogenetics, and medical services. When the Ivory Coast found sugar exports unprofitable, it moved quickly into the production of palm oil. When Hong Kong's textile exports were threatened, the city-state strengthened its role as a world financial center. These regions planned ahead, seizing new opportunities in world trade.

Fourth, the more successful fourth way areas demonstrated a great capacity for saving. In some regions, this was the result of individual proclivities: the Punjab's rate of savings and reinvestment in land or small industries was, for example, the highest in India. The traditional prudence of the Sikhs rather than deliberate public policy accounted for this phenomenon. In Hong Kong, people voluntarily saved an average of 13 percent of their current incomes—four times that of America. Dengist China saved about 10 percent of its annual income both through various tax measures and the initiative of peasants and workers.

Singapore provided the most impressive example. Through the mandatory Central Provident Fund and personal savings accounts, the island republic accumulated reserves almost equal to those of the United Kingdom. Such huge reserves protected Singapore from down-turns in world trade by providing the funds for "counter-cyclical spending" on construction or new enterprises.

India and China during the 1970s and 1980s illustrated the immense future possibilities for hybrid economies which contained 40 percent of the world's population. Under Deng and Rajiv Gandhi, both countries have taken the path to freerer markets and greater openess to foreign trade and capital.

Acknowledging that the limits of mercantilism and central planning had been reached, both leaders tried to stimulate growth, dismantle their bureaucracies, and satisfy growing consumer demands through the services of a strong private sector.

Gandhi found that state-owned industries held three quarters of the nation's industrial assets but produced only one third of its industrial output, while operating continually at a loss. He tried to reduce goverment subsidies to them and open up markets to private competition.

Deng favored the decentralization of decision making in industry, the founding of small entrepreneurial enterprises, and the expansion of labor-intensive service enterprises which could absorb the 10 million extra people that swell China's work force every year.

If these policies are continued, projections for the year 2000 indicate what rapid and sustained growth will do for China and India. Assuming that the rates of growth of India, China, and Western Europe continue at the same pace they did between 1980 and 1985, India will have matched the GNP of Britain and Italy. China will have surpassed Italy and Britain and its GNP will almost match that of France and West Germany.

Obviously, even with huge internal markets, these favorable trends may not continue in China and India, energy shortages may develop, and bottlenecks in transportation may slow the pace of growth. If, however, reasonable and pragmatic leaders continue to govern and to favor hybrid economies, there can be little doubt that China and India will emerge as the economic titans of the next century.

Summing Up

Economic growth in fourth way nations could not reasonably or commonly be attributed to unique resources, historical luck or, as in Russia, to the forced achievements of a command economy. No single element in their economies—a high rate of savings, investment in human resources, the possession of oil—could by itself explain their sustained economic expansion.

Rather, a confluence of people, skills, opportunities, wise policies, and reasonable leaders resulted in a virtuous cycle producing greater wealth. Each element in this process reinforced the other:

• An alien influence, sometimes actual migrants, sometimes contact with new ideas galvanized previously stagnant areas.

• Signs of progress, in those regions which had the physical potential, first appeared in the agricultural sector.

• Industrialization, often aided by multinationals, generally progressed, sometimes leaping from labor-intensive enterprises into an information-based economy.

• The successful regions heavily invested in their physical infrastructure, but most importantly, in their human resources.

• Generally, the successful areas became integrated into the larger world economy, using—or often, creating—comparative advantages so that they could export certain goods or services at a profit.

• As their economies grew, the high-growth regions spontaneously or by government intention generated a fund of savings for reinvestment.

As the success stories of Malaysia, Singapore, the Ivory Coast, and Venezuela made clear, a new fourth way economic system emerged. It used entrepreneurs and small land-holders as antennae to market changes while the state provided an infrastructure, development advice and at times, protection for infant industries. Labeling this approach as the "capitalist development state" (CDS), Chalmers Johnson argued that its most brilliant example was postwar Japan which rose from the ashes of war to world economic predominence. Such CDS economies were certainly not run by a clear-cut "commander" at the center but rather by a network of compromising coalitions between bureaucrats, entrepreneurs, large corporations, merchant princes, and politicians who responded to world market forces.

There was no inherent reason—on a planet whose people had yet to exploit its deeper layers, to explore its oceans, or to open the reaches of space—why this approach could not continue to expand wealth well into the future.

The prime obstacle to further economic expansion and improvements in human welfare was the recurring threat that bumbling, repressive dictators—other Maos, Sukarnos, or Gomézes—might again grab power, ignore criticism, and fumble their way into an economic catastrophe.

THE ESCAPE FROM DESPOTISM

> No, I shall not believe that this human race . . . has become a bastardized flock of sheep . . . and that nothing remains but to deliver it . . . to a small number of shepherds who, after all, are not better animals than are we, the human sheep, and who indeed are often worse.
>
> —ALEXIS DE TOCQUEVILLE

The fourth way countries achieved economic growth without the horrors of the first industrial revolution or the inhumanities of a Stalinist regime. They progressed as their people's health and education improved and the gap between rich and poor lessened.

With the possible exception of Dengist China, one of the great imponderables of the contemporary world, such regions advanced in an atmosphere of reasonable dialogue, critical debate, a rule of law, and a willingness to refrain from violence. When governments had to call in their armies—as did India in the Punjab, as well as Venezuela and Colombia in their cities and mountains—the goal was not extermination of enemies but the preservation of a constitutional order which encouraged the revolutionaries to renounce violence and engage in lawful reconciliation.

How did the fourth way regions maintain stable, relatively liberal, and humane governments while still trying to achieve consensus amidst the chaos of rapid economic and social change?

In explaining their political development, conventional wisdom offered little enlightenment:

Economic development per se did not necessarily lead to more liberal governments. South Korea, Taiwan, and South Africa made as much economic progress as Singapore or Hong Kong, yet their dictatorial structures did not noticeably weaken. In Iran, rapid economic development merely led to the replacement of an arrogant shah with an equally repressive theocracy. In fact, in the Punjab, economic development may have exacerbated religious and caste differences, igniting violence.

Some have maintained that the institutional history of a region best explained political evolution. Certainly, Colombia and Costa Rica maintained their liberal traditions in spite of one-crop economies, undermined by the world market. Yet, Venezuela emerged as a full-scale democracy in 1986 without previously developing a literate electorate, multigenerational political parties, or a tradition of democratic institutions. And Chile, while possessing all of these social "preconditions," had not budged from its military dictatorship.

Other observers, such as Samuel Huntington, have argued that certain religious traditions encouraged democratic practices and a more open political order. Yet, as we have seen, no single religious or ethical culture seemed uniquely receptive or antithetical to liberalizing political trends: an "Islamic" Malaysia created a multiparty government; a largely "pagan" Ivory Coast encouraged discussion and reconciliation; a "Catholic" Costa Rica renounced the methods of the Inquisition; and a "Confucian" China produced both the brutality of Mao and the tolerant pragmatism of Deng.

If there were no prerequisities for the development of liberal regimes in the fourth way regions, certain social and economic attributes tended to accompany economic growth in these areas.

Emergence of an Autonomous Middle Class

The economic and social policies of the fourth way leaders, either consciously or indirectly, led to the creation of autonomous middle classes. Such groups, as Aristotle long ago recognized, had the knowledge and independent power to assert their concerns and interests against the will of any tyrant.

In the context of our present inquiry, we recognized as "middle class" those people who 1. had escaped from a basic subsistence level of living, 2. had established their own economic base independent of the government, and 3. had interests which did not necessarily coincide with those of the ruling elite. Typically, these middle classes had achieved a degree of autonomy as free-holding peasants, merchants, industrialists, professionals, or intellectuals.

Such an independent middle class played a critical role in opening up a freer political order in fourth way countries in several, sometimes contradictory ways:

They usually produced statesmen—Houpouët-Boigny, Betancourt, Lee, even Deng—who led the way in political development.

They also filled the ranks of dissenters and critics who ensured that the new leadership could not easily dismiss, imprison, or kill their possible opponents. COPEI in Venezuela, the teachers' union in the Ivory Coast, and the opposition in Malaysia drew their strength from the middle classes.

As the middle classes grew, their importance in the modernization process became increasingly evident and their interests, however materialistic or idealistic, had to be acknowledged by any government which aimed at both the retention of power *and* economic growth. Thus, India's center avoided eliminating the food-producing Sikhs because of the constant risk of famine; the Singapore government gave in to the opposition of university graduates, a key to the island's future, over various ill-conceived policies; and the Ivory Coast had to bow to the demands of its teachers.

In general, as fine studies by Lipset, Almond and Verba, and Inkeles have demonstrated, various psychic qualities—such as tolerance of others, a dislike for hierarchical relations, a willingness to help the weak, dissent from conformity, a feeling of political efficacy—were much more prominent among the members of the middle class in every region.[22]

Clearly, as the experience of pre–Nazi Germany illustrated, the lower middle classes have not always taken a liberal stance and may, under certain historical conditions, form the bedrock for dictatorship. In other situations, as the long failure of Mexico's large middle sector to open up its society showed, the influence of the middle classes may be crushed by a government which does not hesitate to use its police powers.

Nonetheless, as Huntington has emphasized and the fourth way regions' case histories supported, the middle classes played an important part in maintaining a balance between disorder and the worst sort of tyranny.

An Educated Citizenry

As we have remarked, the fourth way nations invested heavily in education. The Latin American countries, the city-states, Dengist China, and parts of India created exceptionally high levels of mass literacy as well as technical institutes and first-class universities.

In addition to its economic function, the educational system—if it went beyond ossified rote learning or the inculcation of propaganda—opened minds to new ideas, new models, and new expectations. In most of the fourth way regions, literate people had access to foreign publications, objective criticism, and "alien" enticements. An educated citizenry, aware of outside trends, enlightened by world thinkers, and informed about the actual performance of its government, could not be treated in the same fashion as the docile pawns of dictatorial regimes.

Leaders in the "fourth way" regions usually welcomed the political impact of education. To be sure, formal education in itself did not necessarily protect a country against dictatorship. Chileans, Uruguyans, South Koreans, Cubans, East Europeans, and Taiwanese all had high literacy rates during the 1980s while dictators ruled them.

Nonetheless, the best forms of education tended to open up new vistas, created a demand for empirical evidence, encouraged a toleration of different views, and allowed reasonable dissent from conventional wisdom.

As the 1980s approached an end, the influence of a new form of education became apparent: computerized satellites. India had launched its own satellite. Russia could broadcast its programs throughout the world, and Japan was about to complete a massive satellite capable of reaching hundreds of channels throughout the world. In an era when almost every village had its own television, this new source of universal knowledge broached old bulwarks of authority. When the possibilities of communication became so broad, it was increasingly difficult for authoritarians of whatever belief to shield their peoples from information, critical views, and objective news. From satellites, Japan could broadcast television programs of every type with exquisite clarity directly into villages throughout Asia.

With such universal accessibility, how could a future Chinese dictator protect his regime from criticism? How could Islamic groups keep out "impure thoughts" from Malaysia and Indonesia? How could deprived peoples be kept ignorant about information concerning their own economies? Perhaps governments could develop "anti-information technology" but it appeared increasingly difficult for any secret police to black out information—or heresy, pornography, and propaganda—when it reached the world at 300,000 km per second, transmitted by a fiber-optic thread.

Even without advanced communications technology, the potentially "subversive" impact of even traditional education was nowhere more evident than in the Ivory Coast, a formerly illiterate country which had devoted 43 percent of its national budget to education since the beginning of independence.

In 1985, embroiled in a worldwide debt crisis, the Ivory Coast had to cut back on expenditures for education. After years of paying all the costs of education, the ministry of education told 3,000 university students and 200,000 secondary pupils that only one third of their number would receive full scholarships. Moreover, the government changed its priorities. After finding that science and mathematics graduates filled only 10 percent of the country's needs, the government put special emphasis on these skills. Meanwhile, the government eliminated about one third of Frenchmen, "cooperants" teaching in the school system, since their cost was four times greater than that of Ivorian counterparts.

Such hard decisions created intense political discontent not only among high civil servants but also poor farmers who had expected a first class and free education for their children. When the government provided only 35,000 places in primary schools for the 400,000 children who wished them, the teachers' union—a completely autonomous organization which acted as the equivalent of an opposition political party—vocally attacked the government.

The teachers listed grievances that included their own economic complaints, dissent from the government policy of favoring affirmative action for the poor, and demands that "moral education," a form of government propaganda, should be abolished.

In its usual fashion of encouraging dialogue, the Ivorian government held open meetings which included everyone from disgruntled teachers to angry parents to discuss the issues. Clearly, while education had been a major ingredient in the Ivorian model, it had also emerged as a volatile political issue which threatened to topple the government.

Thus, in reasonably open societies, education often served to goad discontent and became a political issue in itself. Nonetheless, it was an instrument for liberalization and a necessary crucible for reasonable dialogue.

The Political Impact of Mixed Economies

As we have seen, fourth way regions usually favored a hybrid economic system which allowed a large role for market forces while the government engaged in building a public infrastructure. As Seymour Martin Lipset has argued, the high rate of economic growth which resulted from these economic policies had several political consequences.

Such economies served to moderate political tension by allowing economic outlets to fallen political leaders. In the more abundant countries, it facilitated compromise and conciliation. Thus, in Venezuela, oil revenues allowed the social democratic government to purchase the private lands necessary for a politically motivated land reform. The conservative landed aristocracy might well have tried a revolution if they had not been compensated for their losses. Similarly, the oil revenues bought compliance from the army.

The existence of a large private sector in the mixed economies of the fourth way regions also opened up the possibility for critics to build up their own means of mass communication. In Malaysia, for example, the deposed Tunku controlled his own newspaper which he used to comment acerbically on government actions while PAS imported video cassettes which criticized what the party regarded as the improprieties of a secular government. In Hong Kong, political groups from Maoists to the Kuomintang produced journals which freely expressed their views. Ruling governments always had the power to ban such dissent but, in mixed economies where an attack on a particular political or religious sect might result in economic catastrophe, prudent rulers tended to avoid crushing privately owned publications, however "destructive" their political opinions were.

As such economies became more complex and industrialized, it proved increasingly difficult (although never impossible) for central bureaucracies to control political criticism. They could suppress their technocrats, industrialists, entrepreneurs, and skilled workers, as Mao did, but only at the risk of economic paralysis. During the 1980s, Malaysia moved toward greater privitization of the economy, India loosened its controls over the private sector, and Dengist China experimented with independent management of factories. As this dispersion in economic influence led to the creation of new power centers, more alternatives and counters to absolute state power appeared. So, too, did privately distributed publications that dissented from one or another aspect of the ruling government's policies.

Economic modernization, particularly in mixed economies with decentralized decision makers and important relationships with multinationals, also involved a movement towards a rule of law. Such diversified economies required a stable and universal set of rules to govern the relation between their differing sectors.

Thus, in Dengist China, new economic conditions prompted the growth of a legal system in a country which had previously depended on the arbitrary decisions of its rulers. In dealing with multinational companies, Gan Jihua, a ministry of justice official, admitted in 1985 that, ''In the past the law was often disregarded by powerful institutions and individuals. . . . What we need most at present is knowledge of international economic law.''[23]

This new emphasis on law had concrete manifestations. When a central government ministry, for example, refused to pay a regional factory for some goods in 1984, the factory sued for the payment of 975,000 *yuan*. The ministry's bureaucrats arrogantly tried to ignore the suit and refused even to come to court. Higher judges ruled that the bureaucrats had no right to decline to appear—an impossible judgment in Mao's China. The factory won its suit.

Thus, by leading to a rule of law, opening possibilities for criticism, and dispersing countervailing powers within a society, mixed economies with a strong private sector reinforced the movement toward politically more open regimes.

Compromising Symbolic Issues

While distributing real economic power throughout their societies, the fourth way leaders were remarkably adept at maintaining the symbols of an *ancien régime*, thereby defusing some of the religious, political, and ethnic conflicts which drove other societies into anarchy, revolt, or counterrevolution. In many areas, modernizing rulers divested the old ruling groups of their real power while wisely allowing them to retain their antiquated symbols.

Denmark, for example, kept its aristocratic titles and its monarchy while the freed peasants and urban merchants took over both the economy and the polity.

In Japan, the victorious Meiji allowed Tokugawa nobles to retain their traditional swords while they were stripped of their lands. Militarily, the weapons had no utility against the Maxim guns of the new regime but the swords symbolized that even if the Tokugawa nobles had lost all real influence, they still had their cherished emblems of virility and status.

In contemporary times, Singapore instituted English as the real language of commerce, education, and administration while recognizing Mandarin, Malay, and Tamil as "official" languages. Singapore's rambunctious trade unions continued to elect officers while, in fact, the government curtailed their right to strike. Singapore's presidents came from minority groups. Government offices everywhere featured the president's picture. The figure heads, however, had no real power, as the prime minister (from the dominant population) actually ruled.

The Ivory Coast's government allowed criticism, free discussion, and continuous dialogue while its leader still maintained a lake filled with crocodiles in his ancestral village—a mystical symbol of a tribal chieftan's powers.

Malaysia proved particularly wise in its handling of symbolic ethnic issues. In a nation composed of fifty-two ethnic groups, Malaysians created the most unusual constitutional monarchy in the world. Rotating the kingship among nine dynastic clans in a peaceful fashion, Malaysians also allowed twelve ethnic-based political parties to vie for power. This communal integrity at the ballot box did not preclude political harmony. For example, the governing coalition would typically ask Malays in a predominantly Chinese constituency to vote for an MCA (Malaysian Chinese Association) candidate who would cooperate in the governing alliance. Conversely, Chinese in the overwhelmingly Malay state of Trengganu were encouraged to vote for a Malay.

By this sort of political maneuvering—and by allowing four official languages, opening the economy to deprived Malays and yet not inhibiting the entrepreneurial talents of a Chinese minority—the government encouraged its medly of ethnic groups to avoid communal exclusionism and to adopt a common "Malaysian" identity.

It was only when secular governments trampled on ancient symbols that the fourth way regimes stumbled. Thus, New Delhi's refusal to recognize Sikhism as a separate religion or Amritsar as a Holy City needlessly inflamed the Punjab. The subsequent invasion of Amritsar's Holy Temple served only to aggravate Sikh passions, led to the assassination of Mrs. Gandhi, ignited riots throughout the country, and threatened the disintegration of India. This tragedy could have been avoided if the center had earlier made symbolic concessions which had meaning solely for the most devout Sikh.

In the more successful regions, the leaders managed to portray nationhood itself in new symbols which the people gradually absorbed. In Singapore, a young artificial creation, boys and girls repeated this daily pledge 2,000 times in the course of their schooling:

> We, the citizens of Singapore, pledge ourselves as one united people, regardless of race, language, or religion, to build a democratic society based on justice and equality so as to achieve happiness, prosperity and progress for our nation.

They said it reverently in English after singing their national anthem in Malay. An immersion in national symbols apparently worked in Singapore: intermarriage between Chinese, Malays, and Indians increased since 1959; a majority of all ethnic groups had close friends from other races; and 96 percent of young men believed that universal national service was their justifiable duty.

Even in a society where, as Lee warned, the "gut issues" of race, language, and religion could "unzip the country right down the middle,"[24] symbolic gestures at nation building helped to insure that Singapore's multiracial tensions did not burst into ugly public manifestations. Many of Singapore's economic and social policies—a mixture of peoples in housing estates, national service, and affirmative action for the Malay minority—concretely reinforced the sense of nationhood.

Clearly, people everywhere needed symbols. The wiser statesmen in developing regions recognized this ancient truth and accomodated their secular goals to communal, ethnic, religious and linguistic customs, as well as to the demands of building a national consensus.

Taming the Army

In a variety of ingenious ways, civilian leaders in the fourth way areas have kept their armies—a prime source and sponsor the authori-

tarian influence—on a tight leash. Costa Rica simply disbanded its army.*
The Ivory Coast, by calling in French troops as defenders, undermined
its domestic military. In 1985, Dengist China dismissed a million men
from its armed forces and gave the remaining soldiers gorgeous uniforms with orders to engage in civilian industries. India and Malaysia,
inheriting a British tradition, limited their armies to a distinctly "professional" role but used them to quell internal violence. Venezuela and
Colombia managed to keep their armies out of politics and played the
intricate, dangerous game of buying military allegiance with generous
pay and luxurious privileges.

In general, as the economies of fourth way nations became increasingly complex and diversified, army officers seemed willing to abstain
from seizing political control. In simpler economies, particularly in Africa
and the Islamic areas, the temptations of military rule remained since
the applicaton of brute force still appeared an attractive alternative to
anarchy and a workable solution to economic problems.

Singapore remained an anomaly among fourth way regions. For a
small island republic, Singapore invested a disproportionate amount of
its income (about $1.6 billion in 1984) in maintaining a highly sophis-
ticated army, navy, and air force. The country had universal conscrip-
tion, far more tanks than Indonesia or the Philippines, and the capacity
to mobilize 200,000 men overnight. Singapore's armed forces were almost
as large as Australia's although they were charged with defending only
.007 percent of territory.

Singapore's army originated in a desire to end its dependence on
Malaysian forces, after the unsuccessful attempt at federation, and an
eagerness to draw Chinese (who traditionally abhored military service)
into the nation-building process. Over the horizon, Vietnam loomed as
a potential threat.

In spite of its size, the Singapore army kept out of politics and engaged
in many purely civilian activities. (Some officers, such as Lee's son,
made the transition between officer status and politics but they were
required to relinquish their commissions before running for office.)
National service helped to unify the ethnically diverse country, created
a pool of technically skilled personnel, and provided labor on public
projects. Like those other fourth way countries, Singapore's leaders had

---

*In 1985, there were dangerous signs in Costa Rica that militarism might reemerge.
Pressured by the Central American crisis, the government called in 200 American "advisers" to train its civilian police as an army.

managed to control the potential domestic influence of this relatively large army.

The Pattern

Our inquiry has not produced a solid set of "preconditions"—economic affluence, cultural consensus, an educated citizenry, a vigorous middle class, or a free enterprise economy—which had to *preceed* the emergence of more liberal political orders.

Places like the Ivory Coast, Colombia, and Singapore were much poorer than some of their neighbors three decades ago and yet they did not succumb to the more brutal forms of dictatorship.

Malaysia lacked the ethnic homogeneity of Indonesia just as India suffered from more cultural divisions than Maoist China but they managed to maintain democracies.

Education and literacy were far less common in Venezuela and Colombia at the beginning of their contemporary political evolution than in Chile, Uruguay, and Argentina which (at least, temporarily) fell into the hands of military dictators.

The middle classes in all fourth way regions were minuscule in 1950. They grew in size and influence as they simultaneously advanced in political maturity and gained a degree of economic independence.

The emergence of mixed, market-oriented economies went hand in hand with the defusion of traditional hostilities and the creation of a rule of law. But hybrid economies were accessories rather than prerequisites to political liberalization.

Reasonable people cannot doubt that the possession of certain social advantages—an independent middle class, an informed citizenry, a mixed economy which distributed affluence (and power) widely, an historical tradition which calmed communal passions and subordinated warriors to civilians, and an economic cushion which provided for peaceful political transitions—were helpful in avoiding bloodshed, creating an atmosphere of voluntary consent (or even consensus), and ensuring that people observed a rule of law.

Nonetheless, back at the middle of this century, none of the fourth way countries had all of these attributes. Only Costa Rica possessed many of them. The more general pattern since 1950 was that a liberal political order, epitomized by a fair rule of law and a distribution of economic rewards, generated a series of social and economic changes. As a broad upturn in economic vitality and welfare began to gain urgency, educated, autonomous middle classes grew in size and importance. They, in turn, provided both the leadership and the critics which allowed for sustained economic growth. This was the common pattern of all fourth way countries, even China after 1976.

Here again, one may legitimately detect a virtuous cycle at work where economic growth reinforced various social changes and allowed the continuance of an open political order. At times, of course, as in the Punjab, unwise political decisions diverted the natural course of change.

THE RICH AND THE POOR

The need is to remove the work of world development from the subsidiary attention of the wealthy nations and to make it a central theme of their diplomacy, their international relations, their philosophy of world order.

—BARBARA WARD

However Promethean the effort of exceptional leaders and their hard-working peoples, it was clear that developing countries could bring their quest for bread and freedom to a triumphant conclusion only with the cooperation of the world's richer nations. Successful collaboration between the rich regions and the fourth way areas proceeded along three routes: direct foreign aid, encouragement of "south-to-south" links, the reduction of barriers to trade and the defusion of the debt crisis.

Foreign Aid

A transfer of funds, skills, and knowledge, whether privately or publicly sponsored, played a critical role in fourth way development.

The Punjab's economic successes (and its copies in Uttar Pradash and Haryana) were primarily due to the wisdom of New Delhi's economic policies and the responsiveness of millions of newly awakened peasants. It could not have been achieved, however, without decisive aid from the outside world:

The Rockefeller Foundation sponsored research on hybrid, highly productive forms of wheat and rice. Originally conceived in Mexico and the Philippines, this knowledge spread to the Punjab. Readily adopting new agricultural technologies, the people brought about a "green revolution'' which saved India from famine.

The new seeds and techniques would, however, have been useless if the British had not originally introduced a complex array of dams and canals to provide irrigation for fallow lands. Loans from the World Bank in the 1960s later allowed for the modernization of this system throughout the Indus valley.

Eventually, teams of U.N. experts in both India and Pakistan furnished the techniques of desalinization, tube-welling, and canal maintenance which allowed the reconditioned land to blossom.

Without these injections of foreign knowledge, financing and skills, the Punjab and its adjoining states would have remained the deserts they were in 1880.

In their own ways, the Ivory Coast (primarily using French assistance and capital), Colombia (building schools with Alliance for Progress monies), Venezuela (modernizing its infrastructure with American aid), and Malaysia (taking advantage of Japanese schooling for managers and technicians) also demonstrated the important role which foreign assistance had in generating a cycle of economic progress.

Foreign aid, particularly bilateral governmental assistance, did not usually draw its inspiration from pure altruism. From the Marshall Plan of 1945, the philosophy of foreign aid was based on the sober realization that the enhanced prosperity of the richer regions depended on the trade, commerce, and future prosperity of the entire world. Statesmen in the richer countries recognized that the economic self-interest of their own societies required erasing abject poverty wherever it existed and expanding world markets. As the decades went on, the mutuality of interests between rich and poor nations—in trade, commodities, broadened markets, transportation, telecommunications, and energy—became increasingly apparent to scholars and international businessmen. Alas, many Western politicians—with the exception of Canada's Lester Pearson and Germany's Willie Brandt—ignored the growing interdependence of the world economy.

The magnaminity of the Marshall Plan (which intitially amounted to 2.79 percent of American GNP) was not matched in later years. Except for Sweden and the Netherlands, Western nations never approached the modest level of aid (0.7% of GNP) recommended by the Pearson and Brandt Commissions. The United States and Italy ignominiously brought up the rear of the ranks of the industrial democracies with a contribution of 0.2% of GNP. The Eastern bloc donated a miserly 0.14% of GNP to developing areas.

This Scrooge-like attitude toward foreign aid was not due to a lack of money in the developed nations. In 1985, for example, experts noted that the standard of living of people in all of the developing regions could immediately be doubled if only 20 percent of the capital devoted to war preparations were diverted to development aid.

Internal political pressures, rather than actual scarcity, blinded many politicians to the interests of their nations. Corporations mistakenly feared for their futures in a trade-free world where foreign aid had nurtured infant industries. They wished to hoard their existing profits. Union leaders feared that foreign aid and a consequent bolstering of new economies would lead their own rusting industries to drop jobs. Local politicians found more votes in their constituencies by supporting wine subsidies in the Lorraine or a Chrysler bail-out in Detroit than in advocating world development.

Nonetheless, a few far-sighted statesmen recognized that we live in one world. Suggestions abounded for improving the conditions of poor nations by increasing the flow of aid from the richer regions. Too often, however, these proposals exceeded the legitimate bounds of economic prudence and political credulity.

In 1969, for example, Nobel Laureate Linus Pauling suggested that an international income tax of 8 percent annually should be levied on the rich nations and devoted to development (a proposal repeated in modified form by the Brandt Commission in the 1980s). The richer countries dismissed the proposal as utopian.

In 1974, the U.N. General Assembly suggested establishing a "New Economic Order" which included, among other items, a world commodity reserve, an automatic subsidy from rich nations to poor, and international control over space and ocean exploration. The proposals—based as they were on castigation of "neocolonialism," multinationals, and the presumed guilt of richer nations for the plight of poorer regions—met with indifference in the West. The industrial countries had, after all, just witnessed the exploiting of their own economies by OPEC.

In the 1980s, the prestigious Brandt Commission again urged raising the level of aid to poor countries and increasing the capacity of world financial institutions to issue "soft," low-interest loans. Yet, the question remained whether the richer countries, lacking in apparent reasons of self-interest, would simply parcel out their wealth for the asking.

On a more rational level, substantive criticism of foreign aid policies emerged even among those who defended the general principle that the West had a moral responsibility to aid in creating a more humane world.

Since 1945, about 40 percent of all American foreign aid was spent on military preparations in underdeveloped countries. Such donations, particularly to dictatorships in Latin America and Africa were spent as Sowell observed "to acquire arms to be used principally in suppressing political critics and movements without their own country."[25]

Foreign aid all too often contributed to a country's problem by artificially distorting its economy. Thus, Bangladesh received about $1.7 billion from the United States, much of it in the form of food. Corrupt officials used the aid to support artificially low food prices in urban areas, decreasing the incentive of their own farmers to produce for the market. Domestic food production fell in a region which could once support itself. Bangladesh began importing one to three million tons of food each year to feed its exploding population. Similarly, in the opinion of some experts, enormous donations to Israel contributed to a staggering rate of inflation (at times, 1,000% a year) and helped to support the colonization of the West Bank.

Subracting military expenditures, direct economic aid went disproportionately to those countries—Israel, Egypt, Turkey, and Pakistan—which various American governments believed served "strategic" interests. Critics argued that it would have been in the country's own economic interest to direct money instead to less developed areas which bought 39 percent of all United States exports.

Further, foreign assistance often merely covered over the mistakes and inefficiencies of dictatorial governments. Tanzania received more aid per capita than any other country in the world, primarily from Sweden. Since independence, however, worker productivity declined, the government bureaucracy grew, and Tanzania's dictator imprisoned thousands. The once productive country turned from being an exporter of food to its new status as an importer.

Deficiences of this sort—wasting aid on guns, using foreign income to distort an economy, directing the flow of aid on dubious assumptions of strategic utility, and using aid to support crumbling dictatorships—were real but correctible. A consideration of these criticism—balanced by a recognition of the tangible achievements of foreign aid in fourth way regions—indicated that a humane but reasonable policy of foreign aid included these elements:

• Aid was directed to encouraging those sectors of an economy, particularly agriculture, which showed immediate promise of increasing a peoples' self-sustained growth.

• Aid in building a rudimentary infrastructure, again emphasizing agricultural supplements such as feeder roads and irrigation, received priority.

• Aid which directly increased a people's knowledge, whether transmitted through satellites or schools, was emphasized.

• Military aid, particularly to the Somozas and Zias of the world, based on "strategic" consideration was vastly curtailed or eliminated.

• Aid was bilateral so that a donor nation was sure that the recipients did not waste their funds in corruption, inefficiency, or repression.

In the future, emergency humanitarian aid—such as food for Ethiopians stricken by drought and dictatorship—will have to be provided. Yet the aid must not become a long-term crutch for debilitated nations. Rather, the donor countries must seek to insure that the economic and political conditions which provoke such calamities are eliminated.

This means that the donor nations should not hesitate to use their aid as a way to end genocide, to promote human rights, and to free political prisoners. Whether in South Africa or Zaire, Poland or South Korea, the West should moderate its flow of foreign aid (as well as trade and private investments) with conditions which help to free the faceless thousands who are held as prisoners of conscience throughout the world.

To use foreign aid as a means of influencing dictatorial governments will incur charges of "neoimperialism." This rhetorical penalty is well worth it if, as in Argentina, such a campaign for human rights gets prisoners out of jail and brings to trial the generals who have effected mass "disappearances."

The record of the fourth way areas indicates that foreign assistance—when it truly goes to aid the poor rather than inefficient, irresponsible, or tyrannical rulers—can add a crucial impetus to economic growth.

Balancing World Trade

Hong Kong and Singapore achieved great economic progress without the benefit of large gifts from foreign governments. Their success depended primarily on finding a profitable, if everchanging role in world trade.

Their leaders understood the interdependence of the world economy, and their peoples strikingly benefited from this recognition. The continued success of such economies depended critically on the preservation of a free trade system throughout the world, sustained growth of exports, and the lowering of protectionist barriers. The crucial lesson of Hong Kong and Singapore was this: when trade grew, the world economy, including its poorest segments, also grew.

De facto cooperation among the world's economic powers was nowhere more apparent than along the "Pacific Rim," stretching from Japan in the north to New Zealand in the south, from China in the east to California in the west.

East Asian nations, including Hong Kong and Singapore which had once been counted as among the more backward in the world, emerged as dramatically expanding economies.

By 1980, two-way trade between America and the Pacific Rim nations began to exceed trade between America and Western Europe. By 1984, the current of trade between the United States and Pacific Rim nations had jumped to $136 billion while trade with Europe remained relatively stable at $110 billion, and the gap continued to widen. Between 1974 and 1984, the average compounded growth rate in Asia's "miracle economies"—Japan, Singapore, Hong Kong, Taiwan, South Korea, and Malaysia—was 8.2 percent annually, while the great markets of China beckoned.

By 1986, the Asian nations traded more with one another than with non-Pacific regions, thereby pumping further energy into their home markets which already composed six out of ten people living on the planet.

Although disunited ethnically and politically, economic interdependence of the Pacific Rim nations urged them towards increasing cooperation. By 1986, over one hundred private and public organizations sought greater economic and political cooperation in the Pacific. Bilateral agreements secured ad hoc cooperation between the various countries on matters ranging from fisheries to reduction of protectionist measures within the region.

This dynamic growth in trade was hardly due to Japan's preeminent position. In fact, by 1986, the Japanese growth in trade had slowed while the combined export–import trade of Hong Kong, Taiwan, South Korea, and the ASEAN countries was, for the first time in history, higher than that of Japan.

Thus, with a great surge in trade and cooperation, the Pacific Rim countries began to fulfill one of Karl Marx's last and most perceptive prophecies about the future: "The Pacific Ocean will then play the same role as at present the Atlantic and that of the Mediterranean in classical antiquity."

In the early 1980s, however, worldwide recession threatened even the Pacific Rim, and its handmaiden was the prospect of increasing protection for ailing industries in the West. America and Japan, the twin pillars for world trade, began to emerge as protectionist villains while many developing nations closed their doors on imports from industrialised areas. As many countries were forced to reduce consumption and increase unemployment, exports were stifled and the risks of political instability compounded. No one gained.

One major symptom of this threat was the continuing debt crisis. Fueled by excess capital from the OPEC countries, New York and London banks extended major loans to developing countries from 1975 until 1983. (Ironically, much of this new money in oil-poor nations went for paying increased energy costs.)

The bankers were all too willing to lend out their monies. By 1982, loans from nine major United States Banks to non–oil-producing states soared to a level of 224 percent of their *total* capital. Obviously, if the debtor nations defaulted, many banks in the richer regions would go with them.

Why did the bankers gamble so heavily in developing areas? Essentially, they were impressed by the spectacular economic performance of many developing countries, particularly in Latin America, in the years between 1970 and 1978. In the 1970s, for example, Mexico averaged 6.4 percent real growth annually while its exports grew 10.9 percent annually. Brazil advanced during this period at 6.7 percent each year and even Argentina expanded its exports by 10.7 percent a year. If the growth had continued at this pace, there was little question that the bankers would reap a profit.

The creditors, however, did not anticipate the oil crisis, the extent of corruption (particularly in Latin America), the inefficiencies entailed by the "corporatist" ideology entertained by military dictators, or the propensity of centralized states to waste money on prestige projects.

Significantly, the bankers made their worst mistakes by investing money in supposedly "stable" dictatorial regimes. Ideology made little difference, as long as a military figure or a single party dominated the economy. Thus, the world banks lent as liberally to Poland ($26 billion in 1983) as to the Philippines ($17 billion). Out of the world's twenty-one largest borrowers, only two (Venezuela and Israel) could have been considered as liberal democracies. In the early 1980s, the top four debtor nations (Brazil, Mexico, Argentina, and South Korea) were all either military regimes or one party dictatorships.

The supposedly realistic financiers made the political mistake of gambling on dictatorships.

Their miscalculations soon became apparent as military regimes in Latin America demonstrated their inefficiency, and the "threat" of liberalization spread. Simultaneously, between 1980 and 1982, recession set in among industrial countries and demands for imports including commodities, oil, and manufactured goods, began to drop. Latin America's export trade declined by 30 percent during this period. Even the oil-exporting countries had to cut back on their development projects.

Scared by the teetering nature of their investments, the bankers raised the interst rates in "high-risk" areas to a level of about 3 percent more than prevailing world rates.

This "scissors effect" of declining export earnings and, at the same time, higher interest costs nearly caused Mexico to default in 1982. By 1983, the twenty-one major borrowing countries were paying nearly 80 percent of their foreign exchange earnings merely for "debt service" (interest on the past loans and repayment of short-term debts). Obviously, this left little room for imports from the industrial world and had a "domino effect" of increasing recession in the developed countries.

By 1984, the debts reached astronomical proportions: Brazil owed $93 billion, Mexico $89 billion, Argentina $44 billion, and South Korea $40 billion. In some cases, repayment of the debts appeared simply impossible: Brazil's debt service payments amounted to 133 percent more than *all* of its earnings of foreign exchange from exports of goods and services. In the worst case, Zambia, debt service payments in 1983 were 195 percent greater than export revenues.

By prudent planning and, in some cases, enormous foreign reserves, the fourth way regions survived the debt crisis. Singapore, India, China, and Hong Kong escaped virtually unscathed. Others had to modify their more ambitious development plans. Between 1982 and 1984, for example, the Ivory Coast reduced investment by 40 percent; Malaysian customs revenues fell 24 percent while debt servicing rose by 23 percent; Costa Rica and Colombia spent 32 percent of their foreign exchange on debt interest in 1984, requiring austerity in health and educational services; and Venezuela postponed payment on $9 billion due in 1984, risking a default which would have cut the growing nation off from needed imports of technology and machine tools.

The other debt-burdened countries seemed caught in an unsolvable dilemma:

They could simply default on their gigantic debts. In that event, they could import nothing—medicines or machine replacements, guns, or food—from the West. Their own economies would spin downward into anarchy and the world financial system, as it did in the 1930s, would collapse.

Conversely, they could attempt to pay their debts—or, at least the debt service charges—in return for a long-term rescheduling of the loans, usually under the supervision of the International Monetary Fund (IMF). This alternative required a reduction in internal spending, higher taxes, curbs on inflation, and more unemployment. Politically, such austerity crippled the poor and adversely affected powerful groups within the middle class. Schools in the Ivory Coast could not be staffed, doctors in Costa Rica could not receive wage increases, and subsidies to Venezuela's military evaporated. This approach created political instability, including the possibility that reckless demagogues would take power and default.

The developing regions, including the fourth way countries, chose the politically and socially unpalatable path of austerity, in the hope that their economies would keep or regain their momentum. Balancing the requirements of the IMF and world trade against domestic pressures was an enormously difficult task but, at least in the short run, the solution worked: the financing requirements of indebted developing countries fell from $150 billion to $47 billion between 1981 and 1985, exports in many areas rebounded, and the world began its recovery from another recession.

Yet, the world debt crisis left little margin for error. The lures of a mass default were still enticing and the dangers of a world depression did not go away. A variety of proposals were made, and some were implemented, to ensure that developing regions could sustain or regain their pace of growth.

With megre room for maneuvering on their own ground, private banks rescheduled loans, allowing a longer period of repayment, and contemplated various measures—issuing long-term bonds which would make their own central governments the "creditor" or discounting existing loans to a new international institution—which would avoid further crises.

The IMF received additional financial support, imposed reforms on unbalanced economies and, in return, rescheduled their debt payments.

The World Bank increasingly supported high-yielding sectors of various economies, particularly in agriculture, and devoted a larger proportion of its monies to structural reforms.

Those countries which were too poor to borrow from commercial sources or even the World Bank but had a great potential for growth, received loans (often at zero interest) from the International Development Association.

Only such measures of world cooperation coupled with internal reforms, a resistance to protectionism, and a continued expansion of capital flows would allow other developing regions to join the ranks of fourth way nations.

Watching the slow, uneven but steady progress of the European Economic Community, perceptive commentators urged that another avenue of cooperation—collaboration among the developing countries themselves—should be realistically explored.

"South-to-South" Linkages

In spite of the grotesque failure of past efforts such as the Organization of African States, leaders in some developing areas encouraged a "south-to-south" dialogue leading to the mobilization of complementary strengths or to the compensation for one country's weaknesses by the strength of another nation in particular sectors.

As OPEC demonstrated during the 1970s, the world market responded most dramatically to those who dealt from strength. The oil cartel forced an increase of prices simply because industrialized nations, at that particular time, had no other choice. OPEC's experience could not be repeated or even prolonged indefinitely because there were far too many alternative sources of raw materials as well as substitutes for the world's basic commodities.

Nonetheless, although in embryonic stages, a new "south-to-south" dialogue began over ways in which developing regions could mutually benefit from their various comparative advantages. The more serious developments included:

Regional institutions for investment and development banking were formed, particularly by Arab states seeking other regions capable of absorbing a gush of oil revenue.

Interregional councils of health, research, and education were established, especially in Latin America, which allowed one nation to capitalize, say, on the advanced health services of its region while receiving in return sophisticated assistance in agriculture.

"Third world" multinationals ballooned in the 1970s and 1980s. India's Birla and Tata Engineering complexes built manufacturing and paper plants in Africa. South Korea's Hyundai Group and Dong Ah Construction became major forces in the Middle East. Hong Kong's textile firms set up plants in Malaysia while Malaysia's quasi-nationalized Sime Darby expanded into Indonesia. Although their nations lacked diplomatic relations, a consortium of Singapore firms invested some $1 billion in oil exploration off China's coastal rim and received a 17 year guarantee of their investment.

Like their Western counterparts, the developing countries' multinationals sought to expand stagnant markets at home, find a cheaper production base, exploit new opportunities and, as in India, to escape from cumbersome government bureaucracies.

They tended to operate in neighboring regions, often had cultural affinities with their new customers, and sometimes possessed expert knowledge of "local" conditions, labor, and materials. Consequently, as the "third world" multinationals grew phenomenally, they not only filled new niches in the world market but, at times, displaced their Western competitors.

The more advanced fourth way countries often cooperated with their neighbors in mutually beneficial ways. In Southeast Asia, for example, Indonesia sent crude oil to Singapore for refining, Malaysia bought petrol products for its new automobile industry from Singapore, while Indonesia and Singapore bought the Malaysian cars. A distribution of labor of this sort allowed each country to profit while concentrating on doing what they knew best and producing at the lowest costs.

Such regional cooperation was vital but it often floundered on nationalism, mistaken visions of self-sufficiency and traditional hostilities. In the Middle East, for example, Egypt imported potash at great expense from Canada when nearby Jordan had large supplies. In Africa, Nigeria refused to enter a common market for oil and helped to bankrupt Ghana. ASEAN linkages were weakened when Indonesia established its own less economic refineries and rendered some of Singapore's existing facilities redundant. This, in turn, reduced the capacity of Singaporeans to buy Malaysian cars. While Indonesia still wanted Singapore's collaboration in exploiting islands off Sumatra, the Singapore businessmen instead turned much of their energies to building radar equipment, helicopters, and ships needed for China's off-shore oil exploration. The eventual loser in Indonesia's nationalistic venture was its own bloated, state-owned oil industry.

Thus, "south-to-south" linkages depended on hard-headed considerations of mutual economic interest, a recognition of interdependence, the abandonment of nationalism, and often, an easing of traditional religious and ethnic hostilities. As Tanzania's attack on Uganda, Iraq's invasion of Iran, and Sukarno's policy of "confrontation" too often demonstrated, these conditions were hard to fulfill. Only as the "south" became cooperatively stronger, however, could it realistically deal with the "north" in creating a genuinely affluent world order.

CONCLUSIONS

Just because a man is poor and maybe cannot read does not mean that he cares nothing for his human rights.

—An Indian villager (quoted by William Borders)

Contrary to the pessimists of the twentieth century, some leaders of developing countries have brought both bread and freedom to their peoples. The successful regions have not followed the orthodoxies of either the right or the left. They have dared to experiment with mixed economies, welcomed the intrusion of alien ideas and technologies, built up their agriculture rather than glittering steel plants, and expressed a willingness to mediate old hatreds in a search for mutual prosperity. Above all, they have carried forward their quest for affluence without sacrificing the living for the debatable benefit of future generations. Instead, they have pursued policies which promoted the health, the education, and the liberties (under law) of their citizens.

Our study, then, points to a central lesson: the humane policies and the wisdom of individual leaders were of sovereign importance in the process of development. They actively promoted freedom for individual ambition and intelligence.

In the fourth way regions, political decisions took precedence over objective economic conditions and social obstacles. Dengist China moved toward rapid economic growth only after pragmatic political leaders had released the peasantry from collectivism. Venezuela used her resources after, not before the ascendency of the AD. The Ivory Coast progressed because Houphouët-Boigny, unlike Touré and Nkrumah, opened his poor economy to world influences and conducted a dialogue with his enemies. Singapore's PAP made political decisions which invigorated an economy which many observers had written off as hopeless in 1959.

None of this was inevitable or dictated by specific economic or social conditions. As philosopher John Plamanetz has warned the newer nations:

The recipe, *first* raise productivity and material well-being and abolish illiteracy, doing whatever needs to be done to these ends, and *afterwards* set about establishing freedom and democracy is bad . . . history gives us no example of a nation that first grew prosperous and acquired a strong centralized government and then afterwards became free and democratic. It is not true of the Greeks or the Romans or the Dutch or the English or the Swiss or the Americans; of any of the people who have cared most for freedom or democracy, or have enjoyed them the most securely.[26]

Those who desired both bread and freedom for their peoples had to work simultaneously to establish a rule of law, the right to criticize, the right of privacy *and* they had to build a pluralistic social structure with depositories of power independent of the group which controlled the government.

While creating a politically open society, the leadership also stimulated a growing economy, educated its people and encouraged individuals to pursue their own destinies. Aspiring tyrants hesitated to attack the complex, interdependent social and economic structure which resulted from these efforts.

The preservation of a diversified, free economy was, as Massimo Salvadori warned, an important element in protecting political freedoms:

Since the beginning of civilization there have been numerous collectivist societies. Not a single one has enjoyed free institutions. Miracles can happen; but it is wiser to believe in miracles (especially economic and political miracles) after they have happened and not before.[27]

To maintain a robust economy and to sustain politically free institutions—buffeted by world economic trends, religious enthusiasms, threats from army generals on the right and guerrillas on the left—was a challenge for Atlas.

Yet, men of courage and compassion, rare people of moderation and vision—Figeures and Betancourt, Lee and the Tunku, Pearson and Brandt—have demonstrated for three decades that solutions to these grim and difficult tasks need not elude human grasp.

Will the achievements of these people last? Only the next generations, freely choosing their destinies, will decide.

ACKNOWLEDGMENTS

The generosity of the National University of Singapore, Clare Hall (Cambridge), the Rockefeller Center of Italy, and the City University of New York provided the means and the time for carrying out this project. The Ford Foundation, Stanford University, the American University in Cairo, and the Rice University Center for the Study of Social Change made possible our initial work in India, Indonesia, Africa, and the Middle East. We gratefully acknowledge their essential backing.

Intellectually, four individuals, sadly departed from this world, played a decisive role in our lives: Hans Kohn taught us the value of Western civilization; Gordon Allport informed us about the humaneness, yet diversity of mankind; Abdullah Lutfiyya introduced us to the complexities of the Middle East; and Zakir Hussain, late president of India, offered hope and evidence that his nation would survive triumphantly from its turmoil.

Edward Sagarin of the City University of New York, Randolph and Sharon Mengchee Phillips of Cornell, Geoffrey Sayre-McCord of the University of North Carolina, and Robert McCord of the Congressional Center for the Study of the Future graciously—well, at times, acerbically—criticized the manuscript. John and Stellah Quah, Ko Yui Chung, and Francis and Ester Heng of the National University of Singapore gave us their kindness and knowledge.

Myron Kolatch, the pioneering editor of *The New Leader,* meticulously crafted several chapters which originally appeared in his journal. As he has done so often in the past, Eric Swenson, editor of W. W. Norton, provided the initial support and careful editing for the manuscript.

We wish to thank, too, some dear friends who so cheerfully enriched our lives but will never have a chance to read this book. We think particularly of Adam in a Polish prison, Ah Heng in Singapore, Ahmed in Egypt, and Joshua in Ghana. And for those who tried to obstruct this project—transparent secret policmen in Egypt, petty bureaucrats in Asia, timid or arrogant academicians in America and the "third world"—we hope that this book will serve as a gentle reproof, another small piece of evidence that attempts at free inquiry cannot ultimately be stifled.

ABOUT THE AUTHORS

William McCord is professor of sociology at the City University of New York and a member-for-life of Clare Hall, Cambridge University. He has been a visiting fellow of Clare Hall and the Institute of Criminology at Cambridge University; a distinguished lecturer at the Warsaw Academy of Arts and Sciences; a Fulbright professor at Trinity College, Dublin; a visiting professor at the American University in Cairo and at the National University of Singapore; and a Ford public affairs fellow in India, Indonesia, the Middle East, and Africa.

Arline Fujii McCord is professor of sociology and dean of social sciences at the City College of New York. She has traveled in Singapore, Malaysia, Hong Kong, Europe, Japan and China.

They and their family live in Orangeburg, New York, near the Hudson River.

Notes

Part I

1. Robert Heilbroner, *An Inquiry into the Human Prospect.* (New York: W. W. Norton, 1974), pp. 13 and 22.
2. Charles Frankel, *The Case for Modern Man* (New York: Harper and Row, 1955), p. 41.
3. Henry James, quoted in *ibid.*
4. Peter Berger, "Democracy for Everyone," *Commentary*, September 1983, pp. 34 and 36.
5. Raymond Aron, *In Defense of Decadent Europe* (Paris: Plon, 1978).
6. Max Lerner, "On Being a Possibilist," *Newsweek,* October 8, 1979.

Chapter One

1. Sir Charles Metcalf, Report of the Select Committee of the House of Commons, 1832, Vol. III, appendix 84, p. 331.
2. Kussum Nair, *Blossoms in the Dust* (London: Gerald Duckworth and Co., 1961), p. 135.
3. Karl Marx, *Capital,* Vol. 1 (Chicago, 1906), p. 834.
4. John Kenneth Galbraith, *The Voice of the Poor* (Cambridge: Harvard University Press, 1983), p. 13.

5. Trevor Fishlock, *Ghandi's Children* (New York: Universe Books, 1983), p. 107.

6. P. T. Bauer, *Reality and Rhetoric* (Cambridge: Harvard University Press, 1984), pp. 136 and 157.

7. Fishlock, *op. cit.*, p. 138.

8. Irving Louis Horowitz, *Beyond Empire and Revolution* (New York: Oxford University Press, 1981), p. 262.

9. Alex Inkeles and David H. Smith, *Becoming Modern* (Cambridge: Harvard University Press, 1974), pp. 315–316.

10. William McCord and Abdullah Lutfiyya, "Urbanization and World View in the Middle East," in *Essays on Modernization of Underdeveloped Societies,* ed., A. R. Desai (Bombay: Thacker & Co., 1968).

11. Clark Kerr, *The Future of Industrial Societies* (Cambridge: Harvard University Press, 1983), p. 23.

12. *Ibid.*, p. 96.

13. Colin Turnbull, *The Lonely African* (New York: Simon & Schuster Inc., 1962), p. 53.

14. *Ibid.*, p. 83–84.

15. Peter Berger, Brigitte Berger, Hansfeld Kellner, *The Homeless Mind* (New York: Random House, 1973).

16. Galbraith, *op. cit.*, p. 16.

17. See, for example, Rati Ram and Theodore Schultz, "Life Span, Health, Savings, and Productivity," *Economic Development and Cultural Change,* April 1979, 27, 399–421; Theodore Schultz, *Investing in People* (Boulder: University of Colorado Press, 1980); Theodore Schultz, "The Value of the Ability to Deal with Disequilibria," *Journal of Economic Literature,* 13 September, 1976, pp. 827–846.

18. Inkeles and Smith, *op. cit.*

19. Theodore Schultz, Presidential Address, *The American Economic Review,* Vol. II, No. 1, March 1961.

20. Sir Arthur Lewis, in *Restless Nations* (New York: Dodd Mead & Co., p. 81).

21. Richard Critchfield, "Science and the Villager; The Last Sleeper Awakes," *Foreign Affairs,* Fall, 1982, Vol. 61, No. 1, p. 40.

CHAPTER TWO

1. Larry Minear, "Hunger's Tangled Roots Require Concerted Attack," *International Herald Tribune,* August 6, 1984, editorial page.

2. Aurelio Peccei, Introduction to *On Growth II,* William L. Oltmans, ed. (New York: Putnams, 1975), p. xi.

3. D. S. Halacy, *Earth, Water, Wind and Sun* (New York: Harper, 1977), p. 5.

4. Peccei, *op. cit.*

5. Council on Environmental Quality and the Department of State, *The Global 2000 Report to the President* (New York: Penguin Books, 1982), p. 1.

6. William W. Kellog and Robert Schware, "Society, Science, and Climate Change," *Foreign Affairs,* Summer, 1982, Vol. 60, No. 5, pp. 1022–1037.

7. Fouad Ajami, "The Fate of Nonalighment," *Foreign Affairs,* Summer, 1982, Vol. 60, No. 5, pp. 1022–1037.

8. Garrett Hardin, "The Case Against Helping the Poor," *Psychology Today,* September 1974, p. 126.

9. Karl Sax, *The World's Exploding Population* (Boston: Beacon Press, 1960), pp. 133, 140, 142.

10. Lester R. Brown, et.al. *State of the World 1984* (New York: W. W. Norton, 1984), pp. 13–14.

11. Julian Simon, *The Ultimate Resource* (Princeton: Princeton University Press, 1981).

12. Peter Odell, quoted in Richard Barnet, *The Lean Years* (New York: Simon and Schuster, 1980), p. 30.

13. Barnet, *ibid.,* p. 30.

14. Julian Simon, *The Ultimate Resource.* Princeton, N.J.: Princeton University Press (1981), p. 209.

15. Ben Bova, *Voyages.* New York: Doubleday (1981), p. 300.

16. Amartya Sen, *Poverty and Famine.* Oxford: Clarenden Press (1982).

17. Vaclav Smyl, "Introduction," *Energy Conservation.* Edited by Vaclav Smyl and William Knowland. Oxford: Oxford University Press (1980).

18. John Gribben, *Weather Force.* London: Hamlyn (1979).

19. Robert McClosky, quoted in the *International Herald Tribune,* August 10, 1984.

20. *Ibid.*

21. Barbara Ward, *Progress for a Small Planet.* New York: W. W. Norton (1979), p. 293.

Chapter Three

1. Marshall Shalins, *Stone-Age Economics* (New York: Aldine-Atherton, 1972).

2. Uli Schmetzer, "Quietly, Albania Allows an Opening in Its Wall," *International Herald Tribune,* 20 August, 1984, p. 1.

3. Haroon Siddiqui, "The Islamic Revival," *World Press Review,* August, 1984.

4. Ayatollah Khomeini in Fouad Ajami, "The Fate of Nonalignment," *Foreign Affairs,* Winter 1980–1981, Vol. 59, No. 2, 1981.

5. Abdul Karim Risalpuri, "An Eye for an Eye," *Far Eastern Economic Review,* 6 September, 1984.

6. Adjami, *op. cit.,* p. 379.

7. Hussain Haqqani, *Far Eastern Economic Review,* 16 August, 1984.

8. Abdul Karim Risalpuri, *op. cit.*

9. D. Sears, "The Meaning of Development," *International Development Review,* 11, 4, 1969, p. 6.

10. Paul Baran, *The Political Economy of Growth,* New York, Monthly Review Press, 1957.

11. *Ibid.,* p. 11.

12. *Ibid.,* p. 12.

13. Ibid., p. 28.

14. Sir Arthur Lewis quoted in Stephen A. Marlin, "The Wealth of Nations," *The New York Review of Books,* July 19, 1984.

15. P. T. Bauer, *Reality and Rhetoric* (Cambridge: Harvard University Press, 1984), p. 5.

16. Ian M. D. Little, *Economic Development* (New York: Basic Books, 1982).

17. Bauer, *op. cit.,* p. 57.

18. Sylvia Ann Hewlett, *The Cruel Dilemma of Development* (New York: Basic Books, 1980), p. 45.

19. *Ibid.,* p. 43.

20. *Ibid.,* p. 207.

21. Richard Fagen, "Equity in the South in the Context of North-South Relations," in Albert Fishlow et al., *Rich and Poor Nations in the World Economy* (New York: McGraw-Hill, 1978), p. 172.

22. Hewlett, *op. cit.,* p. 208.

23. *Ibid.,* p. 24.

PART II

1. See Morris Davis Morris, *Measuring the Condition of the World's Poor* (New York: Pergamon Press, 1979), and Clark Kerr, *The Future of Industrial Societies* (Cambridge: Harvard University Press, 1983).

2. Amnesty International, *Amnesty International Report* (London: Amnesty International Publications, 1983).

3. John Kenneth Galbraith, *The Voices of the Poor* (Cambridge: Harvard University Press, 1982), p. 23.

CHAPTER FOUR

1. London Observer Service, November 15, 1984.
2. Peter Onu, Associated Press dispatch, November 12, 1984.
3. David Lamb, *The Africans* (New York: Random House, 1982), p. xiv.
4. "There Is a Better Way," *The Economist,* November 3, 1984.
5. *Ibid.*
6. Jim Hogland, "Tattered Angola Appears Ready to Take Gambles for Self-Respect," Washington Post Service, November 14, 1984.
7. Sékou Touré, quoted in Lamb, *op. cit.,* p. 211.
8. Anonymous letter in *West Africa,* No. 4, 1967, p. 321.
9. Samir Amin, *Le developpement du capitalisme en Cote d'Ivoire* (Paris: Editions de Minuit, 1967).
10. Felix Houphouët-Boigny, quoted in Lamb, *op. cit.,* p. 218.
11. V. S. Naipaul, *Finding the Center* (New York: Alfred A. Knopf, 1984), p. 76.
12. *Ibid.,* p. 85–86.
13. *Ibid.,* p. 78.

CHAPTER FIVE

1. Tunku Abdul Rahman, *Contemporary Issues in Malaysian Politics* (Pelunduk Publications: Petalung Selangor, Malaysia, 1984), p. 6.
2. Barbara Watson Andaya and Leonard Y. Andaya. *A History of Malaysia* (London: Macmillan, 1982), p. 288.
3. See Clark Kerr, *The Future of Industrial Societies* (Cambridge: Harvard University Press, 1983).
4. Hamish McDonald, *Suharto's Indonesia* (Fontana Books: Blackburn, Victoria, Australia, 1981), p. 216.
5. James Clad, "The Other Malaysians," *Far East Economic Review,* July 26, 1984, p. 22.
6. Amnesty International, *Amnesty International Report, 1983,* Amnesty International Publications, London, 1983.
7. Tan Boon Kean, "Orwell's Year in the Malaysian Press," *Far Eastern Economic Review,* September 20, 1984, pp. 40–41.

CHAPTER SIX

1. John Quincy Adams, quoted in Walter La Feber, *Inevitable Revolution* (New York: W. W. Norton, 1983), p. 23.
2. Glen Dealy, quoted in Jonathan Power, "No Tears for Bygone Caudillos," *International Herald Tribune,* Jan. 11, 1985.

3. Ricardo Jiménez, quoted in *ibid.*, p. 30.

4. Eduardo Ulibarri, "Costa Rica: An Unlikely Oasis of Latin Stability," *World Paper*, Dec., 1984, p. 8.

5. Luis Alberto Monge, quoted in *ibid.*, p. 8.

6. James Chace, *Endless War* (New York: Vintage Books, 1984), p. 51.

7. Luis Alberto Monge, quoted in Marc Edelman and Jayne Huthcroft, "Costa Rica: Resisting Austerity," *NACLA Report*, Jan./Feb., 1984, p. 40.

8. *Miami Herald*, Dec. 26, 1982. Also see *The Future of Latin America*, ed. Richard Fagen and Olga Pellicu (Stanford: Stanford University Press, 1983).

9. Thomas E. Weil, *et al.*, *Area Handbook for Colombia* (Washington, D.C.: Government Printing Office, 1977), p. 321.

10. Clark Kerr, *The Future of Industrial Societies* (Cambridge: Harvard University Press, 1983).

11. See Harry Kline, *Colombia* (Boulder, Col.: Westview Press, 1983).

12. Ramon Jimeno and Steven Volk, "Colombia: Whose Country Is This, Anyway?" *NACLA Report*, May/June, 1983, p. 15.

13. *Financial Times*, Feb, 19, 1982.

14. Jimeno and Volk, *op. cit.*, p. 9.

15. Comité Permanence por la Defensa de los Derechos Humanos, *Repression y tortura en Colombia* (Bogotá: Fondo Editorial Suramérica, 1980).

16. Jimeno and Volk, *op. cit.*, pp. 23 and 29.

17. Daniel H. Levine, "Venezuelan Politics," in Robert Bond, ed., *Contemporary Venezuela* (New York: New York University Press, 1977), pp. 7 and 35.

18. John V. Lonbardi, *Venezuela* (New York: Oxford University Press, 1982), p. 228.

19. See Amnesty International, *Amnesty International Report*, London, Amnesty International Publications, 1983.

20. Lombardi, *op. cit.*, p. 267.

21. Bond, *op. cit.*, p. 231.

22. Ruth Leger Sivard, *World Military and Social Expenditures, 1982* (Leesburg, Va.: World Priorities, 1982).

23. Lombardi, *op. cit.*, p. 248.

24. *Ibid.*

25. Gary W. Wynia, *The Politics of Latin American Development*, (Cambridge: Cambridge University Press, 1984), p. 200.

26. Valentin Hernandez, quoted by Kim Fuad, "Venezuela's Role in OPEC," in Bond, *op. cit.*, p. 143.

27. James Le Moyne "Venezuelan Workers Find the Well Has Run Dry," *New York Times*, Dec. 19, 1983, p. A2.

28. Wynia, *op. cit.*, p. 190.
29. Thomas Jefferson, quoted in La Feber, p. 22.
30. Wynia, *op. cit.*, p. 206.
31. James Chace, *op. cit.*, p. 136.

CHAPTER SEVEN

1. *The People's Daily,* Peking, November 4, 1958.
2. Chester Bowles, *The New York Times,* November 16, 1963.
3. Felix Greene, *Awakened China* (Garden City: Doubleday and Co., 1961), appendix.
4. William K. Stevens, "India's 'Forced March' to Modernity," *The New York Times Magazine,* January 22, 1984, p. 28.
5. *Ibid.,* p. 40.
6. Kemal Pateek, quoted in "Bhopal: High Tech Risks for Third World," *New York Times Service,* February 4, 1985.
7. Trevor Fishlock, *Gandhi's Children* (Universe Books: New York, 1983), p. 110.
8. *Ibid.,* p. 112.
9. Stevens, *op. cit.,* p. 34.
10. Bashiruddin Ahmed, quoted in Stevens, p. 35.
11. See Jan Myrdal, *India Waits* (New Delhi: Sangan Books, 1984).
12. James Traub, "The Sorry State of India," *The New Republic,* June 4, 1984, p. 19.
13. Swaminathan S. Aiyer, quoted by Edward Behr, "The Price of Obedience," *Newsweek,* November 19, 1984.
14. *The Indian Express,* November 12, 1984.
15. Selig Harrison, *India: The Most Dangerous Decades* (Princeton: Princeton University Press, 1960), pp. 326–28.
16. N. A. Palkhivala, *Time,* July 2, 1984.
17. *The Economist,* February 2, 1985, p. 11.
18. *Ibid.*
19. James Traub, *op. cit.,* p. 23, and James Traub, *India: The Challenge of Change* (New York: Julian Messner / Simon and Schuster, 1984).

CHAPTER EIGHT

1. Quoted in Paul Johnson, *Modern Times* (New York: Harper and Row, 1983), p. 545.
2. *Ibid.,* p. 544.

3. See William Hinton, *Fanshen* (New York: Random House, 1966).

4. Fox Butterfield, *China* (London: Hadden and Stoughton, 1982).

5. William L. Parish and Martin King Whyte, *Village and Family in Contemporary China* (Chicago: University of Chicago Press, 1978).

6. Deng Xiaoping, quoted in *Asiaweek,* October 19, 1984, p. 37.

7. Paul Johnson, *op. cit.,* p. 548.

8. W. R. Geddes, *Peasant Life in Communist China,* The Society for Applied Anthropology, Monograph No. 6, Ithaca, New York, 1963.

9. Wilfred Malenbaum and Wolfgang Stopler, "Political Ideology and Economic Progress: the Basic Question," *World Politics.* Vol. XII, No. 3, April, 1960.

10. Mao Zedung, quoted in Bill Brugger, *China: Liberation and Transformation* (Princeton: Princeton University Press, 1981), p. 174.

11. Butterfield, *op. cit.,* p. 42.

12. Among the best treatises on Mao's China are Roderick MacFarquhar, *The Origins of the Cultural Revolution* (London: Oxford University Press, 1983); Randolph Barker and Radha Sinha, *The Chinese Agricultural Community* (Boulder Col.: Westview Press, 1982); and John Frasier, *The Chinese* (New York: Summit Books, 1980).

13. The better descriptions of post-Maoist China are Orville Shell, *To Get Rich Is Glorious* (New York: Pantheon Books, 1983); *Roses and Thorns* ed. Perry Peck (Berkeley: University of California Press, 1983); Roger Garside, *China After Mao* (New York: McGraw-Hill, 1981); and David Bonavia, *The Chinese* (New York: Lippincott, 1980).

14. Deng Xiaoping, quoted by Eric Hall, Reuter's Service, August 20, 1984.

15. *The Economist,* February 2, 1985, p. 11.

16. Qian Jiaju, quoted in *Asiaweek,* October 19, 1984, p. 41.

17. Wang Zizhen, quoted in Christopher Wren, "Zigong Plant Is Industrial Model," *International Herald Tribune* August 1, 1984.

18. Clark Kerr, *The Future of Industrial Societies* (Cambridge: Harvard University Press, 1983).

19. *The China Daily,* February 1, 1985.

20. *The People's Daily,* December 7, 1984.

21. *The People's Daily,* December 8, 1984.

22. *Social Sciences,* July 1984; *Red Flag,* August 21, 1984; *The People's Daily,* December 3, 1984.

23. Den Xiaoping, quoted in *Asiaweek,* October 19, 1984, p. 28.

24. Deng Xiaoping, quoted in Liang Heng and Judith Shapiro, *Intellectual Freedom in China After Mao* (New York: Fund for Free Expression, 1984).

25. Hu Qili, *The People's Daily,* January 20, 1985.

26. *The People's Daily,* January 25, 1985.

27. Amnesty International, *China: Violations of Human Rights,* London, Amnesty International Publications, 1985.

28. Deng Xiaoping, quoted in *Asiaweek,* October 19, 1984.

29. Deng Xiaoping, *People's Daily,* March 9, 1985.

30. Arthur N. Waldron, "Taiwan Economy May be Blueprint for China's Growth," *International Herald Tribune,* November 10–11, 1984.

31. *Asiaweek,* October 19, 1984, p. 22.

32. Kent Morrison, "Intellectuals Given More Rein in China," *The Straits Times,* September 14, 1984, p. 18.

33. *Ibid.*

34. Flora Lewis, "A Red Reformation vs. Red Orthodoxy," *International Herald Tribune,* January 26–27, 1985.

35. Wei Jinsheng, "Democracy or a New Dictatorship," in *China: Violations of Human Rights, op. cit.*

Chapter Nine

1. Capt. Charles Eliot, English Superintendent of Trade in China, proclamation of January 29, 1841.

2. Clark Kerr, *The Future of Industrial Societies* (Cambridge: Harvard University Press, 1983).

3. Roy Hofheinz, Jr., and Kent Calder, *The East Asia Edge* (New York: Basic Books, 1982), p. 108.

4. See N. J. Miners, *The Government and Politics of Hong Kong,* (Hong Kong: Oxford University Press, 1981).

5. See Alvin Rabushka, *Hong Kong: A Study in Economic Freedom* (Chicago: University of Chicago Press, 1979), and P. T. Bauer, "The Lesson of Hong Kong," in Bauer, *Equality, The Third World and Economic Delusion* (London: Methuen, 1981).

6. Hofheinz and Calder, *op. cit.*

7. George Brockway, "The Wages of Exploitation," *The New Leader,* August 8–22, 1983.

8. Fox Butterfield, *China* (London: Hodder and Stoughton, 1982).

9. *Ibid.*

10. *World University Times,* March 19, 1984, p. 9.

11. Lous Kraar, "China," *Fortune,* April 18, 1983, p. 122.

12. Zhang Shi Xiang, quoted in *Ibid.*

13. Mary Lee, "Can Shanghai Regain Its Glory?" *Far Eastern Economic Review,* March 21, 1985, pp. 76–77.

14. Joseph Chai in *China and Hong Kong,* ed. A. J. Youngson (Hong Kong: Oxford University Press, 1985).

15. Audrey Donnithorne, in *ibid.*

CHAPTER TEN

1. Goh Keng Swee, "Decade of Achievement" (Singapore: Ministry of Culture Publications, 1970).

2. Albert Winsemius, "From a Distance," *National Exhibition,* (Singapore: Ministry of National Development, 1984), p. 43.

3. David Bonavia, *Far Eastern Economic Review,* Feb. 23, 1963, cited in John Drysdale, *Singapore Struggle for Success* (Singapore: Times Books Intern'l, 1984).

4. Iain Buchanan, *Singapore in SouthEast Asia: An Economic and Political Appraisal,* quoted in Goh Chok Tong, "People's Action Party 1954–1979," Singapore, Petir 25th Anniversary Issue, p. 65.

5. Wee Hock Ong, *Job Creation or Job Loss* (Singapore: Eurasia Press, 1977).

6. Chok Tong Goh, "We Must Dare to Achieve," Information Division, Ministry of Culture, Singapore, March 1980.

7. Ong, *op. cit.* Chapter 3.

8. *The Straits Times,* Tuesday, October 16, 1984, p. 5.

9. Goh Keng Swee, "Modernizing in Singapore: Impact on the Individual," address, University of Singapore, June 16, 1972.

10. Roy Hofheinz, Jr., and Kent Calder, *The Eastasia Edge* (New York: Basic Books, 1982).

11. Clark Kerr, *The Future of Industrial Societies,* (Cambridge: Harvard University Press, 1983).

12. Jan M. D. Little, *Economic Development* (New York: Basic Books, 1982), p. 108.

13. Fong Sip Chee, *The PAP Story* (Singapore: Times Periodical (Pte) Ltd., 1979), p. 13.

14. *Amnesty International Report—1983,* London, Amnesty International Publications, 1983.

15. Lee Wah Hin, "Out of the Ruins," Letters to the Editor, *Far Eastern Economic Review,* Feb. 28, 1985.

16. *The Straits Times,* February 10, 1985.

PART III

1. George Orwell, *1984* (London: Seker and Warburg, 1949), p. 87.

2. Abdus Salam, *Ideals and Realities* (Singapore: World Scientific, 1984), p. xvi.

3. Tam Kok Seng, *Son of Singapore* (Singapore: Heinemann, 1972), p. 6.

4. *Ibid.*, p. 42.

5. *Ibid.*, cover sheet.

6. *Ibid.*, p. 117.

7. *Ibid.*, p. 115.

8. Tan Kok Seng, *Man of Malaysia* (Petaling Jaya, Malaysia, Heinemann Asia, 1974), p. 184.

9. *Ibid.*, p. 201.

10. *Ibid.*, p. 205.

11. John Kenneth Galbraith, "Ideology and Agriculture," *Harpers*, February 1985, p. 16.

12. "Peasants Rising," *The Economist*, Feb. 2, 1985, p. 11.

13. R. W. Apple, "Hungary Reaps Harvest of its Showplace Farms," *New york Times*, Oct. 18, 1982, p. A2.

14. Albert Winsemius, "From A Distance," National Exhibition Forum, National Ministry of Development, Singapore, 1984, p. 43.

15. Galbraith, *op. cit.*,, p. 16.

16. *Ibid.*

17. Thomas Sowell, "Second Thoughts About the Third World," *Harpers*, November, 1983.

18. Quoted in Dan Herman, "Trieste: World Rendezvous for Physicists," in Abdus Salam, *op. cit.*

19. "Riding the Wind," *Asiaweek*, Sept. 7, 1984, p. 25.

20. Sowell, *op. cit.*,

21. *Ibid.*

22. See Alex Inkeles and Larry Diamond, "Personal Development and National Development," in A. Szalai and F. Andrews, eds., *The Quality of Life* (London: Sage Publications, 1980); Gabriel Almond and Sidney Verba, *The Civic Culture* (Princeton: Princeton University Press, 1963); and S. Martin Lipset, *Political Man*, (Garden City: Doubleday, 1960).

23. Gan Jihua, quoted in *Beijing Review*, Feb. 18, 1985, p. 6.

24. Lee Kuan Yew, Aug. 24, 1984.

25. Sowell, *op. cit.*

26. John Plamenetz, *On Alien Rule and Self-Government* (London: Longmans, Green, and Co., 1960), pp. 138–40.

27. Massimo Salvadori, *Liberal Democracy* (London, Pall Mall Press, 1958), p. 85.

Index